STUDIES IN MODERN BRITISH RELIGIOUS HISTORY

Volume 23

THE REFORMATION AND ROBERT BARNES: HISTORY, THEOLOGY AND POLEMIC IN EARLY MODERN ENGLAND

STUDIES IN MODERN BRITISH RELIGIOUS HISTORY

ISSN: 1464–6625

This series aims to differentiate 'religious history' from the narrow confines of church history, investigating not only the social and cultural history of religion, but also theological, political and institutional themes, while remaining sensitive to the wider historical context; it thus advances an understanding of the importance of religion for the history of modern Britain, covering all periods of British history since the Reformation.

Previously published volumes in this series are listed at the back of this volume.

THE REFORMATION AND ROBERT BARNES: HISTORY, THEOLOGY AND POLEMIC IN EARLY MODERN ENGLAND

KOREY D. MAAS

THE BOYDELL PRESS

First published 2010
The Boydell Press, Woodbridge

ISBN 978–1–84383–534–9

The Boydell Press is an imprint of Boydell & Brewer Ltd
PO Box 9, Woodbridge, Suffolk IP12 3DF, UK
and of Boydell & Brewer Inc.
Mt Hope Avenue, Rochester, NY 14620-2731, USA
website: www.boydellandbrewer.com

A CIP catalogue record for this book is available
from the British Library

This publication is printed on acid-free paper

Printed in Great Britain by
CPI Antony Rowe, Chippenham and Eastbourne

CONTENTS

For Kate

ACKNOWLEDGEMENTS

It has become a commonplace for authors to acknowledge that no book is the product of a single mind, and this is most certainly true. Not only does every scholar 'stand on the shoulders of giants', but many others assist in keeping him or her balanced there, with support both moral and material. From the beginning to the end of this project I have received the able assistance and unflagging support of more people than can here be named. It would, however, be an egregious sin of omission to leave certain individuals and institutions unacknowledged.

In various ways and at various times throughout the stages of research and writing, financial support was very kindly provided by, and very gratefully received from: the Oxford University Humanities Division; the Sir Richard Stapley Educational Trust; St Cross College, Oxford; Westfield House, Cambridge; and Concordia University, Irvine, California.

Academic colleagues in a number of countries have earned my enduring gratitude for the selfless manner in which they also contributed to this work. Blanka Frydrychova Klimova cannot be thanked enough for translating some Czech sources, without which an unpardonable lacuna would be found in this volume. Alec Ryrie was also especially gracious in allowing me to read a pre-publication version of his essay 'A saynt in the devyls name'. John Craig and Christian Moser are in my debt for providing me with copies of little known manuscripts. The Chairman and Governors of Shrewsbury School must similarly be thanked for giving me access to the only surviving copy of an important broadsheet. Nor can I forget the able and efficient assistance of the librarians and archivists of the Bodleian Library, Oxford; the University Library, Cambridge; and the British Library and Public Record Office, London.

Those whom I owe favours for very kindly answering a host of obscure (and sometimes probably naive) questions, as well as offering unsolicited but never unappreciated advice, include: Irena Backus, Stefan Bauer, T.A. Birrell, Peter Newman Brooks, Daniela Solfaroli Camillocci, Maria Dowling, Ronald Feuerhahn, Adam Francisco, Tom Freeman, Christopher Haigh, Felicity Heal, Robert Kolb, Judith Maltby, Tom Mayer, John McDiarmid, Sophie Murray, Oliver Olson, Helen Parish, Judith Pollmann, Richard Rex, Rod Rosenbladt, Ethan Shagan, Nick Thompson, Susan Wabuda, and Bill Wizeman. Most especially, though, I wish to express my gratitude to Diarmaid MacCulloch, who encouraged this project from the start, who read through the whole of more than one draft, and whose critical eye and wise counsel prevented some embarrassing blunders. He is one of the giants on whose shoulders I happily stand.

Finally, the eternal patience of my saintly wife must be gratefully acknowledged. Not only did she allow our 'long honeymoon' to become very much a working holiday, but she has more than once endured transatlantic moves for the sake of my research and writing. It is to her that this work is dedicated.

ABBREVIATIONS AND SHORT TITLES

Aarsberetninger	*Aarsberetninger fra det Kongelige Geheimearchiv*, 7 vols, ed. C.F. Wegener Copenhagen, 1852–83)
AE	*Luther's Works, American Edition*, 56 vols, ed. J. Pelikan and H. Lehmann (Philadelphia and St Louis, 1955–86)
A&M	John Foxe, *Actes and Monuments* (London, 1563 and 1583 editions; 1583 edition cited unless otherwise noted)
A&M (Pratt)	*The Acts and Monuments of John Foxe*, 7 vols, ed. J. Pratt (London, 1877)
BL	British Library, London
Correspondance Politique	*Correspondance Politique de MM. de Castillon et de Marillac, Ambassadeurs de France en Engleterre*, ed. Jean Kaulek (Paris, 1885)
CR	*Corpus Reformatorum, Philippi Melanthonis Opera*, 28 vols, ed. C.G. Bretschneider (Halle, 1836)
CSPS	*Calendar of State Papers, Spanish*, 15 vols, ed. P. de Gayangos et al. (London, 1862–1954)
CWM	*The Complete Works of St. Thomas More*, 15 vols, ed. C.H. Miller et al. (New Haven, 1963–97)
DER	*Documents of the English Reformation*, ed. G. Bray (Cambridge, 1994)
English Austin Friars	Francis Roth, *The English Austin Friars, 1249–1538*, serialised in *Augustiniana*, vols 8–17
Lisle Letters	*The Lisle Letters*, 6 vols, ed. Marie St Clare Byrne (London, 1981)
LP	*Letters and Papers, Foreign and Domestic, of the Reign of Henry VIII*, 23 vols, ed. J.S. Brewer et al. (London, 1862–1932)
Original Letters	*Original Letters Relative to the English Reformation*, 2 vols, ed. H. Robinson (Cambridge: Parker Society, 1846–7)
PRO	[The National Archives] Public Record Office, London
Sentenciae	Antonius Anglus [i.e., Robert Barnes], *Sentenciae ex doctoribus collectae* (Wittenberg, 1530)
STC	A.W. Pollard and G.R. Redgrave, *A Short-title Catalogue of Books Printed in England, Scotland and Ireland, and of English Books Printed Abroad, 1475–1640*, 3 vols, 2nd edition (London, 1976–91)

Supplicatyon (1531)	Robert Barnes, *A supplicatyon made by Robert Barnes* (Antwerp, 1531)
Supplicacion (1534)	Robert Barnes, *A supplicacion unto the most gracious prynce kynge Henry the .viii.* (London, 1534)
Vitae	Robert Barnes, *Vitae romanorum pontificum* (Wittenberg, 1536)
WA	*D. Martin Luthers Werke, Kritische Gesamtausgabe, Schriften*, 62 vols (Weimar, 1883–1986)
WABr	*D. Martin Luthers Werke, Kritische Gesamtausgabe, Briefwechsel*, 10 vols (Weimar, 1930–47)
Wing	D.G. Wing, *A Short-title Catalogue of Books Printed in England, Scotland, Ireland, Wales and British America, and of English Books Printed in Other Countries, 1641–1700*, 4 vols, 2nd edition (New York, 1982–98)

INTRODUCTION

The life, thought, and influence of the Henrician reformer Robert Barnes have not received overabundant attention from historians of the sixteenth-century reformations. Though he never attained the prominence or exerted the influence of some of his closest contemporaries and associates – influential figures such as Thomas Cranmer, Thomas Cromwell, and Martin Luther – his place in the early English evangelical movement was by no means insignificant. To the contrary, Barnes has been recognised as 'one of the most important, and among the most controversial, of the early reformers'.[1] As a Doctor of Theology, prior of the Cambridge Augustinian friary, and one of the 'most important of the group' associated with the White Horse Inn, Barnes figures prominently in treatments of Cambridge University and its early role in the promotion of Luther's idea in England.[2] It is in this context that Barnes's Christmas Eve sermon of 1525, preached in the Cambridge church of St Edward's, has been identified by some as the first 'public manifesto' of the Cambridge evangelicals.[3] One recent work goes even so far as to suggest that the subsequent conservative reaction to this sermon was 'the most important event of the period between 1526 and 1529'.[4]

The conservative response to Barnes's sermon, resulting in his trial, imprisonment, and eventual escape to the continent, also proved to be the most immediate cause of yet another unique contribution to the early English reformation. Attempting to justify his fugitive status by sharply critiquing the treatment he had received at the hands of his judges, Barnes, from the safety of Germany, penned a 'supplication' to Henry VIII. Appended to this defence of his preaching and later flight was a series of theological commonplaces which comprised 'the nearest thing to a work of systematic theology that the Henrician reformers produced'.[5]

1 Susan Wabuda, ' "Fruitful Preaching" in the Diocese of Worcester: Bishop Hugh Latimer and his Influence, 1535–1539', in *Religion and the English People, 1500–1640: New Voices, New Perspectives*, ed. Eric Joseph Carlson (Kirksville, MO, 1998), 61.

2 H.C. Porter, *Reformation and Reaction in Tudor Cambridge* (Cambridge, 1958), 46. For Barnes's importance in the early Cambridge reformation, see also E.G. Rupp, *Studies in the Making of the English Protestant Tradition* (Cambridge, 1966), 31–46, and Richard Rex, 'The Early Impact of Reformation Theology at Cambridge University, 1521–1547', *Reformation & Renaissance Review* 2 (1999), 38–71.

3 Allen G. Chester, *Hugh Latimer: Apostle to the English* (Philadelphia, 1954), 212.

4 Douglas H. Parker (ed.), *A Critical Edition of Robert Barnes's* A Supplication Unto the Most Gracyous Prince Kynge Henry The .VIIJ. *1534.* (Toronto, 2008), 12–13.

5 C. Trueman, *Luther's Legacy: Salvation and English Reformers, 1525–1556* (Oxford, 1994), 3.

The distinctively Lutheran emphases evident in this treatise, combined with the significant fact of Barnes's exile having led him to Wittenberg and into a friendly association with its leading reformers, would also further draw Barnes into the centre of ecclesiastical events not only in England but also abroad.

The esteem in which he was held by the Wittenberg Lutherans, and by his later English patrons, Cranmer and Cromwell, made him especially suited to the role of messenger, ambassador, and negotiator between the English and German churches. From 1531, when he was first engaged by the Crown to seek out Luther's opinion on Henry's divorce, up until his death in 1540, Barnes was integrally involved in each stage of the negotiations to bring England into an alliance with the Lutheran Schmalkaldic League. Similarly in the service of the Crown, as a commissioner for the examination of Anabaptists in England he would also play a prominent role in attempting to establish the boundaries of Henrician orthodoxy. Appointments such as these both reflected and strengthened the perception – held by evangelicals and conservatives alike – that, by the late 1530s, 'Barnes was English evangelicalism's leading theologian and one of its most prominent spokesmen.'[6]

Even his untimely death in 1540 contributed significantly to Barnes's reformation significance. Not only was he 'one of the very few major magisterial Reformers to be executed anywhere in the European Reformation';[7] but his status as an evangelical martyr quickly became capital for the influential Protestant propaganda produced throughout the sixteenth century. Such was the significance of his death that even fifteen years later it would continue to be the most memorable landmark by which Londoners dated past events.[8] It is this prominent and often central role in the early unfolding of England's reformation which accounts for the recent assertion that, 'With the possible exception of Tyndale, Barnes is probably the most important reformer of the 1520s and 1530s in England.'[9]

Yet this mention of William Tyndale also partially reveals the probable cause of the infrequent attention given Barnes by modern scholars. Unlike Tyndale, or even Barnes's own Cambridge student Miles Coverdale, Barnes would leave to posterity no influential translation of Scripture, or even commentary upon it. Unlike his patron Thomas Cranmer, he produced no liturgical works which would leave an indelible mark on the English church. Nor, in contrast to close associates such as Hugh Latimer or Edward Foxe, would his service to the Crown ever be rewarded with elevation to the episcopate. Indeed, it has recently been suggested

6 Michael Riordan and Alec Ryrie, 'Stephen Gardiner and the Making of a Protestant Villain', *Sixteenth Century Journal* 34 (2003), 1048.
7 Diarmaid MacCulloch, 'Putting the English Reformation on the Map', *Transactions of the Royal Historical Society* 15 (2005), 81.
8 Susan Brigden, *London and the Reformation* (Oxford, 1989), 322.
9 Parker, *A Critical Edition*, 13.

that, at the time of his death in 1540, he was best known in his native country as a preacher.[10] Since, however, he was only sporadically in his own country during the height of his reforming activities, and even then rarely in one place for long, his preaching was by its very nature itinerant. Unlike other notable preachers, therefore, he exercised no formative influence in a particular parish, diocese, or university. Nor were his sermons ever collected or published, by which means they might have made an impact on evangelical communities even after his death.

Barnes did publish, however. During the final decade of his life he wrote and saw into print four treatises touching on the faith and history of the church. Those few researchers who have turned their attention to Barnes have therefore quite naturally focused much of their energy on these treatises. The same focus will remain evident in the present work; Barnes's writings, however, will here be approached from a decidedly different angle than that of previous scholarship. Earlier generations of scholars, both theologians and historians, were especially intent on dissecting the doctrinal content of Barnes's works in an attempt to define his own theological leanings. The thesis most often set forth – and which is undoubtedly correct – is that Barnes is best labelled a proponent of Lutheranism, at least to the extent that this term can be used in any narrowly confessional sense in the early years of the reformation.

In this context it is not insignificant that a fair number of the modern authors who have made this thesis the foundation of their research were themselves Lutheran; and it must be noted that much of the twentieth-century writing on Barnes is infused with an unmistakably hagiographical air.[11] This must be noted because the fact has affected the interpretation of Barnes's significance in at least two important ways.

Notably, most investigations of Barnes have concluded with his death. This is, quite obviously, a reasonable point of conclusion for a biographer. But in the case of Barnes, a further, though implicit, logic seems also to lay behind this decision. Beginning from the premise that Barnes was a rare English Lutheran, many have assumed that his active promotion of the Lutheran faith in England – as a preacher, polemicist, and diplomat – constitutes his primary if not his sole significance for the reformation. The further conclusion is then reached that his public execution in 1540 (and that of his patron and protector Thomas Cromwell two

10 Alec Ryrie, ' "A saynt in the devyls name": Heroes and Villains in the Martyrdom of Robert Barnes', in *Martyrs and Martyrdom in England, c. 1400–1700*, ed. Thomas S. Freeman and Thomas F. Mayer (Woodbridge, 2007), 146–7.

11 Notable examples include William Dallmann, *Robert Barnes: English Lutheran Martyr* (St Louis, n.d.; repr. Decatur, IL, 1997), and an abbreviated version titled 'Dr. Robert Barnes: The English Lutheran Martyr', *Theological Quarterly* 9 (1905), 22–32; R.G. Eaves, 'The Reformation Thought of Dr. Robert Barnes, Lutheran Chaplain and Ambassador for Henry VIII', *The Lutheran Quarterly* 28 (1976), 156–65; M.L. Loane, *Pioneers of the Reformation in England* (London, 1964), 49–89; James McGoldrick, *Luther's English Connection* (Milwaukee, 1979); and N.S. Tjernagel, *Lutheran Martyr* (Milwaukee, 1982).

days earlier) signalled in a very dramatic manner the end of any hopes for England entering the Lutheran fold. That is, Barnes's programme died with him. Since that time, more than one attempt to resurrect Barnes seems to have had the implicit (and sometimes explicit) agenda of resurrecting his assumed programme.

A confessional or hagiographical treatment of Barnes is by no means new. It was precisely this approach to his life and death which was taken already in the sixteenth century by influential martyrologists such as John Foxe; and it is Foxe's work which has done much to influence a second prominent emphasis evident in much previous scholarship. His *Actes and Monuments* was of course extremely influential in early modern Britain; and the fact that it remains even today an important source of information about Barnes has given rise to the thesis that Barnes's primary significance for the reformation was the simple fact of his death. In this context, it has been recognised that Barnes did indeed have a continuing significance after 1540 – no longer on account of his peculiar theological leanings, but for the propaganda purposes to which his death was later put. Modern publications guided by this thesis have therefore turned attention from what Barnes himself wrote to what contemporaries and successors wrote about him.

The present examination has been guided by two fundamental and, one hopes, uncontroversial assumptions. First, the important question is not 'What significance, if any, does Barnes have for today?', but 'What significance, if any, did Barnes have in his own era?' Second, any attempt to answer this question must take into account both Barnes's own writings and those which later comment upon his life, death, and work. Therefore, after preliminary surveys of his life and thought (chapters 1 and 2), his own works will be examined in some detail (chapters 3 and 4). On this basis a tentative thesis will be set forth (chapter 5) suggesting that Barnes's conscious programme entailed not only the promotion of a particular theology, but also a particular methodology – what today might variously be called 'confessional historiography' or 'historical theology': that is, the employment of historical sources and methods for specifically confessional or theological ends. (The irony of Barnes's own methodology being the cause of many less-than-objective modern evaluations of his significance is duly noted.) This tentative thesis will then be tested in two final chapters, in which the reception, evaluation, and use of Barnes's works by sixteenth- and seventeenth-century Protestants is examined (chapters 6 and 7).

In concluding that it was indeed as an historical-theological polemicist that Barnes was most often remembered, praised, and recommended in the century after his death, I make no claim to having discredited or overturned previous interpretations. But the view expounded here will, it is hoped, serve to complement received interpretations of Barnes's significance. This is especially the case in two respects. Whereas Barnes has traditionally been studied almost solely within the context of the English reformation, the evidence here presented begins to reveal the extent to which Barnes also played an influential role in the development of historical-theological polemic even on the continent. A related corrective is also offered. Having studied Barnes with the assumption that his significance is to be found primarily in the context of England's reformation, an earlier generation of scholars gave most of their attention to those works which Barnes produced in the English language. A relative neglect of Barnes's Latin works – his most popular, as will be seen – has hitherto partially prevented the interpretation here put forward. The acceptance of these small correctives will, it is hoped, suggest new avenues of research pertaining to Robert Barnes and his reformation significance.

* * *

While much of what follows will be self-explanatory, a few brief notes of guidance might be appreciated by readers. Where they exist, every effort has been made to cite printed sources. In those cases where documents, whether in print or in manuscript, have been abstracted in *Letters and Papers*, references to this resource are also included in brackets for ease of reference. Multi-volume works are cited according to the following format: volume, full stop, page number(s). Some exceptions to this rule occur in the citation of correspondence, where document numbers rather than page numbers are provided. Unless otherwise indicated, therefore, the following works will be cited by volume and document number: *Aarsberetninger fra det Kongelige Geheimearchiv*; Luther's *Briefwechsel*; *Calendar of State Papers, Spanish*; *Corpus Reformatorum*; *Correspondance Politique*; *Letters and Papers*; *Life and Letters of Thomas Cromwell*; *Lisle Letters*; *Original Letters Illustrative of English History*; and *Original Letters Relative to the English Reformation*. Also deserving an explanation are the citations of Francis Roth's *The English Augustinian Friars, 1249–1538*, which was originally published serially in several editions of the journal *Augustiniana*. Citations will note volume and page numbers; page numbers followed by asterisks denote primary sources appended to Roth's text.

All translations, unless otherwise noted, are my own; again for ease of reference, translated quotations are provided in their original language in the footnotes. I have in most cases taken no liberties with the transcription of quotations; but some exceptions do occur. The letters i, j, u, and v are consistently rendered in accordance with modern convention, except in Latin quotations where the letter i has been allowed to stand. In English quotations the common contractions y^e and y^t have also been expanded. The only other liberty I have allowed myself in transcription is the replacement of ß with ss in Latin quotations. Finally, in keeping with modern convention, all dates are rendered 'new style', accepting 1 January as the beginning of the new year.

PART I

THE LIFE AND THEOLOGY OF ROBERT BARNES

1

THE LIFE OF ROBERT BARNES

Robert Barnes stepped on to the stage of the reformation drama on Christmas Eve 1525; though never one of the most famous players in that drama, he would for the next fifteen years remain very close to the centre of the reformation, both in England and abroad. His patrons at home included the architects of English reform, Thomas Cranmer and Thomas Cromwell, as well as Henry VIII himself, who would for a brief period name Barnes his chaplain and occasional diplomat. His associates on the continent were no less eminent, including not only the Wittenberg theologians Martin Luther and Philip Melanchthon, but also princely protectors of early Lutheranism such as Johann Friedrich of Saxony, Philip of Hesse, and Christian III of Denmark.

As his personal association with such individuals intimates, Barnes travelled frequently – not only as a diplomat, however, but also at times as an exile. This fact, combined with the perennial problems posed by an incomplete documentary record, has resulted in confusing and often conflicting accounts of his life. Indeed, despite his recognised importance, no authoritative biography of Barnes yet exists. Rather shockingly, the most reliable account to date remains that of James Lusardi, which exists only as a brief appendix in the collected works of Barnes's early nemesis Thomas More.[1] Several other substantial biographical surveys were produced earlier in the twentieth century;[2] and while far more objective than the hagiographical accounts noted above in the introduction, these too remain less than authoritative: primarily because they exist only as unpublished theses and therefore remain relatively inaccessible, but also partly for methodological reasons. Most notably, each relied overwhelmingly upon the abstracted versions of primary sources found, for example, in the *Letters and Papers, Foreign and*

[1] J.P. Lusardi, 'The Career of Robert Barnes', in *CWM*, 8.1365–1415. Also reliable, though older and much more brief, is the biographical sketch found in E.G. Rupp, *Studies in the Making of the English Protestant Tradition* (Cambridge, 1966), 31–46.

[2] N.H. Fisher, 'The Contribution of Robert Barnes to the English Reformation' (unpublished M.A. Thesis, University of Birmingham, 1950); Charles Anderson, 'The Person and Position of Dr. Robert Barnes, 1495–1540: A Study in the Relationship between the English and German Reformations' (unpublished Th.D. Thesis, Union Theological Seminary, New York, 1962).

Domestic, of the Reign of Henry VIII. Furthermore, the theses forwarded in these dissertations make it evident that none is intended primarily to be a critical biography of Barnes. Charles Anderson, for instance, 'deals with the general problem of the relationship between the German and early English Reformation'.[3] The same is true of Neelak Tjernagel's *Henry VIII and the Lutherans*, the revised and expanded version of his own doctoral thesis.[4] Its subtitle, 'A Study in Anglo-Lutheran Relations from 1521 to 1547', advertises a trajectory very similar to Anderson's. For each author, Barnes's life and thought serve largely to illustrate in distilled form the perceived nature of theological relations between England and Germany in the reign of Henry VIII.[5] Far more influential than these works, however, is William Clebsch's *England's Earliest Protestants*.[6] While Barnes figures as only one of a half-dozen reformers surveyed in some detail by Clebsch, the unique and ostensibly authoritative nature of his work has long ensured that any investigation of Barnes must give it due attention. Indeed, though his brief biographical summary is reliable in its details, the interpretation built upon it has arguably obscured the understanding of Barnes more than any other single volume. Like Anderson and Tjernagel, Clebsch sees in Barnes a distillation of larger and more complex phenomena. Rejecting the received opinion that he was most significantly a conduit for German theology in England, however, he instead (and somewhat anachronistically) sees in Barnes a reformer who 'stamped English-speaking Christianity with ... a concern for morality as the clue to theology and the core of religion'.[7] A number of Clebsch's questionable assertions have been effectively challenged in the last generation – and will receive further attention in the following pages – yet no critical or comprehensive treatment of Barnes's life and thought has since been published. Although the present volume is not primarily biographical, and though this introductory chapter cannot pretend to provide an exhaustive account of Barnes's life, any attempt to evaluate Barnes and his significance for the reformations of the sixteenth century does first make necessary the more mundane task of locating him in the chronology and geography of those reformations.

Early years to exile

Born in King's Lynn, Norfolk, in the year 1495, Robert Barnes was sent to Cambridge only a decade later, where he entered the house of the Augustinian

3 Anderson, 'The Person and Position', 2.

4 N.S. Tjernagel, *Henry VIII and the Lutherans: A Study in Anglo-Lutheran Relations from 1521 to 1547* (St Louis, 1965); cf. N.S. Tjernagel, 'Dr. Robert Barnes and Anglo-Lutheran Relations, 1521–1540 (unpublished Ph.D. Thesis, University of Iowa, 1955).

5 Cf. Anderson, 'The Person and Position', 303–4, and Tjernagel, *Henry VIII and the Lutherans*, 250.

6 W.A. Clebsch, *England's Earliest Protestants: 1520–1535* (New Haven, 1964).

7 Clebsch, *England's Earliest Protestants*, 3.

friars.[8] The fact that his native King's Lynn did not lack its own prominent Augustinian friary – among others – would indicate that it was the presence of the university, and the friary's close ties to it,[9] which prompted his early move. And Barnes's aptitude for learning, suggested by this early move, was later confirmed by those who knew him in Cambridge; even his early associate and later episcopal foe Stephen Gardiner begrudgingly confessed that he had 'some savour of lernynge',[10] while the Carmelite friar John Bale would admit that Barnes 'greatly surpassed' him in learning.[11] Such judgements were evidently shared by his Augustinian superiors, for sometime after 1514 he was sent to Leuven for further study.[12]

It has often been noted that Barnes's time in Leuven coincided with that of the much celebrated Dutch humanist Desiderius Erasmus. Though no evidence exists to associate these two personally,[13] there is good reason to believe that Barnes was influenced by the Leuven humanism of this period, during which the famous *collegium trilinguae* was founded by Erasmus himself. Soon after his return to the Cambridge friary, for instance, it is recorded that Barnes consciously took pains to replace the scholastic study of Duns Scotus and Nicholas de Orbellis with a more immediate study of the text of Scripture itself. John Foxe also notes that this religious return *ad fontes* was preceded by, and took place in conjunction with, an emphasis on the reading of classical Latin authors such as Terence, Plautus, and Cicero.[14] The significance of this classical emphasis is easy to overestimate, however, and was certainly not unique to Barnes; nor is it necessarily indicative of a humanism inconsistent with theological orthodoxy. Already in 1495, for instance, Terence had entered the university curriculum, replacing an earlier statute's more general mention of 'libros humanitatis'.[15] In 1523, the unquestionably

8 The location of Barnes's birth is given in the brief biography found in John Bale, *Scriptorum Illustrium maioris Brytanniae ... Catalogus* (Basle, 1557), 666–7, from which the date is also inferred. The year in which he entered the Cambridge friary is assumed to be 1505: Bale describes him as 'impubes'; and Barnes himself says that, before he left Cambridge in early 1526, he had remained there 'continually .xx. yearis'. *Supplicatyon* (1531), fo. 21r.

9 *English Austin Friars*, 8.40.

10 Stephen Gardiner, *The Letters of Stephen Gardiner*, ed. J.A. Muller (Cambridge, 1933), 166.

11 Bale, *Catalogus*, 667: 'multis praecurrit'.

12 Foxe makes note of his time in Leuven in *A&M*, 2.1021 and 2.1192. No date is recorded by Foxe, but Bale, *Catalogus*, 666–7, mentions that they were students together at Cambridge in 1514. It is possible that Barnes's arrival occurred as late as 1520, the year in which the Prior General of the Augustinians notes in his register that Barnes is 'to stay at the college of Louvain'. *English Austin Friars*, 10.414*–15*. It is not until the next year, on 24 May, that 'D. Robertus Beeren, Anglus in Theologia, Noorwicensis dyoces', is listed among those matriculating. *Matricule de L'Université de Louvain*, 10 vols, ed. A. Schillings et al. (Brussels, 1903–80), 3.648.

13 Indeed, Barnes's matriculation date allows only for a five-month overlap with Erasmus at the university itself, as the latter departed at the end of October 1521. Emiel Lamberts et al. (eds), *Leuven University, 1425–1985* (Leuven, 1990), 23.

14 *A&M*, 2.1192.

15 Christopher Brooke et al. (eds), *A History of the University of Cambridge*, 4 vols (Cambridge, 1988–2004), 1.249.

orthodox Stephen Gardiner was one of those drafting statutes relative to the university lectures on Terence.[16] By 1522, the probable date of Barnes's return from Leuven, Plautus had also become a university standard.[17]

It must also be pointed out that, despite Leuven's humanist bent during Barnes's stay, the university itself remained unquestionably orthodox. Its faculty would, for example, quickly and vigorously condemn Martin Luther's *Ninety-Five Theses* of 1517, which themselves had more in common with contemporary humanist critiques of ecclesiastical practice than they did with later Protestant critiques of medieval doctrine. This is not to suggest, however, that Barnes would have remained ignorant of the nascent Luther affair while on the continent. To the contrary, Leuven's early pronouncement on the German's theology would certainly have brought it to the attention of the university's students. Similarly, though there is no independent evidence to support the suggestion that Barnes and Luther had met at the Heidelberg Disputation of 1518,[18] Luther's increasingly public protest could hardly have remained a secret in continental Augustinian circles. Indeed, though the suggestion must remain tentative, it is entirely possible that it was Leuven's unyielding stance in the Luther controversy which prompted Barnes's return to England only a year after his matriculation.[19]

It is upon his return from Leuven to Cambridge in the early 1520s that slightly more information concerning Barnes's activity, and his increasingly evangelical sympathies, becomes available. Having been approved by the Augustinian Prior General for promotion to the doctorate in June of 1523,[20] Barnes was incorporated at Cambridge as a Bachelor, and simultaneously made Doctor of Theology.[21] In the same year he was elected to the position of prior in his Cambridge house and began to institute the changes to the syllabus above noted. Foxe also associates Barnes with the informal meetings then taking place at the White Horse Inn. Despite the amount of attention the White Horse has received by subsequent scholars, little is in fact known about either the make-up of the group which met there or the nature of the meetings themselves. Some authors have attempted to downplay any explicitly evangelical bent, preferring instead to

16 J.A. Muller, *Stephen Gardiner and the Tudor Reaction* (London, 1926), 9.
17 Brooke, *A History of the University of Cambridge*, 1.317.
18 Clebsch, *England's Earliest Protestants*, 43.
19 Based upon Barnes's 1531 statement that he had neither been in Amsterdam 'nor yet in the contrye thys ten yearys', his return to Cambridge can be dated c.1521–22. See his *Supplicatyon* (1531), fo. 33v, and Lusardi, 'The Career of Robert Barnes', 1369. The oddity of Barnes's return to England so soon after his matriculation is compounded by the Leuven regulation which normally required students progressing from bachelor to licentiate status to remain in Leuven for their doctorates. See Lamberts, *Leuven University*, 93.
20 *English Austin Friars*, 10.425*.
21 *English Austin Friars*, 10.435*. See also *Alumni Cantabrigienses*, 10 vols, ed. J. Venn and J.A. Venn (Cambridge, 1922–54), 1.93, and C.H. Cooper and T. Cooper, *Athenae Cantabrigienses*, 2 vols (Cambridge, 1858–61), 1.74.

interpret the gatherings as an opportunity to discuss more broadly academic questions. As Foxe remains the only source of information regarding the White Horse meetings, however, some weight must certainly be given to his statement that the inn soon came to be known as the Cambridge 'Germany', undoubtedly referring to a common belief that the Luther affair was a prominent topic of conversation.[22] Perhaps even more illuminating, however, is Richard Rex's observation that from 1523, when Barnes became prior, the previously commonplace bequests to the friary for the singing of *Scala Coeli* Masses seem to have ceased.[23] The coincidence of these two events suggests that, by 1523, signs of Barnes's discomfort with some traditional piety were becoming evident, at least within his own friary.

Some small evidence of growing reformist leanings can also be found in Barnes's activities outside Cambridge during this time. Upon his return to England Barnes did not break contact with the friends and scholars he had met at Leuven. In addition to bringing back with him the young scholar Thomas Parnell, he also maintained a close relationship with the former Leuven student Edmund Rougham, a Benedictine of the abbey of Bury St Edmunds, to whom Barnes made frequent visits in the early 1520s.[24] It was during one of these visits, in the company of London brickmakers and known Lollards Lawrence Maxwell and John Stacy, that Barnes also met the abbey chamberlain Richard Bayfield, with whom he left a Latin New Testament, presumably the recent edition of Erasmus. Exactly what prompted a confrontation is unknown, but after studying this work for 'two yeares space' Bayfield fell afoul of his superiors and was imprisoned in the house.[25] What seems likely is that he was reading and discussing this new translation with interpretations which were also new, presumably the very interpretations previously discussed in his presence by Barnes and his associates. Later events in the lives of all involved would support such a reading, as does the fact that it was Barnes himself who eventually interceded on Bayfield's behalf, both securing his release and bringing him back to Cambridge.[26]

In spite of the above, however, there are notable indications that Barnes had

[22] *A&M*, 2.1192.

[23] Richard Rex, 'The Early Impact of Reformation Theology at Cambridge University, 1521–1547', *Reformation & Renaissance Review* 2 (1999), 49 n. 41.

[24] Rougham, like Barnes a Norfolk man, had matriculated at Leuven the year before Barnes on 2 October 1520. *Matricule de L'Université de Louvain*, 3.638.

[25] For this paragraph see *A&M*, 2.1021. The initial meeting of Barnes and Bayfield cannot be dated with precision. Foxe records that Bayfield travelled to London when Barnes was 'in the Fleete', i.e., sometime between February and August of 1526. He had previously spent 'a good while' in Cambridge after his release from an imprisonment that had lasted '.iii. quarters of a yeare'. Two years had passed between his arrest and his first meeting with Barnes. If 'a good while' encompasses even the space of a year – and it must have lasted more than a few months, as Barnes could only have secured his release before his own troubles of late 1525 – the dating of this first meeting can safely be placed in 1522.

[26] For the story of Bayfield, see *A&M*, 2.1021–4; for Rougham's evangelical activities, see *A&M* (Pratt) 4, Appendix, 767–8.

yet to be wholly or outspokenly converted to opinions that could be called explicitly evangelical. He had fallen under no suspicion from the university authorities, who at the beginning of 1524 even gave him early release from typical requirements of regency.[27] Likewise, in Foxe's brief mention of George Stafford's 1524 Bachelor of Divinity disputation, a picture is painted of Stafford confounding 'the great blynde Doctors' who examined him, but who could not refute his evangelical opinions.[28] Barnes himself was one of these doctors, the individual in fact appointed to act as moderator in the disputation. In this light it is perhaps not surprising that Foxe says it was only under the later influence of Thomas Bilney that Barnes was truly 'converted', though also worthy of note is John Bale's emphasis on Luther's works having been the primary factor in Barnes's conversion.[29]

Whatever the immediate cause of Barnes's evangelical leanings, over the next year Bilney certainly did have a growing influence on the young Augustinian, to the extent that it was Bilney who in 1525 persuaded a not altogether willing Barnes to preach before an audience beyond the safe walls of his friary. Arrangements were made in which Barnes, on 24 December, would preach in the Cambridge church of St Edward's while Hugh Latimer, the scheduled preacher, would occupy Barnes's pulpit in the house of the Austin friars. Why this exchange of pulpits should have been arranged is rather puzzling, since it was surely not precipitated, as John Foxe claims, by Latimer having been prohibited from preaching in St Edward's.[30] The most probable explanation is that the exchange was conceived not to oblige Latimer at all, but to accommodate Barnes. On more than one occasion Latimer would liberally praise his preaching, and Bilney is described in this episode as eagerly encouraging Barnes to enter the pulpit.[31] What seems most likely, therefore, is that Bilney and his fellows saw in Barnes a convincing preacher and desired to place him before a public audience where his persuasiveness might serve the slowly growing evangelical cause. If this was indeed their hope, they disastrously misjudged both their situation and their preacher.

Shortly after the sermon Barnes was censured, and only six weeks later committed indefinitely to the Fleet. The rush of events leading to his imprisonment took Barnes quite by surprise; he was convinced that the content of his sermon was entirely within the bounds of orthodox proclamation. Indeed, examining the twenty-five articles eventually brought against him, one is led to believe

27 See *A&M* (Pratt) 7, Appendix, 772.

28 *A&M*, 2.1192; and cf. *A&M* (1563), 477.

29 *A&M*, 2.1192, and cf. Bale, *Catalogus*, 667.

30 Chester, *Hugh Latimer*, 22–4.

31 *A&M* (1563), 477. For Latimer's praise of Barnes's preaching, see, e.g., Hugh Latimer, *Sermons and Remains of Hugh Latimer*, ed. G.E. Corrie (Cambridge: Parker Society, 1845), 378 (*LP*, 12/2.258) and 389 (*LP*, 12/2.1259).

he was largely correct in this assumption.[32] The sermon was primarily a denunciation of clerical pomp and ecclesiastical abuses; in this he was hardly original, though perhaps more than usually effective. He was quick with a pun or an intentional verbal slip; even those with whom he would later fall out could not fail to acknowledge his 'merye skoffynge witte'.[33] Even when this was aimed at prominent figures like Cardinal Thomas Wolsey, it could hardly have been unexpected from a friar. Indeed, Stephen Gardiner, then in the employ of Wolsey, would later specifically note, 'that raylynge, in a frere, had ben easely pardonned'.[34] It was the unexpected, however, which led Barnes into the first of his troubles with ecclesiastical authority.

Barnes did not anticipate, for example, that one of those present for his Christmas Eve sermon would be an individual with whom he had that very week come into conflict. The man, as Barnes later related, was a churchwarden who had brought a lawsuit against the executor of an impoverished man's will. The will had stated that a kettle was to be left to the man's parish church; but the executor, being poor himself, retained it. He soon found himself imprisoned on the action of the churchwarden. His wife asked Barnes to intercede, which he did unsuccessfully on 23 December. Barnes recalls his surprise upon the next day seeing that 'the selfe man stode afore me in the churche'. Departing therefore from the text on which he was preaching, Barnes claims to have announced a condemnation of the man 'in a parable, that no man knewe what I ment, but he, and I'.[35] Barnes, however, in addition to a quick wit also had a quick temper. Apparently unable to leave the point after his parable, he 'spake so much the more violently' and continued to denounce all lawsuits brought by Christians against fellow believers. This, as his critics would later point out, sounded not at all unlike the condemned opinions of the Anabaptists.[36] Less damning, perhaps, but certainly not helpful to Barnes's case was the fact that his denunciation of lawsuits had been made in the church associated with Trinity Hall, traditionally known as the lawyers' college.

Barnes could also not have suspected that, even before he entered the pulpit, Wolsey was setting in motion new plans to curb the importing and distributing of heretical literature.[37] The testimonies of four Steelyard men examined early in

[32] The ideas for which he was eventually charged are outlined in his *Supplicatyon* (1531), fos 22v–35v, and *Supplicacion* (1534), sigs F1r–H1r.

[33] Gardiner, *Letters*, 165.

[34] Gardiner, *Letters*, 166.

[35] *Supplicacion* (1534), sig. F3r. The discussion of the context of the will and the lawsuit does not appear in the 1531 *Supplicatyon*, where Barnes presented a more general case against lawsuits. His defence was rewritten in the 1534 edition, adding the context in which he spoke, and arguing that his sermon did not in fact denounce all lawsuits between Christians, but only 'uncharitable sewtes' (sig. F3v).

[36] Gardiner, *Letters*, 166; cf. *CWM*, 8.944–7.

[37] For Wolsey's campaign against heretical literature, see Craig D'Alton, 'The Suppression of Lutheran Heretics in England, 1526–1529', *Journal of Ecclesiastical History* 54 (2003), 228–53.

1526 bear witness to the fact that Luther's books, banned now for nearly five years, were still making their way into the country with an easy regularity.[38] Only a short while earlier, in August 1525, a Paul's Cross preacher had complained about Londoners who were expressing a willingness to die for the sake of Luther's works.[39] And as Tyndale's English translation of the New Testament began to roll off a Cologne press at the end of 1525, Wolsey had good reason to believe that it too would soon become available in England in disturbing quantities.[40] He therefore intended a 'secrete serch ye wuld this terme make in diverse places', with the confiscated works to be burned at Paul's Cross with preaching 'contra Lutherum, Lutherianos, fautoresque eorum, contra opera eorum et libros, et contra inducentes eadem opera in regnum'.[41] Though evidence indicates that very few Lutheran books were in fact uncovered, what was discovered was an influential preacher publicly expounding what could, through a lens of suspicion, be seen as Lutheran ideas.[42]

Barnes was first summoned by the university vice-chancellor, Dr Edmund Natares, for a hearing in the schools.[43] The hearing was a private, informal event, for the purpose of gaining a retraction from the preacher and bringing a swift end to the matter. Barnes maintained his innocence, however, and before he could be persuaded to reconsider a student mob consisting, according to the accused, of 'the hoole body of the universite' interrupted the proceedings.[44] A second examination was convened a few days later in Natares's chambers, at which the authorities took precautions against another fruitless adjournment; a notary was present – unknown to the accused himself – to record the conversation. The examiners were proved to have planned wisely when students again interrupted the meeting and forced its end. Using the transcript of this second meeting, in addition to the original points of offence taken from his sermon, twenty-five articles together with a revocation were formally drawn up and presented to Barnes at yet a third meeting. When he refused to read the recantation at St Edward's on the following Sunday, he was given eight days to reconsider. University authorities had no reason to be optimistic, however, and at the same time despatched a messenger to London, to Wolsey, in the likely event that Barnes would again refuse.

38 See PRO SP 1/37, fos 130–7 (*LP*, 4.1962); cf. PRO SP 1/38, fo. 14 (*LP*, 4.2073).

39 Susan Brigden, *London and the Reformation* (Oxford, 1989), 158.

40 Letters from Johannes Cochleaus and Edward Lee, both then on the continent, had explicitly warned the Crown of the New Testament's imminent arrival in England. See *Records of the English Bible*, ed. A.W. Pollard (London, 1911), 107–10.

41 *Original Letters Illustrative of English History*, 1st series, 3 vols, ed. H. Ellis (London, 1824–46), 1.65 (*LP*, 4.995).

42 For the convincing argument that Barnes's arrest was essentially an afterthought, see A.G. Chester, 'Robert Barnes and the Burning of the Books', *The Huntington Library Quarterly* 3 (1951), 211–21.

43 For the events of this paragraph, see the account provided in *Supplicacion* (1534), sigs H1v–H4r.

44 *Supplicacion* (1534), sig. H2v.

As the timely interference of student supporters on two separate occasions indicates, no small controversy had been aroused in Cambridge. Foxe further testifies that the ensuing debate over the content of Barnes's sermon led to 'one preachyng agaynst another ... until within vi. dayes of Shrovetyde'.[45] It must have been with some relief to city and university authorities, then, that on Monday 5 February 1526 Barnes was very visibly arrested in the Convocation House, and on the next morning removed to London. After a brief interview with Wolsey on Wednesday evening, during which Stephen Gardiner and Edward Foxe assured the cardinal that Barnes was 'reformable', his formal examination before the bishops of Rochester, St Asaph, and Bath and Wells commenced on Thursday 8 February.[46] The reactions of Wolsey and the bishops to the prepared articles offer further indications that Barnes's sermon had not been overtly or explicitly heretical. Even Robert Ridley, the secretary of London Bishop Cuthbert Tunstall, confessed that he heard no clear heresy when the sermon was first preached.[47] Similarly, Bishop John Fisher declared that, even if paid a hundred pounds, he could not be persuaded to condemn as heretical some of Barnes's words.[48] Wolsey, understandably, was drawn especially to those points which called his own actions or authority into question. He chastised Barnes for criticising the accoutrements of his office, and questioned the wisdom of some particularly stinging witticisms having been made in the presence of unlearned townspeople. But he was rather dismissive of other articles and, again being assured that Barnes was 'reformable', released him for the night into the custody of Cambridge friends rather than detaining him.[49] The bishops who heard Barnes's case over the next three days – John Clerk, Henry Standish, and John Fisher – were not always so charitable; but neither were they explicit in their charge of particular heresies. The revocation to which Barnes finally subscribed noted vaguely that, of the articles taken from his sermon, 'some be sclaunderous, some be erroneous, some be contencyous, some be sedicious, some be folyshe, and some be hereticall'.[50] There is no disputing that many were slanderous, contentious, and foolish. But to Barnes's request that his examiners be clear about which were in fact heretical, he would receive no answer.

In spite of their refusal to be explicit, and despite the vagueries of Barnes's own Christmas Eve proclamation, the suspicions of his examiners are entirely understandable when the circumstances of his sermon and trial are taken into consideration. Not only might the lawyers of Trinity Hall have found Barnes's condemnation of lawsuits objectionable, but, more decisively, while the

45 *A&M*, 2.1192.
46 *A&M*, 2.1192.
47 *Supplicatyon* (1531), fo. 22v.
48 *Supplicatyon* (1531), fo. 23v.
49 *A&M*, 2.1193.
50 *Supplicacion* (1534), sig. I2r.

staunchly orthodox Fisher remained chancellor of the university any public criticism of the ecclesiastical order, explicitly heretical or not, was bound to be heard unfavourably. Furthermore, that Barnes's sermon was in some sense intended to be an official declaration of his evangelical sympathies appears to have been advertised in advance, which explains the attendance that evening of his accusers Robert Ridley and Walter Preston.[51] Most importantly, however, as previously noted, Barnes's arrest took place in the context of Wolsey's organised campaign to discover and destroy heretical literature imported from the continent. His arrest was, in fact, carried out concurrently with a search for such books in Cambridge itself. On the very day his trial began four Steelyard men – Hans Ellendorpe, Herbert Bellendorpe, Hans Reusell, and Henry Prykness – were also examined by the panel of bishops who sat in judgement of Barnes. Each admitted to having owned and read certain works of Luther.[52] No less significant is the fact that Chancellor Fisher, who had for five years now been publishing against Luther and his heresies, and who was one of those commissioned by Wolsey to curb the trade in Luther's books, sat among those questioning Barnes. With Luther's dangerous opinions at the forefront of everyone's mind it can hardly be surprising that similarities, intended or not, were readily found in the articles compiled against Barnes. He had questioned the importance of holy days and inveighed against ecclesiastical wealth, clerical pride, and rampant pluralism; he criticised the church's trafficking in indulgences and dispensations; he questioned the benefit of mumbled Masses; and he dispensed with prayers to the Virgin Mary and for souls in purgatory. Barnes, by the time of his public abjuration at St Paul's on Sunday 11 February, should hardly have been surprised that Fisher's sermon was directed almost entirely 'agaynst Lutherians, as though they had convicted me for one'. Nevertheless, as late as 1534 Barnes was still claiming that at the time he was 'as farre from those thyngs as any man coulde be'.[53]

As Fisher's sermon indicates, Barnes's attempt to deny any connection with explicitly Lutheran ideas was not entirely convincing. Further evidence also suggests that it was not entirely honest. John Foxe, for example, would later assert that Barnes's sermon had been preached 'folowyng the scripture and Luthers postill'.[54] Though not always reliable in details, Foxe seems to have been correct on this point, as Barnes's commentary on lawsuits is strikingly similar to the printed text of Luther's 1521 sermon on Philippians 4:4–7. The similarities are especially significant since the text upon which both preached does not especially lend itself to an attack on litigiousness.[55] To be sure, even the text of Luther's own homily is not overtly evangelical in its theological content; yet Barnes's use of it

51 See Rex, 'The Early Impact', 49.
52 PRO SP 1/37, fos 130–7 (*LP*, 4/1.1962).
53 *Supplicacion* (1534), sig. I2v.
54 *A&M*, 2.1192.
55 See Rex, 'The Early Impact', 47–8.

was in clear contravention of the English ban on Luther's writings, a ban which had been made quite explicit in Cambridge itself with the burning of Luther's books in 1521.

Whether truly a 'Lutherian' or not, Barnes was finally persuaded that 'to rede the rolle ... was but a smalle thynge, and I was never the worse man'.[56] He therefore recanted before his examiners, was absolved, and the next day did public penance at St Paul's.[57] But if Barnes had believed 'that they wold have required no more of me, but for to have redde the rolle afore the face of the worlde', he had again seriously misjudged the times.[58] At the conclusion of the ceremony he was once again returned to the Fleet, the first of a series of locations at which he would remain imprisoned for nearly three years.

Barnes remained in the Fleet, he recalled, for 'the space of halfe a yeare', at which time he was, for reasons unexplained, transferred to the London house of his order. Though now able to enjoy again the company of his fellow friars, this was for Barnes no return to the life of a prior. He was here to remain a 'free prisoner', confined but allowed to receive visitors.[59] Even this lenient treatment is rather surprising in several respects. Not only was Barnes's presence apparently resented by some of the London friars, but the former Augustinian Prior General, Gregory of Rimini, scandalised by the laxity in some houses of the order, had mandated that all prisoners remain chained in their cells, hold no conversation, and neither send nor receive letters.[60] Perhaps emboldened by his lenient treatment, though still rather naively for an abjured heretic, Barnes enquired of the Bishop of London, Cuthbert Tunstall, whether he might be allowed to put this privilege to good use and during his confinement 'teache chylderne to wryte and to reade / and lerne them theyr gramer / and soo too gett my lyvynge wyth truth and honestye / and not ydlye to lyve in preason'. Tunstall responded negatively (though rather tactfully avoiding any mention of Barnes's heresy), saying this was not a task he would entrust to one he had never met.[61] Whether Tunstall suspected that Barnes's recantation was suffered as a mere formality is unknown; but had he then been aware of what he was to learn a year and a half later his reply surely would not have been so polite. Late in April 1528 Tunstall heard the confession of John Tyball, a Lollard of Steeple Bumpstead in Essex. Tyball informed the bishop that at Michaelmas 1526 he and his associate Thomas Hilles came to London with the intent of acquiring the newly printed English New

56 *Supplicacion* (1534), sig. I2r.
57 *A&M*, 2.1193; Edward Hall, *Hall's Chronicle Containing the History of England* (London, 1809), 708.
58 *Supplicacion* (1534), sig. I2r.
59 *A&M*, 2.1193.
60 *English Austin Friars*, 14.186. For Foxe's suggestion that the London friars were hostile to Barnes, see *A&M*, 2.1193.
61 *Supplicatyon* (1531), fos 19v–20r.

Testament from friar Barnes. They found him in the Augustinian house, made the desired purchase, and further persuaded Barnes to enter into correspondence with their curate, Richard Fox. The episode is enlightening not only in demonstrating that Barnes maintained some contact with those he knew to be religious dissenters, but in also faintly illuminating his own mindset at this time. In marked contrast to his attitude four years earlier, when he had provided Richard Bayfield with a Latin New Testament, he now disparagingly compared the Latin text to 'a cymball tynkklyng, and brasse sowndyng'.[62] While Barnes's preference for the English might reveal him to be a proponent of vernacular Scripture, his explicit warning to Tyball and Hilles to keep the Bible hidden also shows him fully aware that the distribution and possession of such Scripture was in contravention of secular and ecclesiastical prohibitions. Similarly, while the evidence of Tyball's examination seems to suggest that only one New Testament was purchased, the October 1528 examination of Hilles makes clear that 'eche of them bowght a new testament in English of hem, and paid iii s for a pere'.[63] Clearly Barnes was not simply parting with his own personal Bible, but was acting as a known distributor of contraband literature.[64] To whatever extent Barnes was sincere in his protestation of innocence some months earlier, by October 1526 he had, at least on this decisive point concerning Scripture, consciously sided with the evangelical programme of reform against the official position of the English church.

The Bumpstead men were drawn to Barnes by his reputation; and it would appear that a broader awareness of Barnes's leanings was becoming increasingly common at this time. It was probably also in 1526 or shortly thereafter that Barnes had not only discussed with the Augustinian Provincial the question of whether St Ambrose had maintained the doctrine of justification by faith alone, but had also disputed the veneration of images with Tunstall's secretary Robert Ridley.[65] Despite such advertisement of his opinions, even to those closely associated with Tunstall, Barnes yet again appealed to the London bishop. Hoping to maximise the chances of a charitable response, a number of prominent Londoners – including a city burgess, a former mayor, and a former sheriff – approached Tunstall on his behalf. Though precise details of the bishop's reply are not recorded, something of its nature can be guessed by the fact that Barnes's intercessors were left, as he relates, 'a frayd too speake wyth me and also to speake for

62 John Strype, *Ecclesiastical Memorials*, 3 vols in 6 (Oxford, 1822), 1/2.55 (*LP*, 4/2.4218).

63 BL Harleian MS 421, fo. 35r, extracted in Margaret Aston, 'Lollards and the Reformation: Survival or Revival?', in *Lollards and Reformers*, ed. Margaret Aston (London, 1984), 240. As two books were purchased for the above price, rather than one, it is necessary to correct Lusardi's suggestion that Barnes was significantly overcharging his customers. See Lusardi, 'The Career of Robert Barnes', 1386 n. 1.

64 For the connection between Lollards and the Lutheran book trade, which was first being discovered by authorities in 1528, see Craig D'Alton, 'Cuthbert Tunstal and Heresy in Essex and London, 1528' *Albion* 35 (2003), 210–28.

65 *Supplicatyon* (1531), fos 43v and 134v.

me to any man / yee they were a frayde to geve me meate and dryncke'.[66] If Tunstall's response was prompted by rumours of the friar's opinions and activities, the revelations of Tyball and Hilles in 1528 would have provided evidence both to substantiate the rumours and to encourage swift consequences. Barnes was moved once again, this time to the Augustinian house at Northampton, where he was 'to remayne, as in a perpetuall prison'.[67] Foxe suggests that the perpetuity of this imprisonment would have been severely curtailed, asserting that Barnes's relocation was merely a prelude to a planned execution. Being apprised of the situation, however, Barnes concocted a successful plan for escape. He feigned a short but noticeable bout of desperation; then, by means of a letter left in his cell, he explained that he had gone to end his life by drowning. He also explained that next to the river they would find, with his clothes, another letter and, when his body was recovered, yet a third letter. So convincing was the ruse that an entire week was spent dragging the river, by which time Barnes had made his way in disguise to London and set sail for the safety of the continent.[68]

From exile to ambassador

By the summer of 1530 Robert Barnes can be found in Wittenberg, but his travels between his late 1528 escape and this time cannot be charted with any great certainty. When it was finally discovered that he was still very much alive, Bishop Tunstall voiced a belief that he had gone to Amsterdam. Barnes, however, later denied this, saying he had never in his life visited that city.[69] Thomas More, who took great pains to stay informed of Barnes's comings and goings, indicates Antwerp as a more likely stop on his way to Wittenberg. He claimed that a reliable source told him about 'suche tyme as frere Barons and Tyndale fyrste mette and talked to gether beyond the see, after that he fledde out of the freres where he was enjoynded to tarye for his penaunce after he had borne his fagot'.[70] Despite the trust he placed in his informant, More's account of this meeting is not altogether accurate in its details, as Barnes himself would later complain.[71] But with More, unlike with Tunstall, Barnes did not make a point of denying that his location had been accurately ascertained. And More's belief that Barnes spent time in Antwerp is supported by Foxe, who maps his route 'by long Seas to Antwerpe, and so to Luther'.[72] More certain is Barnes's location in 1529. At least part of this

66 *Supplicatyon* (1531), fo. 20r–v.
67 *Supplicacion* (1534), sig. I3r; cf. Gardiner, *Letters*, 167.
68 *A&M*, 2.1193. Based upon Barnes's own calculation that he was imprisoned for 'two yeres, and thre quarters', his flight can be dated to late 1528. *Supplicacion* (1534), sig. I2v.
69 *Supplicatyon* (1531), fo. 33v.
70 *CWM*, 8.302.
71 See *CWM*, 7.255.
72 *A&M*, 2.1193. The proposed route from Antwerp through Lübeck and Hamburg to Wittenberg

year he spent in Lübeck, where a local chronicler notes that he cared for a number people suffering the sweating sickness, introducing to the city the then novel 'English treatment' for the illness. Barnes's advocacy there for vernacular Scripture, however, did not meet with the same success as his medical advice. The same chronicler, Reinmar Kock, recalls Barnes making an unsolicited visit to the home of a city councillor. Enquiring whether the councillor would ensure that a man's testament be faithfully upheld, Barnes proceeded to produce a German New Testament. He was promptly turned away and, according to Kock, banished from the city the following day.[73] It would appear that he then proceeded to Hamburg, where similar reports of the English method of treating the sweats come to light in the summer of 1529.[74] As both William Tyndale and Johann Bugenhagen were present in the city this year, it is probable that here Barnes took leave of the one and continued on with the other;[75] it is in Bugenhagen's home that Barnes is lodged by the summer of 1530.

Though frustratingly little evidence exists with which to detail Barnes's first stay in Wittenberg, it is clear that he quickly made a positive impression on the city's reformers. Not only did he live with Bugenhagen in 1530, but in the same year his host would happily contribute a preface to Barnes's first published work of theology.[76] Later recalling Barnes's early days in Germany, Luther described him as 'our good pious table companion', commended his 'noteworthy humility', and numbered him among those 'saints who have eaten with us, drunk with us (as the apostles say of Christ, Acts 4), and joined in our happiness'.[77] Though Luther's remembrance here is especially warm as it was offered in the immediate wake of Barnes's death, when Barnes left Wittenberg to visit England in early 1531 Luther – making use of the name by which Barnes was known on the continent – was already fondly referring to him as 'mi Antoni'.[78]

While thus temporarily enjoying the patronage of the Wittenbergers, Barnes could at last return to a similitude of the academic life he had once enjoyed in Cambridge. Here he soon set to work on two of the books he would publish in his lifetime. The first, his *Sentenciae ex doctoribus collectae*, published under his continental pseudonym Antonius Anglus, was compiled during the summer of

mirrors that which Barnes would travel from Wittenberg on his way back to England in late 1531, when he passed through Lübeck en route to Antwerp.

73 See J.L. Flood, '"Safer on the battlefield than in the city": England, the "Sweating Sickness", and the Continent', *Renaissance Studies* 17 (2003), 173–5.

74 See Flood, 'Safer on the battlefield', 173, for the English method of treating the sickness coming to light at Hamburg in the summer of 1529.

75 See J.F. Mozley, *William Tyndale* (London, 1937), 153.

76 It is in his preface to Barnes's *Sentenciae* that Bugenhagen notes the work was compiled that summer 'in aedibus nostris' (sig. A2v).

77 *WA*, 51.448: 'unser guter, fromer tischgeselle'; 'sonderlicher demut'; 'Heiligen werden, die mit uns gessen, getruncken (wie die Apostel von Christo sagen, Act. iiij) und ehren frölich gewest sind'.

78 *WABr*, 6.1861.

1530 and published by the Wittenberg printer Joseph Clug later that autumn. The second, *A supplicatyon made by Robert Barnes*, was published late in the following year and can in some respects be considered an amplified edition of his first work. Most obviously different, however, was the intended audience of this second publication. Barnes addresses his King – and, implicitly in his choice of the vernacular, a wider English audience – with an appeal for the reformation of the church. In an attempt to illustrate the corrupt state of the contemporary English church he also offers an extended commentary on the handling he had himself received during the trial and imprisonment preceding his exile. If Henry, convinced by the *Supplicatyon*, is willing to promise him protection from the bishops, Barnes in turn promises to 'presente my selfe un to oure most noble prynce / there offeringe my selfe to his grace that I wyl eyther prove these thynges by godes worde agenst you al / or els I wyl suffer at hys graces plesure'.[79] Despite his growing affinity for the theology of the Germans (or, indeed, perhaps because of it), Barnes clearly desired to return to his homeland.

If Barnes feared he had no friends in high places at home, he was soon proved happily wrong. Even as he completed work on the *Supplicatyon* in the summer of 1531, an unknown English messenger sought him out in Germany. Henry VIII, who had been violently opposed to Luther for the last decade, had suddenly become interested in that reformer's thoughts on his marital status. Barnes was asked to ascertain Luther's opinion and relay it to England. In his desire to gain Henry's favour, he attempted an even greater service. In late August or early September he visited Landgrave Philip of Hesse, asking him to correspond with Luther in a bid to influence his answer to the King.[80] Philip happily obliged, noting that an alliance with Henry was not without political advantages. His letter, however, only arrived at Wittenberg some two weeks after Luther had given Barnes his answer in writing. By the first week in September Barnes and Luther had already discussed the matter in person, and Barnes could not have been surprised at receiving Luther's unfavourable verdict. Luther, though, was well aware that his judgement would not advance Barnes's standing with Henry, and his letter concludes with the advice that Barnes confer with others about whether to present it to the King or, for his own sake, to suppress it.[81] Upon receipt of this letter, and perhaps yet undecided about his course of action, Barnes made for Antwerp.

From Antwerp Barnes could readily set sail for England with Luther's reply. But he also had business of his own in the city, namely the printing of his now finished *Supplicatyon*. By mid-October 1531 this work had come off the press of

[79] *Supplicatyon* (1531), fo. 34r.
[80] Erwin Doernberg, *Henry VIII and Luther: An Account of their Personal Relations* (London, 1961), 85.
[81] *WABr*, 6.1861.

the Antwerp printer Simon Cock; by mid-November copies were present in England; and by mid-December Barnes himself had again set foot on English soil.[82] Stephen Vaughan, a merchant-adventurer with evangelical leanings, was the man responsible for bringing the *Supplicatyon* to the attention of those at court. Vaughan had left England for Antwerp nearly one year earlier with hopes of convincing Tyndale to return to England, and of convincing Henry VIII to guarantee his return a safe one. As part of this programme Vaughan provided the King with regular copies of Tyndale's works and provided Thomas Cromwell, the King's minister, with regular reports of his progress.[83] Yet serious problems arose after only a few months in Antwerp. On 20 May 1531 Cromwell, who had thus far been supportive of Vaughan's efforts, wrote to insist that he stop courting Tyndale.[84] While he assured Vaughan that both he and the King appreciated his efforts, he also made it unmistakably clear that Henry despised Tyndale's opinions and had no desire for his return to England. Cromwell did indicate, however, that Vaughan would earn the King's favour if he were to make progress with John Frith, another English evangelical in exile.

Unless he later received additional instructions, Vaughan seems to have interpreted this as giving him a certain licence also to seek out other exiles. On 24 October he sent Cromwell 'suche a piece of worke as I yet have not syn one like unto it'.[85] The work was Robert Barnes's *Supplicatyon*, and it was accompanied by Vaughan's request that it be specially presented to the King. When three weeks later he learned that it remained undelivered, Vaughan became almost obsessed with the idea of it being read by Henry. He wrote to Cromwell twice on 14 November.[86] He not only begs the minister to enquire about the fate of the first copy sent, but also forwards a second. Again he implores Cromwell to present it to the King and, in a postscript, offers some explanation for his plea.

> How good a dede shulde you do to healpe that Doctour Barnes might declare thepinions of his booke before the Kynges magestye and the worlde that men lokyng upon the same booke, and moved with his opinions (being good) maye be suffered to holde them for such, and being

[82] It is generally agreed that Cock was the printer, though Martinus de Keyser cannot be ruled out. De Keyser printed Tyndale's *Exposition of the Fyrste Epistle of Seynt Jhon* (STC 24443), which was included with the *Supplicatyon* in a parcel sent by Stephen Vaughan to Thomas Cromwell. Whoever was responsible for Barnes's work seems also to have printed John Frith's *Disputacion of Purgatory* (STC 11388) and Tyndale's *Answere unto Sir Thomas Mores Dialoge* (STC 24437), which bear the same type and ornamentation. For the debate, see M.E. Kronenberg, 'Forged Addresses in Low Country Books in the Period of the Reformation', *The Library*, 5th series, 2 (1947), 81–94, and Anthea Hume, 'English Protestant Books Printed Abroad, 1525–1535: An Annotated Bibliography', in *CWM*, 8.1063–91.

[83] For Vaughan's correspondence, see, e.g., BL Cottonian MS Galba B.X, fos 46–7 (*LP*, 5.65); PRO SP 1/65, fo. 169 (*LP*, 5.153).

[84] R.B. Merriman, *Life and Letters of Thomas Cromwell*, 2 vols (Oxford, 1902), 1.21 (*LP*, 5.248).

[85] PRO SP 1/68, fo. 51 (*LP*, 5.533).

[86] BL Cottonian MS Titus B.I, fo. 373 (*LP*, 5.532); PRO SP 1/68, fos 51–2 (*LP*, 5.533).

> evyle maye be therwith induced to detest and abhorre them accordyngly. I thynke verily the comen people have never byn so muche moved to geve credence to any worke that before this, hathe byn put forthe in thenglishe tongue, as they wil be unto this, by cause he presumithe to prove his lernyng as well by the scripture, as by the Doctours and the popes law. If it be true that he writeth, as it is not in my judgement to know (albeit that I rather thinke na, then yea) let all the worlde thinke that in nothing prevaylethe any prince of the worlde be he never so myghtye, to thinke that he can destroy it, for heaven and yerthe shall sonner perish than one iota of godes worde (crist being ther of witness) shall fayle. / If it be false, let the world agayn thinke, that god being thereunto most mightiest and most able shall bothe destroy it and the makers mayntaynours and upholders therof. ... Mennys errours in my poore judgement shulde from hensforthe cesse, wer it so that it myght please the Kynges magestye, to have this man examyned both before his highness and the worlde, wherby his grace shulde show hym self seryously to regard the truthe of goddess worde.[87]

Vaughan is obviously enthusiastic about the work; but after his embarrassment with Tyndale he wisely qualifies his praise. He wonders whether the first copy may have gone undelivered due to the carrier's fear of being associated with it, and famously suggests that Barnes 'shall seale it withe his bloode'.[88]

Rather than earning Henry's wrath, however, the work seems to have been well regarded. Barnes very quickly received a royal safe conduct, and on 21 December 1531 the imperial ambassador Eustace Chapuys writes that:

> An English Austin friar, who has lived for a length of time with Luther and others of his sect, has lately arrived in this city. He has come with a safe conduct, and it is added, at the King's express solicitation (*au tres grand porchas du roy*). He goes about court dressed as a layman (*en habit de seculier*) in the company most times of another Italian friar of the Order of St Francis, one of those who are known to have written in favour of the King.[89]

Without being specific, Chapuys indicates that Barnes must have arrived at least several days before 21 December. But his arrival may be pushed back even further on information from Thomas More, who says that Barnes only adopted his secular attire after he had been nearly six weeks in England, when his safe conduct neared its expiration.[90] Until this point, says More, he was 'monstrousely dressed ... because he wold be wondred on'.[91]

87 PRO SP 1/68, fo. 52 (*LP*, 5.533).
88 PRO SP 1/68, fo. 51 (*LP*, 5.533).
89 *CSPS*, 4/2.865 (*LP*, 5.593). Nicholas de Burgo is the Franciscan to whom Chapuys here refers.
90 *CWM*, 8.885.
91 *CWM*, 8.845.

While Barnes was yet in England, the *Supplicatyon* continued to receive attention. It certainly received that of Stephen Gardiner, who, having consistently spoken on Barnes's behalf throughout his 1526 trial, was understandably disgruntled by the manner in which he had been portrayed in the *Supplicatyon*. There, referring back to the events of his trial, Barnes had accused Gardiner of selectively quoting and therefore misrepresenting St Augustine's opinion on litigation.[92] Yet Gardiner would later recall that, during Barnes's brief return to England in 1531, the two had met by chance, in the presence of Thomas Cranmer, at Hampton Court. There Gardiner, now the Bishop of Winchester, challenged Barnes's recollection of the matter and showed him the Augustine text in question. In response, Gardiner reported, 'Barnes fyl downe on his knees and asked me instantlye forgeveness'.[93] That Gardiner's report is credible cannot be doubted; not only is its substance earlier attested by Thomas More, but Barnes would silently excise his earlier criticism of Gardiner from the 1534 republication of his work. But Gardiner was not the only one to feel he was being misrepresented in recent publications; Barnes too was receiving negative press and felt the need to defend himself. Thomas More had written, in the summer of 1531, that when Tyndale and Barnes first met on the continent they had some small falling out over the sacrament of the altar. According to More, Barnes shared the doctrine of the Swiss reformer Ulrich Zwingli, a view which Tyndale had found distasteful.[94] This, according to Barnes, was not at all the case, and before he returned to the continent he wrote to More and strongly denied that he held the Swiss position.[95] Though clarifying issues with Gardiner and More, Barnes failed to make any positive progress with his King. Understandably displeased with the communication from Luther concerning the royal marriage, Henry seems to have considered Barnes of no further use. Chapuys, who had noted his arrival only a month before, wrote on 22 January that Barnes left England with 'the dislike and displeasure of these people'.[96]

Barnes returned in 1532 not to Wittenberg, however, but again to Hamburg, where he would lodge with the pastor and later city superintendent Johannes Aepinus. For more than a year Barnes would call Hamburg home, finally returning to Wittenberg in mid-June 1533 to participate in the disputation leading to the conferral of a doctorate on Aepinus.[97] Barnes's decision to remain in

92 *Supplicatyon* (1531), fo. 26v.
93 Gardiner, *Letters*, 166–7; cf. More's mention of the episode in *CWM*, 8.10.
94 *CWM*, 8.302.
95 *CWM*, 7.255. Tyndale also clarified their respective positions one year later. Writing to John Frith, who unquestionably affirmed the sacramental theology of the Swiss, Tyndale warned him not to cross Barnes on this point. The tone of this admonition suggests that Tyndale spoke from experience. See *A&M*, 2.1081 (*LP*, 6.403).
96 *CSPS*, 4/2.888 (*LP*, 5.737).
97 See *Dr Johannes Bugenhagens Briefwechsel*, ed. O. Vogt (Stettin, 1888), 127, 205.

Wittenberg is revealed in his own matriculation at the university on 20 June.[98] On the basis of this matriculation, it is most likely that Barnes remained in the city through the second half of 1533 and into 1534, probably taking advantage of the university library as he began work on that which would be published in 1536 as his *Vitae romanorum pontificum*.

Only one year after his matriculation, however, Barnes would again return to England. He travelled this time not alone on the King's safe conduct, but in the company of ambassadors from his previous place of residence, Hamburg, and from the city of Lübeck.[99] Both cities looked to Henry as a beneficial ally in opposition to the emperor, and Henry for his part encouraged their support of his marital decisions. By May Hamburg and Lübeck had agreed to send ambassadors to England, and in mid-June they arrived in London.[100] Given the circumstances of all involved, the negotiations could surely not have been limited to political issues. Already on 7 July 1534 Chapuys voiced a fear that the embassy's intention was to refute any who would make 'difficulties about entering the Lutheran sect'.[101] And indeed, by August daily disputations were taking place with England's bishops and doctors of theology. Intriguingly, in a letter written by Thomas Warley to Lady Lisle on 13 August, Robert Barnes is the only disputant mentioned by name.[102] Similarly revealing is the fact that, even when most of the ambassadors returned to the continent in September, Barnes was one of those left behind to continue the theological discussions which took place through to the year's end.[103] But he also had further reason to remain in the country; in November, and almost certainly at Cromwell's instigation, he saw through John Bydell's London press a radically revised edition of his previously published *Supplicatyon*. With this task completed, and with theological discussions coming to a frustratingly fruitless end shortly thereafter, Barnes and his remaining cohorts returned to the continent near the end of January 1535.[104]

From ambassador to martyr

With the Hamburg and Lübeck embassy of 1534 Robert Barnes received a foretaste of the theological and political negotiations that were to consume most of his remaining years. And despite the failure of the delegates to reach an agreement with the English bishops in 1534, Barnes at least seems to have proved himself a valuable Anglo-Lutheran mediator. Only one month after departing for Germany

98 See P. Smith, 'Englishmen at Wittenberg in the Sixteenth Century', *English Historical Review* 36 (1921), 423.
99 See *A&M*, 2.1193, where Foxe mentions this embassy but has many of the facts confused.
100 *CSPS*, 5/1.68 (*LP*, 7.871).
101 *CSPS*, 5/1.70 (*LP*, 7.957).
102 *Lisle Letters*, 2.245 (*LP*, 7.1064).
103 *CSPS*, 5/1.87 (*LP*, 7.1141); *CSPS*, 5/1.112 (*LP*, 7.1482).
104 *LP*, 8.121.

he was again acting as intermediary between England and continental Lutherans. He arrived in Wittenberg on 11 March 1535, approaching not Luther this time, but Melanchthon. Again the topic was the King's marriage. The meeting was brief, and only two days later Barnes was on his way back to England with both letters and praise from Melanchthon.[105]

Though Barnes remained well regarded by the Wittenbergers, he was not without enemies both in England and on the continent. In April 1535, making his way through Antwerp en route to London, Barnes, being forewarned, managed to avoid being taken in the plot that resulted in Tyndale's arrest by Henry Phillips. That Phillips also had a commission for Barnes's arrest demonstrates that the latter had not entirely shaken off his status as an abjured heretic; but the brief correspondence resulting from the affair also reveals that he had by this time come to be increasingly favoured by prominent evangelicals at the English court. When Cranmer's agent Thomas Theobald learned the details of Phillips's commission, he wrote immediately to the Archbishop. Summarising a conversation he had with Phillips, Theobald mentioned that Phillips's servant, who had travelled to England, still remained unaccountably absent. Phillips feared that 'he be taken & commen in to master secretays handlyng'.[106] Being obviously at odds with these two men, it seems evident that Phillips's commission for Barnes's arrest did not originate in the court circle of Cranmer and Cromwell. In fact, it appears that Cranmer and Cromwell sent Barnes on the mission to Melanchthon in the first place, as he made a point of writing to both of them the day after leaving Wittenberg.[107]

Barnes's standing in the eyes of these two men becomes even clearer upon his arrival in England. By 25 May 1535 he had been appointed to a commission charged with examining the theological opinions of a number of recent immigrants.[108] Two months later he is found on another such commission; though several others were also appointed, an extant memorandum specifies that 'oon of the which [is] allwae to be my lorde of Canterbury master Secretary or doctor barnes'.[109] And despite sporadic complaints about what conservative clergy impugned as 'abhomynable sermons' by a 'false felowe and a noughty wretche', Barnes grew even in the estimation of his King.[110] Thus when Henry learned in

105 *CR*, 2.1263 (*LP*, 8.375); *CR*, 2.1264 (*LP*, 8.384).
106 BL Cottonian MS Galba B.X, fo. 119 (*LP*, 8.1151).
107 See PRO SP 1/91, fo. 76 (*LP*, 8.385). A contemporary rumour had the commission for Barnes's arrest originating with the procurator general of Brussels. See PRO SP 1/92, fo. 115 (*LP*, 8.652). Mozley, *William Tyndale*, 300, has suggested that the conservative Bishop Stokesley was behind the commission.
108 *Lisle Letters*, 2.396 (*LP*, 8.771).
109 PRO SP 1/94, fo. 97 (*LP*, 8.1063). That Barnes's opinion was especially respected by Cromwell seems to have been common knowledge by this time. See, e.g., PRO SP 1/93, fo. 40 (*LP*, 8.854).
110 PRO SP 1/94, fo. 1 (*LP*, 8.1000); cf. also BL Cottonian MS Cleopatra E.V, fo. 397 (*LP*, 9.230) and PRO SP 1/99, fo. 174 (*LP*, 9.1059).

July that the French were making arrangements for Philip Melanchthon to visit, he immediately despatched Barnes to thwart any such plans. This was not merely a defensive mission, however; in addition to persuading Melanchthon to come instead to England, Barnes was also to learn the German position regarding the possibility of a general council and to impress upon the Wittenbergers Henry's interest in joining the Schmalkaldic League of the Lutheran estates. Though it was apparently not part of his official duties, Barnes was also eager to prove his loyalty by debating the conservative polemicist Johannes Cochlaeus, who had recently written against the Royal Supremacy.[111] In some respects, this mission can be regarded as Barnes's first formal embassy on behalf of the Crown; as such he was sent with letters of credence designating him the King's chaplain.[112]

Barnes set sail from England on Sunday 25 July 1535.[113] By late August he had arrived in Hamburg, and on 6 September Luther wrote from Wittenberg that 'Doctor Antonius is here'.[114] At the behest of Luther and other university theologians, Barnes was granted a private meeting with Saxon Elector Johann Friedrich near the end of the month.[115] If the Elector was unwilling to give unqualified answers to Barnes's requests, it was still, according to both parties, a fruitful first meeting. Melanchthon could not be freed to travel to England, but neither would he be going to France. And though Johann Friedrich could not speak by himself on matters pertaining to the Schmalkaldic League or a general council, these would be taken up when the League met in December.[116] Thus Barnes could write to Cromwell early in October and announce that his mission was progressing positively.[117] Luther and Melanchthon relay the same, both praising Barnes and noting that the Elector had shown his own pleasure by dismissing him with gifts.[118] Johann Friedrich himself further confirmed Barnes's diligence in correspondence with the English King.[119]

Until the League's scheduled meeting at Schmalkalden, and until ambassadors

[111] Though this desire is frequently mentioned, it seems it was never fulfilled. See, e.g., *CSPS*, 5/1.190 (*LP*, 9.18); BL Cottonian MS Vitellius B.XXI, fos 127–8 (*LP*, 9.153); BL Cottonian MS Vitellius B.XXI, fos 120–1 (*LP*, 9.543); *CR*, 2.1355 (*LP*, 9.825).
[112] See BL Cottonian MS Cleopatra E.VI, fos 337–8 (*LP*, 8.1062). For Cromwell's notes relating to Barnes's mission, see also BL Cottonian MS Titus B.I, fo. 476 (*LP*, 8.1061); PRO SP 1/94, fo. 97 (*LP*, 8.1063); PRO SP 1/94, fo. 108 (*LP*, 8.1077). In addition to Melanchthon's high opinion of him, the choice of Barnes was undoubtedly influenced by Cromwell, who only one month earlier had made a point of reminding Henry of Barnes's recent service in Germany. See BL Cottonian MS Titus B.I, fo. 475 (*LP*, 8.892).
[113] Cf. PRO SP 1/94, fo. 109 (*LP*, 8.1078) and PRO SP 1/94, fo. 135 (*LP*, 8.1109).
[114] *WABr*, 7.2235: 'hic est Doctor Antonius' (*LP*, 9.294). For his correspondence at this time, see BL Cottonian MS Vitellius B.XXI, fos 127–8 (*LP*, 9:153); BL Cottonian MS Vitellius B.XXI, fo. 126 (*LP*, 9:177); PRO SP 1/95, fo. 171 (*LP*, 9.181).
[115] *WABr*, 7.2241 (*LP*, 9.355); *CR*, 2.1326 (*LP*, 9.363); *CR*, 2.1328 (*LP*, 9.389).
[116] *CR*, 2.1329 (*LP*, 9.390).
[117] BL Cottonian MS Vitellius B.XXI, fos 120–1 (*LP*, 9.543).
[118] *CR*, 2.1332 (*LP*, 9.503).
[119] *CR*, 2.1330 (*LP*, 9.468).

Edward Foxe and Nicholas Heath arrived from England to join him in further discussions, Barnes was temporarily freed to busy himself with academic concerns. On 10 September 1535 he penned the introduction to his *Vitae romanorum pontificum*, a history of the papacy dedicated to Henry VIII. In the same month he would participate in university disputations at Wittenberg.[120] But, strangely for one so keen on debate, and especially one so anxious to dispute with the papal theologian Cochlaeus, Barnes chose to forego an invitation extended by the papal legate Pietro Paolo Vergerio. This is especially difficult to understand since the legate arrived in Wittenberg to discuss the convening of a general council – a matter of definite interest to Barnes and his King. Nevertheless, Luther, who met with Vergerio in November, explained that he had to act as Barnes's representative.[121] Whatever Barnes's reason for declining the invitation, it is clear that as the month progressed he became increasingly anxious about the forthcoming meeting of the League and the delay of his fellow Englishmen.[122] He was greatly relieved, then, when they finally arrived late in November and when, in the first week of December, a flurry of activity signalled preparations for the move to Schmalkalden.[123]

Having travelled from Wittenberg to Erfurt the week before, Barnes moved on to Weimar on 9 December 1535, there to meet Foxe and Heath, as well the Saxon Elector, his chancellor, and the vice-chancellor. After a series of preliminary conferences in which the English ambassadors were assured that Johann Friedrich was not acting contrary to the King's interests, the three continued on to Schmalkalden in the Elector's company, arriving on 13 December.[124] They remained spectators through much of the meeting that there took place, but began to take an active part in the proceedings in the days before Christmas, when discussions turned to Henry's interest in the League. In response to this interest, members conferred with the King's delegates and together drafted a series of articles outlining the conditions upon which England might enter the Schmalkaldic League.[125] Though Barnes's signature is affixed to these articles, he also makes clear that Foxe had taken the lead in negotiating with the Lutheran representatives. Writing to Cromwell three days after Christmas, Barnes praises Foxe's handling of the political matters at Schmalkalden and notes that they are moving on to Wittenberg where discussion of theological matters will continue. He indicates that Foxe will there again act as head of the delegation, but hints that even the English delegates are not all of the same mind. Though he and Foxe are not in

120 See *AE*, 34.108.
121 *WABr*, 7.2270 (*LP*, 9.805).
122 *WABr*, 7.2276 (*LP*, 9.929).
123 *CR*, 2.1372 (*LP*, 9.930); *CR*, 2.1374 (*LP*, 9.928).
124 BL Cottonian MS Vitellius B.XXI, fo. 179 (*LP*, 9.1018).
125 For the articles, see *CR*, 2.1383 (*LP*, 9.1016).

complete theological agreement, Barnes voices his confidence that he will be able 'to drawe hym at length to me'.[126]

What the English embassy was agreed upon, much to the distaste of the Germans, was the desire yet again to argue the merits of Henry's case for an annulment – this in spite of the fact that the King had long been remarried and, as Luther would learn later in the month, Catherine herself was now dead.[127] Luther expressed a hope that this would take no more than three days; but he also observed that the delegates displayed no intentions of leaving soon.[128] And indeed, when Melanchthon arrived in mid-January 1536, he complained that the English were still pursuing the matter. It was only the promise that they would move on to more specifically doctrinal concerns that prompted him to stay.[129] Even then, however, theological discussions were delayed until March, due perhaps in small part to Barnes's engagement with seeing his *Vitae romanorum pontificum* through the press.

In contrast to the consideration of Henry's annulment, doctrinal matters, when finally addressed, were concluded fairly quickly. Melanchthon announced on 9 March that they were being discussed; a day later he noted that articles had been drawn up; and by 20 March it was reported that each article had been discussed except those few touching what the Germans considered to be abuses in English ecclesiastical practice.[130] Discussion continued until the end of the month, and though Melanchthon noted that the English and Germans had 'no unimportant differences', he also confirmed that they had agreed on most articles.[131] Luther was not overly optimistic, however, and mentioned that even the English were unsure whether Henry would favourably receive the articles on which they had agreed.[132] His scepticism was partially confirmed when, shortly thereafter, Henry's response to the earlier articles of 25 December arrived. He informed the Lutherans that he did not 'thinketh it meet to accept at any creature's hand, the observing of his and his realm's faith'.[133] Nevertheless, early in April his delegates returned to England to present him with a final draft of the new 'Wittenberg Articles'.[134]

Though Barnes had for several months acted as ambassador for the English King, not a few people in England suspected at this time that he was more closely

126 BL Cottonian MS Vitellius B.XXI, fo. 123 (*LP*, 9.1030).
127 *WABr*, 7.2287.
128 *WABr*, 7.2289 (*LP*, 10.180).
129 *CR*, 3.1393 (*LP*, 10.158).
130 *CR*, 3.1405 (*LP*, 10.447); *CR*, 3.1406 (*LP*, 10.448); F. Prüser, *England und die Schmalkaldner* (Leipzig, 1929), 296. The so-called abuses were clerical celibacy, the withholding of the eucharistic cup, private Masses, and monastic vows.
131 *CR*, 3.1409: 'non leves contentiones' (*LP*, 10.584).
132 *WABr*, 7.3003.
133 Gilbert Burnet, *History of the Reformation of the Church of England*, 7 vols, ed. N. Pocock (Oxford, 1865), 6.155 (*LP*, 9.1016/3).
134 *WABr*, 7.3013 (*LP*, 10.644). For the articles themselves, see *DER*, 118–61.

allied with the German theologians. Thus the abbot of Coggeshall, denouncing prominent heretics, specifically mentions Luther and Barnes together.[135] Likewise, an English evangelical who criticised the recently executed Thomas More noted that More had written 'against Luther, Melanchthon, Pomeranus, and Barnes'.[136] But those who associated Barnes with the Lutherans did not necessarily regard this as detrimental to his standing with the King. In fact, rumours had been circulating since February 1536 that Henry had made Barnes a bishop.[137] Such rumours proved false, but there is some reason to believe that the King was indeed considering the granting of such a benefice. In mid-May, when Barnes requested that Cromwell acquire for him the mastership of Bethlehem Hospital, he specifies that he would rather receive this post than a bishopric.[138] In the event, he received neither; and in the next few months he instead experienced a considerable downturn in his fortunes.

No longer acting on behalf of the King, and without a benefice, Barnes soon found himself in financial straits, as his letters to Cromwell testify.[139] But evidence also indicates that financial problems soon became the least of Barnes's difficulties. He wrote to Melanchthon in June that, although he was still preaching, England was becoming unsafe for outspoken evangelicals.[140] This pessimistic view of English affairs was confirmed the next month by the Scots evangelical Alexander Alesius, who, writing from London to Barnes's Hamburg friend Aepinus, vaguely explained that his correspondence was brief because dangerous times allowed no more.[141] Indeed, by September Barnes himself told Luther that he was no longer preaching openly.[142]

Just how dangerous England could be at the time was vividly illustrated when, in mid-November, the London evangelical Robert Packington was murdered in Cheapside.[143] Packington, an economically and politically prominent London mercer, had been active in broadly reformist circles since 1529, when he had a hand in drafting articles presented to the 'Reformation Parliament' commencing that year. He was brought into Cromwell's service in the early 1530s by Stephen Vaughan, the same merchant adventurer who had brought Barnes to Cromwell's attention in 1531. And while it was Robert's younger brother Augustine who had previously and more prominently advertised evangelical leanings, effectively

135 PRO SP 1/103, fo. 212 (*LP*, 10.774).
136 PRO SP 1/103, fo. 50: 'adversus Lutherum Melanthonem Pomeranum Baronum' (*LP*, 10.587).
137 *CSPS*, 5/2.38 (*LP*, 10.528); cf. *LP*, 10.283.
138 PRO SP 1/103, fo. 293 (*LP*, 10.880).
139 PRO SP 1/113, fo. 138 (*LP*, 11.1448); PRO SP 1/104, fo. 193 (*LP*, 10.1185).
140 *CR*, 3.1439 (*LP*, 10.1034).
141 *CR*, 3.1450 (*LP*, 11.185).
142 *WABr*, 7.3082 (*LP*, 11.475).
143 On Packington and his death, see especially Peter Marshall, 'The Shooting of Robert Packington', in *Religious Identities in Henry VIII's England*, ed. Peter Marshall (Aldershot, 2006), 61–79.

conning Bishop Tunstall into funding the printing of Tyndale's New Testament, Robert Packington was also later remembered as an importer of Tyndale's Bible.[144] His unsolved shooting shocked the city of London, not least its evangelical community. London conservatives were also somewhat surprised when Barnes himself called an end to his recent sabbatical in order to preach a typically fiery sermon at Packington's funeral. He was promptly arrested.[145]

The fear felt by evangelicals at the time is hardly surprising in the light of events such as Packington's murder and, more significantly, Anne Boleyn's execution earlier in May. But evangelical uneasiness is also partially explained by the tension building up to and finally released in the northern uprisings of 1536. Not only had these revolts set authorities on edge and acutely highlighted the possible consequences of radical religious division; they also drew specific attention to men like Robert Barnes. The demands drawn up by Yorkshire rebels in December, for example, mentioned him by name and called for the destruction of his printed works.[146] A bad end for Barnes himself was also predicted by Robert Aske, the leader of the Yorkshire rebellion.[147] In this light, it is most probable that Barnes's brief imprisonment following Packington's funeral was meant as much for his own protection as it was for his punishment.[148] But upon his release by Cromwell, and again confident in the quiet of summer 1537, Barnes zealously resumed the delivery of public sermons throughout the realm.

Having received word of Barnes's preaching in London on 15 July, the Worcester bishop Hugh Latimer wrote to Cromwell the same day that he had heard it was 'a very good sermon', suggesting that 'no one man shall do more good' for the gospel than Barnes.[149] His explicit comment on the sermon's 'great moderation and temperance', though, highlights his assumption – apparently shared by Barnes – that caution was still warranted on the part of prominent evangelicals. The same concern is perhaps evident in Latimer's further comments on Barnes's preaching in December 1537. Having himself heard Barnes preaching at Hartlebury, he was willing to say that 'he is alone in handling a piece of Scripture,

[144] M. Dowling and J. Shakespeare, 'Religion and Politics in mid-Tudor England through the Eyes of an English Protestant Woman: The Recollections of Rose Hickman', *Bulletin of Historical Research* 55 (1982), 97.

[145] For Packington's funeral and Barnes's arrest, see *Lisle Letters*, 3.783 (*LP*, 11.1097); *CR*, 3.1518 (*LP*, 12/1.181). Though specifics are not recorded, it is also evident that Barnes's imprisonment coincided with a dispute he was having with the Bishop of London. See PRO SP 1/113, fo. 20 (*LP*, 11.1355). For Barnes's eventual release, see PRO SP 1/120, fo. 172 (*LP*, 12/1.1260) and *CR*, 3.1597 (*LP*, 12/2.433).

[146] PRO SP 1/112, fo. 119 (*LP*, 11.1246).

[147] PRO E.36/122, fo. 26 (*LP*, 12/1.853); PRO E.36/119, fo. 109 (*LP*, 12/1.901).

[148] See Susan Brigden, 'Thomas Cromwell and the "Brethren" ', in *Law and Government under the Tudors*, ed. C. Cross, D. Loades, and J.J. Scarisbrick (Cambridge, 1988), 45; cf. Diarmaid MacCulloch, *Thomas Cranmer: A Life* (New Haven, 1996), 171.

[149] Latimer, *Sermons and Remains*, 378.

and in setting forth of Christ he hath no fellow'.[150] On this basis he also sent Barnes to preach at Worcester and Evesham. But the apparently unique circumstances of Latimer's first requesting that Barnes preach with him at Hartlebury may reflect some continuing wariness about his preacher's tendency toward unguarded statements.[151]

The clearly Christocentric, if sometimes overly combative, nature of Barnes's sermons was also recognised and again rewarded in late 1537, this time by a prominent layman. When the London alderman Humphrey Monmouth died on 23 November, his will stipulated that Barnes be one of those considered to preach 'to the laude and prayse of my Lord and Saviour Jesus Christ' at the funeral.[152] In addition to leaving Barnes ten pounds and a gown, and naming him to oversee bequests to the will's executors, Monmouth also left money to pay for thirty sermons in his parish church of All Hallows, Barking.[153] Again Barnes was named as one of the preachers. Two months later, Barnes was even being requested as a preacher in Calais, where it was hoped that he might counter the recent influence of the conservative chaplain of the city's high marshal.[154] This request, being addressed to Cranmer in January 1538, is not only indicative of the esteem in which Barnes was held as a preacher; it also highlights the fact that, in spite of repeated complaints by conservative critics, and his own brief imprisonment in 1536, Barnes retained the favour of his patrons at court. Though Cranmer did not send him to Calais, Cromwell continued to employ him throughout 1538, more than once in Wales, where Barnes was in conference with Bishop William Barlow in early spring and again in late summer.[155]

Not only the King's minister but the King himself would also call upon Barnes in 1538, once again to take part in negotiations with the German Lutherans. Despite Henry's often expressed wish to receive a German embassy, especially one that included Melanchthon, negotiations with the Lutherans had until 1538 taken place only on the continent. Finally, in May of that year, though without Melanchthon, German ambassadors arrived in London to take up theological discussions once again. In meetings that lasted until the end of August, they debated with English theologians appointed by the King. Barnes himself was one

150 Latimer, *Sermons and Remains*, 389.

151 See Susan Wabuda, ' "Fruitful Preaching" in the Diocese of Worcester: Bishop Hugh Latimer and his Influence, 1535–1539', in *Religion and the English People, 1500–1640: New Voices, New Perspectives*, ed. Eric Joseph Carlson (Kirksville, MO, 1998), 61.

152 Strype, *Ecclesiastical Memorials*, 1/2.369.

153 Strype, *Ecclesiastical Memorials*, 1/2.372–3. Monmouth's specific request that the *Te Deum* be sung after each sermon also seems to have been granted, with Barnes himself perhaps introducing its singing in English. Cf. Strype, *Ecclesiastical Memorials*, 1/2.369, and Charles Wriothesley, *A Chronicle of England during the Reigns of the Tudors*, 2 vols, ed. W.D. Hamilton (London, 1875–77), 1.83.

154 PRO SP 1/128, fo. 96r (*LP*, 13/1.108).

155 See, e.g., PRO SP 1/137, fo. 201 (*LP*, 13/2.614); PRO SP 1/141, fo. 126 (*LP*, 13/2.1223).

of those appointed, though, significantly, Henry requested that he join the Germans in representing the position forwarded by the Lutherans.[156] Despite this implicit acknowledgment of notable differences between the two parties, the German delegates informed those back home that they were dealing with friendly and learned men, and that the first meetings concluded very satisfactorily. These early meetings seem to have avoided discussion of the controversial abuses, however, and Melanchthon, remembering the results of earlier dialogue, would negatively comment: 'we expect catastrophe'.[157] By August it seems that the delegates themselves were growing sceptical of reaching an agreement on the abuses. On 5 August they drew up their opinion for the last time and asked Cromwell to acquire the King's leave for them to depart.[158] This they did on 1 October 1538, optimistic that, despite their failure to conclude, England under Henry was being led further into the evangelical camp.[159]

As Henry came increasingly to rely upon the counsel of Cuthbert Tunstall and his fellow traditionalists, this optimism was proved naive. But Barnes – perhaps because his name did not appear on the German opinion regarding ecclesiastical abuses, which Henry quickly and forcefully rejected – remained at least tentatively in favour. He continued to be regarded as a trustworthy deputy of Cromwell,[160] and Cranmer also voiced his support of Barnes by asking Cromwell in late August to obtain for him the deanery of Tamworth College, Staffordshire, because he had thus far received 'very small preferment for his pains and travail as he most willingly hath sustained in the king's affairs'.[161] Like the mastership of Bethlehem, it was a benefice ultimately denied him; but Barnes was not wholly ignored. On the day the German embassy departed London he was appointed to a royal commission charged with the examination of English Anabaptists, a commission to which Cromwell also appointed the Archbishop.[162] Barnes's appointment itself is some indication that, however fiery his rhetoric might occasionally be, the substance of his theology continued to remain within the vague boundaries of Henrician orthodoxy. Even more telling in this regard, however, is the uncompromising role Barnes would play in this capacity, leading

156 Wriothesley, *A Chronicle of England*, 1.81–2.
157 *CR*, 3.1699 (*LP*, 13/1.1437): 'Sed καταστροφην expectemus.'
158 BL Cottonian MS Cleopatra E.V, fos 186–221 (*LP*, 13/2.37). Barnes's signature is not included with those of the German delegates. This might simply reflect the fact that he would not leave with the ambassadors, though perhaps it also indicates his awareness of Henry's suspicions and an attempt to distance himself from those at odds with the King.
159 See *CR*, 3.1475 (*LP*, 13/2.741).
160 See, e.g., PRO SP 1/135, fo. 244 (*LP*, 13/2.209).
161 Thomas Cranmer, *Miscellaneous Writings and Letters of Thomas Cranmer*, ed. J.E. Cox (Cambridge: Parker Society, 1846), 381 (*LP*, 13/2.204).
162 *Concilia Magnae Britanniae et Hiberniae*, 4 vols, ed. David Wilkins (London, 1737), 3.836 (*LP*, 13/2.498).

in November to the execution of fellow evangelical John Lambert on Sacramentarian charges.[163]

Partly on account of his anti-Sacramentarian credentials, Barnes's fortunes continued to hold into 1539. He emerged unscathed even when, early in the year, he crossed John Stokesley, Bishop of London, by speaking for a man Stokesley had accused of heresy.[164] Though this can perhaps be credited to his standing with Cranmer and Cromwell, it is also evident that Barnes had not fallen from the King's favour. Early in March Henry again called upon him to act as ambassador to continental Lutherans, not only to the Germans this time but also to the King of Denmark, Christian III.[165] This latter mission seems to have been his primary responsibility, and in a speech before Christian on 12 May he impressed upon the Danish King both Henry's religious zeal and his desire to enter into a defensive alliance against pope and emperor.[166] Christian's reply was positive, if hesitant. While praising Henry's faith, he informed him that the Danish upheld the Lutheran confession presented at Augsburg in 1530 and encouraged Henry again to consider the benefits of joining the Schmalkaldic League. He hoped to send delegates to England, but wished first to confer with his German allies.[167] While he did so, and while his reply was forwarded to England, Barnes made for Hamburg to await further developments.

Barnes was considerably delayed in Hamburg. He wrote to Henry on 12 July 1539, both explaining his delay and further outlining the benefits the English King could expect should he be allied with Denmark.[168] Four days later Christian wrote to Barnes with his own apologies, explaining that he still had no reply from the German princes.[169] Both letters reveal their authors to have been ignorant of recent events in England, where the official tide had turned decidedly against the theology of Barnes and those to whom he had been sent. On the very day that Barnes wrote to Henry the Act of Six Articles, passed in Parliament on 28 June, came into force in England. By mid-July news of the Articles and their effects had reached Germany. Prominent evangelicals, including Latimer, had resigned their sees; Cranmer had sent his wife into exile; Alesius fled to Wittenberg; and Barnes, finally apprised of the situation, strongly doubted whether he should leave Hamburg and return to England.[170]

The next month he did return and, presumably much to his surprise, was finally

163 *A&M*, 2.1121–3.
164 *A&M*, 2.1185.
165 For his letters of credence, see PRO SP 1/144, fo. 34 (*LP*, 14/1.441), and *Aarsberetninger*, 4.131 (*LP*, 14/1.442).
166 *Aarsberetninger*, 4.132 (*LP*, 14/1.955).
167 *Aarsberetninger*, 4.134 (*LP*, 14/1.981); *Aarsberetninger*, 4.133 (*LP*, 14/1.956).
168 BL Cottonian MS Nero B.III, fos 99–100 (*LP*, 7.970). Though the *LP* editors place this among the correspondence of 1534, both internal and external evidence suggest 1539 as the true date.
169 *Aarsberetninger*, 4.138 (*LP*, 14/1.1273).
170 *CR*, 3.1830 (*LP*, 14/1.1278).

granted the living he had been so often denied. William Barlow, Bishop of St David's, had offered the prebend of Llanboidy to Cromwell for one of his chaplains. In doing so he indicated a preference for Barnes, calling him 'not the unfaythfullest' of Cromwell's men.[171] If such praise and preferment suggested to Barnes that he was out of danger, though, he sorely misjudged both Cromwell's position and his own. Rumours had circulated widely in his absence – more than one patently false, but undermining his credibility nonetheless. He had been accused of preaching subversion in late March 1539, an accusation in which Cromwell was also implicated.[172] He was also accused of preaching in July against the Act of Six Articles.[173] But perhaps most damaging was the recollection of a sermon nearly fifteen years in his past, that which had led to his initial trial, abjuration, and imprisonment in early 1526. Recalling Barnes's status as an abjured heretic, and making reference to his recent embassy, Stephen Gardiner protested that an 'herytik' should have been appointed a royal ambassador. Gardiner's protests were answered by Cromwell, who successfully moved to have him displaced from the Privy Council.[174] This was a snub not to be forgotten by Gardiner, who soon made his own move to topple Cromwell's defendant.

In spite of news reaching the continent in February, which indicated that the evangelical movement was progressing unhindered in England, and that 'the word is powerfully preached by an individual named Barnes', conservatives like Gardiner were coming increasingly into the King's favour in early 1540.[175] Therefore, despite Barnes having been the one scheduled to preach, it was no great difficulty for Gardiner, who had been appointed to preach weekly before Henry throughout Lent, to enter the pulpit at Paul's Cross as his replacement on 15 February, the first Sunday in Lent.[176] And despite Gardiner's later denial that he was responsible for the change in schedule, it is hard to imagine that his sermon, a denunciation of the evangelical emphasis on justification by faith, was preached without the man he replaced in mind. Barnes certainly heard it this way; when he entered the same pulpit two weeks later he took up the very text upon which Gardiner had preached, interpreted it in opposition to him, and even unwisely mentioned his opponent by name, handling him, Gardiner would complain, 'somewhat rudely'.[177] When Henry was made aware of the controversy

[171] PRO SP 1/153, fo. 58 (LP, 14/2.107); PRO SP 1/155, fo. 117 (*LP*, 14/2.688).

[172] See Burnet, *History of the Reformation*, 4.419–20 (*LP*, 15.498); cf. BL Lansdowne MS 515, fo. 49. The accusation, it would appear, was false, since Barnes remained on the continent until August 1539.

[173] See *LP*, 14/2.400. Again, Barnes was in fact out of the country on the date of the alleged sermon.

[174] PRO SP 1/155 fo. 156 (*LP*, 14/2.750). See MacCulloch, *Thomas Cranmer*, 257.

[175] *Original Letters*, 2.288 (*LP*, 15.259).

[176] Gardiner, *Letters*, 168–70; Raphael Holinshed, *Holinshed's Chronicles of England, Scotland, and Ireland*, 6 vols (London, 1807–08; repr. New York, 1976), 3.815.

[177] There are several accounts of this sermon, which was preached on 29 February 1540. Most significant are the recollections of Barnes and Gardiner themselves. For Gardiner's account, see his

he promptly summoned both Gardiner and Barnes to appear before him at Hampton Court. They appeared on 5 March, presented their cases, and Barnes, understanding that he did not have the King's sympathy, requested time to consider Gardiner's arguments. The next morning, meeting again, Barnes would replay the scene enacted at his Hampton Court encounter with Gardiner some nine years earlier; 'he fell on bothe his knees and desyred me to have pytye upon hym', Gardiner recalled.[178] Barnes revoked the opinions expressed in his sermon and uncharacteristically volunteered to become the bishop's 'scoler', taking up residence with him to be instructed.[179] This he did on the following Monday, 8 March, at which time he was presented with nine propositions Gardiner had authored as the basis for their study.[180]

Notwithstanding his dramatic display of contrition, it quickly became evident that Barnes had only been playing for time. Only two days into their arrangement – and despite the bishop's promised stipend of forty pounds, more than twice the annual income of Barnes's Llanboidy appointment – Barnes rejected the agreed terms and removed himself from Gardiner's house.[181] It is hardly probable that he could have assumed the matter would thus be concluded. But having heard his evangelical associate William Jerome preach at Paul's Cross the previous Sunday, revisiting the themes of his own earlier sermon, Barnes may have believed popular opinion to be on his side. That Jerome had also been appointed to preach by Cranmer, and that he was the vicar of Cromwell's own Stepney parish, perhaps further suggested to Barnes that they were well protected. Barnes's hope, however, was also Gardiner's fear. The bishop, who had first complained to the King following Barnes's sermon of 29 February, approached Henry once again, warning him that:

> if you allow Dr. Barnes to preach much, all the nation will be lost, and the people will become such heretics that they will not recognize either God or your Majesty.[182]

The suggestion that Barnes's opinions might be read as undermining Henry's authority was further highlighted by Gardiner in his annotated summary of

Letters, 170; for Barnes's, see his letter to Johannes Aepinus in *Original Letters*, 2.282. For the sermon's mention in the chronicles, see *Hall's Chronicle*, 837–8, and *Holinshed's Chronicles*, 3.815.

178 Gardiner, *Letters*, 172.

179 Gardiner, *Letters*, 165.

180 BL Cottonian MS Cleopatra E.V, fo. 107 (*LP*, 15.312). John Foxe also records a tenth article; see *A&M*, 2.1199.

181 Gardiner, *Letters*, 173, and cf. PRO SP 1/153, fo. 58 (*LP*, 14/2.107).

182 The words attributed to Gardiner are found in the conservative mid-sixteenth-century *Chronicle of King Henry VIII of England*, ed./tr. M.A.S. Hume (London, 1889), 194, though the anonymity of its author prevents one from knowing just how accurately he records Gardiner's opinion.

Jerome's sermon, where he observed that both Jerome and Barnes denied that one's conscience could be bound by human laws.[183]

Henry, always touchy where his own authority was concerned, was not amused. Similarly, when Thomas Garrett entered the pulpit at Paul's Cross on 14 March, once again reiterating the themes of Barnes and Jerome, it became all too apparent that the religious uniformity so desired by the King was being thwarted in a very public manner. No less worrying, the evangelicals at the centre of the disturbance were both prominent and popular. Not only was Jerome the vicar in Cromwell's parish, but Garrett – a former distributor of illicit books and, like Barnes, an abjured heretic – was now a chaplain of the Archbishop. The popularity of Barnes himself, identified by the French ambassador as the 'principal preacher of these German doctrines',[184] had once again been affirmed at the conclusion of his own Paul's Cross sermon: Bartholomew Traheron would report, though certainly with some exaggeration, that it was met 'with almost universal applause'.[185] The King's patience had been worn thin. Even before Garrett preached on 14 March, Barnes had been refused any further audience with Henry.[186] Following Garrett's sermon, all three men were ordered to make recantations in Easter week, with Henry specifying that reports of each were to be presented to him.[187] This seems finally to have opened Barnes's eyes to his tenuous position, for he wrote to Aepinus on 21 March, 'I have been deceived.'[188]

Just over a week later, the recantations commenced at St Mary Spital, with Jerome preaching on 29 March. While retracting the specifics of his Lenten sermon, his prefatory homily made clear enough that his opinions had not in fact changed.[189] Barnes's recantation and sermon on the following day were even more explicitly contradictory. Following the formal retraction of his own previous preaching, he once again took the opportunity to make public sport of Stephen Gardiner. He then, according to Gardiner, began 'playnlye and directlye [to] preacheth the contrarye of that he had recanted; so evidentlye as the Mayour, of hym self, asked whither he shuld from the pulpete send him to warde'.[190] Barnes was not immediately arrested; but following Garrett's performance on the following day, in which he also 'recanted nothing', all three were committed to

[183] For the similarities between the sermons of Barnes and Jerome, and for Gardiner's recognition that the two were of a like mind, see *A&M* (Pratt), 5, Appendix, no. 8 (*LP*, 15.345).
[184] *Correspondance Politique*, 205: 'principal prédicateur des cens doctrines d'alemans' (*LP*, 15.306).
[185] *Original Letters*, 2.316 (*LP*, 15.383).
[186] PRO SP 1/158, fo. 29 (*LP*, 15.335).
[187] Gardiner, *Letters*, 174; cf. PRO SP 1/158, fos 95–6 (*LP*, 15.414).
[188] *Original Letters*, 2.282. The letter is signed 'May 21. From the house of Thomas Parnell', but this must be incorrect as Barnes was in the Tower by 21 May.
[189] For the summary report of Jerome's recantation sermon, see *A&M* (Pratt) 5, Appendix, no. 21.
[190] Gardiner, *Letters*, 174.

the Tower, at the King's order, on 3 April.[191] In the light of such public defiance, and the popular reaction to it, nothing less than imprisonment could have been expected. It had been obvious to all that Barnes especially had recanted 'more out of obligation and in order to satisfy his master the King than on account of a change of opinion'.[192] Most annoying for those such as Gardiner, even evangelicals at court were celebrating 'howe gaily they had all handled the matter'.[193] There arrests, however, did not put an end to the controversy begun with the Lenten sermons. When Gardiner took to the pulpit again a week later, his sermon was interrupted when a scuffle broke out among those present.[194] Increasing the confusion, when the previously appointed preacher was arrested, Archbishop Cranmer himself preached at Paul's through May; his sermons, not unlike Barnes's, were delivered as refutations of Gardiner's.[195]

Such confusion naturally gave rise to rumour. Continental Protestants heard English evangelicals lament that three of their best preachers were in the Tower; but their fate, it seemed, remained open to speculation.[196] Others writing from England noted that some of those recently arrested had been released without punishment.[197] In early June some speculated that Barnes himself was on the verge of being released; and by the middle of the month it was rumoured that this had not only happened, but that he had been elevated to the post of King's almoner.[198] Such rumours – soon proved false – were prompted in part by two assumptions: that Barnes had Cromwell's favour, and that Cromwell's own position was sure. Even the first of these assumptions, however, was now questionable, as Cromwell had cautiously refrained from any vocal support of Barnes throughout the controversy.[199] Indeed, even at its climax on the day of Barnes's recantation sermon Cromwell was attempting to restore his own relationship with Gardiner.[200]

It was his failure to do so, however, which most decisively undermined the further assumption of Cromwell's own security. This assumption was dramatically refuted on 10 June, when Cromwell was suddenly arrested on the accusation

[191] Wriothesley, *A Chronicle of England*, 1.114.
[192] *Correspondance Politique*, 211: 'plus par contraincte et pour satisfaire au roy son maistre que pour changement d'opinion' (*LP*, 15.485). Cf. Wriothesley, *A Chronicle of England*, 1.114, who also notes that, by recanting, Barnes was 'not doing the Kinges commandment so syncerelie'.
[193] Gardiner, *Letters*, 174.
[194] Wriothesley, *A Chronicle of England*, 1.115.
[195] *Correspondance Politique*, 225 (*LP*, 15.737). See also M. Maclure, *The Paul's Cross Sermons, 1534–1642* (Toronto, 1958), 189.
[196] *Original Letters*, 2.291 (*LP*, 15.734).
[197] *Correspondance Politique*, 215 (*LP*, 15.566).
[198] BL Harleian MS 288, fo. 47 (*LP*, 15.792); *Correspondance Politique*, 225 (*LP*, 15.737).
[199] Susan Brigden, 'Popular Disturbance and the Fall of Thomas Cromwell and the Reformers, 1539–1540', *The Historical Journal* 24 (1981), 266.
[200] G.R. Elton, 'Thomas Cromwell's Decline and Fall', *Cambridge Historical Journal* 10 (1951), 172.

of working 'contrary to his graces most godly entent'.[201] The otherwise vague charges made against him notably include his support of Barnes's preaching, preaching which his accusers claimed he had promised to defend even with violence, even against his King.[202] Though hardly credible in its specifics, the more general suggestion that Cromwell's fall was intimately intertwined with that of Barnes is not without warrant. The very ambiguity of the charges against both, however, prevent the development of any clear causal relationship. The supposition that the King's move against his minister was prompted by the prolonged and public disturbance inaugurated by Barnes cannot be dismissed out of hand;[203] neither, however, can that which suggests the deaths of Barnes and his fellow preachers were primarily intended to justify the charge that Cromwell had knowingly protected heretics.[204] Whatever the motivation, Cromwell and Barnes were attainted within a week of each other.[205] When Henry announced a general pardon for prisoners on 16 July, exceptions were made for both.[206] Any further rumours concerning Barnes's favoured position, or assumptions about Cromwell's ability to protect him, were put to rest when, two days after the death of Cromwell, Barnes met his own end at the stake on 30 July 1540.

[201] PRO SP 1/160, fo. 141 (*LP*, 15.765).
[202] Burnet, *History of the Reformation*, 4.419–20 (*LP*, 15.498); cf. PRO SP 1/160, fos 141–2 (*LP*, 15.765).
[203] G.W. Bernard, *The King's Reformation: Henry VIII and the Remaking of the English Church* (New Haven, 2007), 570.
[204] Brigden, 'Popular Disturbance', 257 and 267.
[205] PRO C.65/148, caps 58 and 60 (*LP*, 15.498).
[206] *The Statutes of the Realm*, 12 vols, ed. A. Luders et al. (London: Record Commission, 1963), 3.812 (*LP*, 15.498).

2

THE THEOLOGY OF ROBERT BARNES

On the evidence of even a brief survey of his life, Robert Barnes is clearly seen to have been a proponent of the early modern evangelical movement. His commitment to this movement for the reform of the church is seen even more plainly when examining his theology proper, whether on the basis of his published works or of other extant evidence. The details of Barnes's biography also indicate that he was aligned especially with the Lutheran wing of reformation evangelicalism. And again, an examination of his theology bears this out. Not all have agreed that Barnes can be so easily categorised, however. Having already placed him in the history and geography of the early reformation, then, it is necessary to attempt to locate him theologically.

While his stance on every controversy of the day cannot here be examined, a brief look at three particular issues is warranted before moving on to address the subject of his overall historical and theological programme. A fresh appraisal of Barnes's positions with regard to the doctrine of justification, the theology of the eucharist, and the understanding of Royal Supremacy is desirable, in part, because each has been the subject of some dispute. More importantly, his stance on these issues is intimately related to his particular theological method, both influencing it and in turn being influenced by it.[1]

The doctrine of justification

When Robert Barnes first came to public attention with his sermon of December 1525, his preaching gave little evidence of a programme going beyond a moral reform of the clergy. Indeed, later recounting the articles with which he was then charged, he noted that offences 'agenst theyr abomynable lyvynge and damnable pompe and pryde be the moste parte of them all. Those ware the thynges / that I

[1] Ironically, it is methodology that bears much of the blame for the confusion existing in modern studies of Barnes's theology. Most authors have approached his thought as theologians, that is, giving attention only to the few theological works that Barnes himself published. Important historical and circumstantial evidence has thus often been ignored.

toke in honde to dystroye'.[2] As he came increasingly under the influence of the Wittenberg reformers, however, Barnes's emphasis on 'abominable living' gradually gave way to more specifically doctrinal emphases. Unquestionably, of the many theological articles he would address in the final decade of his life, none was granted such consistent attention as that concerning the doctrine of justification. Not only does it receive its own heading in each of his topical dogmatic works, but in each of these it also comes first in the order of theological points addressed. On this basis alone one might concur with Carl Trueman that, for Barnes, the doctrine of justification by faith was 'the necessary foundation for any correct understanding of the Christian faith'.[3] Any understanding of Barnes's theological programme will therefore make necessary a correct understanding of his doctrine of justification. A survey of his thought on this point is especially necessary in the light of suggestions that, in successive years, he 'shifted ground', 'changed his mind radically', and made 'extreme alterations' in his confession of this central doctrine of the reformation.[4]

The first evidence for Barnes's emphasis on justification is found, as one might expect, in the work written and published during his first stay in Wittenberg. In his *Sentenciae* of 1530 he arranges a number of biblical and patristic quotations under the proposition they are meant to support: 'Faith Alone Justifies'.[5] To further emphasise his claim that this teaching is no novelty, he takes the liberty of highlighting the relevant vocabulary. Thus he quotes Hilary, the fourth-century bishop of Poitiers, who also confessed that 'faith ALONE justifies'.[6] Likewise, when calling upon Ambrose of Milan's definition of the saints, he notes that they are those who 'without labouring or working have their iniquities remitted and sins covered, not on account of works of penitence, but ONLY by believing'.[7] In addition to this simple quotation and capitalisation, Barnes also includes his own marginal annotations for further emphasis. Next to Augustine's claim that

> men are not justified by the precepts of a good life, but by faith in Jesus Christ, that is, not by the law of works, but by the law of faith, not the letter, but the spirit, not by merit of deeds, but freely by grace

he adds his own concurring confession that 'nothing is profitable for justification but faith'.[8] With monotonous regularity, '*sola fides*' appears by itself next to

2 *Supplicatyon* (1531), fo. 19r.
3 C. Trueman, *Luther's Legacy: Salvation and English Reformers, 1525–1556* (Oxford, 1994), 158.
4 Clebsch, *England's Earliest Protestants*, 67, 59, 58.
5 *Sentenciae*, sig. B1v: 'Sola Fides Iustificat'.
6 *Sentenciae*, sig. B3r: 'Fides enim SOLA iustificat'.
7 *Sentenciae*, sig. B3r: 'sine labore, vel opere aliquo remittuntur iniquitates, & peccata teguntur, nulla ab his requisita poenitentiae opera, nisi TANTUM ut credant'.
8 *Sentenciae*, sig. B3v: 'non iustificari hominem praeceptis bonae vitae, nisi per fidem Iesu Christi, hoc est, non lege operum, sed lege fidei, non litera, sed spiritu, non factorem meritis, sed gratuita gratia', and, 'Nihil conducit ad iustificationem nisi fides.'

selected quotations, noting that which Barnes intends his readers to understand as full patristic agreement with his own theology. While leaning heavily on the theologians of the early church, Barnes also finds supporting evidence in the writings of medieval authors. He even shows himself willing to call upon the scholastics he had previously rejected while at Cambridge. He favourably quotes the Scotist Nicholas de Orbellus, for instance: 'good works are not more pleasing to God than sin is displeasing to him; therefore they do not justify, nor are they any aid in fulfilling righteousness'.[9]

The argument Barnes had outlined by quotation in 1530 was expanded upon one year later in the fuller treatise that appears in the first edition of his *Supplicatyon*. The title, though now in English, has changed little: 'Only faythe Justifyeth by fore god'.[10] What does differ slightly – though without altering his fundamental argument – is a more focused emphasis on the object of justifying faith. It is, he here argues, faith alone in Christ alone that justifies: 'we have nede of nothing but of hym only / and we desyer no nother salvacion / nor no nother satisfaccion / nor any helpe of any other creature / other hevynly or erthely but off him onlye'.[11] Defining justification as 'nothyng but remission of synnes',[12] he goes on to summarise the place of Christ and of faith in the *ordo salutis*.

> The verye trew waye of justificacyon ys this / fyrst comythe God for the love of Chryste Jhesus / and alonly of his mere mercy / and gevythe us frely the gyfte of faythe where by we doo beleve God and hys holy worde / and stycke faste un [*sic*] the promyses off God / and beleve that though heven / and erthe and all that is in them shulde perishe and come to nought / yet god shalle be founde trew in hys promises: for this faithes sake be we the elect childern of god.[13]

This continuing emphasis on faith alone and Christ alone, over against any claims made for human works in the order of salvation, results in part from Barnes's consistently negative assessment of free will. Both in his *Sentenciae* of 1530 and his *Supplicatyon* of 1531, the proposition that faith alone justifies is paralleled with articles insisting that 'free will by its own strength can do nothing but sin'.[14] Undoubtedly considering the common late medieval slogan that 'God will not deny grace to those who do what is in them', Barnes had previously called upon Augustine: 'It is not, therefore, in order for him to love us that we first keep

[9] *Sentenciae*, sig. B6r: 'bona opera non sunt magis grata deo quam peccatum est displicens, ergo nec iustificant, nec aliquod adiutorium prestant ad iustitiam'.
[10] *Supplicatyon* (1531), fo. 36v.
[11] *Supplicatyon* (1531), fo. 38r.
[12] *Supplicatyon* (1531), fo. 47r.
[13] *Supplicatyon* (1531), fo. 48r–v.
[14] *Sentenciae* (1530), sig. C2r: 'Liberum Arbi. Ex Suis Virib. Non Posse Non Peccare'; *Supplicatyon* (1531), fo. 81r: 'Fre wille of man / after the faulle of Adam / of hys naturalle strength / cane doo nothynge but synne'.

his precepts; but unless he loves us, we cannot keep his precepts.'[15] By way of explanation, a fuller passage from Augustine's *Enchiridion* is also cited in the *Sentenciae*.

> What good work can a lost man perform, unless he has been delivered from ruin? None voluntarily by free will. This is impossible. For it was by evil use of his free will that man destroyed it and himself. For, just as a man who kills himself is alive when he kills himself, but after he has killed himself no longer lives and cannot resuscitate himself, so also when man sinned by his own free will, and sin was victorious, the freedom of his will was lost.[16]

Barnes takes up this very thought again in the *Supplicatyon*, where, as he had done with justification, he weaves the substance of his patristic citations into a more comprehensive argument. Taking his cue from Augustine, he states in his own words that by free will one 'cane no more do unto goodnes / than a dede man cane do to make hym selfe a lyve agayn / yee he cane doo nothynge but delyght in synne'.[17] Reacting to the Scotist theology in which he had been trained, Barnes rejects the assertion that original sin has affected only the lower human faculties while leaving some freedom to the higher faculty of the will.[18] Thus he concludes that 'all that you can do / is but hyppocrisy / and dubbille sinne a fore god tyll the tyme / that he of hys mercy chousyth you'.[19]

Barnes's 1530 and 1531 assertions of justification by faith alone and his attendant denials of free will closely and consistently parallel Martin Luther's far more famous statements on the same, and it can hardly be doubted that, while composing his works in Wittenberg, Barnes was substantially influenced by the theology of Luther and his circle. Like Luther, Barnes had even attempted to strengthen his 1531 arguments by denying the canonical status of the epistle of James.[20] But by 1534, when a greatly revised edition of the *Supplicatyon* was printed in London, Barnes had been drawn once again into close contact with those supporting evangelical reform in his native England. Changes made in the 1534 *Supplicacion* are almost certainly attributable to Barnes's assessment of the political and theological climate of his homeland. That such changes amount to a 'modification of the Wittenberg theology' or a 'withdrawal from a strict Lutheran

[15] *Sentenciae*, sig. B7v: 'Non ergo ut ui nos diligat, prius eius praecepta servamus, sed nisi nos diligat, praecepta eius servare non possumus.'

[16] *Sentenciae*, sig. C5v: 'Quid enim boni opari potest perditus, nisi quantum fuerit a perditione liberatus? Ninquid libero voluntatis arbit. Et hoc absit. Nam lib. arb. male utens homo, & se perdidit & ipsum. Sicut enim qui se occidit, utique vivendo se occidit, sed se occidendo non vivit, nec se ipsum potest resuscitare cum occiderit, Ita cum lib. peccamus arbitrio victore peccato, amissum est & lib. arb.'

[17] *Supplicatyon* (1531), fo. 83v.

[18] *Supplicatyon* (1531), fo. 84r–v.

[19] *Supplicatyon* (1531), fo. 94r.

[20] *Supplicatyon* (1531), fos 52r–53r. See Clebsch, *England's Earliest Protestants*, 66.

stand on justification by faith alone', however, is not at all supported by the available evidence.[21]

Most of the changes in the 1534 *Supplicacion* have little or no direct bearing on the doctrine of justification that Barnes had outlined in 1530 and amplified in 1531. He expands on the description of his dispute with the bishops at his 1526 trial; he revises his discussion of the church in response to criticism by Thomas More; he excises articles on vernacular Scripture, adiaphora, utraquism, and images; and he adds a lengthy article on the right of clerical marriage. That no substantial modifications were made to the important article on free will suggests Barnes left himself little room for any radical change regarding the related article of justification. In fact, most of the alterations evident in the discussion of justification itself are inconsequential. That which does stand out, the 'most important difference', is the elimination of those arguments which had cast doubt on the canonicity of James.[22] In their place is found an attempt to reconcile the Pauline insistence on justification by faith without works with James's assertion that there can be no faith without works.[23] William Clebsch has highlighted what thus seems to be a 'new connection between faith and works', and has therefore argued that by 1534 Barnes abandoned his former stance on justification by faith alone.[24] A close reading of Barnes's comments on good works, however, reveals that no such radical change has been made.

The revised conclusion to the 1534 article on justification states that 'I have declared unto youre grace, howe that I wolde have good workes done, and wolde not have a christen mans lyfe, to be an ydle thynge, or elles a lyfe of unclennes'.[25] A more explicit discussion of good works had been made necessary, Barnes explains, because his adversaries had charged him with forbidding such deeds as fasting, prayer, alms, and other penitential works.[26] But such accusations had been made, and were denied, already in 1531. At that time Barnes faced the accusation that 'thou dystroyest all good workes and wylt that no man shall worke well / but alonly beleve'. He responded then, as in 1534, by calling such accusations 'open lyes'.[27] When his critics persisted in their charge, he was forced to explain his position on works more clearly. Thus he wrote in the second edition of the *Supplicacion* that 'workes shulde declare, and shewe the outward faythe, and workes shulde be an out warde declaracion, and a testimonie of the inwarde justificacion'. But this justification, he insisted, is 'recevyed of faythe, not that workes can or may take awaye our synne, or elles be any satisfaction, for any

21 Clebsch, *England's Earliest Protestants*, 67, 60.
22 Clebsch, *England's Earliest Protestants*, 66.
23 Cf. *Supplicatyon* (1531), fos 52r–53r and *Supplicacion* (1534), sig. L4r–v.
24 Clebsch, *England's Earliest Protestants*, 67.
25 *Supplicacion* (1534), sig. M2v.
26 *Supplicacion* (1534), sig. M2v.
27 *Supplicatyon* (1531), fo. 51r; *Supplicacion* (1534), sig. L3v.

parte of synne, for that belongeth alonely to Christe'.[28] Even this description of works as external testimony to an internal justification by faith, which Clebsch calls a 'new connection between faith and works', is not new at all. Virtually the same had been stated in 1531: 'the workes of the lawe be no cause of justificacyon / but allonly an outward testimonye'.[29]

Clebsch is indeed correct to observe that in 1534 Barnes had forsaken his earlier arguments in rejection of the epistle of James. But the conclusion drawn from this, that a withdrawal from Luther's stance on the epistle indicates a new withdrawal from Luther's stance on justification, is further flawed on two counts. The first is quite simply that by 1534 Luther himself was greatly downplaying his earlier rejection of James.[30] Rather than reading Barnes's revision on this point as a move away from Luther, then, it can reasonably be interpreted as yet another step taken with his German mentor. Equally problematic for Clebsch's thesis is his interpretation of that which replaces the former arguments against James. The 1534 *Supplicacion* replaces these arguments with a lengthy appeal to St Augustine, who had provided a useful harmonisation of James and Paul on faith and works.

> S. Augu. doth declare in dyverse places, that blessed S. Paule, and S. James, semed for to be contrary in this matter, And therfor S. Aug. wyllyng to save the estimacion of this epistle, doth declare, how that S. Paule doth speake of workes, that go before faythe, and S. James speaketh of workes, that folowe faythe, And yet S. Augu. wyll not be compelled by the words of this epistle, to graunt, that my workes do justifie.[31]

But neither the source nor substance of this harmonisation is new to Barnes's thought in 1534. Not only is reference made to it in the *Supplicatyon* of 1531,[32] but already in his 1530 *Sentenciae* Barnes had quoted Augustine at length on this very point.

> Therefore, the two judgements of the apostles Paul and James are not contradictory when one says man is justified by faith without works and the other says faith without works is dead. Because one speaks concerning works which precede faith, the other concerning those which follow faith.

[28] *Supplicacion* (1534), sig. L4r–v.
[29] *Supplicatyon* (1531), fo. 54r.
[30] Changes are evident both in his general New Testament preface and the preface to James itself. The well-known reference to James as 'an epistle of straw', which had appeared in each edition of his New Testament since 1522, is first excised in the 1534 edition of the whole Bible. See *AE*, 35.362 and 358 n. 5. The strong language of the 1522 preface to James – e.g., 'he mangles the Scriptures and thereby opposes Paul and all Scripture', and, 'I will not have him in my Bible to be numbered among the true cheif books' – disappears in all editions after 1530. See *AE*, 35.397 nn. 54, 55.
[31] *Supplicacion* (1534), sig. L4r.
[32] *Supplicatyon* (1531), fo. 53v.

Barnes adds his own comment in the margin: 'Thus neither works preceding nor following justify, because they follow righteousness and are effects, not causes, of righteousness.'[33] Again, contrary to Clebsch, this emphasis on works as a necessary effect of justification is by no means absent in Barnes's work of 1531. He insists that 'a juste man must nedes do them',[34] and that 'those men that wyll do no good workys by cause they be Justyfyde alonly by fayth / be not the chylderne of god nor the chylderne of Justyfycacyon'.[35] Likewise, even while heightening the emphasis on good works in 1534, he takes equal pains to deny them any role in salvation. He rejects them as 'damnable and very sinne, if there be no fayth',[36] and concludes 'that the glorye, and prayse of justification belongeth onely to fayth in christes bloude, and not to workes in any wyse'.[37]

Had Barnes truly shifted ground by 1534 one could reasonably expect to see a modification of his doctrine reflected in later statements concerning justification. What is seen instead, up to the time of his death in 1540, is a consistent reiteration of the profession he had first offered in his works of 1530 and 1531. Preaching in London in 1535, for example, he stresses the sole sufficiency of faith in Christ by stating that 'Christ dyed alone and rose ageyn alone and went to hell alone, savyd us alone etc.'[38] Over against any confidence in the human will or good works, he asks pointedly, 'who is not desperat in the law for who is able to fulfyll it? who doth love god above all thyngs?'[39]

Similar emphases are evident in the Wittenberg Articles of the next year, which were the result of negotiations in which Barnes took part and to which his signature is affixed. Here again free will is denied and the consequent assertion made that 'the godly would be driven to despair if they had to think that they please God only when they satisfy the law'.[40] Rather, Barnes and his fellow ambassadors confess, 'we are justified and accounted righteous and become sons of God, not because of the worthiness of our contrition or of other works, but freely for Christ's sake'.[41] This same profession, with some slight amplification,

33 *Sentenciae* (1530), sig. B4v: 'Quamobrem, non sunt sibi contrarie duae apostolorum sententiae Pauli & Iacobi, cum dicit unus iustificari hominem per fidem sine operibus, & alius dicit inanem esse fidem sine operibus. Quia ille dicit de operibus quae fidem praecedunt, iste de his, quae fidem sequuntur', and, 'Ita nec opera praecedentia nec sequentia iustificant, quia sequuntur iusticiam & sunt effectus non caussa iusticiae.'

34 *Supplicatyon* (1531), fo. 49r.

35 *Supplicatyon* (1531), fo. 50r.

36 *Supplicacion* (1534), sig. K4v.

37 *Supplicacion* (1534), sig. L4v.

38 Warwickshire Record Office, DR 801/12, fo. 68r. For commentary on this sermon, as well as a discussion of its date and location, see J. Craig and K. Maas, 'A Sermon by Robert Barnes, c. 1535', *Journal of Ecclesiastical History* 55 (2004), 542–51.

39 Warwickshire Record Office, DR 801/12, fo. 68r.

40 *DER*, 133.

41 *DER*, 125.

is made three years later in the Thirteen Articles.[42] Again, Barnes played a prominent role in the theological discussions of which they were the culmination; the articles can thus safely be assumed to represent his own thought. And again, as he had in his own publications, Barnes consents to the opinion that good works are necessary 'not because they justify the ungodly, nor because they are a price paid for sin, or a cause of justification; but because it is necessary that one who is already justified by faith and reconciled to God though Christ, should strive to do God's will'.[43] That the Wittenberg Articles, saying nearly the same thing, were approved by both Luther and Melanchthon is further evidence that such a position cannot be interpreted as a 'modification of the Wittenberg theology'.[44]

The events surrounding the sermon and trial that led eventually to Barnes's death further illustrate his consistency in the proclamation of justification by faith in Christ alone. It was this doctrine that the conservative Bishop of Winchester, Stephen Gardiner, had publicly attacked from Paul's Cross on the first Sunday of Lent, 1540. And it was in response to this attack that Barnes preached his own critical sermon from the same pulpit two weeks later. He notes as much in his brief summary of the controversy for the Hamburg theologian Johannes Aepinus, where he describes the dispute as

> respecting justification by faith and purgatory. He holds that the blood of Christ cleanseth only from past sins previous to baptism, but that those committed since are blotted out partly by the merits of Christ, and partly by our own satisfactions. He adds too, that voluntary works are more excellent than the works of the ten commandments. As to purgatory, he says, that if a woman shall have caused Masses to be celebrated, and shall have bestowed alms for the soul of her husband, she may boldly demand his soul in the day of judgment, and say that she has paid the price of his redemption. But I, on the other hand, in opposition to all these things, vindicate the efficacy of the blood of Jesus Christ my Lord.[45]

At least one contemporary chronicler who makes mention of this homiletical duel also points out that the doctrine of justification stood at the centre of the dispute.[46] It is not at all surprising, then, that it formed the substance of the articles with which Gardiner presented Barnes in the following days. The first of the propositions to which the bishop expected him to agree was that the benefits of Christ's death are conditional; the remaining nine follow suit.[47] As noted in the previous chapter, Barnes soon found reason to reject Gardiner's attempts to school him.

42 *DER*, 187.
43 *DER*, 188.
44 Clebsch, *England's Earliest Protestants*, 67; cf. *DER*, 128.
45 *Original Letters*, 2.282.
46 *Hall's Chronicle*, 837. Foxe, following Gardiner's own account, also notes that the question in dispute was 'Whether a man coulde doe anye thynge good or acceptable, before the grace of justification or not?' *A&M*, 2.1198; cf. Gardiner, *Letters*, 169–70.
47 BL Cottonian MS Cleopatra E.V, fo. 107 (*LP*, 15.312); cf. *A&M*, 2.1199.

His position on the matter was reaffirmed for the last time in the moments before his death. At the stake he confessed once again his belief that Christ's death 'was the sufficient price and ransom for the sin of all the world' and that 'there is no other satisfaction unto the Father, but this his death and passion only'.[48] Allowing himself a rare argument from personal experience, he once more denied good works any place in the order of salvation, 'for I knowledge, the best work that ever I did is unpure and unperfect'.[49] But he is also quick to affirm their necessity after justification:

> Take me not here, that I speak against good works. For they are to be done: and surely they that do them not, shall never come to the kingdom of God. We must do them, because they are commanded us of God, to shew and set forth our profession, not to deserve or merit; for that is only the death of Christ.[50]

On the basis of this brief survey of his confession of justification between 1530 and 1540, it is evident that, despite occasional assertions to the contrary, Barnes's doctrine underwent no discernible change during this time. He consistently argued, both in his publications and in his preaching, that justification is achieved by faith alone. This faith has its object in Christ alone, whose death is judged sufficient to atone for both original and actual sin. This profession of faith in Christ alone is consistently paralleled with a denial of free will and the related confession that, without faith, one is incapable of performing even the least of good works. Having been justified by faith, however, the Christian not only will engage in good works, but indeed must do so.

The sacrament of the altar

Barnes's confession of justification closely followed that of Luther and the Wittenberg theologians. Also in agreement with the German reformers, Barnes understood the chief doctrine of justification to be intimately entwined with the theology and practice of the church's sacraments. Barnes's understanding of this relationship is evident, for example, in the confession of the sacraments found in the Thirteen Articles of 1538. 'Through them', the ninth article states, 'God

48 Miles Coverdale, *Remains of Myles Coverdale*, ed. G. Pearson (Cambridge: Parker Society, 1846), 352, 355. No independent version of Barnes's 'Protestation' remains extant. The first extant printed version is that embedded within the conservative John Standish's reply to it, *A lytle treatise composyd by Johan Standysshe one of the felowes of Whyttington Coledge in London, again the protestacion of Robert Barnes at the tyme of his death* (London, 1540 [STC 23209]). Coverdale's subsequent work, *A confutacion of that treatise which one John Standish made agaynst the protestacion of D. Robert Barnes* (Zurich, 1541 [STC 5888]), is reprinted in his *Remains* and includes the full texts of both Barnes's 'Protestation' and Standish's treatise.

49 Coverdale, *Remains*, 383; cf. 379 and 397.

50 Coverdale, *Remains*, 402.

works in us invisibly, and pours his grace into us invisibly, if we receive them rightly, and faith is also awakened through them and confirmed.'[51]

Barnes's sacramental interests lie chiefly with the eucharist, and in his various works he wrote on several aspects of this sacrament. He addressed the nature of the elements after consecration, the sacrifice of the Mass, and utraquism, as well as outlining the history of the eucharistic liturgy. In the middle of the decade Barnes brought his views to the Anglo-Lutheran dialogues previously discussed, dialogues which continually ran aground on the theology and practice of the Mass. Again at the end of the decade he was employed by the Crown, this time in the suppression of English Sacramentarianism. Barnes's significance in the eucharistic controversies of the 1530s is further acknowledged by his contemporaries; his sacramental theology was debated in the correspondence of men like Thomas More, William Tyndale, and John Frith. Even after his fall from royal favour and consequent death, reference to his views would make their way into polemical pamphlets and broadsides designed to discredit his theology. It is clear, then, that the eucharist held an important place in Barnes's theological programme.

In a letter addressed to Thomas More in the early 1530s, Barnes promised that he would soon publish a book outlining his theology of the sacrament. Unfortunately, this was a promise which went unfulfilled.[52] Yet a fair amount of evidence does remain extant, enough to compose a satisfactory if less than comprehensive description of his thought. As with his doctrine of justification, this is made especially necessary by claims that Barnes's sacramental theology underwent significant changes throughout his life.[53] The basis for such suggestions is once again the dissimilarities between the two editions of his *Supplication*; but differences between the *Supplications* and the earlier *Sentenciae* also raise important questions. In the 1530 work, Barnes arranged his patristic citations under nineteen *loci*, three of which pertain to the eucharist. These address reception in both kinds, Christ's presence in the sacrament, and the origin of the Mass. The 1531 edition of the *Supplicatyon* includes only the first of these articles. The *Supplicacion* of 1534 omits even this.[54]

[51] *DER*, 198.

[52] *CWM*, 7.255–6.

[53] Clebsch, *England's Earliest Protestants*, 68–9; B. Hall, 'The Early Rise and Gradual Decline of Lutheranism in England', in *Reform and Reformation: England and the Continent, c.1500–c.1750*, ed. D. Baker (Oxford, 1979), 110.

[54] Contrary to Clebsch and Hall, Rainer Pineas, *Thomas More and Tudor Polemics* (Bloomington, IN, 1968), 121, and C. Trueman, ' "The Saxons be sore on the affirmative": Robert Barnes on the Lord's Supper', in *The Bible, the Reformation and the Church*, ed. W.P. Stephens (Sheffield, 1995), 296, 300–1, maintain that Barnes's personal convictions remained unchanged, and that the revisions are simply the result of cautious politics in the face of uncertainty regarding Henry's views. If, as seems likely, it was the ever cautious Cromwell who prompted the revising and republishing of the *Supplicacion*, this suggestion has much to recommend it. See A.G. Dickens and J.M. Tonkin, *The Reformation in Historical Thought* (Oxford, 1985), 63; Pineas, *Tudor Polemics*, 122.

Perhaps partly because of such changes, confusion over Robert Barnes's eucharistic theology existed even among his sixteenth-century contemporaries. Thomas More charged him with being 'of zwynglius secte agaynste the sacrament of the auter, bylevynge that it is nothynge but bare brede'.[55] Richard Mekins claimed to believe on the basis of Barnes's teaching that the bread remained present even with Christ's body. John Foxe seems to indicate that Barnes never ceased to confess transubstantiation.[56] Such confusion does not disappear with Barnes's modern commentators. He has been variously described as a Zwinglian, as 'the orthodox Lutheran', and as one who reveals 'an unblushing avowal of belief in transubstantiation'.[57] In the attempt to clarify where Barnes stood on sacramental matters, a chronological look at the textual and historical evidence will prove helpful.

In Barnes's fullest treatment of the eucharist, his *Sentenciae*, there can be little doubt that he holds to a belief in Christ's true, corporal presence in the sacrament.[58] This is made clear not only in the patristic citations he chose to include, but also in the brief commentary he provides. Even while denouncing certain emphases in the Roman theology of the Mass, he does not hesitate to refer to the eucharist as the sacrament of Christ's body, noting that 'the words by which the body is made were given by the Lord himself'.[59] Justifying such language are the catechetical questions and answers of the fourth-century Athanasius:

> What in fact is the bread? It is the body of Christ.
> What is given to those who partake? Without a doubt, the body of Christ.[60]

Against opinions that the bread merely represents the Lord's body, or that this is simply a 'virtual' or 'spiritual' body, the graphic language of the Byzantine father Theophylactus is brought forward:

55 *CWM*, 8.302.

56 See below at p. 57 n. 79.

57 J. Gairdner, *Lollardy and the Reformation in England*, 4 vols (London, 1908–13), 1.530 n. 1; H.C. Porter, *Reformation and Reaction in Tudor Cambridge* (Cambridge, 1958), 65; Fisher, 'The Contribution of Robert Barnes', 327. In many respects the confusion increases in the secondary sources. Porter, for instance, calls Barnes 'the orthodox Lutheran' while also stating that 'Frith and Lambert were of the school of Robert Barnes'. This is clearly not the case, as will be seen below.

58 The choice of the adjectival 'true' is simply governed by Barnes's own use of the term in the title of article seventeen in his *Sentenciae*: 'In Sacramento altaris est verum corpus Christi'. It should not, *a priori*, be construed as something other than what may be called a 'real' presence. In an otherwise fine work, P.N. Brooks misleadingly implies a clear sixteenth-century distinction between a real (corporal) presence and a true (spiritual) presence. P.N. Brooks, *Thomas Cranmer's Doctrine of the Eucharist*, 2nd edn (Basingstoke, 1992), 38, 43, *et passim*. For a corrective analysis, see especially MacCulloch, *Thomas Cranmer*, 181–3, 392.

59 *Sentenciae*, sig. K5r: 'Verba enim quibus corpus conficitur, ab ipso domino sunt tradita'.

60 *Sentenciae*, sig. K4r: 'Quid enim est panis? Est corpus Christi. Quid autem huius participantes redduntur? Nimirum Christi corpus.'

> He certainly did not say, this is a figure, but this is my body. Although it seems to us bread, it is in fact transformed by an ineffable operation. Because we are weak and loathe to eat raw flesh, especially human flesh, it therefore appears to be bread; but it is flesh.[61]

By way of explanation, Christology is introduced with Augustine's opinion that just as 'of the virgin the body of Christ was made true flesh by the Holy Spirit, so also by the same is the body of Christ mystically consecrated from the substance of bread and wine'.[62] Not only does Barnes thus compare Christ's incarnational body with that of the consecration; he goes on to equate them. He calls upon the testimony of Augustine and Ambrose in support of the contention that the body on the altar is that born of the virgin, which suffered, died, rose, and ascended.[63]

While Barnes's quotations and commentary point unequivocally to a belief in a corporal presence, and while they denounce a Roman theology of sacrifice, they nowhere give an indication of his thoughts regarding the status of the bread after consecration. A belief in transubstantiation therefore cannot wholly be excluded on the basis of the text alone. However, circumstances related to the production of the *Sentenciae* mitigate against associating it too closely with any position other than Lutheran. Johann Bugenhagen notes in his glowing preface that Barnes was at work on the book while living under his roof. That it was written in Wittenberg, published there, and promoted by the town pastor suggests that the Lutherans understood it to harmonise with their own position. In 1530, only a few months after the presentation of the Augsburg Confession and only one year after the Marburg Colloquy, the Wittenbergers certainly would not have been reading sacramental theology uncritically.

Although Barnes does not take up Christ's sacramental presence under a separate heading in his *Supplicatyon* of the next year, his references to the eucharist in other articles give no hint of a changed opinion. He constantly speaks of the 'blessyd boddy' and 'holy bloude' of Christ;[64] when mentioning the cup, he variously refers to Christ's 'blessyd bloud', 'glorious bloud', and 'swet bloude'.[65] In some respects, it seems that Barnes actually makes his position of 1530 more explicit. Whereas he had previously quoted Athanasius to the effect that all who partake of the bread receive Christ's body, he now even more specifically allows for a *manducatio impiorum*. Criticising Rome's explanation that withholding the

61 *Sentenciae*, sig. I7r: 'Non enim dixit, hoc est figura, sed hoc est corpus meum. Ineffabili enim operatione transformatur, etiamsi nobis videatur panis. Quoniam infirmi sumus et abhorremus crudas carnes commedere, maxime hominum carnem, et ideo panis quidem apparet, sed caro est.'

62 *Sentenciae*, sig. I6r: 'ut sicut de virgine per Spiritum Sanctum vera caro sine coitu creatur, ita per eundem ex substantia panis et vini mystice idem corpus Christi consecretur'.

63 *Sentenciae*, sig. I8r.

64 *Supplicatyon* (1531), fo. 128v.

65 *Supplicatyon* (1531), fo. 130r.

cup from the laity prevents Christ's blood from being spilled, he argues that there are far greater dangers in offering Christ's body to unbelievers.[66] Such a position not only distances Barnes from those who hold a symbolic view of the elements; it also distinguishes him from those who might argue that the body of Christ is present virtually and only on account of the communicant's faith.

As noted above, the second edition of the *Supplicacion* contains no article on eucharistic doctrine or practice. The suggestion that this omission indicates a revision of Barnes's theology has also been noted. Against this argument from silence, however, stands evidence found in the correspondence of his contemporaries. Letters related to the arrest and trial of John Frith shed light on Barnes's thought between 1531 and 1534. Thomas More, who had charged Barnes with sharing the Sacramentarian heresy of Frith, tentatively admits that he may have been mistaken. His comments on a letter received from Barnes in 1532 deserve to be quoted at length.

> And also frere Barns, albe it that as ye wote well he is in many other thinges a brother of thys yonge mannes secte / yet in thys heresye he sore abhorreth hys heresye / or ellys he lyeth hym selfe. For at hys laste beynge here, he wrote a letter to me of hys own hand / wherin he wryteth that I lay that heresye wrongfully to his charge / and therin he taketh wytnesse of god and his conscyence / and sheweth hym self so sore greved therwyth, that any man shold so repute hym by my wrytyng, that he sayth he wyll in my reproche make a boke agaynst me, wherin he wyll professe and proteste hys fayth concernyng thys blessed sacrament. By whych boke it shall he saith appere, that I have sayd untrewly of hym, and that he abhorreth thys abomynable heresy.[67]

Their divergence on this point was also apparent to William Tyndale, who clearly understood how such differences could be exploited by polemicists such as More. He wrote to Frith:

> Of the presence of Christes body in the Sacrameut [*sic*], meddle as little as you can, that there appeare no division among us. Barnes will be whote agaynst you. The Saxons be sore on the affirmative.[68]

Perhaps more enlightening than Tyndale's mention of the division between Frith and Barnes is his association of the latter with the theology of the Saxons. In the light of Barnes's matriculation at Wittenberg in 1533, he is undoubtedly correct in alluding to Barnes's Lutheranism. The Frith controversy also provides one more bit of evidence linking Barnes with Luther, and distancing the former from the position of transubstantiation. Attempting to downplay the obvious division

66 *Supplicatyon* (1531), fo. 132r. Cf. 1 Corinthians 11:27–30, which Barnes apparently has in mind.
67 *CWM*, 7.255–6.
68 *A&M*, 2.1081 (*LP*, 6.403).

between the more conservative reformers and himself, Frith insisted that both Barnes and Luther 'did both agree with him, that the sacrament was not to be worshipped'.[69]

In addition to these comments on Barnes's thought in the years leading up to the 1534 *Supplicacion*, there are further clues to be found in the events following its publication. As he was a member of the embassy taking part in the drafting of the 1536 Wittenberg Articles, Barnes's opinion can be seen in their conclusions. Though no consensus was reached on utraquism or private Masses, Barnes and his English companions did confess with the Germans:

> We firmly believe and teach that in the sacrament of the Lord's body and blood, Christ's body and blood are truly, substantially and really present under the species of bread and wine, and that under the same species they are truly and bodily presented and distributed to all those who receive the sacrament.[70]

The same would be confessed again in the Thirteen Articles of 1538.[71] It is not insignificant that in this last round of discussions, which took place in England and included several traditionalist bishops, Barnes was assigned by the King to argue on the German side of the debate. This implicit acknowledgement that Barnes's theology did not accord with traditional doctrine is especially revealing in the light of another royal decision of the same year, one which makes plain that his theology did not differ from tradition to the point of Sacramentarianism.

In October 1538 Thomas Cranmer was appointed head of a commission for the suppression of English Sacramentarianism. Also appointed to the commission was Robert Barnes, who, before the next month had passed, would set in motion events leading to the condemnation and subsequent death of John Lambert.[72] Lambert, who had previously spent time with Tyndale and Frith in Antwerp, returned to England as a proponent of their eucharistic theology. His views became the centre of public controversy in 1538 when he challenged the sacramental preaching of John Taylor, rector of St Peter's Cornhill. When Taylor turned to Barnes for support, he was encouraged to bring the matter before Cranmer. With Barnes's awareness of the King's intent and Cranmer's theology, it cannot be doubted that he was in disagreement with Lambert, who denied 'the very body of God to be in the said sacrament in corporal substance as flesh and blood *realiter et effectualiter* but only to be there spiritually'.[73] Far more probably, Barnes was of the same mind as Cranmer, to whom he referred the case.

69 *A&M*, 2.1034.
70 *DER*, 137.
71 *DER*, 192.
72 For the text of the commission, see *Concilia Magnae*, 3.836 (*LP* 13/2.498); for the Lambert affair, *A&M*, 2.1101–30.
73 *Lisle Letters*, 5.1273 (*LP* 13/2.851).

Some hint of Cranmer's position on the sacrament at this time is evident in a letter of August 1538. He wrote to Thomas Cromwell, commenting on the trial of Adam Damplip, whose confession of the eucharist had also been questioned. He reports that Damplip did not deny the bodily presence of Christ; he did however deny transubstantiation. Cranmer confesses that 'therein I think he taught but the truth'.[74] John Foxe draws what seems the logical conclusion in his summary of the Damplip affair; he refers to Cranmer as 'then yet but a Lutheran' in sacramental theology.[75]

Ten years after his first published confession of the eucharist, Barnes would reaffirm his belief in Christ's bodily presence one last time. Before being burned at Smithfield in 1540, he made his last profession of faith. A witness records his confession of the sacrament:

> After this there was one that asked him, what he said of the sacrament of the altar. Then said he to Mr. Pope, which was there present: 'Mr. Pope, ye know, and Mr. Riche, if ye be alive, that there was one accused before my lord chancellor for denying of the sacrament; and for fault of a better, I was assigned to the examination of him in the gallery. And after long reasoning and disputation I declared and said, that the sacrament being rightly used and according to scripture doth, after the word spoken by the priest, change the substance of the bread and wine into the body and blood of Christ. Were not these my words?' said he. 'Yea', said Mr. Pope. 'Then bear me witness', said he, 'that I err not in the sacrament'.[76]

That Barnes here mentions the substance of bread and wine being *changed into* the body and blood of Christ has been read by some as a clear confession of transubstantiation. This is indeed what the words seem to suggest, and it would not be unheard of for an early English evangelical to maintain such a belief; Barnes's Cambridge mentor Thomas Bilney was, according to Foxe, of this opinion.[77] There are also indications that those who read and reprinted this confession were uncomfortable with the overtones in the language. Luther's fond remembrance of Barnes was prefaced to a translation that considerably modified his last words. Here Barnes was only allowed to confess that 'the true body of Christ, which was conceived and born of the virgin Mary, exists in a miraculous manner'.[78] John Foxe also records Barnes's last words. Unlike Luther, however, he does not

[74] Cranmer, *Miscellaneous Writings*, 375 (*LP* 13/2.97). On the weight of this phrase, see MacCulloch, *Thomas Cranmer*, 182.

[75] *A&M*, 2.1224.

[76] Coverdale, *Remains*, 417.

[77] See *A&M*, 2.1011. For another possible interpretation, however, see Korey Maas, 'Thomas Bilney: "simple good soul?" ', *The Tyndale Society Journal* 27 (July 2004), 14–16.

[78] *Bekanntnus dess Glaubens die Doctor Robertus Barus* (Wittenberg, 1540), sig. A3r: 'wunderbarlicher weis / der warhafftig leiB Christi / welcher von Maria der Junckfrawen empfangen und geporn ist'.

modify his confession of the sacrament; he simply omits it altogether. It is not unreasonable to think he did so in order to avoid the embarrassing language of transubstantiation.[79]

Though an understandable aversion to transubstantiationary language very probably played some part in Foxe's editorial decision, a complementary and even more substantive factor in this decision can be located in the context in which Barnes's words are found. It is noteworthy that his involvement with commissions for the suppression of Sacramentarianism is nowhere mentioned in the martyrologist's life of Barnes. Yet Barnes himself alludes to this involvement in his confession of the sacrament.[80] This may have been reason enough for Foxe to omit it, especially as it occurs at the point of Barnes's own death. Foxe's keen sense of divine providence may have persuaded him to avoid the obvious irony of the judge having become the judged. Reference to his role as an examiner may even explain Barnes's own choice of words. Interestingly, he makes no mention of the sacrament until asked by a bystander. Then, rather than simply offering his confession, he requests confirmation of words spoken in the course of a previous examination. As Barnes was commissioned by the Crown, and was well aware of Henry's own views on the matter in question, it would not be surprising if he had at that time phrased his opinion so as not to offend orthodox ears. Indicative of his desire to avoid conflict in the matter is his contemporary Richard Hilles's indication that Barnes had spoken against the Six Articles, though only in private.[81]

Hilles, who himself disagreed with Barnes on the sacrament, also provides enlightening commentary on another episode relative to Barnes's eucharistic theology. In 1541, shortly after a second commission for enforcing the Act of Six Articles went into effect, the young Richard Mekins was brought to trial. Hilles explains Mekins's heresy, saying that he did not reject Christ's corporal presence, but merely denied that the accident of the bread remained without its substance; by way of clarification, he refers to this as 'the Lutheran opinion'.[82] Mekins claimed to have learned this opinion from Robert Barnes.[83]

Upon a review of the evidence, it is not surprising that there should be some confusion regarding Barnes's theology of the sacrament. Even the anonymous sixteenth-century polemicist whose broadside rejoiced at Barnes's downfall

79 Foxe seems to believe Barnes had held to transubstantiation. He knew, for example, that Barnes was not in agreement with the opinion held by Frith; but he also states that Barnes did not hold the view of Richard Mekins, discussed below. See *A&M*, 2.1202.

80 It is not entirely clear to which examination Barnes refers. There is no evidence of the Lord Chancellor's involvement with the Lambert trial of 1538 or the 1535 examination in which Barnes took part. Likewise, though Chancellor Audley was involved with Lambert's questioning in 1536, there is no evidence connecting Barnes with this examination.

81 *Original Letters*, 1.105 (*LP*, 16.578).

82 *Original Letters*, 1.106 (*LP*, 16.1204).

83 *A&M*, 2.1202.

could only say, 'But what he thought (the Sacrament was) I wyll not judge'.[84] Some conclusions can be made, however. Between 1530 and 1540 Barnes consistently maintained a belief in the true, corporal presence of Christ in the sacrament. He was decidedly anti-Sacramentarian, but never wholly in agreement with Rome. There is perhaps some merit to the description of his theology 'not as Lutheran, but as anti-papal, although there is not sufficient evidence to enable us to determine exactly how he conceived of the mode of the eucharistic presence'.[85] However, contrasting Rome's insistence on transubstantiation with Luther's consistent refusal to define a mode of presence, Barnes's very ambiguity argues for a Lutheran interpretation.[86] This last point should not be pressed too far, but, when weighed together with the extant literary and circumstantial evidence, the Lutheran interpretation remains far more satisfying than the alternatives.[87]

Church, state, and supremacy

While Robert Barnes is seen to uphold a consistently Lutheran position in specifically doctrinal matters, it is also obvious that, from the beginning, he was faced with a social and political context which differed greatly from that of the German reformers. Unlike the Wittenbergers, who had enjoyed princely support from the first, Barnes and his English fellows were subject in the 1520s to a magistrate who loudly voiced his opposition to evangelical reform. Even when Henry VIII softened his resistance to such reform in the early 1530s, it was clear that he had no intention of falling into line with his continental counterparts. Rather than merely striking a defensive posture for the protection of English theologians, the King early on made it evident that he intended to occupy a central place in the ecclesiastical administration of his realm. Any programme of reform set forth by English evangelicals, therefore, had not only to avoid his displeasure; it had to gain his favour and his active support. Such support could hardly be expected, however, unless the question of royal authority had been clearly and persuasively addressed.

One practical implication of the different contexts with which Luther and

84 Anon., *This lytle treatyse declareth the study and frutes of Barnes borned in west smyth felde* (London, 1540 [STC 1473.5]).

85 C.W. Dugmore, *The Mass and the English Reformers* (London, 1958), 96; cf. James McGoldrick, *Luther's English Connection* (Milwaukee, 1979), 165.

86 For Luther on this point, see especially his *Babylonian Captivity of the Church*; *AE*, 36.28–35 (*WA*, 6.508–12).

87 It also makes unnecessary any explanation of why Barnes should be out of step with his closest associates on the continent and in England: the Wittenberg theologians and the circle of Cranmer and Cromwell. For the eucharistic views of his English associates, see R. McEntegart, 'England and the League of Schmalkalden 1531–1547: Faction, Foreign Policy and the English Reformation' (unpublished Ph.D. Thesis, London School of Economics, 1992), 293–7, 348; Brooks, *Thomas Cranmer's Doctrine of the Eucharist*, 3–37.

Barnes were faced can be seen in the prefaces and introductions to their various works. Whereas Luther would only occasionally address his prince, and then only for the sake of strengthening his resolve or offering practical advice in temporal matters, Barnes was moved to be more direct. Three of his four extant published works are either dedicated to or written specifically for his sovereign. One might suspect – and indeed, some have suggested – that, as a result of these dissimilar circumstances, the two reformers held disparate opinions concerning the relationship between secular authority and ecclesiastical reform. Whether this is indeed the case cannot be decided until Barnes's position is understood. It has been examined before, but, as with his views on justification and the sacrament, contradictory interpretations of the evidence have been offered. Likewise, the argument has again been made that Barnes radically modified his stance on the issue throughout his lifetime. To test this and other interpretations, then, Barnes's thought on four issues must be addressed: the questions of obedience and non-resistance; the distinction between temporal and spiritual power; the response to issues judged adiaphora or indifferent, that is, matters neither prescribed nor proscribed by Scripture; and the question of who bears responsibility for the reform of the church.

There is little doubt that Barnes maintained a consistently high view of the obedience all subjects owe their King. Though he did not address the topic before he began writing in the 1530s, his actions in the years following his 1526 trial do conform to the opinions he would later outline in print. Writing in the 1531 *Supplicatyon*, for example, he insists that 'it is clear made that we can not resyst this temporalle power in no wysse by vyolence / but if we have wrong either we must do the thyng that is commanded us or els flye'.[88] Obedience or flight were the only two options for which Barnes allowed. In view of the disobedience he had himself shown by distributing forbidden English Bibles in the late 1520s, this may seem somewhat disingenuous. And in fact it has been claimed that Barnes excluded the possession of Scripture from those things in which princes must be obeyed.[89] He did indeed constantly discourage Christians from relinquishing Scripture, but he also made clear that anyone choosing to retain their Bibles must be willing to suffer the consequences without any thought of violent resistance. He wrote that 'They shalle kepe their testament with alle other ordinance of christ / and lett the kyng exercysse his tyranny (if they can not flye) and in no wisse under the payne of damnacion shalle they withstonde hym with violence but suffer paciently alle the tyranny that he layth on them'.[90] When he learned in 1528 that Henry might indeed be planning to 'exercise his tyranny', Barnes himself chose to flee.

88 *Supplicatyon* (1531), fo. 118r.
89 Clebsch, *England's Earliest Protestants*, 64.
90 *Supplicatyon* (1531), fo. 115r.

It cannot be doubted that when Barnes wrote to his King in 1531 he was taking pains to justify his earlier actions. Consistency between his words and deeds therefore comes as no surprise. But this cannot be judged his sole reason for addressing the topic; he goes beyond a simple defence of his own flight to outline the doctrine of non-resistance he would maintain until his death. Royal authority 'was geven to kynges of god and not by man'; therefore, Barnes insists, 'there may be no resystaunce / nor rebellion in ony wyse agenst oure prince for orderinge of these temporal goodis / no though he do unryght / but all must be lefte to god and we must only suffer'.[91] There were of course those who doubted his sincerity; and the consistently fiery rhetoric of Barnes's preaching, combined with the effect this often produced in his hearers, might partially justify the contemporary perception of Barnes as subversive. This is especially the case as he had already noted in the *Supplicatyon* of 1531 that the higher clergy were fond of charging as rebels and traitors any who dared criticise them.[92] By 1534, as it was becoming clear to Barnes's adversaries that he would not be held accountable for the transgressions with which he had previously been charged, the accusation of treason was levelled against him. 'For men hath not ben ashamed to reporte, that I wolde (which am but a wretche, and poore symple worme, and not able to kyll a catte, though I wolde do my uttermoste) to make insurrecion agaynste my noble and myghtye prynce.'[93] He responded by reiterating and even heightening his earlier rejection of all forms of resistance and rebellion.[94]

Barnes also had opportunity in later years to restate his conviction. The twelfth of the Thirteen Articles of 1538 is in clear conformity with his earlier statements.

> Even if a bad prince or governor should order the subject to do something wrong or unjust, and although he may be abusing his power, contrary to the will of God, to the hurt of his own soul; yet the subject must endure such rule and suffer it, however hard it may be (unless it is clear that it is sin), rather than disturb public order and peace by resisting.[95]

Even at the point of death, when it was all too clear that he had nothing to gain by supporting such a doctrine, he would once again defend his belief in non-resistance and deny that he had ever taught otherwise.

[91] *Supplicatyon* (1531), fo. 18r.
[92] *Supplicatyon* (1531), fo. 2v.
[93] *Supplicacion* (1534), sig. D3v. Hereafter it seems that insurrection would often be associated with Barnes. It was, as previously noted, mentioned at Cromwell's fall in connection with his preaching. Even after Barnes's death, the author of *This lytle treatyse* asserted that, if Barnes would have had his way, 'Both gods lawe, and mans lawe, wold have ben subvertid'. See also the accusation by John Standish in Coverdale, *Remains*, 349.
[94] See W.D.J. Cargill Thompson, 'The Sixteenth-Century Editions of *A Supplication Unto King Henry the Eighth* by Robert Barnes, D.D.: A Footnote to the History of the Royal Supremacy', *Transactions of the Cambridge Bibliographical Society* 3 (1960), 140.
[95] *DER*, 205.

> I have been reported a preacher of sedition and disobedience to the king's majesty: but here I say to you, that you are all bound by the commandment of God to obey your prince with all humility and with all your heart, yes, not so much as in a look to show yourselves disobedient unto him; and that not only for fear of the sword, but also for conscience sake before God.[96]

He concludes by further emphasising that 'if the king should command you anything against God's law, if it be in your power to resist him, yet may you not do it'.[97] Such a confession is all the more noteworthy in the light of an unguarded statement made by the otherwise irenic Philip Melanchthon. Though he too agreed with Barnes's doctrine of obedience, upon hearing of the Englishman's death he voiced a wish that someone less scrupulous might be tempted to regicide.[98]

This desire, so uncharacteristic of Melanchthon, was also untypical of his fellow Wittenbergers. Barnes's last words, summarising his long-held opinion, better represent Luther's own position with respect to secular rule. In the related matter of distinguishing between the realms of secular and spiritual rule, Barnes was also very much in agreement with Luther. As early as his Christmas Eve sermon of 1525, for example, he had criticised the English clergy for usurping authority that rightly belonged only to the Crown.[99] It was not a unique charge, but when moved to defend himself in 1531, he took the opportunity to outline his thought further. Speaking of the temporal and spiritual estates, he explained that 'The mediator betwene god and man Christ Jesus / hathe devydyd the offices of bothe powers in to their proper actes and in to dystincte dygnityes.'[100] This division and distinction meant that 'the bysshops neither have nor yet may have any power temporal',[101] and that, likewise, those entrusted with temporal power 'have wonly the temporalle swerde'.[102] That these two swords or powers were not to be co-mingled Barnes makes clear when addressing his King: 'as youre grace maye not usurpe to preache the worde of god / no more maye they usurpe any power that belongeth to youre swerde'.[103]

Even this 1531 argument is less than novel. It very obviously parallels popular medieval opinions, and Barnes's terminology undoubtedly betrays the influence of medieval categories.[104] But in an often cited essay W.D.J. Cargill Thompson

[96] Coverdale, *Remains*, 436–7.
[97] Coverdale, *Remains*, 438; cf. also 335.
[98] *CR*, 3.1995.
[99] See the charge laid against him, which he later discusses in the *Supplicatyon* (1531), fo. 28v.
[100] *Supplicatyon* (1531), fo. 16r.
[101] *Supplicatyon* (1531), fo. 16r.
[102] *Supplicatyon* (1531), fo. 112v.
[103] *Supplicatyon* (1531), fo. 16r.
[104] For important medieval texts and commentary, see Brian Tierney, *The Crisis of Church and State, 1050–1300* (Toronto, 1988).

was right to point out that this argument was not simply a medieval inheritance; Barnes's version had been formulated along specifically 'Lutheran lines'.[105] That he chose to retain traditional medieval terminology partially obscures this fact. Cargill Thompson himself, however, introduces further confusion by describing the shared position of Barnes and Luther as one that 'defined the limits of temporal government in such a way as to exclude the magistrate from all participation in ecclesiastical affairs'.[106] This conclusion was later adopted (and simplified) by William Clebsch, who also argued that between 1531 and 1534 Barnes made 'extreme alterations in his view of the King's rôle in ecclesiological matters'.[107] While Barnes in 1534 made no explicit reference to limitations upon royal authority, he had in 1531, according to Clebsch, made obedience to the King 'applicable only to temporal matters'.[108] This perceived change was described as a 'shift from a Lutheran to a Rhenish or "proto-Calvinist" understanding of civil magistracy'.[109]

These interpretations must be challenged, however. There is no doubt that Barnes's 1531 *Supplicatyon* strongly emphasises Henry VIII's rule in the temporal realm. This is especially so in the opening of his treatise, which is largely devoted to denouncing the clerical usurpation of the King's power. But to read his argument as a rejection of any royal involvement in ecclesiastical affairs ignores important evidence to the contrary. It also involves a misunderstanding of the Lutheran position upon which Barnes's own is based. What is regularly called Luther's 'two-kingdoms doctrine' is far more subtle than either Clebsch or Cargill Thompson seems to allow.[110] It does not posit a simple distinction, in modern terms, between church and state, nor even between church and world. Closer to the centre of Luther's thought on the two realms is his distinction between law and gospel. The spiritual realm concerns only the gospel, but the gospel in its narrowest sense: the proclamation of salvation. All beyond this – including even ecclesiastical administration – belongs properly to the temporal sphere, which is governed by reason and law, princely or other.[111] Thus, even in

[105] Cargill Thompson, 'The Sixteenth-Century Editions', 141.
[106] Cargill Thompson, 'The Sixteenth-Century Editions', 141.
[107] Clebsch, *England's Earliest Protestants*, 58.
[108] Clebsch, *England's Earliest Protestants*, 64.
[109] Clebsch, *England's Earliest Protestants*, 60. See also F. Oakley, 'Christian Obedience and Authority, 1520–1550', in *The Cambridge History of Political Thought, 1450–1700*, ed. J.H. Burns (Cambridge, 1994), 177.
[110] Cargill Thompson does, however, present a more nuanced assessment in 'The "Two Kingdoms" and the "Two Regiments": Some Problems of Luther's *Zwei-Reiche-Lehre*', in *Studies in the Reformation*, ed. C.W. Dugmore (London, 1980), 42–59. More recently, see J.M. Estes, 'Luther on the Role of Secular Authority in the Reformation', *Lutheran Quarterly* n.s. 17 (2003), 199–225; and for what remains a very thorough analysis, see Gustaf Wingren, *Luther on Vocation*, tr. C. Rasmussen (Edinburgh, 1958).
[111] Thus, for example, the visitation of the Saxon churches was carried out by princely authority; and Luther (though not until 1539) would occasionally refer to evangelical rulers as 'emergency bishops'. See Estes, 'Luther on the Role of Secular Authority', 19.

1531, when Barnes speaks of the spiritual realm he does not broadly equate it with the visible or institutional church, but states very precisely that it is 'alonly a mynystracyon of the worde of God'.[112]

Misunderstandings of Barnes's distinction between temporal and spiritual authority has also influenced confused and contradictory interpretations of his related stance on adiaphora, or things indifferent. Barnes had first addressed the issue in his 1530 *Sentenciae*, where the title of his tenth article summarises his position: 'Human Constitutions Cannot Bind Men In Sin.'[113] Following Hilary's allegorical interpretation of Matthew 15:13 – 'Every plant that my heavenly Father has not planted will be pulled up by the roots' – Barnes concurs with the church father's conclusion: 'The traditions of men will be uprooted'.[114] He has specifically in mind those 'human constitutions which rule the consience',[115] and insists that 'If they wish us to be bound under penalty of sin, they are not to be obeyed.'[116] He further detailed his position in the *Supplicatyon* of the next year. There he explained that there are two kinds of bad statutes: those that are plainly against God's word, and those 'whan serten thynges that be called indifferent be commanded as thinges to be done of necessite and under the paynes of deedly synne'.[117] Again he notes that such statutes are not necessarily to be obeyed, an opinion Cargill Thompson associates with 'the standard Lutheran thesis'.[118]

It is indeed noteworthy, then, that this thesis disappears in the revised *Supplicacion* of 1534. William Clebsch labels this the 'most striking single change' in Barnes's expression of political thought, and holds that there are 'irreconcilable contradictions' between his positions of 1531 and 1534.[119] He here again follows the conclusions of Cargill Thompson, who understood the article on adiaphora as having 'contained an implicit denial of the whole conception of the Royal Supremacy'.[120] The author concludes, therefore, that in 1534 'the article was suppressed as a matter of deliberate policy, because its contents were potentially subversive'.[121] It is indeed likely that the article was excised because critics might interpret it as conflicting with the claims of royal authority.[122] But whether it actually did undermine 'the whole conception of the

112 *Supplicatyon* (1531), fo. 118r. Barnes seems to have understood this ministration as Luther did, as encompassing the word in its written and preached forms, as well as when bound to the sacraments. See fo. 115r.
113 *Sentenciae*, sig. G1r: 'Constitutiones Humanae Non Obligant Conscientiam Ad Peccatum.'
114 *Sentenciae*, sig. G3r: 'Traditiones hominum eruendas'.
115 *Sentenciae*, sig. G1r: 'Constitutiones humanae que conscienciis dominentur'.
116 *Sentenciae*, sig. G2v: 'Si voluerint nos stringere sub pena peccati non sunt audiendi.'
117 *Supplicatyon* (1531), fo. 119v.
118 Cargill Thompson, 'The Sixteenth-Century Editions', 140.
119 Clebsch, *England's Earliest Protestants*, 64, 64–5 n. 6.
120 Cargill Thompson, 'The Sixteenth-Century Editions', 140.
121 Cargill Thompson, 'The Sixteenth-Century Editions', 141.
122 In fact, Stephen Gardiner would later interpret it in this manner. See *A&M* (Pratt), 5, Appendix, no. 8 (*LP*, 15.345).

Royal Supremacy' is highly debatable. In fact, one author points to this article in particular, notes its emphasis on a 'national church', and concludes that Barnes's entire argument is constructed 'in terms that would certainly please his king'.[123] In light of the fact that it was this *Supplicatyon* that prompted Henry VIII to grant the exiled Barnes a safe-conduct in late 1531, it must at least be granted that the article did not wholly displease the King.

Interpretations to the contrary can be attributed to an oversimplification of both Barnes's true argument and, again, the Lutheran position he echoes. The position shared by Barnes and the Germans is concisely summarised in their discussion of adiaphora in the Wittenberg Articles of 1536. Here, in the context of discussing church ordinances, the authors state that 'Christian freedom should be maintained, that is, that people should understand that they are to observe such usages not as if they were necessary for salvation'.[124] The reformers do not condemn or prevent the observation of ordinances deemed adiaphora; rather, they imply that things indifferent are indeed to be observed, but that their observation is not to be understood as necessary for salvation. This is perhaps more clearly stated than in Barnes's *Supplicatyon*, but by no means in disagreement with his earlier judgement. Even in 1531 he had insisted that 'yf the cause be right / lawfull / or prophitable to the common welth / thou must obey',[125] and that 'thys thyng shalte thou do of thy cherite / by cause thou wilte not breke the outward order / nor make any disquietnes'.[126] He argues in fact that one is bound by things otherwise indifferent 'in such a cause where as brotherly cheryte / or the common peace shuld be offended' by their neglect.[127] This emphasis on obedience for the sake of charity had also been highlighted in his earliest publication, where he notes that 'it is lawful to obey on account of charity' and that 'we do all freely, that is, on account of charity'.[128]

Also noteworthy in the above is Barnes's consistent emphasis on 'the common peace', the 'outward order', and those things 'profitable to the commonwealth'. These are of course the foremost concern of temporal rulers. It is significant that Barnes should highlight their importance in his discussion of matters primarily ecclesiastical; this raises the question of where exactly he stood on the subject of church reform enacted and supervised by temporal authority. Evidence for his final position on the matter is found in the recantation he signed in 1540:

123 Anderson, 'The Person and Position', 224 n. 2.

124 Though the Latin text of this particular article is no longer extant, the German text is only slightly more ambiguous than the English translation above. '[C]hristliche Freiheit behalten sole, nämlich dass die Leute verstehen, dass solche Satzungen nicht der Meinung zu halten, als seien sie nötig zur Seligkeit'. Both texts are found in *DER*, 142.

125 *Supplicatyon* (1531), fo. 113r.

126 *Supplicatyon* (1531), fo. 122v.

127 *Supplicatyon* (1531), fo. 119v.

128 *Sentenciae*, sig. G2v: 'licet audire ex charitate', and 'libere omnia facimus, id est ex charitate'.

> [I] also do confess with my heart, that laws and ordinances made by Christian rulers, ought to be obeyed by the inferiors and subjects, not only for fear, but also for conscience; for whoso breaketh them, breaketh God's commandments.[129]

Though this was of course a confession prepared for him, it does not differ greatly from the statement to which he had voluntarily agreed two years previously. With the Thirteen Articles he had professed that rulers

> should provide and enact by statute, wholesome and just laws (as far as human power permits), by which not only equity, justice and peace may be preserved in the state, but also that piety towards God may be furthered. They are also, as stated above, to have responsibility for upholding the law of God and the Christian religion.[130]

If necessary, the articles further state, princes are even to 'compel all priests and everyone else to perform their duties properly'.[131]

Because it has been argued that Barnes only arrived at this position 'as Henry's hold of the Church became evident', it must be asked whether he showed any consistency on this point.[132] While Clebsch asserts that 'Between 1531 and 1534 Barnes changed his mind radically ... on kingship',[133] Charles Anderson has argued that already in 1531 he had 'laid out a strong case for royal supremacy'.[134] It cannot be doubted that at least by 1535 Barnes was strongly supportive of Henry's claim to be supreme head of the church in England. While engaged in business on the continent that year he constantly voiced his desire to engage in public debate with Johannes Cochlaeus, the papal theologian who had recently published against the Royal Supremacy.[135] And as has already been noted, any passages that might have been read as a challenge to the Supremacy were excised from the *Supplicacion* of 1534. There is evidence, however, that already in 1531 Barnes favoured the sort of top-down reform that Royal Supremacy might make possible. In fact, even evidence brought forward to dispute this claim can be offered in its support. It has been noted, for example, that in revising his 1531 arguments Barnes later eliminated remarks that appeared critical of the King's claim to be Defender of the Faith.[136] What Barnes had criticised, however, was the means by which Henry originally came by the title. His status as such is never disputed; to the contrary, Barnes prays that God give the King the necessary

129 Burnet, *History of the Reformation*, 4.498.
130 *DER*, 203.
131 *DER*, 204.
132 Clebsch, *England's Earliest Protestants*, 65.
133 Clebsch, *England's Earliest Protestants*, 59.
134 Charles Anderson, 'Robert Barnes on Luther', in *Interpreters of Luther*, ed. J. Pelikan (Philadelphia, 1968), 39.
135 See above at p. 29.
136 Cargill Thompson, 'The Sixteenth-Century Editions', 137.

strength to perform his duty in defence of the true faith.[137] This duty is further emphasised when he explains that if the bishops reject the teaching of Christ and his apostles, 'than ys the kinges grace sworn to expelle you his realm and to defend the church from you'.[138]

Because Barnes had in 1531 so strongly rejected clerical claims to temporal power, it has been suggested that this issue defined for him the limits of royal reform. That is, Henry had a prerogative only to deny the clergy any temporal rule; but if he thus reformed the political sphere, ecclesiastical reform would happily and inevitably occur as a result.[139] Barnes certainly did believe that the church would benefit by the King's ejection of clergy from temporal rule, but his argument in fact goes beyond this. Henry not only had a right to deny them political power, but also to deny them ecclesiastical power. The King had appointed bishops, Barnes noted; therefore it was within his right also to depose them.[140] And indeed he should: 'yf youre grace wolde doo them ryght / you shulde returne them home ageyne'.[141] As the King has authority over appointment to the offices of the church, so too does he have a claim to the property of the church. Thus Barnes asked of his opponents, 'by what auctorite / have you made that princes shal make no statute as concernynge the goods of the church'?[142] And already in 1531 Barnes had hinted that the King might have certain rights even with regard to judging doctrine. Therefore those questioning his authority should beware, for 'the kynges highnes (if it pleased him) myght laye hie tresone to youre charge / and also the abomynable cryme of heresye'.[143]

By granting that the King wields authority with respect to church offices, church property, and to some extent even church teaching, Barnes showed himself to be supportive of the Royal Supremacy even as it was unfolding. It is also evident that, on account of this authority, he sees Henry as bearing much of the responsibility for the reform of the church. This responsibility and its benefits are expressed most clearly when Barnes addresses the reform of the clergy:

> youre grace is bounde in consciens to see amendment / and to se them reformyd / and to sett them to do their mynistracyon that they be callyd un to in the churche off god. ... And if youre grace do thus reforme them / no doute but you shall have the favore of god: and prosper in all thynges / and have a commen welthe welle ordered.[144]

137 *Supplicatyon* (1531), fo. 56r–v.
138 *Supplicatyon* (1531), fo. 11r.
139 Clebsch, *England's Earliest Protestants*, 63. See also R. O'Day, *The Debate on the English Reformation* (London, 1986), 11.
140 *Supplicatyon* (1531), fos 9v–10r, 47v.
141 *Supplicatyon* (1531), fo. 10r.
142 *Supplicatyon* (1531), fo. 12v.
143 *Supplicatyon* (1531), fo. 13r–v.
144 *Supplicatyon* (1531), fo. 17v.

This sentiment, stated already in 1531, would be reiterated quite consistently throughout the remainder of Barnes's life.

Upon an examination of these few topics, each central to the programme of reform that Robert Barnes would advance in the 1530s, it is evident that his thinking was relatively consistent throughout the years of his public life. Particular emphases might have changed slightly in response to changing circumstances, but his conclusions remained fundamentally unaltered. Although notable revisions were indeed made to his published works, such revisions provide no firm basis for speaking of 'radical' or 'extreme' modifications to his theology in the 1530s. Discussion of any decisive change in Barnes's thought should thus be limited to the period preceding his arrival in Wittenberg, at which time any lingering concern with a reformation of morals was overtaken by a more focused emphasis on specifically doctrinal reform.

Of the doctrines judged in acute need of reform, Barnes gave special attention to those touching the article of justification. On this article, and the related topics of sin, free will, and good works, he has been seen to hold a position very much in conformity with the confession of Luther and his Wittenberg associates. With regard to the sacrament of the altar Barnes is again quite evidently a proponent of what can fairly be called the Lutheran position. And though England and Germany presented very different contexts in which to promote reform, Barnes is not radically out of step with Wittenberg on questions of princely involvement in matters of ecclesiastical reform – though his treatment of this subject especially is most evidently framed with his King's own temperament in view. In the light of his frequent association with Luther and his circle, it is not at all surprising that Barnes should share their views on some fundamental matters of reform. And it can hardly be doubted that he arrived at his conclusions under the influence of the German reformers. But whether Barnes's theological programme was simply one of popularising for English readers an already formulated Lutheran doctrine can be determined only after some attention has been given to the methodology evident in his published works.

PART II

BARNES'S PROGRAMME: HISTORY, THEOLOGY, AND POLEMIC

3

HISTORY IN THEOLOGY: *SENTENCIAE* AND *SUPPLICATIONS*

Historians of the early reformation in England have long noted the manner in which history was called upon to bolster the Crown's case for independence from Rome. Few, for example, fail to reference the 1533 Act in Restraint of Appeals and its mention of 'divers sundry old authentic histories and chronicles'.[1] It is this use of history for political ends which has most often been noted; and indeed, F.J. Levy seems to speak for many when he writes that 'the use of history during the early period of the English Reformation was essentially secular, simply because, in the eyes of the government, matters of theology were not at issue'.[2] While it has been more recently argued that matters of theology were very much at issue for the Henrician government, any detailed investigation of history's employment in these matters has yet to be made.[3] The argument of this and the following chapters, however, will be that Robert Barnes made just such a use of historical argumentation.

1 *DER*, 78. Maurice Powicke, for example, treats the 1533 Act as illustrative of his famous contention that 'the one definite thing which can be said about the Reformation in England is that it was an act of State'. See Maurice Powicke, *The Reformation in England* (London, 1941), 1 and 44–9. A.G. Dickens, who would just as famously argue that 'the English Protestant Reformation arose and grew largely in opposition to the will of Henry VIII', nevertheless calls the Act Cromwell's 'most critical piece of legislation'. A.G. Dickens, *The English Reformation* (London, 1964), 83 and 117. The more recent 'revisionist' historians, for whom Dickens's work often serves as a foil, do not disagree. Richard Rex, for instance, cites the Act as a prime example of 'reform by statute' and describes its content as 'programmatic' for the Henrician reformation. Richard Rex, *Henry VIII and the English Reformation* (Basingstoke, 1993), 19 and 28.

2 F.J. Levy, *Tudor Historical Thought* (San Marino, 1967), 86–7. G. Nicholson, 'The Nature and Function of Historical Argument in the Henrician Reformation' (unpublished Ph.D. Thesis, Cambridge, 1977), also ignores specifically theological history. Even the few brief examinations of Barnes's polemical use of history focus almost solely on his critique of clerical power. See, e.g., R. Pineas, 'Robert Barnes' Polemical Use of History', *Bibliotheque d'Humanisme et Renaissance* 26 (1964), 55–69.

3 For Henry's theological concerns see especially McEntegart, 'England and the League of Schmalkalden', and the revised and published edition of this thesis, *Henry VIII, the League of Schmalkalden and the English Reformation* (Woodbridge, 2002).

On the evidence of his early biography one might assume that Barnes would naturally be disposed to a programme of theological reform based on an appeal to historical sources. The academic leanings evident in his reform of the Cambridge Austin friary clearly point to an interest in both the sources and methods of contemporary humanism. Though it is impossible to say how wholeheartedly or how consistently he embraced the *studia humanitatis* in the 1520s, it is probable that even at this stage he shared the renewed interest in history that was common to most humanist curricula. And indeed, unlike Luther, who at the imperial diet of Worms vowed to stand on the evidence of Scripture and conscience, Barnes claimed that at his own trial in 1526 he could not modify his confession because he had not been proved a heretic 'by godes worde nor by holy doctours'.[4] This certainly cannot be read as an unqualified acceptance of patristic authority; but it does betray his early willingness to give at least some weight to extra-biblical historical sources. And the willingness to weave such authorities into the source and substance of his theology was to become only more evident in later years.

The suggestion that Barnes made a distinct contribution to the methodology of sixteenth-century theological polemic is, however, faced with numerous opinions to the contrary. He has been described as 'a plodding culler of proof texts' in whose writings one looks 'in vain for a flash of originality'.[5] His citation of patristic authors is judged 'rather pedestrian',[6] and his appeal to chronicles and histories has been dismissed as 'commonplace'.[7] One author sums up Barnes's methodology under the bluntly uncomplimentary heading 'Scissors and Paste'.[8] Whether this common judgement of Barnes's thought as derivative and largely superfluous is in fact warranted can only be determined after a careful examination of his own writings. The uncontrived approach is chronological; this also offers the benefit of being further able to distinguish between his works according to genre. The *Sentenciae* and separate editions of the *Supplication* are quite evidently meant to be topical presentations of evangelical theology, while the later *Vitae romanorum pontificum* is ostensibly a work of history. As will be seen, however, a great deal of historical argument is introduced into his theological works, while at the same time his historical writing addresses primarily theological concerns.

Sentenciae ex doctoribus collectae (1530)

Robert Barnes's first published work, his *Sentenciae ex doctoribus collectae* of 1530, provides an early but clear indication of his literary agenda. Here one

4 *Supplicatyon* (1531), fo. 21r.
5 Anderson, 'The Person and Position', 169, 262.
6 Pineas, *Tudor Polemics*, 140.
7 Clebsch, *England's Earliest Protestants*, 76.
8 Clebsch, *England's Earliest Protestants*, 73.

glimpses not only the theological positions he will consistently hold throughout the remainder of his career, but also the method by which he arrives at and promotes these positions. As with his doctrinal conclusions, so also with his method there is an evident consistency. Indeed, such methodological consistency has been observed even by those who consider it commonplace or unoriginal. Charles Anderson has noted that 'The method most often used by Barnes was set when he put out his first production, the *Sentenciae*'.[9] W.A. Clebsch concurs by admitting, 'The task Barnes set for himself by his 1530 *Sentenciae*' was also 'carried out in the rest of his publications'.[10] Yet the only existing studies of Barnes's methodology – as distinct from his theology, that is, his expressed views on various doctrinal *loci* – suffer in part because this has been inadequately recognised. Rainer Pineas's analyses give particular attention to the *Supplications* and *Vitae*, but the *Sentenciae* receive no comparable mention.[11] An examination of Barnes's first publication will thus serve not only to complement Pineas's research, but may also provide some correctives to his particular conclusions.

As its title indicates, the *Sentenciae* is not a work of original scholarship. Barnes's modest intent was to collect opinions from the writings of the church doctors and to arrange them under topical theological headings. Though his selection and arrangement – and the very choice of topics themselves – are meant to support decidedly evangelical convictions, he offers comparatively little by way of personal commentary or interpretation. This slim volume is thus best viewed as a handy reference work to be made use of in theological controversy. The fact that Barnes's own controversies had, at the time of his writing, been with the traditionalist bishops of the English church informs his choice of authorities and the use to which he puts them. That is, he largely constrains himself to citing only those authors and works accepted by his opponents. Before describing the type of historical and theological arguments found in the *Sentenciae*, it is therefore worth briefly commenting on his sources.

Among the historical sources to which Barnes appeals in his theological works, the writings of the church fathers are naturally the most abundant. They are so prevalent, one author concludes, that 'The influence of the patristic writers upon the work of Robert Barnes can scarcely be overestimated'.[12] Though certainly true, such a conclusion should not necessarily lead one to assume that Barnes was always, or even regularly, making use of original sources. Bugenhagen wrote in the preface to Barnes's *Sentenciae* that the work was

9 Anderson, 'The Person and Position', 168.
10 Clebsch, *England's Earliest Protestants*, 74.
11 Pineas's choice of emphases is partly responsible for his conclusion that Barnes's use of history has primarily secular aims.
12 Trueman, *Luther's Legacy*, 33.

produced during a summer in Wittenberg. While he was in that university town Barnes surely would have had access to the works of the fathers;[13] it is rather more likely, however, that he worked primarily from previously compiled collections. That he often quotes the fathers as they are cited in Gratian's *Decretum* is evident from the references he includes in both the *Sentenciae* and the *Supplications*. Barnes's general reliance upon the recently published *Unio Dissidentium* has also been observed.[14] This collection of nearly six hundred patristic quotations, 'heavily weighted on the Protestant side', became almost instantly popular among early English evangelicals.[15] First published in two parts by the Antwerp printer Martin de Keyser in 1527, it was already found among the illicit books seized at Oxford in 1528.[16] In the next decade John Lambert was bold enough to make reference to the work in his interrogation before Archbishop Warham,[17] and Tyndale would lean heavily upon it in producing his *Answere* to Thomas More. The work's early condemnation by Bishop Tunstall – highlighted by Tyndale with some polemical effect[18] – as well as the number of editions subsequently published, further testify to its recognised utility for evangelical propagandists.[19] Barnes was no exception. Clebsch has pointed out, for example, that half of the topical headings found in the *Sentenciae* appear also in the *Unio Dissidentium*. Likewise, most of the patristic citations found under the locus of justification in Barnes's work are paralleled in this earlier publication.[20]

The use of such anthologies, however, cannot simply be judged the mark of indolent or incompetent scholarship. The utilisation of such tools was rather typical of Barnes's contemporaries. Thomas More, for example, did not hesitate

[13] Augustine, to whom Barnes most frequently appeals, was especially well represented in Wittenberg. Moreover, his former Cambridge friary quite probably had not only Augustine's complete works, but also indices to aid in their study. For the prevalence of indices or *tabulae* to Augustine's works in Austin friaries, see, e.g., M.R. James, 'The Catalogue of the Library of the Augustinian Friars at York', in *Fasciculus Joanni Willis Clark dictatus*, ed. J.W. Clark (Cambridge, 1909), 2–96, esp. 42–3.
[14] See S.L. Greenslade, *The English Reformers and the Fathers of the Church* (Oxford, 1960), 15; Clebsch, *England's Earliest Protestants*, 75–6.
[15] Greenslade, *The English Reformers and the Fathers*, 15. Though unquestionably compiled to support Protestant theology, the patristic quotations are, with few exceptions, culled from editions compiled by humanists who remained faithful to the old church. See Robert Peters, 'The Enigmatic *Unio Dissidentium*: Tyndale's "Heretical" Companion', *Reformation* 2 (1997), 236.
[16] See *A&M* (Pratt) 5, Appendix, no. 6.
[17] *A&M*, 2.1117.
[18] See, e.g., William Tyndale, *An Answer to Sir Thomas More's Dialogue, The Supper of the Lord ... and Wm. Tracy's Testament Expounded*, ed. H. Walter (Cambridge: Parker Society, 1850), 187.
[19] For analyses of the *Unio Dissidentium* and its evangelical use, see the whole of Robert Peters, 'The Enigmatic *Unio Dissidentium*', his earlier treatment of the work, 'Who Compiled the Sixteenth-Century Patristic Handbook *Unio Dissidentium*?', in *Studies in Church History*, vol. 2, ed. G.J. Cuming (London, 1965), 237–50, and Anne M. O'Donnell, 'Augustine in *Unio Dissidentium* and Tyndale's Answer to More', *Reformation* 2 (1997), 241–60.
[20] Clebsch, *England's Earliest Protestants*, 76.

to make use of patristic testimonies compiled by John Fisher.[21] Likewise, it has been suggested with reference to More's use of the *Glossa Ordinaria* that this work 'became a kind of index to the fathers for him'.[22] In his debate with More on the sacrament, John Frith would also employ a collection of patristic citations, the *Dialogus* of Oecolampadius. This text, a revision of and response to Philip Melanchthon's writing on the eucharist, proved so popular among early English Sacramentarians that it has been not unjustly labelled 'their chief armoury for this topic'.[23]

Barnes's use of patristic citations, whether culled from collections or original sources, is by no means unique. But neither are the writings of the fathers the only historical sources employed in his works. In addition to dealing with the medieval schoolmen and with papal and conciliar decrees, of which he displays more than superficial knowledge, Barnes also calls on the testimony of national and ecclesiastical histories. Apparently this is something for which he was especially known even by his adversaries. A not entirely flattering ballad published after his death, for example, puts the following rhyme in his mouth:

> who lyst to seke about
> may in chronicles sone finde oute
> what sedes the popish route
> in yngland hath sowen
> because the time is short
> I shall brefely report
> and wright in dewe sort
> them what I have knowen.[24]

The anonymous author probably has in mind the arguments that introduce Barnes's 1534 *Supplicacion*, where the historical conflicts between the papacy and English kings are addressed in some detail. But even in the *Sentenciae* Barnes makes great use of the sixth-century *Tripartite History* of Cassiodorus, for example, as well as more recent histories such as Hartmann Schedel's *Liber Cronicarum*, Werner Rolewinck's *Fasciculus Temporum*, and the *Saxonia* of Albert Krantz.[25]

21 R. Marius, 'Thomas More and the Early Church Fathers', *Traditio* 24 (1968), 396.
22 Marius, 'Thomas More and the Early Church Fathers', 385.
23 Greenslade, *The English Reformers and the Fathers*, 14. Clebsch, *England's Earliest Protestants*, 126, refers to Frith's eucharistic argument as 'hardly more than a rearrangement and abbreviation of Oecolampadius' work'.
24 Anon., *The metynge of Doctor Barons and Doctor Powell at Paradise gate* (London, 1548 [STC 1473]), sig. A5v.
25 Rather than the *Liber Cronicarum*, Barnes actually refers to the *Cronica Cronicarum*, the title of a 1521 Parisian abridgement of Schedel's work. However, R.J. Schoeck, 'The *Cronica Cronicarum* of Sir Thomas More and Tudor Historians', *Bulletin of the Institute of Historical Research* 35 (1962), 84–6, has pointed out that it was customary for Tudor historians to refer to Schedel's complete work by the title of its abridgement.

Equally as important as the sources Barnes employs is the manner in which they are put to use. In common with most theologians of the magisterial reformation, he frequently calls upon his theological predecessors in countering charges of novelty. As is frequently noted, from the start the reformers often faced the hostile question: 'Where was your church before Luther?' Since Barnes and his co-religionists quite consistently conceived of the church as a theological rather than merely an institutional entity, the question they in fact endeavoured to answer is: 'Where was your theology before Luther?' It is obviously in response to this sort of question that Barnes goes about selecting his quotations from early church fathers, ecclesiastical councils, and even medieval schoolmen. Some examples of this defensive use of historical authorities have already been observed in the survey of Barnes's doctrine. He had attempted to show, for instance, that his own teaching on free will was neither more nor less than that of Augustine, that his profession of justification by faith was merely that of Ambrose, and that his sacramental theology was simply Athanasian.

As noted, this defensive use of authorities is something Barnes shares with the majority of his fellow reformers. Where he begins to show some hints of originality is in what might be called his offensive use of these sources. Here Barnes not only attempts to prove the antiquity of evangelical doctrine, but also forwards evidence in support of the contention that it is the Roman church which is guilty of novelty. Even in this Barnes is not entirely original; already in the previous decade this line of attack had been advanced, for example, by the Swiss author of *Vom alten und nüen Gott*. When this work went into English in 1534, its translator would praise the author for 'deducynge all thynges by a very godly ordre of hystoryes' and thereby demonstrating that it was papal theologians, rather than evangelicals, who 'through the fraudes of Sathan have brought forthe newe goddes'.[26] It was not until the latter half of the century, though, that this programme would begin to find its most coherent English expression, in the works of the 'official apologist' of Elizabeth's reign.[27] Beginning with his 'challenge sermons' of 1559–60, the Salisbury bishop John Jewel would challenge conservative theologians to establish by 'any one sufficient sentence out of any old catholic doctor, or father, or out of any old general council, or out of the holy scriptures of God, or any one example of the primitive church' that the 'old faith' was in fact the faith of antiquity.[28] Convinced that this was impossible, he charged them with 'having without cause renounced the judgment and orders

26 Joachim Vadianus [attr.], *A worke entytled of ye olde god [and] the newe* (London, 1534 [STC 25127]), sig. A5v, A3r.

27 W.M. Southgate, *John Jewel and the Problem of Doctrinal Authority* (Cambridge, MA, 1962), 121.

28 John Jewel, *The Works of John Jewel, Bishop of Salisbury: The First Portion*, ed. John Ayre (Cambridge: Parker Society, 1845), 20.

of the primitive church and ancient fathers', and erected instead a novel church of their own creation.[29] Assertions of evangelical antiquity and conservative novelty were of course two sides of the same coin, and in Barnes's works especially the distinction between a defensive and offensive use of historical authorities is not always clear. It appears that on more than one occasion he thinks the novelty of Roman doctrine has been proved simply by showing the antiquity of the contrary. His selective quotation of the sources, being primarily polemical, ignores the fact that opinions diverged even among the earliest fathers. To cite Ambrose, for instance, does not prove that justification by faith alone was the unanimous opinion of the ancients, or even that Ambrose himself was always clearly consistent on this point. Barnes's opponents quickly seized upon this fact and pointed out the weakness of such an argument, prompting him to make a reply in his *Supplicatyon* of the next year.[30]

Barnes's offensive use of history typically rests on a much surer foundation when he is attacking rites and practices either grounded in particular theological assertions, or which, on account of their antiquity, are cited in support of the legitimacy of the same. His commentary on private confession and absolution offers one example of the manner in which Barnes moves from a defensive to an offensive posture, calling upon historical evidence both to bolster and to undermine theological claims. In support of his own proposition, that 'auricular confession is not necessary for salvation', he especially calls upon patristic sermons and biblical commentaries.[31] He is thus able to show that prominent fathers of both the eastern and western churches had interpreted the scriptural mandates for confession without making auricular confession a binding necessity. As Barnes begins to move from the support for his own position to the evidence against that of his adversaries, he introduces a passage from Augustine that more explicitly drives a wedge between ancient and modern opinions. The contemporary applicability of what could be construed as anti-clerical polemic was no doubt a deciding factor in its inclusion:

> Therefore who am I to men that they should hear my confession, as if all my weakness were to be healed by them? They are the sort curious to know about the lives of others, but inactive in correcting their own. Why do they demand to hear who I am? Why do they not wish to hear from you who they are?[32]

At least as late as Augustine, then, there were orthodox fathers who not only did

29 John Jewel, *The Works of John Jewel, Bishop of Salisbury: The Fourth Portion*, ed. John Ayre (Cambridge: Parker Society, 1850), 901.

30 See *Supplicatyon* (1531), fo. 44r.

31 *Sentenciae*, sig. G3v: 'Confessio Auricularis Non Est De Necessitate Salutis.'

32 *Sentenciae*, sig. G5v: 'Quid mihi ergo cum hominibus? ut audiant confessiones meas? quasi ipsi sanaturi sint omnes languores meos? Curiosum genus ad cognoscendam vitam alienam, desidiosum ad corrigendam suam. Quid a me quaerunt audire qui sim? qui nolunt a te audire qui sint?'

not insist upon auricular confession, but who even rejected those who would deem it necessary.

Certain questions naturally arise with such information. If early exegetes found no biblical mandate for private confession, and if later fathers rejected its necessity, then when and why did it nevertheless become binding upon those Christians under the authority of Rome? Barnes finds some revealing answers recorded in Cassiodorus's *Tripartite History*, a compilation and continuation of earlier ecclesiastical histories. Here he reads an account of the origins of private confession.

> We see, therefore, that faults were disclosed to the ancient pontiffs as in a theatre, under the testimony of the people of the church. And [then] for this thing they appointed wise presbyters, of good conversation and who could keep secrets, to whom the delinquent went in order to confess their faults. And according to the guilt of each he also imposed punishment. This is diligently observed even to this time in the western churches, and especially at Rome.[33]

Though the practice is clearly of ancient origin, Barnes is convinced that the seemingly arbitrary circumstances of its introduction undermine any claim that it is a necessary practice. But his marginal comment sheds important light on his attitude towards ancient tradition, contemporary practice, and binding dogma.

> Here you have the origin of secret confession, of which the church of God was ignorant for three hundred years. I do not say this in condemnation; no, I very much approve it. But I do not teach that it is commanded, that it is necessary for salvation.[34]

That private confession, regardless of Barnes's approval, is a practice which may legitimately be set aside is further supported by the evidence of the *Tripartite History*. Eusebius's fifth-century continuer Sozomen, the source for the *History* at this point, relates the story of its fourth-century abrogation by Nectarius, the bishop of Constantinople. According to his account,

33 *Sentenciae*, sigs G8v–H1r: 'propterea visum est antiquis pontificibus ut velut in Theatro sub testimonio ecclesiastici populi delicta pandantur. Et ad hanc rem, presbyterium bonae conversationis, servantemque secretum, ac sapientem virum statuerunt, ad quem accedentes qui deliquerant, delicta propria fatebantur. At ille secundum uniuscuiusque culpam indicebat & mulctam. Quod etiam hactenus diligenter in occidentalibus servatur ecclesiis, & maxime apud Rhomam.'

34 *Sentenciae*, sigs G8v–H1r: 'Hic habetis originem clanculariae confessionis, quam ecclesia dei ignoravit per. CCC. annos. Haec non dico quod damnem imo valde eam probo, sed doceo eam non esse urgendam ut necessariam ad salutem.' Unless he has in mind Sozomen's mention of private confession's introduction only after the Decian persecution and subsequent Novatianist controversy – information not included in the *Tripartite History* – it is unclear why Barnes fixes upon the span of 'three hundred years'.

> A presbyter was over the penitents until that time when a woman of nobility had confessed her sins and the presbyter commanded that she fast and pray to God with works. Having observed this, she confessed that she had frequently lain with the deacon in the church. When the people learned of this they were furious with the priests, as if they had injured the church. Then Bishop Nectarius removed the impious deacon and, being advised to leave to each one's conscience the decision of when to commune, he appointed no more presbyters over the penitents. And from then the ancient custom ceased.[35]

Sozomen's account serves a dual purpose for Barnes. Most importantly, it offers evidence in support of his claim that the prescribed western form of confession, absolution, and satisfaction is unnecessary. Otherwise, the ancient eastern church could hardly have abrogated the practice without controversy. But the scandalous circumstances under which the practice was abolished also afford Barnes the opportunity to comment sarcastically on the 'admirable deed of the religious celibate', further strengthening his case for clerical marriage.[36]

Earlier in the *Sentenciae* Barnes had shown himself well versed in the historical literature that points up the relative novelty of enforced clerical celibacy. The cited sources certainly affirm that there were many in the church, from the earliest days, who indeed would have preferred a celibate priesthood. But equally clear is the fact that conciliar canons, along with both episcopal and papal decrees, consistently forbade the laws which would have effected such a priesthood.[37] Barnes notes that the fourth-century council of Gangra went even further, anathematising any who would judge the Masses of married clergy invalid or who abstained from the Mass for this reason.[38] Likewise, even as late as the early thirteenth-century papacy of Innocent III, clergy were being condemned not for marrying, but for dissolving their own legal marriages.[39] Ecclesiastical practices such as private confession and mandates such as clerical celibacy were certainly not unrelated to the official theology of the Roman church. Thus by questioning the history of such practices, Barnes was also raising implicit but important questions about the dogma with which they were entwined. Confession especially,

35 *Sentenciae*, sig. H1v: 'presbiter super penitentes fuit, usque ad illud tempus, quo quedam mulier nobilissima, cum peccata sua fuisset confessa, & ei a presbytero fuisset praeceptum ut ieiunaret, & deo operibus supplicaret, cum hoc observaret, crebrius in ecclesia cum diacono se concubuisse confessa est. Hoc cum populus cognouisset, saviebat in sacerdotes quasi per eos facta fuisset iniuria ecclesiae. Tum Nectarius episcopus removit diaconum sceleratum, & quibusdam suadentibus, ut singulos ad communicandum iudicio conscientiae suae relinqueret, etiam presbyterum nequaquam super paenitentes esse praecepit. Et ex illo, antiquitatis consuetudo sublata est.'

36 *Sentenciae*, sig. H1v: 'Egregium facinus casti celibatus'.

37 See, e.g., *Sentenciae*, sig. F1r–v on the council of Nicaea.

38 *Sentenciae*, sig. F2v.

39 *Sentenciae*, sig. F4v. Barnes addresses the history of clerical marriage again in his *Supplicacion* of 1534. The fuller presentation there will provide an opportunity to discuss his argument in some detail.

being one of the seven sacraments, stood at the heart of the church's theology.[40] This was of course also the case with the Mass, to which Barnes gives a great deal of attention. In fact, Barnes's writing on the history of the Mass particularly stands out among the articles of his *Sentenciae*. Here, rather than simply arranging quotations from the doctors, he allows himself the liberty of extended commentary. Perhaps even more telling, Barnes's research on the subject of the Mass appears to be wholly original. There is no discernible dependence upon the previously mentioned *Unio Dissidentium*, a fact which is less than surprising since the sacramental theology of that work was without question 'that of Strassburg and Switzerland'.[41] What is surprising, though, especially given their geographical and theological proximity, is that there appears to be no dependent relationship even between Barnes's eucharistic sentences and those collected by Philip Melanchthon earlier in the same year.[42] Barnes, then, seems to have his own agenda.

Though not promulgated as binding dogma until the council of Trent, the sacrifice of the Mass did not lack official sanction in the church of the early sixteenth century.[43] The language of sacrifice was enshrined in the canon of the Mass, which liturgy in turn was granted authoritative status by canon law. This code of law cited as its own authority that of an earlier council. It was thus to the history of councils, canon law, and liturgy that Barnes turned.

According to the decretalists, the shape of the eucharistic liturgy originated with and was handed down by James, the brother of Jesus. In support of this assertion, the sixth synod of Constantinople was cited as authoritative.[44] Barnes immediately protests this claim with an assertion of his own: 'of the Mass (as they understand it) no mention was made in the church for two hundred years'.[45] Regarding the first century at least, he shows no lack of confidence in his knowledge of custom. Without naming him, he addresses Thomas More's claim that the Mass was celebrated a thousand times even before St Matthew's Gospel was written; Barnes challenges his opponents to 'provide evidence of one apostolic Mass, and they shall be victorious'.[46] As the canonical gloss had also attributed

40 Not only was confession and absolution one of the church's sacraments, but by the early sixteenth century it had in many respects become the primary sacrament of the church. On this see T.N. Tentler, *Sin and Confession on the Eve of the Reformation* (Princeton, 1977).
41 MacCulloch, *Thomas Cranmer*, 468.
42 For Melanchthon's *Sententiae*, see *CR*, 23, cols 733–52.
43 See F. Clark, *Eucharistic Sacrifice and the Reformation* (London, 1960), 76–7.
44 The 'sixth synod' to which Barnes refers is actually the third council of Constantinople, the sixth ecumenical council. Though convened as a synod in 680, it was declared ecumenical upon its opening.
45 *Sentenciae*, sig. K5r–v: 'et missae (ut ipsi eam intelligunt) nulla in ecclesia fit mentio per ducentos annos'.
46 *Sentenciae*, sig. K5r: 'Adducant unum ex apostolis missantem, et vicerint'. See More's claim in *CWM*, 5.599.

the origin of the Mass to Basil, fourth-century bishop of Caesarea, Barnes offers a further challenge. He asks hostile readers to explain which parts of the Mass originated with James, and which were added by Basil. The challenge, of course, serves only a rhetorical purpose. The author fully intends to answer himself. He does so first by denying James and the apostles any role in liturgical development. He appeals to the testimony of St Gregory, 'who says the apostles had no special way of celebrating Mass, but said only the Lord's Prayer'.[47] He then ends as he had begun, with a statement meant to be left unanswered: 'Now where is your tradition of James?'[48]

Having dismissed the claim that the Mass originated with James, Barnes goes on to deal with Basil's alleged additions. Here he enters his element as a liturgical historian, stating his aim and intent before proceeding: 'Because the Mass is so dear to you ... I myself will describe for you the originators of your patched-together Mass, and this from your own authors'.[49] This he does, covering the development of the rite from the second through the eighth century. He provides dates for the various introductions and notes whether they developed out of local custom, were borrowed from divergent rites, or were imposed by papal decree.[50] Unsurprisingly, not so much as a word of the liturgy is ascribed to Basil. The sixth synod, Gratian's authority for naming him its author, is mentioned in Barnes's catalogue only to note that there the bishop of Porto sang the first recorded Latin Mass. In Barnes's mind, it becomes evident, this synod is ultimately most important for what it does not say. It was neither convened to settle controversy regarding the Mass, nor did it address the subject in its canons and decrees. 'Their writings are among us', he notes, 'in which is read not a syllable regarding the Mass'.[51] For those still doubtful of his evidence and interpretation, he simply urges them to 'read the acts of the synod, and you will discover as much'.[52]

It is perhaps surprising that, having spent some time outlining the growth of the Mass, Barnes spends little time at all drawing out the implications of its mutability or attacking what he judges to be its questionable theological content. Aside from a few passing references to sacrifice, and particular mention of the sacrificial language introduced by Leo the Great in the mid-fifth century, he seems content to let his readers draw their own conclusions based on the evidence. Though he may not go into great detail about specifically theological errors

47 *Sentenciae*, K6r: 'qui dicit apostolos nullum peculiarem modum habuisse in celebranda missa, sed tantum dixisse dominicam orationem'.
48 *Sentenciae*, sig. K6r: 'Ubi iam est traditio Iacobi vestri?'
49 *Sentenciae*, sig. K6r–v: 'Quia missa vobit tam chara est ... ego describam vobis auctores vestrae consutae missae, idque ex vestris scriptoribus'.
50 This exercise is repeated in a more expanded form in Barnes's 1536 *Vitae romanorum pontificum*, and so will be discussed in further detail in the next chapter.
51 *Sentenciae*, sig. K5v: 'Scripta eorum apud nos sunt, in quibus de missa ne syllaba quidem legitur'.
52 *Sentenciae*, sig. K5v: 'legite acta Synodi et ita invenietis'.

resulting from additions to and modifications of the eucharistic liturgy, he is clear about the historical errors. Those who falsely claim that the Mass is of apostolic origin 'stand against the clear truth of God'.[53] Before closing, however, Barnes cannot resist at least brief acknowledgement of the intimate relationship between faulty history and false theology: 'here you now have the first Latin Mass – however patched together – and the originators of each part, which our wicked [opponents] so impiously assert is a sacrifice'.[54] Without this allegedly authoritative liturgy, so confusedly composed and so long in the making, what would be left to the church? Barnes answers, 'Nothing at all, except the words of Christ'.[55]

The argument implicit throughout the whole of the *Sentenciae* is twofold. First, the historical record – from Scripture, through church fathers and church councils, and even among some later medieval doctors – offers evidence that the evangelical propositions derided as 'new learning' are not new at all. This common defensive use of tradition is also complemented by an offensive use that goes one step further. Again appealing to those sources that had been accepted through the ages, Barnes marshals evidence in support of his assertion that it is the Roman church which has introduced novel doctrines and rites. As he largely limits himself in the *Sentenciae* to quotations without extended commentary, however, it is not until his later publications that he begins to make more explicit the presuppositions and implications inherent in this line of argument.

A supplicatyon made by Robert Barnes (1531)

That the *Supplicatyon* was intended to be something of an extended commentary on the evidence first published in the *Sentenciae* is clear upon even cursory comparison of the two works. Though Barnes never explicitly refers back to his previous publication, the theses selected for explication in 1531 are simply lifted and translated from the contents page of the 1530 work. The title page of the *Supplicatyon* provides an early indication that the sources and methods to be employed will not differ greatly from those of the previous year; Barnes will again rely upon 'the scripture / holye doctoures and their awne lawe'. And indeed, as one moves through the body of his 1531 publication, it becomes obvious that Barnes's citations from Scripture, fathers, and canon law are quite often the same as those first forwarded in the *Sentenciae*. Despite a noticeably different style,

[53] *Sentenciae*, sig. K8r: 'contra apertam veritatem dei se opponunt'.

[54] *Sentenciae*, sig. K7v: 'hic iam habes missam primam latinam utcunque consutam, et auctores singularum partium, quam nostri impii tam impie defendunt pro sacrificio'.

[55] *Sentenciae*, sig. K8r: 'Omnino nihil nisi verba Christi'. Though it is possible to read this as a call for the abolition of liturgy in its entirety, doing so would, I believe, miss Barnes's point. His argument is not an attack on rites *per se*; it is a rejection of any fallible authority's right to make the Mass – and any false theology embedded therein – binding on the church. In this context, his appeal to Christ's words is probably best read as a defence of his principle of *sola scriptura*.

then, it can safely be argued that much of what has been said above about the *Sentenciae* holds true also for the *Supplicatyon*.

It is noteworthy, however, that some of the theses treated in the earlier work are not brought forward and reiterated in 1531. Especially significant is the absence of those articles on clerical marriage, auricular confession, and the development of the Mass, some of the topics in which Barnes's historical bent had been especially evident. And in fact it has been suggested that the historical argument has little place in the 1531 *Supplicatyon*. Rainer Pineas, for instance, has noted that the first edition of Barnes's *Supplicatyon* contains merely one historical reference. While perhaps true in an unnecessarily narrow sense – Barnes only once refers to a 'secular' historical event, the crowning of Pepin – this observation is particularly misleading if meant to imply that it was only near the end of his publishing career, and only at the prompting of others, that Barnes turned to the study of history and the use of specifically historical argumentation.[56] He had of course already in 1530 made beneficial use of ancient and modern historians from Sozomen to Schedel. And though direct appeal to the modern historians is noticeably absent in 1531, he continues to reference the ecclesiastical histories of the ancient church. Taking even these facts into account, Barnes's assertion that he could further prove certain points 'both by auncient cronicles / and also by the practes of youre awne law / yff it were not to longe a processe', cannot be hastily dismissed as a rhetorical bluff.[57]

That Barnes does not in fact go on to provide proof from such chronicles might perhaps be explained by the obvious change in his audience. The *Supplicatyon*, unlike the *Sentenciae*, was not intended to be a debating handbook. That is, it was not written for evangelical academics who could often expect to find themselves engaged in disputes with learned opponents. Instead, while formally addressing this tract to his King, Barnes makes clear that he also writes for 'alle trewe chrysten men', including those 'pore men that be unlerned'.[58] Hence his decision to compose in English rather than in the Latin of the *Sentenciae*. While the poor and unlearned of England would not necessarily be familiar with the content or concerned with the relevance of the chronicles – especially those written by foreign authors for a foreign audience – they would certainly be aware of the claims to authority made by the church in which they were raised. Rather than parading details of specific historical events, then, Barnes focuses much of his attention on this question of authority and its underlying presuppositions. In

56 *Supplicatyon* (1531), fo. 5r; but even on this point also compare fos 5v and 8v, where Barnes appeals to 'the cronycles' in support of his argument. Pineas's claim that this is the only historical reference is largely determined by his focus on Barnes's use of secular history for political purposes. It does indeed seem Pineas's intent to date Barnes's use of history to the mid-1530s and to associate it with Cromwell's influence. See Pineas, *Tudor Polemics*, 121–2.

57 *Supplicatyon* (1531), fo. 8r.

58 *Supplicatyon* (1531), fo. 131v.

doing so, however, he also makes evident that this method of defence and attack serves as prolegomena to the historical arguments forwarded from patristic and conciliar sources, as well as from the ancient customs and laws of the church.

This method of argument was, in many ways, also dictated simply by the rhetoric of those with whom he was engaged in controversy. Barnes describes what he heard from his detractors:

> Crye theye heresy / heresy / an heretyke / an heretyke / he ought not to beharde for his matters be condemned by the churche / and by holy fathers / and bi alle longe customs and by alle maner of lawys.[59]

Barnes's case – presumably to be presented with a characteristically evangelical appeal to Scripture – need not be heard and ought not be heard because it had already been judged and condemned in the courts of church, fathers, custom, and law. In such a context there was little room for him to doubt that matters of doctrine were as much matters 'of the nature of ecclesiastical authority as of the interpretation of Scripture'.[60] In addressing doctrine, therefore, he would necessarily have to address the nature of the church and its traditional authorities. Only then would he be free to present his own historical evidence and to ask if his opinions had indeed been condemned by church, fathers, custom, and law. After taking up the issue of authority he would also find himself in a better position to ask once again whether he or Rome was in fact guilty of theological novelty.

Regarding the nature of traditional ecclesiastical authority, Barnes makes no attempt to hide his presuppositions.

> Crye / the church / the church / and the counsels / the counsels that were lawfully gathered in the power of the holye gost (alle this may you say and yet lye) and yf you have not in dede the holly goste with in you / and iff you do heare any other voyce than christes / thane are you not of the church / but of the devylle.[61]

Without the authority of Christ and his Holy Spirit, Barnes argues, the authority of church and councils is null and void. Lest he be misunderstood, he makes clear that his appeal to the Holy Spirit and to the 'voice of Christ' is not that of a radical. It is not an appeal to any special, immediate revelation, but rather to the accepted words of Scripture. He argues that

> you see opinly / that I have the holy worde of god / and oure Master Christ / which is elder than oure fathers I have also the practis of the holy apostillis that understonde thys thyng better than all youre counsellis.[62]

It will be self-evident, Barnes believes, that the words of the fathers are more

59 *Supplicatyon* (1531), fo. 36v.
60 Trueman, 'The Saxons', 299.
61 *Supplicatyon* (1531), fo. 63r.
62 *Supplicatyon* (1531), fo. 76r–v.

recent than those of Christ, and that the authority of councils is lesser than that of the apostles. But more pointedly, he goes on to assert that any such extra-biblical authority might stand in direct contradiction to Christ's. In fact, asserting such authority against that of Scripture, to the deception and ruin of the church, is precisely the charge Barnes levels against his opponents. Thus he continues: 'But let us graunte that you have fathers and counsellys for you / That ys the next way to dysseve the church of god'.[63]

Nor does Barnes shy away from identifying what he believes to be the true source of this deception:

> if all youre councellis / All youre fathers / All youre customs / brevely all that you bringe for you be compared [with Scripture] / than shal we se whether it be trew and of god or not / for of them selfe they have no truth / but be invencions of corruptid reson and persuasions of the devell to perverte the holy church of god.[64]

Thus he introduces not only the possibility, but also the assertion that the devil himself has been at work in and against the visible church on earth. He further sharpens this assertion by stating that the devil and his ministers may remain present even yet in the church, not only tempting the weak and ignorant among the laity, but even working in and through those who make up the highest courts of appeal. Thus, Barnes says again:

> we can not be delyvered / with these glorious wordes / Concilium / Concilium / Patres / Patres / Episcopi / Episcopi / for alle these may be the minysters of the devylle.[65]

Significantly, however, such a conclusion does not lead him to dismiss the sayings of such authorities out of hand. To do so, in fact, would be to dismiss the very evidence upon which he will build his case. Instead, it is Barnes's intention to present this historical evidence to his readers and ask them to make their own conclusions. In a particularly revealing passage, he summarises the respective responsibilities of himself and his readers:

> thys one thynge I do require off the / that thou wylte compare these sayinges of doctoures / holye fathers and of the popes awne lawe unto the sayinges of the pope and bysshopes that be nowe / and unto the practice of thys present worlde / and then geve sentence thy selfe howe they do agre.[66]

Should modern authorities be shown not to agree with the ancients, Barnes is willing to suggest what he believes the appropriate conclusion should be:

63 *Supplicatyon* (1531), fo. 76v.
64 *Supplicatyon* (1531), fo. 77r.
65 *Supplicatyon* (1531), fo. 124v.
66 *Supplicatyon* (1531), unnumbered folio = sig. U1r.

> yf they agre not / then mayest thou suspecte that yt ys amysse and that the devell hathe transfygured hym selfe in too an angell of lyght and that they are hys mynysters.[67]

Barnes's frequent insistence that both Christ and Antichrist may be present and active in the visible church leads him quite naturally to de-emphasise its authority: 'this', he says, 'is not the church that we wille greatly speke of'.[68]

But Barnes does indeed have plenty to say with regard to this church. The presence and activity of Antichrist in its midst cannot simply be asserted as self-evident. Nor is this a claim that might be supported by appeal to dogmatic theology, for it was the accepted dogma of the church itself that proclaimed it infallible. If Barnes's assertion were to be given convincing weight then support of another kind would have to be found. He thus turns to the historical record for anecdotal evidence to buttress his claim. Before doing so, however, he is quick to reject the sort of counter-claim he might reasonably expect to hear from his opponents. Appeals to ancient tradition or long-standing custom cannot, by themselves, be admitted as conclusive proof of divine sanction. To the contrary, Barnes answers with the legal maxim that 'a custom with out the verite ys but an olde erroure'.[69] This theoretical point, Barnes notes, is granted even by the canon lawyers. But the task he sets for himself is not simply to prove that 'old errors' might possibly have crept into the church, but rather to show that they indeed have. This is made evident when he turns his attention specifically to the ecclesiastical councils, those ecumenical gatherings understood to be representative of the whole church and thus authoritative: 'yf they have not the worde of god / I wylle not alonly say they may erre / but also that they do erre in verye dede'.[70]

In support of the contention that even plenary councils are not beyond reproof, Augustine is cited at some length:

> those counselles that be gethered in everie province must with out geve place to the auctorite of the full counsellis which be gethered of all chrystendom / and also those ful counsellis oft timis must be a mendyd by the full counsellys that come after / yf any thynge be openyd by any experience that was a fore shyt / and yf any thyng be knowen that was hyddyn. And this may be done with out any shaddow of supersticious pryde / with out any bostyd Arrogancye with out any contencyon of malycius envye / but with holy meknes / wyth holy peasse / and with chrystened cheryte.[71]

The implication of such an admission is further drawn out by Barnes:

67 *Supplicatyon* (1531), unnumbered folio = sig. U1r.
68 *Supplicatyon* (1531), fo. 58v.
69 *Supplicatyon* (1531), fo. 15r.
70 *Supplicatyon* (1531), fo. 63v.
71 *Supplicatyon* (1531), fo. 64r–v.

> Here it is playne that youre full counselles may be a mendyd and reformyd / the wyche thynge nede not / yf they coulde not erre ye and if they did not erre in dede.[72]

Given the esteem in which Augustine was held by all, Barnes can confidently highlight the conclusion he finds implicit in the saint's words. He is well aware, however, that Augustine only explicitly supports the previously stated contention that conciliar error is a theoretical possibility. Further evidence must be adduced if error is to be asserted as an historical fact. For such testimony Barnes turns to an unwilling witness in the person of his old antagonist John Fisher, the bishop of Rochester. Fisher, Barnes notes, though himself holding conciliar authority in high regard, had been forced to acknowledge that the council of Constantinople, for example, 'had .330. bisshops and yet did erre'.[73] If even the conservative Rochester could reach such a conclusion, Barnes feels confident that he can rest his case. His argument is succinctly summarised with the statement: 'the counselle *may* erre as it *hath* erred'.[74]

If even a council comprised of more than three hundred bishops has erred, Barnes recognises that significant problems can also be identified in any claims regarding episcopal authority. Not surprisingly then, he turns his attention immediately to the highest episcopal office in the church, that of the bishop of Rome. Returning to his previously forwarded claim that 'many pryncis and many popes / and other inferior persons have swervyd from the faithe',[75] he continues again with reference to the bishop of Rochester. Barnes claims that Fisher's reluctant willingness to question the authority of certain councils was predicated on 'no nother cause / but by cause the pope dyd not agre to them'.[76] While agreeing with his ultimate conclusion, Barnes takes issue with the premise on which it was founded. He appeals once again to conciliar history, as well as canon law:

> is not thys a resonable cause? can not the pope erre? lett hym rede his awne lawe. Dis. 19. Anastasius / and Dis. 40. Si papa and also. 24.q.1 A recta in the glosse / and there shall he finde that the pope hathe erred wherfore than shulde the matter stonde in hys judgement? Now how wille he by this rule save the counselies of constance / and of basel where in both counsels the popes were condemned for heretykes? as the same counsels make mencion / also that the counsels have erred that graunteth he hym self.[77]

72 *Supplicatyon* (1531), fo. 64v.
73 *Supplicatyon* (1531), fo. 63r. For Fisher's views on conciliar authority, see especially R. Rex, *The Theology of John Fisher* (Cambridge, 1991), 102–3. See also B. Gogan, 'Fisher's View of the Church', in *Humanism, Reform and the Reformation*, ed. B. Bradshaw and E. Duffy (Cambridge, 1989), 137.
74 *Supplicatyon* (1531), fo. 63v. Italics are my own.
75 *Supplicatyon* (1531), fo. 60v.
76 *Supplicatyon* (1531), fo. 63r.
77 *Supplicatyon* (1531), fo. 63r–v.

Barnes is therefore convinced that the very history of the visible church illustrates that its own authorities are unreliable guarantors of truth. In this light, even if his detractors are correct in asserting that 'his matters be condemned by the churche / and by holy fathers / and bi alle longe customs and by alle maner of lawys'[78] (something which Barnes is in any case unprepared to admit), he may, as he had already stated, 'ryghtously denye there church / their lawys and their customs'.[79] Erroneous judgements are by no means divine judgements. Error in Christ's church and deception of the same is rather, in Barnes's analysis, undoubtedly the work of Antichrist. What remains for him, then, is to point out some of those errors which have occurred in the church's historical doctrine and practice, and thus to show that deceit and novelty are charges more appropriately lodged against his opponents than against himself and his fellow evangelicals.

Having already argued that the authorities of tradition pale in comparison to that of Scripture, and that they might in fact contradict this supreme authority, Barnes unsurprisingly finds Antichrist most evidently at work in the church's history when and where access to Scripture is forbidden.

> How cane antichryst be better knowyn / than be this tokyn that he condemnithe scripturs and makythe it heresy and hye treason agenst the kynges grace for lay men to rede holy scripture As though it were alonly a possession and an heritage of sertyn men that be markyd allonly with exterior sygnys. ... If this be not the doctryne of Antichrist I knowe not his doctryne.[80]

But, Barnes takes pains to illustrate, this was not always the doctrine of the church. He points immediately to the examples of the New Testament itself, noting that the Ethiopian eunuch of Acts 8 was no clergyman, and that even Apollos was instructed in Scripture by the lay teachers Priscilla and Aquila (Acts 18).[81] Nor were these exceptions, as the later history of the church makes evident. Even at the turn of the fifth century Augustine was exhorting his readers to take up the Scriptures. Of any who do not, Augustine asked, 'Is he any better than an horsse or a mule the whych hath no understondynge'?[82] Citing the letter to 'the brothers' in which this comment is found, Barnes is quick to point out the disjunction between the prescription of Augustine and the proscription of the contemporary church:

> Here S. Augustyn movythe men to rede holy scripture And you commande them not to rede it S. Augustine sayth They shall know in

78 *Supplicatyon* (1531), fo. 36v.
79 *Supplicatyon* (1531), fo. 15v.
80 *Supplicatyon* (1531), fo. 100v.
81 *Supplicatyon* (1531), fo. 106v.
82 *Supplicatyon* (1531), fo. 107r.

> them what to do / and what not to do / and you say they shalle lerne nothyng there out but heresys.[83]

Lest his opponents fix on or misinterpret the fact that he exhorted only 'the brothers', Barnes also brings forth the similar exhortation of Augustine's contemporary Jerome, 'wrytten to two wemen'.[84]

In addition to the abundantly available examples showing that the laity of the early church had not only been allowed to read Scripture but even encouraged to do so, Barnes is also eager to present what he believes to be even more damning evidence. The fathers – those authorities who his adversaries claimed stood in condemnation of him – had in fact condemned the very position the Roman church was now trying to defend. Those who reserved Scripture for the clergy alone were rejected on the practical basis that the laity had even greater need of its teaching. This is the argument of the Alexandrian father Athanasius, which Barnes cites in his favour:

> But thou shalt not saye that it belongyth alonly to religious men to studdy scriptures / but rather it belongythe to every christen man and specially un to hym / that is wrappyd in the busynessis of this world / and so muche the more / by cause he hathe more nede of helpe for he is wrapped in the trubbilles of the world.

Further commentary by Barnes is deemed unnecessary: 'These wordes be playne ynough agenste you / They nede no exposicion'.[85] Athanasius's words may be plain, as Barnes believes, but he also feels it necessary to show that they are not uncommon. Thus he brings forward the even more emphatically stated judgement of the later Chrysostom:

> but men wille defend this myschiffe with this excuse / I am no religious man I have a wyfe and chylderne / and a house to care for / This is the excuse where with you doo (as it were with a pestelence) corrupt alle thynges for you do rekkyn that the studdy of holy scripture belongythe alonly unto religius men / whane they be much more necessary un to you than unto them.[86]

While Chrysostom's words illustrate that even the early church was tempted to make Scripture a book of the clergy only, they are all the more pertinent for emphasising the manner in which the godly reacted to such temptations. Again, their contemporary relevance is highlighted by Barnes:

> Here may you se that youre damnable institucion was in the hartes of men in chrysostums days / and how they wolde rede no scripturs / but you se

83 *Supplicatyon* (1531), fo. 107v.
84 *Supplicatyon* (1531), fo. 109r.
85 *Supplicatyon* (1531), fo. 107v.
86 *Supplicatyon* (1531), fo. 108r.

> he condemmyth it / and callithe it a pestilense / and wille you now bryng it in agayn?[87]

The reservation of Scripture for the clergy, in addition to being in itself a dangerous novelty, also opened the door for further deception. Barnes thus responds to subsequent innovations in the same manner. He points out that error arises first from a neglect of Scripture, whether by laity or clergy. Holding up historical practice and the writings of the early fathers, he goes on to highlight notable divergences in the doctrine and practice of the contemporary church. And where the contemporary church is found to contradict that of the apostles and fathers in word or deed, Barnes concludes that Antichrist is at work. Something of this method and conclusion is evident in his attack on the practice of withholding the eucharistic cup from the laity.

> If men had stucke to the open scripturs of gode / and to the practys of christes holy church and to the exposicion of old doctours as yt dyd become christen men to doo / than had yt not byn nedefulle for me to have taken these paynys and laboures in thys cause / nor yet to have layd to theyr charges those thynges that Antichrist dothe wonly.[88]

As his complaint indicates, Barnes did have to take 'pains and labours in this cause'. But the cause was not simply that of a particular doctrine or practice; it turns out once again to be that of the fundamental question of ecclesiastical authority. He again insists that, ultimately, Scripture offers the only normative judgement. And likewise, he once again calls on the testimony of history to undermine any attempts to forward an alternative authority.

In the matter of the disputed eucharistic practice, Barnes rejects out of hand the authority of 'carnal' or 'damnable' reason, which might hold utraquism unnecessary on account of Christ's blood being present naturally within his body.[89] But he gives little attention to this logical justification, recognising that it is not in fact the ground on which the cup had been denied to the laity. The basis for doing so, he points out, is the fifteenth-century declaration of the council of Constance. He thus turns to ecclesiastical history, to 'the very use and practes of the holye appostles and of holye churche', in an attempt to prove 'by the practes of holly churche / that this counselle / ys false and damnable'.[90] Lest his readers have any doubt about the legal origins of current ecclesiastical practice, he offers the council's own words:

> that everye man maye know / by what auctoryte they did it / and what thing did move them to condemne so blessed and so glorious an

87 *Supplicatyon* (1531), fo. 108r.
88 *Supplicatyon* (1531), fo. 123r.
89 *Supplicatyon* (1531), fos 125v, 130v; 129r, 131v.
90 *Supplicatyon* (1531), fo. 124r.

> ordinance of oure lorde Jesus christ / here wylle I wryte their awne wordes whiche be these / as thys custome for avoydynge serten sclaunders and parrelles was resonably broughte in notwithstondinge in the begenynge off the church this sacrament was reseved of christen men under both kyndes / and afterwarde yt was reseved alonly under the kynde of brede / wherefore seyng that suche a custom off the church / and of holy fathers resonably brought in and longe observed must be taken for a law the whych shall not be lawfulle to repreve.[91]

Having made evident that even the council acknowledged utraquism as the practice of the early church, Barnes raises the fundamental question of why this was the ancient custom. He asks 'of whome the church had reseved this manner: of christe? or hys holy appostles'? His own answer – 'doughtles she did' – allows him to stress the obvious conflict between Christ's authority and conciliar authority, ancient practice and modern practice. He continues:

> than what auctoryte had the counselle to change the institucion of christ / and of his holy appostles / and also the use and practys of holy churche / was not the fyrst churche of god? Dyd she not kepe Christes institucion? dyd she not fulfyll christes worde? Dyd not the holy appostles lerne hare so? and now shall the counsell of constanciens fyrst condemme Christ and his blessed word / and thane the lerninge of Christes holy appostles? and also the longe use and practes of christes blessed churche.[92]

Some had tried to dismiss this appeal to the words of Christ by pointing out that the command to 'take and drink' was spoken not to the laity, but only to the apostles. But Barnes is quick to insist that the church had never interpreted this to exclude those outside of the apostolic office. In addition to pointing out that it was not so interpreted even by the contemporary church (as only bishops, not the lower clergy, stood in succession to the apostles), he simply asks, 'yf this thing were alonly lawfulle unto the appostles / how wylle you dyscharge the primatyve churche'?[93]

Throughout his treatment of utraquism, Barnes's emphasis is clearly on the witness of this primitive church. He pits the evidence of its historical practice against the legal declaration of a later council, constantly singing a refrain of 'holy church and holy fathers'. In his reading of the evidence, the practice of communion in one kind is so manifestly against 'the usse of holy churche and contrary to the exposycion of alle holy doctours' that he simply asserts it would never have been introduced if men had remained aware of and faithful to 'the practys of christes holy church and to the exposicion of old doctours'.[94] The fact

91 *Supplicatyon* (1531), fo. 123r–v. Barnes had provided the full text of the decree in the *Sentenciae*, sigs E5v–6v, where he also noted the day, month, and session in which it was formalised.
92 *Supplicatyon* (1531), fo. 125r.
93 *Supplicatyon* (1531), fo. 126r.
94 *Supplicatyon* (1531), fo. 130r; 123r.

that they have not done so, he concludes, makes them 'shamfulle and detestable sclanderars bothe of holye churche and also of holye fathers'.[95]

The manner in which Barnes addresses the topic of utraquism, like the manner in which he attempted to undermine the prohibition on the lay reading of Scripture, is typical of his historically driven attack on traditional ecclesiastical authority. At the heart of the task he had set for himself was the attempt to show that the stance of the contemporary church contradicted, and in some cases even condemned, earlier authorities. As did many of his reformist and humanist contemporaries, Barnes held the 'old doctours' and 'holye fathers' in especially high regard, and not only as effective polemical allies. But his respect for the ancient church did not extend so far as to deem it normative in matters of doctrine or rites. Thus, by establishing that even the church of his opponents had in many cases contradicted or condemned such authorities as ancient custom, early fathers, church councils, canon law, and papal decrees, he effectively bolstered his claim that such authorities were at least potentially unreliable and therefore ultimately non-binding. They could thus be rejected just as legitimately by evangelicals as by their conservative counterparts. If his opponents insisted that, to the contrary, these were the church's highest court of appeal, there was little to prevent Barnes from pressing his claim that the later Roman rejection of previously accepted authorities amounted to a virtual rejection of the historical church itself; those who had effected such changes were 'shamfulle and detestable sclanderars ... of holye churche'. At the very least, the modern reversal of ancient customs and laws – even if his adversaries insisted this was legitimate – provided adequate proof to support his contention that Rome itself was the author of 'new learning' and the instigator of novelty.

Where the authority rejected or condemned was not simply that of human customs or laws, but that of Christ and his apostles, the charge of novelty became all the more serious. Not only were such new prescriptions and prohibitions unknown to Christ, Barnes could argue; they were by their very nature anti-Christ. He had taken preliminary steps toward illustrating this thesis in the brief sketches of historical doctrines and practices provided in his *Sentenciae* of 1530. In the *Supplicatyon* of 1531 he began more clearly to draw out the full implications of changes and contradictions in the same. He would build on these foundations three years later when he revised and republished the *Supplicatyon*. This second edition, significantly altered, would provide the specific historical details he had promised to bring forward if challenged.

95 *Supplicatyon* (1531), fo. 125r.

A supplicacion unto the most gracyous prynce (1534)

The use which Robert Barnes made of historical sources and historical arguments in his specifically theological publications reached its pinnacle in the revised *Supplicacion* of 1534. This culmination is noted by Rainer Pineas, who refers to this edition when he asserts that 'Most of Barnes's polemical use of secular history is contained in one work'.[96] His judgement is undoubtedly correct with regard to Barnes's earlier writings, though it is by no means clear that this work contains more 'secular history' than his later *Vitae romanorum pontificum*. Others, however, have suggested that it does contain better history. A.G. Dickens and John Tonkin conclude that the *Supplicacion*, though not an historical offering like the *Vitae*, was nevertheless written 'with somewhat more historical skill'.[97]

An investigation of the *Vitae* will be reserved for the following chapter, but it certainly is evident upon examining the 1534 *Supplicacion* that the additions incorporated do consist largely of specifically historical material. Where relatively minor changes are made, as for example in the article concerning free will, these typically amount to the inclusion of previously uncited patristic sources. But some of the most striking and significant additions of historical material appear precisely where Barnes had promised they would. When he wrote in 1531 that certain arguments he could 'well prove both by auncient cronicles / and also by the practes of youre awne law', he referred especially to his thesis that Rome and her clergy lived peaceably with secular rulers only so long as such rulers bowed to Roman authority.[98] At that time Barnes had suggested that Henry

> reade all hys cronycles / and not allonly them / but all other noble princes cronicles. And hys grace shall never fynde that they were trewe chyderne off obedyence / yff their prince dyd dyspleasse them.[99]

By 1534, rather than allowing this advice possibly to go unheeded, Barnes had decided it was worth summarising the content of the chronicles himself.

As is by this time typical of Barnes's writing, he also asks that Henry compare his evidence from the chronicles with the testimony of Scripture and church fathers. He particularly wants the King to see that those who hold fast to Scripture and the doctrine of the ancients cannot encourage sedition, and therefore pose no

96 Pineas, 'Robert Barnes', 55; Pineas, *Tudor Polemics*, 121.
97 Dickens and Tonkin, *The Reformation in Historical Thought*, 63.
98 *Supplicatyon* (1531), fo. 8r. Despite the amount of historical material introduced in 1534, Barnes still promises more if necessary: 'yf you thynke I judge a mysse, or els do you wrong, let me be put to my profe / and you shall se, what an hepe of holy facts that I wyl bryng out of your owne cronicles and bokes'. *Supplicacion* (1534), sig. D3v. Barnes's reference to the papacy's 'own' chronicles here in the 1534 *Supplicacion*, like his reference to its 'own' law in the 1531 edition and its 'own' authors in the *Sentenciae* of 1530 (sig. K6v), is a polemical point made frequently throughout his works and effectively illustrates the nature of his programme.
99 *Supplicatyon* (1531), fo. 8v.

possible threat to the peace of the realm.[100] Papal warnings to the contrary, Barnes insists, are entirely without merit:

> Is not this a subtyle crafte of Antychryst / to warne other men of heretykes, and of traytours / and in the meane season, whyle men stande lokyng for traytours / commeth he in and playeth the parte of an open traytour.[101]

This open papal treason consists in the fact that 'they deposed openly Prynces, and Emperours / ye and assoyled all theyr subjectes from the obedyence of them'. After reading the evidence Barnes forwards from the chronicles, Henry is meant to ask himself, 'who hath deposed any kynge syth Chrystes passyon, savynge they onely? Who wyll be kynges felowes / ye and controllers, savynge they onely?'[102]

Barnes begins his own attempt to answer the question by taking up his argument precisely where he had left it in 1531: with the famous eighth-century coronation of Pepin by Pope Zacharias, which first necessitated the deposition of the Merovingian King Childeric III. Against the explanation found in the canonical gloss, that Childeric was deposed on account of a lecherous lifestyle, Barnes asserts that the chronicles give contrary testimony concerning his piety.[103] But, for the sake of argument, Barnes is willing to allow the canonical explanation in order to raise the issue most likely to capture his King's interest. If rulers may legally be deposed for adultery, he asks, then why do the clergy not openly proclaim this? More to the point, why does Rome not consistently force all such princes immediately to step down?[104] Barnes is too careful to insinuate further, but the logic and its possible implications would surely not have been lost on Henry. And lest any think that Childeric's deposition was unique, Barnes is quick to cite additional examples of the same, from what he assures his readers are reliable sources. That Emperor Frederick II was deposed by Innocent IV is 'red openly in your unyversytes';[105] of Pope Urban V's deposition of the King of Spain the 'cronycles maketh mencyon';[106] and that even local bishops have deposed Kings in England 'is wryten by one called Petrus de natalibus, the whiche wryteth the lyves of all sayntes'.[107]

Barnes's address to Henry is also intended to highlight what he believes to be perhaps less obvious, but no less dangerous, clerical threats to national peace and security. He recounts an episode from the reign of Richard II as an example of the

100 *Supplicacion* (1534), sig. B2r–v.
101 *Supplicacion* (1534), sig. B3r–v.
102 *Supplicacion* (1534), sig. B3r.
103 *Supplicacion* (1534), sig. B3r–v.
104 *Supplicacion* (1534), sig. B4r–v.
105 *Supplicacion* (1534), sig. C2v.
106 *Supplicacion* (1534), sig. C1r.
107 *Supplicacion* (1534), sig. C2r.

manner in which papists have historically disregarded both law and order.[108] Not only have they broken the public peace, as when the bishop of Salisbury's servant attacked a London baker; they have also called for the punishment of those lawfully charged with keeping the peace, as in this case when the bishop instigated the removal of the sheriff and mayor who had arrested his servant. Barnes insinuates that such scandals are commonplace, but he also emphasises the even more subtle means by which Rome has historically undermined lawful authority. He mentions, for example, Henry IV's archbishop of York, Richard Scrope, who had been beheaded for going to war against the King. Rather than being denounced by the church as a rebel and a traitor, he was instead elevated to sainthood.[109] Such actions on the part of Rome and her clergy lead Barnes to conclude emphatically, if not altogether accurately, that 'there was no rebellyon in this realme this .v.C. yeres, yf the kynge had displeased them, but they were at the begynnynge of it'.[110]

In further support of this conclusion Barnes draws upon the increasingly popular tale of King John's prolonged thirteenth-century controversy with the papacy. The story was not only there to be read in popular chronicles such as that produced by Fabyan, but by the time Barnes wrote it had also been put to polemical use by fellow evangelical authors such as Simon Fish and William Tyndale.[111] Barnes means it to serve the same purpose as his immediate predecessors: to highlight the self-serving and inevitably treasonous policies of Rome. Loosely following Fabyan's account, Barnes locates the origins of the controversy in John's having requested of the monasteries, 'for the defence of his realm, but a small somme of money'.[112] Instead of receiving this money from the church, the King soon found himself excommunicated, deposed, and then finally restored only after handing over large sums of his own money.[113] By way of contrast, Barnes draws on Froissart's chronicle for an illustration of how willingly the clergy contribute to the papacy's own war chest. In support of Urban VI's campaign against France, he records, there 'was gathered a tunne of golde' from the diocese of London alone.[114]

108 *Supplicacion* (1534), sig. C3r.
109 *Supplicacion* (1534), sig. C1r. See also sig. C3v for a bishop similarly rewarded for treason against Henry II.
110 *Supplicacion* (1534), sig. C3v.
111 For the history of King John in reformation polemic, see especially Julian Lock, 'Plantagenets against the Papacy: Protestant England's Search for Royal Heroes', in *Protestant History and Identity in Sixteenth-Century Europe*, vol. 1, *The Medieval Inheritance*, ed. Bruce Gordon (Aldershot, 1996), 153–73. See also Leslie P. Fairfield, *John Bale: Mythmaker for the English Reformation* (West Lafayette, 1976), 56 and 192 n. 20, who notes that Barnes's retelling 'differs considerably' from that of the Tyndale circle.
112 *Supplicacion* (1534), sig. C4v.
113 *Supplicacion* (1534), sig. C1v.
114 *Supplicacion* (1534), sig. C4r–v. Cf. sig. E2r, where Barnes contrasts the eagerness with which clergy even take up arms for the pope with the hesitancy they display in defending their King.

As his aim was overwhelmingly polemical rather than historiographical, Barnes's use of his sources was rarely critical. Even in those instances when his facts and interpretations would eventually be proved false, however, he could claim to be following widely accepted written sources. Thus, for example, he was quite willing to accept the account of King John's death which laid the blame on monastic poisoning, even claiming that the monk responsible had been absolved before the fact.[115] Though historians writing only a short time later would finally begin to question the credibility of this tale, it was precisely the sort of behaviour Barnes's reading had led him to expect from those loyal to the papacy. But this expectation did not arise from his reading of history alone. Nor did he assume that his historical anecdotes in themselves were sufficient to seal the case he was attempting to make against Rome.

A failure to grasp the true nature of his case itself has often led to a certain amount of misunderstanding on this point. It is commonly asserted that 'The purpose of Barnes's polemical use of secular history was to demonstrate that the clergy always had been and still were a subversive element in every realm'.[116] While this cannot be dismissed as false, it does overlook an important element of Barnes's programme. His writing betrays the fact that his arguments are not simply those of an anti-clerical polemicist. His complaint is not ultimately with the clergy themselves, nor with the unsavoury deeds some chroniclers had ascribed to them. Compared to many of his contemporaries, for example, Barnes shows little interest in tales of clerical ignorance, greed and gluttony, or the lurid details of sexual scandal – all common fare in popular anti-clerical works. In contrast, he is insistent that the fundamental danger posed by papal clergy is to be found in the papal theology to which they adhere.

The historical evidence Barnes takes pains to provide is meant merely to illustrate the inevitable consequences of what he judges false doctrine. Thus, rather than immediately launching into his catalogue of clerical treason, he begins with a recitation of what he titles 'The doctrine of the papist'. Citing chapter and verse from Gratian, he highlights the dogmatic claims that 'Rome gyveth strength and myghte to all lawes, but it is subjecte to none', that 'subjectes may be disobedient to their owne lordes', and that the pope 'hath auctorite to breke all othes, bondes, and oblygacyons'.[117] What the chronicles then provide for Barnes is evidence that the papists, 'as men past shame / beynge both without feare of God and man / spared not to put in execucyon these abhomynable doctrynes'. He thus turns to them in an effort to prove his case for a cause-and-effect relationship between

[115] *Supplicacion* (1534), sig. C1v. See Lock, 'Plantagenets against the Papacy', 161, for discussion of this tale's long acceptance and eventual rejection.
[116] Pineas, 'Robert Barnes', 56. See also Pineas, *Tudor Polemics*, 120; O'Day, *The Debate on the English Reformation*, 11.
[117] *Supplicacion* (1534), sig. B3r.

doctrine and practice: 'But that my wordes shulde the better appere to all men / I shall recyte some of theyr practyse / bothe out of autentycke crownycles / and out of theyr owne lawe.'[118] Therefore, after having brought forward from them the stories noted above, he once again pauses to emphasise what he understands to be a necessary relationship between papal dogma and papal deed: 'This is your facte, this is your dede, this is your doctryne, in this lernynge you be promoted doctours, and in this lernynge you are sworne.'[119]

That the Roman clergy were indeed sworn to doctrines which in application could not but undermine princely authority was a point on which Barnes quickly capitalised in yet another significant addition to his revised *Supplicacion*. Though he had made no mention of it in 1531, the subject of apparently contradictory oaths sworn by bishops to both pope and prince became a prominent point of attack in 1534.[120] The rhetorical but fundamental question he put forward was 'How dothe it stande with your allegyance toward your prynce, to be sworne to the pope?'[121] Barnes had good reason to believe this a fruitful line of questioning; Henry himself had raised the very issue in parliament only two years previously when, having compared the two oaths in question, he reached the conclusion that the clergy 'bee but halfe our subjectes, yea, and sca[r]ce our subjectes'.[122] Parliamentary discussion of the episcopal oath soon stalled, however, and Barnes could see the benefit in now reviving the matter and thus encouraging again the royal suspicion so clearly displayed in 1532.[123] Taking his cue from Henry's own insinuation of treason, he now pointedly asked, 'How agreeth these .ii. othes? you may set them together as well as you can: but I know no wayes to avoyde your perjury'.[124]

Already before raising the issue of oaths Barnes had provided historical examples in support of his contention that 'as sone as there was any varyance, betwene the kynge and the pope, than were you fyrste of all, assoyled of your allegyance dewe unto your kynge'.[125] To further demonstrate the conflict of allegiances, he offers commentary on the origins and histories of the episcopal oaths. He points out the relative modernity of that currently sworn to the pope, noting that for 'a great many of yeres' after the papacy of Gregory III the clergy were sworn only to uphold the faith and unity of the church, and to maintain no fellowship with those

118 *Supplicacion* (1534), sig. B3r.
119 *Supplicacion* (1534), sig. C2v.
120 The texts of both oaths are printed in *Hall's Chronicle*, 788–9.
121 *Supplicacion* (1534), sig. D3v.
122 *Hall's Chronicle*, 788. The 1530 charge of *praemunire*, laid against the whole of the English clergy for their recognition of Wolsey as papal legate, would surely also have been remembered by Barnes in this context.
123 See J.J. Scarisbrick, *Henry VIII* (Harmondsworth, 1968), 390–1; Pineas, 'Robert Barnes', 60.
124 *Supplicacion* (1534), sig. D4r.
125 *Supplicacion* (1534), sig. D4r.

who taught contrary to the old fathers.[126] The origins of the most recent oath, however, Barnes traces to the frequent hostilities between popes and emperors. Gregory's oath, according to Barnes, was finally dismissed as insufficient because

> by it, the bysshoppes were not bounde to betraye theyr prynces / nor to revelate theyr councelles to the Pope. The whiche thynge the Pope muste nedes knowe, or els he coulde not brynge to passe his purpose / that is to say, he coulde not be lorde over the worlde, and cause Emperours, and kynges, to fetche theyr confirmacyon of hym.[127]

Neither Gregory's oath nor even this 'newe othe, nowe in our days made' was hesitantly greeted by the clergy.[128] By way of contrast, Barnes describes their reaction to King Henry II's requirement of an oath of allegiance to be sworn by his bishops. They immediately protested that their rights and dignities were being abused, and finally consented only with the proviso that 'we wyll be under your grace, savynge the honour of God, of the churche of Rome, and of our order'.[129]

That the clergy had not accepted unqualified submission to the King came as little surprise to Barnes. But that their highest allegiance was sworn not simply to 'the church', but specifically to 'the church of Rome', gave him cause to draw out once more the dubious implications of contrary oaths.

> But what meaneth it / that you swere only to the holy churche of Rome? wyll you be traytours to the holy churche of Constantinople? or els to the holy churche of Englande? ... Why are you not rather sworne to kepe? and to fede? to noryshe? and to be trewe to your owne churche?[130]

Though making much of what would have perhaps previously been overlooked as common and acceptable phraseology, Barnes could be confident that his rhetoric would especially resonate with readers in the year of the Royal Supremacy, and particularly with the Supreme Head who for nearly half a decade had conceived of the universal church as 'a federation of autonomous churches' beyond the control of a central or foreign ruler.[131] But Barnes also realised that Henry's position with regard to the papacy – a position he was trying very much to confirm – might not be without undesirable consequences. And to heighten the King's distrust of Rome he could hardly resist spelling these out. Just as Pepin and other princes had been deposed by the pope, the 'same or worse / wyll they attempte to do unto your grace / yf you displease them'.[132] As for what the ambiguous 'worse'

126 *Supplicacion* (1534), sig. D1v.
127 *Supplicacion* (1534), sigs D1v–D2r.
128 *Supplicacion* (1534), sig. E1v.
129 *Supplicacion* (1534), sig. E2r.
130 *Supplicacion* (1534), sig. D2v.
131 Scarisbrick, *Henry VIII*, 379.
132 *Supplicacion* (1534), sig. B3v.

might entail, Barnes suggests one possibility with a memorable play on words: 'yf this wretched Clement coulde drowne our noble prynce with one worde, it shulde not be longe undone, sine clementia'.[133]

It is understandable that, as his King's antipathy towards the papal exercise of power had become increasingly evident, Barnes would revise his original supplication in order to bolster previously forwarded arguments. Nor is it surprising that, having already suggested as much in 1531, his revision would largely consist of newly introduced historical material. What is perhaps surprising is that further alterations, while also consisting largely of new historical arguments, would be made concerning topics on which Henry's attitude was equally well known but decidedly less favourable. The subject of clerical celibacy is particularly noteworthy. Though the King would not place priestly marriage entirely out of bounds for debate until 1539, there was before this time little to suggest that he might be sympathetic to its allowance. As has been noted above, though he had touched on it in the *Sentenciae* of 1530, Barnes did not address the issue at all in his *Supplicatyon* of 1531. Therefore one of the most significant changes evident in the revised edition is the inclusion of a lengthy discussion of the practice's origin, history, and consequences. This newly included article is in fact the longest of those found in his 1534 work, further indicating the increasingly important regard in which Barnes held the issue. And despite the fact that Henry gave no evidence of sharing Barnes's view, the context of the King's recent political and theological manoeuvring does offer some indication as to why the topic was now introduced.

Throughout the summer months of 1534 a panel of bishops and doctors appointed by Henry had been engaged in theological negotiations with representatives of the Lutheran cities of Hamburg and Lübeck. These representatives, invited to England by the King himself, included among them Robert Barnes. Though there was apparently some attempt to keep secret the precise nature of the discussions, it took little guesswork for some at court to conclude that their purpose revolved around 'joining the Lutheran sect'.[134] And indeed, the matter of clerical celibacy was to be a point of debate.[135] Seeing that the topic now had been opened for discussion and debate, Barnes may have viewed the revision of his *Supplicatyon* as a timely opportunity to outline further the evangelical position.

Other events, too, are very likely to have influenced his belief that the time was right to speak out on the subject. Also in the 1534 *Supplicacion* Barnes had rewritten his article on the doctrine of the church; the reason for doing so was Thomas More's criticism of the essay published in 1531.[136] If Barnes found good

133 *Supplicacion* (1534), sig. D3v.
134 *CSPS*, 5/1.70 (*LP*, 7.957).
135 See BL Cottonian MS Cleopatra E.V, fos 207–14 (*LP*, 13/2.37).
136 See *CWM*, 8.831–992.

reason to respond to More on the subject of the church, equally valid motives could be found for replying to More's constantly disparaging references to the evangelical defence of clerical marriage.[137] In fact, More had explicitly related the two doctrines of church and marriage in his criticism of Barnes. Barnes was frequently ridiculed for his association with Luther, the false friar married to a renegade nun. In More's presentation of a fictional dialogue between Barnes and St Gregory, for example, the former is pointedly asked about the membership of this church that he has newly defined; caught up short, Barnes is only able to name himself, Tyndale, Luther, and Luther's wife Katie.[138] Given More's determination to make marriage a prominent topic of debate, it is not surprising that Barnes would again take up the subject in a work partially given over to refuting other of his criticisms. This is even less surprising in the light of More's recent falling out with the King. With More now imprisoned for rejecting the Royal Supremacy, there was good reason for Barnes to believe that Henry might look with some suspicion on his former chancellor's theology. In any case, he is determined to show Henry that clerical celibacy is very much intertwined with the rejected notion of papal supremacy: 'The truth is', he claimed, 'that no man hath forbydden any certeyne state of men to marye, but the Pope onely.'[139]

Whatever Barnes's primary motivation for now introducing the subject, his 1534 attack on enforced clerical celibacy is to this point almost undoubtedly 'the ablest of his disputative works'.[140] It is the least repetitive, most coherent, and best organised of any of the essays included in the two editions of his *Supplication*. But still the 'most remarkable feature' on display here is 'the broad knowledge of church history Barnes reveals'.[141] After explaining the common theological distinction between those things judged necessary and those judged indifferent, he marshals an impressive array of historical material in support of the claim that clerical celibacy was never, until only very recently and even then unconvincingly, demanded as necessary.

As he had in his earlier critique of papal pretensions to power, Barnes insists that his primary complaint is with doctrine, rather than simply with its consequences or possible abuses. He makes clear that he does not wish 'to envey

137 So frequent are these references that Pineas, *Tudor Polemics*, 144, has concluded that 'this device, as much as More's reiterated claim of infallibility for the Church, deserves to be called his *deus ex machina*'. For clerical celibacy in the broader context of English Reformation polemic, see Helen Parish, '"Beastly is their living and their doctrine": Celibacy and Theological Corruption in English Reformation Polemic', in *Protestant History and Identity in Sixteenth-Century Europe*, vol. 1, *The Medieval Inheritance*, ed. Bruce Gordon (Aldershot, 1996), 138–52, and her more recent publication, *Clerical Marriage and the English Reformation* (Aldershot, 2000).

138 *CWM*, 8.936.

139 *Supplicacion* (1534), sig. R2r.

140 Clebsch, *England's Earliest Protestants*, 72.

141 N.S. Tjernagel, *The Reformation Essays of Dr. Robert Barnes* (London, 1963), 109.

agaynst any persone, but alonely to fyghte agaynst, that devyllyshe doctrine'.[142] To this end, his survey begins with the theological history of clerical marriage. He quite logically gives attention first to those biblical passages which indicate that even apostles such as St Peter were married, and that they did not reject their wives after being called into the ministry of the church. Barnes is well aware that these passages are not undisputed, and he quickly cites Athanasius, Cyprian, and Eusebius as respected fathers who agree with his own reading of the texts.[143] Against such biblical authority, he finds in the early church only 'a lousye decree of Pope Siricius', the late fourth-century pope who was the first to issue decretals as binding statements of dogma.[144] But Barnes also highlights the low regard in which Siricius's decree was held even among his contemporaries. Ambrose of Milan, for example, though himself an advocate of celibacy, refused to 'commaund it imperiously'.[145] Ambrose's convert Augustine even condemned those churchmen who sought to prevent clerical marriage or to separate clergy from their wives, a fact on which Barnes hoped he might rest his case:

> Nowe let men admyt this doctrine of s. Augustine, and I wyll require no more. And yf they wyll condempne me, than let them also condempne s. Augustine, for I have lerned it of him.[146]

It is also evident, however, that Barnes learned quite a lot from the conciliar history of the early church. He recalls that the council of Nicaea had attempted to forbid the marriage of priests, but that the highly esteemed confessor Paphnutius persuaded them against such an act.[147] Going even further, the fourth canon of the fourth-century council of Gangra anathematised all who would condemn clerical marriage or abstain from the sacraments of married clergy.[148] Such opinions were held by the heretic Eustachius, whose doctrine the council was specifically convened to discuss. That his doctrine was there condemned allows Barnes to draw out relevant parallels:

> Nowe let every man judge what diversite is betwene this heretyke, and the popes doctrine. This heretyke sayth, that maryage is unpure, and unclene, and that a maryed preest may not touche the sacramentes. The selfe and the same doctrine saythe the Pope in diverse places.[149]

142 *Supplicacion* (1534), sig. R4r.
143 *Supplicacion* (1534), sigs R1r–v; R4v; T1r.
144 *Supplicacion* (1534), sig. R3r. The first of Siricius's decretals, dated February 385, deals with the disputed issues of clerical continence and celibacy.
145 *Supplicacion* (1534), sig. S1r.
146 *Supplicacion* (1534), sigs R4v–S1r.
147 *Supplicacion* (1534), sig. S1v. Barnes also makes it a point to mention a fact found in the *Tripartite History*, that Paphnutius was not married. In an attempt to disassociate himself from any charges of selfish motive, Barnes will also go on later to dispel rumours that he himself has married. See sigs T4v–U1r.
148 *Supplicacion* (1534), sig. S2r.
149 *Supplicacion* (1534), sig. S2r–v. At this point he also cites relevant passages from canon law. For

Having thus compared papal doctrine with previously condemned heresy, Barnes also finds conciliar support for his claim that the evangelical stance is the 'rule of the apostles'. He cites at length from a decree of the sixth ecumenical council, which is particularly notable for its anti-Roman phrasing:

> Consyderyng that it is decreed amongest the lawes made by them of Rome, that no deacon, nor preste, shall company with theyr wyves. Therefore we notwithstandyng that decree, folowyng the rules of the apostles, and the constitutions of holy men, wyll, that from this day forthe, mariage shall be laufull, in no wyse dissolvyng the matrymony betwene them, and theyr wyves, nor deprivyng them theyr familiarite in tyme convenient.[150]

As the authors had also gone on to threaten excommunication for any clergy who set aside their wives, and to announce deposition for any who would order the same, Barnes announces the conclusion which he might reasonably expect to please his King: 'Out of the whiche dothe folowe, that the Pope, and all his adherentes ben ipso iure deposed'.[151] Many readers would have perhaps been unfamiliar with this conciliar decree and would certainly have found Barnes's conclusion hard to accept. He is therefore quick to provide the same premise and conclusion as succinctly stated in the *Corpus Iuris Canonici*. The decretals of Innocent III stated that priests who dissolved their marriages 'ought grevously to be punyshed, seinge that they may use laufully matrimony'.[152] And likewise, it could be read in the *canon apostolorum* that 'Yf any man dothe teache, that a preest by the reason of his ordre ought to forsake his wyfe, cursed be he'.[153] Despite the possible appearance of novelty, then, Barnes could confidently proclaim that 'this doctrine of myne is no newe thynge, but it is elder than theyr lawe'.[154]

The history of doctrine Barnes found in the fathers, councils, and canon law provided strong support for his claim that clerical celibacy was a theological novelty. To buttress this claim further, however, he also turned his attention from dogma to practice, from the pronouncements of the church to the histories of the church: 'Wherfore nowe wyll I go further unto the histories, and prove this thynge by examples, and practise of holy men'.[155] He begins with the early ecclesiastical histories of Eusebius and Cassiodorus. In the former he finds mention of Spiridion, a bishop of Cyprus who had a daughter, 'whyche he could not have, yf

similar comparisons between papal doctrine and that of condemned heretics, see his mention of the Tatianites and Marcionites at sig. R2r.

150 *Supplicacion* (1534), sig. S2v.

151 *Supplicacion* (1534), sig. S3r.

152 *Supplicacion* (1534), sig. S3r.

153 *Supplicacion* (1534), sig. S2r.

154 *Supplicacion* (1534), sig. S4r. Cf. sigs T1v and T2r for similar denials of novelty.

155 *Supplicacion* (1534), sig. S4v.

he had had no wyfe'.[156] In the same is read of the Ephesian bishop Policrates, who claimed that his father before him had been a bishop, as had his father before him, and so on for six consecutive generations.[157] More generally, Barnes refers to the *Tripartite History*'s description of the eastern church, where priests who abstained from marriage did so of their own free will, and where the marriages and children of those who did not abstain were recognised as lawful.[158]

In addition to the ancient histories, Barnes also makes use of more modern works such as the recent world chronicle of Nauclerus and the popular papal lives of Platina. It is to these that he turns to 'se how many popes have ben preestes chyldren, that this matter maybe opened by them and that Popes them selves may be witnesse of this doctrine'.[159] He compiles a list of twelve such popes, including Silverius, Felix III, Deusdedit, Theodore I, Hadrian II, John XV, Agapitus I, Boniface I, Gelasius I, and John XI, this last having the unique distinction of also being the son of a pope.[160] Though the argument requires the presupposition, Barnes does not explicitly state, as he had in the case of the above mentioned Spiridion, that each of these must have been legitimately born. Only shortly before, however, he had highlighted the canon law provision for the children of priests to receive ordination only 'yf they be gotten of laufull maryage'.[161] He can thus leave the question open in the assumption that his critics will not sacrifice nearly a dozen papacies for the sake of what increasingly appears to be an historically insupportable doctrine.

Lest any get the impression that clerical marriage had only been a foreign matter, Barnes also draws the reader's attention to specific examples from the history of the English church. Not only had the pope himself written to past English bishops regarding the children of priests, which letters were now part of canon law,[162] but the chronicles of England also illustrated the previous acceptance of clerical marriage. Fabyan, for example, records a dispute over the patronage of a Plymouth benefice, which was resolved only when one of the claimants showed how often and to whom he had granted the benefice in the past. In doing so he recalled that he had granted it first to a priest, later to the priest's son, and later still to his son.[163] Reading also in the chronicles that it was only in the early twelfth century that Anselm of Canterbury decreed that priests should

156 *Supplicacion* (1534), sig. T1r. Logically, of course, Barnes is incorrect to state that a cleric could have no child without a wife. He had, however, already argued that, lacking any clear evidence to the contrary, Christian charity necessitated the assumption that clergy had not committed adultery. See sigs S1r and S4r.
157 *Supplicacion* (1534), sig. T1r–v.
158 *Supplicacion* (1534), sig. T1r.
159 *Supplicacion* (1534), sig. T1v.
160 *Supplicacion* (1534), sig. T1v.
161 *Supplicacion* (1534), sig. S4r.
162 *Supplicacion* (1534), sig. S4r.
163 *Supplicacion* (1534), sig. T2r.

forsake their wives, Barnes surmises that marriage had been legal for centuries before.[164]

That clerical marriage did seem to have been permissible for at least a thousand years leads Barnes to his final historical investigation. The question he seeks to answer is 'how longe it is that the Pope hath gone about to bring in the vowe of chastite'.[165] Under no circumstances would he admit that celibacy had been accepted as mandatory in the early church. Contrary to Eck's claim that Pope Calixtus I had first enforced celibacy, Barnes replies that 'al cronicles beareth wytnes, that preestes had wyves in the counsel of Nycene the which was almost an hundreth yeares after Calixtus dayes'.[166] He again notes that the fourth-century Siricius had called for celibacy, but reminds his readers that the statute was widely ignored. Again in the sixth century Pelagius II attempted to mandate clerical chastity, but his successor Gregory I refused to enforce the decree since the clergy had made no vow of chastity. Gregory did, however, declare that those who wished to be consecrated in future would have to swear such a vow. Barnes notes that 'Here began the thynge somthynge to sprynge, and to take effecte, but yet it was not fully stablyshed'.[167] He finds the reason why it was not fully established even by Gregory's decree in a letter to the later Pope Nicholas I. He quotes the letter in full, allowing himself an amount of credulity and scurrility thus far untypical of his work.[168] According to Bishop Huldericus of Augsburg, the assumed author of the letter, Gregory's fishermen one day drew in their nets to find them filled with the heads of young children. The pope assumed these were from the offspring of his priests, who had attempted to hide their marriages by murdering their own progeny. He was so repulsed by the consequence of his mandate, said Huldericus, that he promptly repealed it. Clerical marriage then remained a legal adiaphoron until the reigns of Leo IX, who allowed marriage but discouraged sexual intercourse, and Innocent II, who condemned marriage itself.[169]

Even the twelfth-century decree of Innocent II, though backed by a long history of papal attempts to mandate celibacy, was not universally accepted. 'But

164 *Supplicacion* (1534), sig. T2r.
165 *Supplicacion* (1534), sig. T3r.
166 *Supplicacion* (1534), sig. T3r.
167 *Supplicacion* (1534), sig. U1r.
168 *Supplicacion* (1534), sig. T3r–v. But again, he could claim simply to be following previous sources, in this case perhaps Caspar Hedio's *Chronica der altenn Christlichen Kirchen* of 1530. See Pineas, 'Robert Barnes', 65. The better informed John Bale would criticise Barnes for attributing this letter to Huldericus of Augsburg, though he himself had previously been of the same opinion. For Bale's criticism and his own attribution, see T. Graham and A. Watson (eds), *The Recovery of the Past in Early Elizabethan England: Documents by John Bale and John Joscelyn from the Circle of Matthew Parker* (Cambridge, 1998), 28. For critical discussion of the authorship, see Graham and Watson, *The Recovery of the Past*, 48 n. 156, and Parish, *Clerical Marriage*, 100–4.
169 *Supplicacion* (1534), sig. U1r.

al these yet coulde not brynge this matter to passe, as they wolde, for in many places (for all this) preestes had wyves'.[170] Barnes here highlights the disjunction between papal commands and ecclesiastical compliance, going on to point out that national churches had long resisted the desires of the papacy, even when these desires were framed as authoritative decrees. By way of illustration he outlines the conflicts faced by Gregory VII, who went to great lengths to enforce clerical celibacy. The French church, he notes, resisted Gregory's prescription, denounced him as a heretic, and dismissed his decree as 'not of God, but of the devyll'.[171] Though the bishops quickly relented when threatened with the loss of their sees, the lower clergy were less easily persuaded. Those of Germany were not persuaded at all. They rejected the first announcement with little discussion. When the archbishop of Mainz attempted to enforce Gregory's decree six months later they contemplated his assassination as a warning to any others who might try to infringe upon their rights. And again in the next year, when papal legates arrived to attempt what the archbishop had failed to do, they too barely escaped with their lives.[172]

Barnes's invocation of the rights of national churches and of the history of such churches renouncing papal authority was surely calculated to appeal to Henry's own views on national and ecclesiastical sovereignty. Likewise, Barnes had suggested that clerical marriage could reasonably be expected to contribute to the peace and order of the realm.[173] He concludes, then, that there is nothing to prevent Henry from once again allowing what had been for many centuries the common doctrine and practice of the Christian church. In fact, he argues, there is a great deal to recommend it:

> I conclude here yet agayne, that Gods holy worde, olde doctours, holy counsells, themperours lawe, olde decrees of the churche, the practise of the holy apostles the lyvyng of holy men summa summarum Gods law, and mans law, nature, and reason, dothe alowe this article of myn.[174]

Barnes's defence of 'this article' – which he had argued was first and foremost an issue of doctrine – with what is almost entirely an appeal to historical evidence is perhaps the best example of the way in which history and theology are intimately related in his thought. As with his defence of earlier articles, it also demonstrates the manner in which he attempted to capitalise on the uncertain relationship between these two disciplines in the early sixteenth century. So long as critics denounced evangelical theology as heretical novelty while at the same time insisting on the historical authority of fathers, councils, papal decrees, and

170 *Supplicacion* (1534), sig. U1r.
171 *Supplicacion* (1534), sig. U1v.
172 *Supplicacion* (1534), sig. U2r.
173 *Supplicacion* (1534), sig. Q4r.
174 *Supplicacion* (1534), sig. T4v.

canon law, Barnes was motivated to pursue both offensive and defensive campaigns against such claims. Defensively, the charge of novelty was effectively rebuffed by laying out the evidence for 'evangelical' theology in the very sources Rome claimed as its own authorities. Offensively, the same charge was turned back against his opponents as the growth of particular papal doctrines could be demonstrated from the same sources and further supported by the testimony of national and ecclesiastical histories.

Further motivation to call upon history in support of primarily theological claims could be found in the historical circumstances of Barnes himself. Throughout the period from 1530 to 1534, while producing his theological tracts, Barnes was also aware that his King was pursuing political arguments of the same kind. That is, Henry was actively seeking historical arguments that might justify a political break with Rome. The promulgation of the Act in Restraint of Appeals, and finally the declaration of Royal Supremacy, sufficiently indicate that he found such arguments convincing. Barnes, then, had some small reason to believe that the King might be persuaded by the same sort of case made concerning more specifically theological issues. Much of what appears in his *Sentenciae* and the two editions of the *Supplication* could be described in this way, as theology written under the influence of history. If the relationship between these two disciplines is increasingly evident in his publications before 1535, it becomes even more so in his final work of 1536. In the *Vitae romanorum pontificum*, also dedicated to Henry VIII, Barnes will leave behind the former focus on individual doctrinal articles and turn his attention to the genre of history proper; but the result, as might be expected, is definitely history written under the influence of theology.

4

THEOLOGY IN HISTORY: *VITAE ROMANORUM PONTIFICUM* (1536)

As demonstrated in the previous chapter, a sustained use of historical sources and historical argument is evident in Robert Barnes's publications of the early 1530s. The conclusion thus proposed was that such historical argumentation was central to the polemical task Barnes had set for himself, even in those writings which appear distinctly theological in nature. It must be admitted, however, that this is not a widely held conclusion. Partially explaining this is the simple fact that most studies of Barnes have focused almost exclusively on his doctrinal conclusions, especially as they relate to the theology of Martin Luther. Not unsurprisingly, then, most studies have dwelt on Barnes's most explicitly doctrinal publications. But Barnes did not limit his output to the sort of locus by locus commentary on doctrine which is evident in his *Sentenciae* and *Supplications*. His final publication, the *Vitae romanorum pontificum*, offers readers something radically different; and here especially Barnes's historical leanings are unmistakable.

The *Vitae romanorum pontificum*, as its title suggests, is a compilation of and commentary on various acts from the reigns of past popes. Arranging the lives chronologically, Barnes offers short accounts of the pontificates of Roman bishops from the apostle Peter through Alexander III.[1] This drastic change of genre, however, is not necessarily a signal that Barnes had set for himself a new or fundamentally different agenda. In fact, despite differences of appearance, the *Vitae* is best viewed as a continuation of the programme begun even with his 1530 *Sentenciae*. Some small hint of this is evident already in its opening pages; Barnes very nearly begins the body of his last work where his first concluded, with commentary on the post-apostolic development of the Mass.[2] It was also in an earlier work, his *Supplicacion* of 1534, that Barnes first announced his intention

1 These 'lives' are not in any sense true biographies. Information concerning the lives of individuals before they assumed the pontificate, for example, is neglected. Even commentary on individual reigns is largely limited to official acts.

2 Cf. *Sentenciae*, sigs K5r–K8r, and *Vitae*, sig. B1r–v.

to take up the historical issue which occupies him in the *Vitae*. While attacking the bishops of England for swearing allegiance to that of Rome, he paused to announce, 'howe this caterpyller is come to be a lorde … I wylle speake (God wyllynge) after this in a peculier treatyse'.[3]

How competently Barnes answered his own question – and, therefore, how significant the *Vitae* is among his works – is a point of some dispute. It has long been common to ascribe a certain amount of importance to this publication for its sheer novelty. It has been described as 'one of the earliest excursions of the Reformers into Church History',[4] and more definitely as 'the first Protestant history of the papacy'.[5] Although some would qualify this claim,[6] the *Vitae* certainly is unusual among the polemic of this period, especially among that published by Englishmen. Thomas Freeman has pointed out that, although the pope's usurpation of temporal and ecclesiastical power was a major theme of early evangelical polemical tracts in England, 'very few of the ones written in the first half of the sixteenth century dealt with the growth of papal power on the continent before Wyclif's time'.[7] Barnes's publication, however, made this topic its central preoccupation. Therefore the *Vitae*, according to some, 'broke ground',[8] was one of 'the pioneer works in confessional historiography',[9] and was the 'first important contribution of the Protestant camp'.[10] Others, though, have dismissed it as a 'pedestrian offering'[11] and a 'patchwork of earlier sources',[12] saying the work 'has little value'.[13] While one author politely suggests that it 'is not a first-rate achievement in historical writing',[14] another bluntly labels it 'wholly worthless as a work of history'.[15]

The above quotations adequately illustrate the disparate and even contra-

3 *Supplicacion* (1534), *sig. D4r.*

4 E.G. Rupp, *The Righteousness of God* (London, 1953), 39. Cf. also Fisher, 'The Contribution of Robert Barnes', 99.

5 McGoldrick, *Luther's English Connection*, 14. Cf. also Katharine Firth, *The Apocalyptic Tradition in Reformation Britain, 1530–1645* (Oxford, 1979), 29.

6 See C.V. Bostick, *The Antichrist and the Lollards: Apocalypticism in Late Medieval and Reformation England* (Leiden, 1998), 52 n. 14, who takes issue with claims made for Barnes's primacy as a 'Protestant' historian of the papacy, attributing this distinction to the earlier Lollards. See Ernest W. Talbert, 'A Lollard Chronicle of the Papacy', *Journal of English and Germanic Philology* 41 (1942), 163–93.

7 Thomas Freeman, 'A Solemne Contestation of Diverse Popes: A Work by John Foxe?', *English Language Notes* 31 (1994), 37.

8 Fairfield, *John Bale*, 57.

9 C.K. Pullapilly, *Caesar Baronius: Counter Reformation Historian* (Notre Dame, 1975), 50.

10 H.E. Barnes, *A History of Historical Writing* (New York, 1963), 123.

11 Glanmor Williams, *Reformation Views of Church History* (London, 1970), 41.

12 Mark U. Edwards, *Luther's Last Battles: Politics and Polemics, 1531–46* (Leiden, 1983), 78.

13 McGoldrick, *Luther's English Connection*, 146.

14 Anderson, 'The Person and Position', 163.

15 Hartmann Grisar and Franz Heege, *Luthers Kampfbilder*, Heft 5, *Der Bilderkampf in den Schriften von 1523 bis 1545* (Freiburg im Breisgau, 1923), 64: 'als Geschichtswerk gänzlich wertlos'.

dictory estimates of Barnes's final publication. The secondary sources from which they have been drawn, however, do display one notable commonality: each lacks any sustained or detailed analysis of the *Vitae* itself. Almost without exception, this work receives no more than passing mention. This is true even in studies dedicating much of their attention to the life and writings of Barnes himself. It might be rash to assume that this lack of discussion evidences a lack of knowledge, but what little is said concerning the *Vitae* seems to make this assumption warranted. Confusion is commonplace. William Clebsch, for example, suggests that Barnes dedicated this publication to Martin Luther, when in fact the dedicatory epistle is addressed to Henry VIII.[16] More typical are the diverse assertions about the original date and place of publication. Though no evidence is ever cited to suggest that an edition came off the press before that published by Joseph Clug at Wittenberg in 1536, it is quite common to see references to an *editio princeps* of 1535.[17] The usual assertion that this was a Basle edition is likely to have originated in a misreading of the details regarding the later 1555 edition published there, but it is still frequently repeated.[18] In most cases, this seems to be the simple result of secondary sources cross-referencing one another. This same reliance on modern sources is evident in the selective quotations from the *Vitae*. The single most frequently quoted passage comes not from Barnes's text itself, but from Luther's preface.[19] And even here, the quotation is typically lifted from a secondary source rather than from Luther's original Latin.[20] Such borrowing is also evident in the rare translation of Barnes's own words.[21]

The unmistakable impression left by the above is that the *Vitae romanorum pontificum*, though consistently demanding brief acknowledgement, has never

16 Clebsch, *England's Earliest Protestants*, 73. See *Vitae*, sigs A5r–A8r. Luther did provide a preface to the work, which appears before the dedication at sigs A2r–A4v.

17 See, e.g., *Dictionary of National Biography*, ed. L. Stephen and S. Lee, 63 vols (London, 1885–1900), 1.1176; R.G. Eaves, 'The Reformation Thought of Dr. Robert Barnes, Lutheran Chaplain and Ambassador for Henry VIII', *The Lutheran Quarterly* 28 (1976), 164; McGoldrick, *Luther's English Connection*, 19; Tjernagel, *Henry VIII and the Lutherans*, 128; N.S. Tjernagel, *Lutheran Martyr* (Milwaukee, 1982), 101, 166; Tjernagel, *Reformation Essays*, 112.

18 Less common is the suggestion that there was a 1535 Wittenberg edition. See, e.g., Tjernagel, *Lutheran Martyr*, 172. This conclusion may also have arisen from less than careful reading; the dedicatory address to Henry VIII is indeed dated from Wittenberg on 10 September 1535.

19 See, e.g., Anderson, 'The Person and Position', 162; Richard Bauckham, *Tudor Apocalypse* (Oxford, 1978), 69; William Dallmann, *Robert Barnes: English Lutheran Martyr* (St Louis, n.d.; repr. Decatur, IL, 1997), 28; H.E. Jacobs, *The Lutheran Movement in England* (Philadelphia, 1916), 182–3; Tjernagel, *Henry VIII and the Lutherans*, 148.

20 The paragraph of English translation provided by H.E. Jacobs in the nineteenth century comes from Veit Ludwig Seckendorf's *Commentarius historicus et apologeticus de Lutheranismo* (Frankfurt and Leipzig, 1692). Anderson and Dallman simply reproduce Jacobs's translation, while Tjernagel cites an eighteenth-century German translation of Seckendorf for his own English rendering of the same paragraph. Bauckham reproduces Tjernagel's translation.

21 E.g., McGoldrick's only quotation of the *Vitae* comes from a secondary source. Cf. McGoldrick, *Luther's English Connection*, 147, and M.M. Knappen, *Tudor Puritanism* (Chicago, 1929), 64.

been adequately examined by modern scholars. This is perhaps due in part to the fact that the *Vitae* does not appear in the misleadingly titled 'Whole Workes' of Barnes published by John Foxe in 1573, the edition to which many have turned in their examinations of Barnes's thought.[22] The traditional neglect of his final work, however, has undoubtedly led to a skewed understanding of that which Barnes was attempting to achieve with his written works. It is therefore worth examining in some detail.

The nature and use of Barnes's sources

In examining the *Vitae* it is perhaps worth beginning where Barnes himself began: with his sources. One reason for this, as Rainer Pineas has pointed out, is that, 'In his polemical use of ecclesiastical history, Barnes makes his professed attitude to his sources a definite part of his technique.'[23] This was certainly the case in his earliest publication. Before outlining the historical development of the Mass in his *Sentenciae*, he had announced to potential detractors that he would do so 'from your own writers, so you cannot accuse me of being a Lutheran'.[24] A similar approach is taken when Barnes turns his attention to the historical development of the papacy and immediately states his intention of relying upon impartial sources. He notes that numerous histories have previously been written – many meant to do no more than flatter – but insists that he intends to follow 'men worthy of great trust, and excellent authorities, and others who, so that things are stated exactly, write modestly and simply'.[25] There will be no need to embellish the accounts found in such 'proper histories', he claims;[26] by even the briefest reading 'from the histories deserving trust, the deeds of the Roman Popes are brought out into the light and publicly exposed'.[27] This is, of course, precisely the sort of claim to objectivity common to similar polemics of the period; and, as with other such claims, it can hardly be taken at face value. Among his purportedly dispassionate witnesses one finds, for instance, the name of the curiously unfamiliar Didymus Faventinus, which upon investigation turns out to be a pseudonym for the unquestionably Lutheran Philip Melanchthon. Equally suspect is his reliance on the *Chronica Carionis*, a world history initially compiled by Johann

22 John Foxe, *The Whole workes of W. Tyndall, John Frith, and Doct. Barnes* (London, 1573 [STC 24436]). This publication includes only a conflation of Barnes's *Supplications* and select portions of his *Sentenciae*. It is the basis for much of the work done by McGoldrick, Fisher, Anderson, Pineas, and Tjernagel.

23 Pineas, 'Robert Barnes', 63.

24 *Sentenciae*, sig. K6v: 'ex vestris scriptoribus, ne causemini Lutheranum esse'.

25 *Vitae*, sig. A5v: 'homines maiori fide dignos, & auctoritate excellentiores &c. Qui, ut resipsa loquitur, modestius & simplicius scripserunt.'

26 *Vitae*, sig. A6v: 'propriis historiis'.

27 *Vitae*, sig. A6r: 'ex historiis fide dignis, in lucem & publicum producantur res gestae Paparum Romanorum'.

Carion and subsequently revised for publication, again, by Melanchthon.[28] The prophetic interpretation of history apparent in the structure of the *Chronica*, dividing the world's history into three ages, the last of which is introduced by the restoration of the gospel with the reformation, further betrays its evangelical bias.

Citations from the works of former cardinals and even Roman bishops themselves might at first glance seem more in keeping with Barnes's claim to follow sources generally judged friendly to the papacy; but closer inspection reveals that these too are not quite what they seem. Barnes makes use of two works written by the eleventh-century Cardinal Benno, for instance, without making mention of the fact that Benno was a cardinal of the anti-pope Clement III, with whom he shared a bitter hatred of the rival Pope Gregory VII. Conveniently, these previously obscure letters were first translated by Thomas Swinnerton, who quite possibly had been one of Barnes's own students at Cambridge.[29] The title of Swinnerton's original work, with which Benno's texts were published – *A mustre of scismatyke bysshopes of Rome* – leaves little doubt as to the views of both author and translator. Swinnerton himself is quite clear: although he had once subscribed to the notion of papal infallibility, his reading of Benno convinced him instead that the pope was the 'tyrannouse Antychrist of Rome'.[30]

Two years before Swinnerton's English translation of Benno appeared, Benno's writings had also been published together with Aeneas Silvius's record of the council of Basle. Barnes also makes use of Silvius, to whom he refers by his later title: Pope Pius II. This papal title certainly lends an air of unquestionable authority to *De Gestis Concilii Basiliensis*, Silvius's first-hand account of the council's proceedings. And Barnes's use of the work scores high polemical marks since Silvius, at the time of his writing, was a firm proponent of a conciliarist and anti-papal theology; his work not only favourably records the deposition of Pope Eugenius IV, but also offers a detailed outline of the popular position against papal absolutism. What Barnes neglects to mention, however, is that Silvius himself later retracted such views. In fact, as Pius II it was Silvius who later promulgated the bull *Execrabilis*, forbidding all appeals from the pope to a future council.

Having made note of some of Barnes's less than impartial sources, it must also be said that these by no means make up the majority of documents to which he

[28] Melanchthon's name can also be related, *post facto*, to yet another of Barnes's sources, the *Chronica Urspergensis* of the early thirteenth-century Abbot Burchard of Ursberg. This chronicle, which Gerald Strauss, 'The Course of German History: The Lutheran Interpretation', in *Enacting the Reformation in Germany*, ed. G. Strauss (Aldershot, 1993), 670, characterises as 'an early example of partisan anti-papal historiography', was first printed at Augsburg in 1515. After Barnes wrote, in 1537, it was reprinted at Strassburg with a preface by Melanchthon.

[29] Richard Rex, *A Reformation Rhetoric: Thomas Swynnerton's The Tropes and Figures of Scripture* (Cambridge, 1999), 8.

[30] Thomas Swinnerton, *A mustre of scismatyke bysshopes of Rome* (London, 1534 [STC 23552]), sig. C3v.

appeals. Furthermore, some criticisms occasionally levelled at his sources deserve careful qualification. Rainer Pineas, for example, questions his reliance on the *Vitae Pontificum* of Bartolomeo Platina, suggesting that this work was little more than literary revenge for the ill treatment Platina had suffered at the hands of Pope Paul II.[31] While Platina certainly had no love for Paul II – a fact unmistakably reflected in his description of that pope – he did count both his predecessor, Pius II, and his successor, Sixtus IV, as his patrons. His work was in fact dedicated to the latter in return for promotion to the post of Vatican librarian. Whatever Platina's motivation for writing, his completed work can hardly be disqualified as a hostile anti-papal diatribe. Had authorities believed it to be so it would hardly have gone through dozens of unedited and uncensored editions throughout the sixteenth century, the majority of them, even after the reformation was in full swing, being printed on Catholic presses.[32] Equally unfounded are suggestions that the eleventh-century Benedictine Lambert of Hersfeld was an outspoken critic of the papacy. Not only was Lambert's impartiality unquestioned before the nineteenth century, his *Annals* being judged 'the outstanding historical work of the period', but when his biases were finally pointed out they were revealed to be quite the opposite of those sometimes suggested.[33] Unlike Benno, for example, who denounced Pope Gregory VII in support of his protector Henry IV, Lambert's defence of Gregory was clearly motivated by his prejudices against the Emperor.[34]

Equally pro-papal was the Florentine Dominican, and later Archbishop, Antoninus, who with the council of Florence reasserted the primacy of the papacy over ecclesiastical councils. That Eugenius IV requested the counsel of Antoninus on his deathbed, and that Pius II presided at his funeral, is some indication of the favour in which he was held by the bishops of Rome.[35] His *Summa Theologica Moralis*, of which Barnes made use, also reflects his high view of papal authority, as is perhaps even hinted at in the alternative title under which it was published: *Juris Pontificii et Caesarei Summa*. Nor can the early sixteenth-century *Enneads* of Marcus Antonius Sabellicus be dismissed as inherently anti-Roman or anti-papal, as its translation was carried out and promoted by none

[31] Pineas, 'Robert Barnes', 64.

[32] It was not until 1592 that a censored edition, in Italian, was published. See *Biographisch-Bibliographisches Kirchenlexicon*, ed. F.W. Bautz and T. Bautz, 24 vols (Hamm, Herzberg, and Nordhausen, 1975–2005), 22.1100. None of the Latin editions was ever officially censored or placed on the Roman (i.e., universal) Index of Prohibited Books. For the most comprehensive treatment of this subject, see Stefan Bauer, *The Censorship and Fortuna of Platina's* Lives of the Popes *in the Sixteenth Century* (Turnhout, 2006).

[33] *Dictionary of the Middle Ages*, ed. J.R. Strayer, 12 vols (New York, 1982–89), 7.231.

[34] See, e.g., A.J. Carlyle, *A History of Medieval Political Theory in the West*, 6 vols (Edinburgh, 1927), 3.130–2, 3.155–7.

[35] So too is his canonisation in 1523, when the events of the reformation would have made any hint of criticism all the more noticeable.

other than Luther's outspoken opponent Thomas Murner. Likewise, Albert Krantz, upon whose Saxon history Barnes had relied as early as 1530, condemned Luther for even the relatively mild criticisms first voiced in his ninety-five theses.[36]

The views reflected in Barnes's sources are clearly diverse, but the works which he cites were for the most part, as he claimed, generally respected standard authorities which had previously elicited no criticism from the church. For the earliest years of the church's history, as would be expected, he makes much use of the *Chronicle* and the *Ecclesiastical History* of Eusebius, as well as the *Tripartite History* of Cassiodorus. For early canon law he turns to the *Collectio Hispana Chronologica*, the collection of conciliar canons attributed to Isidore of Seville. His medieval sources include not only the previously mentioned Lambert, but also Petrus de Natalibus's *Catalogue of Saints* and the *Chronica Pontificum et Imperatorum* of thirteenth-century Dominican Martin of Troppau. Despite its now obvious naiveté, this latter work, commissioned by Pope Clement IV, whose chaplain Martin was, quickly established itself as the preferred historical handbook of the late Middle Ages.

Following such sources, which were by no means exemplars of critical historiography, Barnes frequently – and no doubt quite happily – repeated much information that was historically inaccurate. His promotion of the legend of the female Pope Joan is only the most blatant example of Barnes's willingness to accept questionable sources where they might serve his purpose.[37] Even here, however, criticism must be qualified; it is Martin of Troppau's favoured *Chronica* which serves as the original source for the information regarding Joan, who throughout the fourteenth and fifteenth centuries was indeed believed by many to have been an historical pontiff. But Barnes's reference to Platina for this story, despite Platina's expressed doubts concerning its veracity, does illustrate Barnes's preference for the most unflattering options.

His factual errors, however, are not always the result of a rejection of learned, humanist sources; just as often they were the result of his reliance upon them. Thus, despite criticism for his inaccurate retelling of the conflict between Barbarossa and Alexander III,[38] Barnes has been defended for basing his account on 'prima facie trustworthy humanist sources'.[39] In fact, just as his early and

36 *Allgemeine Deutsche Biographie*, ed. R. von Liliencron et al., 56 vols (Leipzig, 1875–1912), 17.43–4.

37 See *Vitae*, sigs K5v–K6v.

38 See R.W. Scribner, 'Demons, Defecation and Monsters: Popular Propaganda for the German Reformation', in *Popular Culture and Popular Movements in Reformation Germany*, ed. R.W. Scribner (London, 1987), 291.

39 Kurt Stadtwald, 'Pope Alexander III's Humilation of Emperor Frederick Barbarossa as an Episode in Sixteenth-century German History', *Sixteenth Century Journal* 23 (1992), 766. Barnes cites Nauclerus, for instance, whose history was published with prefaces by such esteemed

medieval sources consisted largely of reputable and accepted authorities, Barnes's more contemporary sources, mostly written by respected humanists, were also deemed at the time to be honest and scholarly productions. The *Chronica Chronicorum* of Hartmann Schedel and the Carthusian Werner Rolewinck's *Fasciculus Temporum* were certainly thought by contemporaries to be so, and this is reflected in their popularity. Between 1474 and 1500 Rolewinck's publication, for instance, went through thirty-three editions in five languages. Two equally prominent authors upon whom Barnes relied were Raphael Maffei of Volterra, a humanist associated with the early sixteenth-century papal court, and Polydore Vergil, whose critical skills were grudgingly admired even by those who attacked his use of them in undermining cherished myths about the antiquity of Britain. Relevant to Barnes's use of the latter, Vergil's conservative religious credentials are as significant as his scholarly reputation. Long uncomfortable with the reforming program of Henry VIII, he quit England for good in the reign of Edward VI and later wrote to Mary I in hopes that she would successfully restore the realm to the old faith.[40]

But more important than sources alone, of course, is the manner in which Barnes put such sources to use. While Barnes's willingness to take an uncritical approach to his sources has already been noted, it must also be asked whether this is always the case, or whether he can and does make any attempt at critical historiography in his *Vitae*. On the whole, and despite the evidence which suggests that Barnes had some pretensions to being a humanist scholar himself, it appears that he had little interest in the increasingly popular questions of historiographical method. This is not to say that he was unaware of the problems raised by conflicting historical accounts; but once he makes note of them he typically opts to ignore them rather than to address them directly. He often notes, for instance, that his sources provide widely differing conclusions regarding the lengths of particular pontificates. Rather than offering an appraisal of the evidence and announcing his own verdict, however, he is usually content to provide his readers with all of the options and then to proceed without comment.[41] When others have already done the critical work for him, on the other hand, he will not despise their conclusions. Barnes was, for example, aware of the debate concerning whether Popes Cletus and Anecletus were the same person. Eusebius had judged them to be the same, but Barnes chooses instead to follow Platina, who had pointed out

humanists as Reuchlin and Erasmus. Strauss, 'The Course of German History', 668, refers to it as 'the model par excellence' of sixteenth-century chronicling.

40 See M. McKisack, *Medieval History in the Tudor Age* (Oxford, 1971), 99. It is also significant that one of the most violent critics of Vergil's historiography was the Protestant polemicist John Bale.

41 The same is true even when he is aware of confusion regarding the order of certain popes, for example, Anicetus and Pius I. See *Vitae*, sigs B7v–B8r.

that differing national origins and different dates of death had typically been ascribed to each.[42]

Barnes quite probably sought to avoid such issues as pedantic, time-consuming, and ultimately irrelevant to his goal. Precise dating, important though it may be for critical scholarship, would do little to support his contention that many pontiffs 'were truly none other than Domitians, Diocletians, and Neros'.[43] This is not necessarily to conclude, as some have, that Barnes's sole priority was to compile 'a wholly uncritical collection of everything unfavorable to the popes'.[44] If a claim to authorial objectivity can be reduced to an emphasis on simply recording the facts (or, at least what are believed to be the facts) rather than being side-tracked by tendentious commentary on or interpretation of the facts, then Barnes can indeed show himself to be more restrained than even some of his less hostile predecessors. Contrary to Ernst Breisach's suggestion, for instance, it is not the case that Barnes simply magnifies the faults recorded by Platina.[45] Quite regularly, in fact, he omits the very criticisms which Platina had provided. Commenting upon Urban I's desire for ecclesiastical wealth to be distributed equally among the clergy, Barnes does not, as Platina had, allow himself a remark about the greed and covetousness which later derailed such pious hopes.[46] Nor does he highlight the clerical envy and pride which Platina believed to have precipitated the Diocletianic persecution, and which he still considered rampant in the church of his own day.[47] There is some warrant, then, in describing the *Vitae* as 'a catena of standard medieval and renaissance sources, to which Barnes brought the originality only of selection'.[48] The originality of his selection, however, lies at least partially in the fact that his concern was not to highlight often repeated – and rarely refuted – charges of clerical immorality, papal corruption, or ecclesiastical abuses. A closer look at the substance of his text will reveal his real concerns and the method by which he sought to address them.

The content and method of the *Vitae*

For what might be obvious reasons, while Barnes begins his history with Peter he does not name that apostle the first pope. Instead, he follows an older tradition in

42 Cf. *Vitae*, sig. B2r and sigs B2v–B4r.
43 *Vitae*, sig. A5v: 'vere nihil aliud quam Domitianos, Diocletianos, & Nerones fuisse'.
44 Grisar and Heege, *Luthers Kampfbilder*, 64: 'eine ganz kritiklose Sammlung alles den Päpsten ungünstigen'.
45 Ernst Breisach, *Historiography: Ancient, Medieval, and Modern* (Chicago, 1983), 167.
46 Cf. *Vitae*, sig. C3r and Bartolomeo Platina, *Lives of the Popes*, 2 vols, tr. W. Benham (London, 1888), 1.42.
47 Cf. *Vitae*, sig. D1r–v and Platina, *Lives of the Popes*, 1.63.
48 Clebsch, *England's Earliest Protestants*, 73.

which Peter's successor Linus receives that title.[49] This is certainly noteworthy, but perhaps even more significant for a proper understanding of the content and method of the *Vitae* is the paragraph which sits between its accounts of Peter and Linus. It is unexpected and, in fact, entirely without context. As the information it provides is found elsewhere in the text of Barnes's history, it is also wholly superfluous. But coming as it does even before he summarises the reign of the first pope, it serves as an important clue; it indicates what sort of information readers should find most significant in his historical survey of the Roman bishopric. He writes:

> The holy eucharist grew with the passing of time. Celestine added the *Introit* of the Mass; Gregory the *Kyrie Eleison*; Thelesphorus the *Gloria in Exelsis Deo*; Gelasius I the offerings; Jerome the Epistle and Gospel readings. The *Alleluia* was taken up from the church in Jerusalem. The creed was added at the council of Nicaea. Pelagius added the commemoration of the dead; Leo III incense; Innocence the kiss of peace; Sergius the *Agnus Dei*. That which other pontiffs added is taught in their place in the acts of the pontiffs.[50]

And indeed, throughout his survey of papal acts – especially through the late seventh-century reign of Agatho, under whose pontificate the sixth general council was held at Constantinople and at which, he notes, 'John of Porto ... celebrated the first Latin Mass, and the use of this order of the Mass was approved by the whole synod'[51] – Barnes makes it a point to notify his readers of any liturgical innovations which come to light. Several, he is quick to point out, were introduced almost immediately by Alexander I, who not only added a recitation of Christ's passion to the words of institution, but also prescribed that the wine be mixed with water and that priests not consecrate leavened bread, which, Barnes says, 'they had used before'.[52] It was Sixtus I who introduced the singing of the *Sanctus* in the second century, and Damasus I by whose statutes the *Gloria Patri* and public confession first entered the liturgy in the fourth century.[53] In addition to Celestine's above noted inclusion of the *Introit*, Barnes also mentions that he ordained the *Gradual*, as well as the singing of Psalm 43 'in initio

49 *Vitae*, sig. B2r. For brief comment on this early tradition see J.N.D. Kelly, *The Oxford Dictionary of Popes* (Oxford, 1986), 6–7.

50 *Vitae*, sig. B1r–v: 'Eucharistiae sacra successu temporis aucta sunt. Celestinus introitum Missae adiecit. Gregorius kyrie eleyson. Thelesphorus Gloria in exelsis Deo. Gelasius I. Collationes. Hieronimus Epistolam & Evangelium. Alleluia sumptum est ab Ecclesia Hierosolomitana. Symbolum addidit Niceanum Concilium. Pelagius commemorationem mortuorum. Leo iii. Thus. Innocentius osculum pacis. Sergius Agnis Dei, Quid alii pontifices addiderint, suo loco in pontificiis actis dicetur &c.'

51 *Vitae*, sig. G6r: 'Ioannes portuensis in ea synodo primam missam latinam celebravit, & ille Misse ordo ac usu a tota synodo tunc approbatus est'.

52 *Vitae*, sigs B4v–B5r: 'quo usi ante fuerant'.

53 *Vitae*, sig. E1v.

sacrificii'.[54] Somewhat surprisingly, however, he does not take this mention of sacrifice (or several others) as an opportunity to offer comments on the Roman doctrine of eucharistic sacrifice. Indeed, throughout the whole of this work Barnes offers very little in the way of explicit commentary, and Leslie Fairfield is not mistaken in his characterisation of the *Vitae*'s methodology as rarely more than a chronological listing of papal acts, 'with little in the way of interpretation'.[55] Thus Barnes immediately returns to simple recitation, though still making careful note of any perceived changes in the liturgy. Leo I, he says, added the *Hanc Igitur*, while the *Te Igitur* and the preface 'vere dignum & iustum est' were instituted in the late fifth century by Gelasius I.[56] Following the medieval *Catalogue of Saints*, he describes the proper prefaces to the Canon of the Mass, those specific to particular festivals of the ecclesiastical year, as a novelty only introduced by Pope Pelagius II at the end of the sixth century.[57] One of the greatest innovators in Barnes's account, however, is Pelagius's successor, Gregory I. In addition to his introduction of the *Kyrie Eleison*, he also instituted the *Diesque Nostros* and further introits from the Psalms. It was Gregory, Barnes says, who was first responsible for introducing Litanies and the Roman Stations, as well as decreeing that the church sing no Alleluias in the seventy days prior to Easter.[58]

Few readers could be expected to find this catalogue engrossing, especially in the light of Barnes's consistent refusal to provide any of the rhetorical flourishes for which his sermons were known, or any of the biting commentary to which readers of his *Supplications* had become accustomed. It is indeed the case that 'nowhere in the work does Barnes descend to the level of unrestrained abuse which at times disfigures his English works'.[59] The unemotional manner in which Barnes records the growth of the Mass, should not, however, be interpreted as an indication that it is any less than a central concern. Nor should the fact that his recital of individual additions is disjointed, being interspersed with a great deal of other historical information. His consistent flagging of each innovation by means of marginal annotation serves not only as a helpful reference aid; by highlighting them as especially worthy of reference he also signifies their particular importance. The reason for their importance finally becomes apparent in yet another marginal note: 'The approval of the first Latin Mass.'[60] This Latin Mass, as noted above, was only recognised for the first time in the late seventh century, at the council of Constantinople. Drawing attention to this fact alone would have perhaps been enough to persuade sympathetic readers of the

54 *Vitae*, sig. E4v.
55 Fairfield, *John Bale*, 57.
56 *Vitae*, sigs E5v, E8v.
57 *Vitae*, sigs F6v–F7r.
58 *Vitae*, sig. F7v.
59 Fisher, 'The Contribution of Robert Barnes', 101.
60 *Vitae*, sig. G6r: 'Missae latine prima approbatio.'

unlikelihood of Roman claims for its apostolic origins. But as noted in the previous chapter, it was to this very council that the decretalists had appealed in asserting that the shape of the Mass originated with and was handed down by James, the brother of Jesus. Barnes's careful record of the origins of the rite's many parts, the great majority of them instituted more than four hundred years after the death of James, is specifically intended to undermine this claim. Without the need to be either caustic or explicit, the evidence provided in the *Vitae* serves the same conclusion Barnes had announced six years earlier in his *Sentenciae*: 'here you now have the first Latin Mass – however patched together – and the originators of each part'.[61]

By detailing the origins of the Mass Barnes not only countered popular claims for its antiquity, but, even more importantly, he was once again able to raise doubts about traditionally accepted ecclesiastical authorities such as canon law. Thus, for good measure, he goes on to point out that further additions were made to this allegedly apostolic rite even after its official approval at Constantinople. It was Pope Agatho's immediate successor, Leo II, Barnes claims, who instituted the sharing of the *Pax* in the celebration of the Mass, and Sergius I, a decade later, who first introduced the *Agnus Dei*.[62] Having established that the liturgy of his day could not be traced to the apostles, or even to a more recent council, Barnes finally allows himself to raise the question of why so many previously unknown elements were now found in the Mass. It should be emphasised that, to this point, Barnes had offered no explicit criticism of the additions themselves. In fact, contrary to intimations by those who have attempted to portray him as a proto-Puritan, there is no evidence to suggest that Barnes found the great majority of changes in any way objectionable. His primary objection was to making necessities of what he understood to be adiaphora.[63] This was a point he had raised already in the *Sentenciae*, where, for example, he had said of the practice of private confession: 'I very much approve it; but I do not teach that it is commanded'.[64] Barnes, however, sees a dubious motive at work in the continuous growth and modification of ceremonies: the desire to increase the power and

61 *Sentenciae*, sig. K7v: 'hic iam habes missam primam latinam utcunque consutam, et auctores singularum partium'.

62 *Vitae*, sigs G7r, H1r.

63 Barnes makes much of what he describes as the early consensus on adiaphora, as especially highlighted in the controversies concerning the date of Easter. Regarding the outcome of dispute between Polycarp and Pope Anicetus, he concludes, 'it is not possible to break the harmony of faith on account of different ceremonies' ['non oportuit propter Ceremoniarum dissonantiam rumpere fidei consonantiam']. *Vitae*, sig. B8r. He finds the same conclusion when the issue was raised again by Pope Victor, 'it not being worth destroying the agreement of faith on account of disagreement in ceremonies' ['indignum esse rati propter dissonantiam Ceremoniarum, fidei consonantiam rumpere']. *Vitae*, sig. C1v.

64 *Sentenciae*, sigs G8v–H1r: 'valde eam probo, sed doceo eam non esse urgendam'.

prestige of the papal office itself. 'They always contrived new ceremonies', he asserts, 'by which the unlearned common folk are kept in wonder.'[65]

And not only wonder, but, apparently, confusion as well. Thus Barnes makes note of the fact that the ancient custom was to consecrate the blood of Christ in a wooden chalice; Severius later insisted that this be done in a chalice of glass; and only shortly thereafter Urban decreed that 'no sacred vessels of glass, but those of either gold or silver, or, in poor churches, pewter, were to be the rule.'[66] Likewise, he notes, Severius's decree concerning the number of times the faithful were expected to commune was also soon reversed. Rather than once a year, Fabian later prescribed that all were to receive the eucharist at least three times yearly. Though Barnes does not here expressly question the popular, if not yet official, concept of papal infallibility, his succinct marginal note – 'Contra decretum Severii' – does suggest that he expects his readers to consider the implications.[67] Also touching on the frequency of communion and apparent contradictions between ancient and modern practice, he recalls that Pope Soter had expressly ordained that 'no priest should celebrate unless at least two people partake.'[68] The implication for private Masses, which Barnes frequently condemned, would have been clear to his readers. And while he consistently draws attention to the confusion and contradiction between individual popes on a variety of matters, his concern for the sacrament finally concludes with a remark on eucharistic doctrine, and the hint that even Christ and his apostles have been contradicted by the papacy. Commenting on the eighth-century pontificate of Gregory III, he claims: 'Here the Mass appears as a sacrifice for the dead, which was not so in antiquity, not according to the institution of Christ or the apostles'.[69] After Gregory's reign Barnes mentions no further additions to the Mass, leaving readers with the impression that the doctrine of eucharistic sacrifice was the culmination of eight centuries of innovation. One might also suspect that, in Barnes's reading of history, it was no coincidence that a doctrine which he held to be particularly loathsome arose at the precise time it did; it was only in his survey of the previous pontificate that he finally located the event many readers had no doubt been anticipating. 'Here', he says, 'the Roman beast began to rule.'[70]

In Barnes's account, the rule of this 'Roman beast' – the closest he ever comes

65 *Vitae*, sig. G8v: 'Semper excogitant novas ceremonias, quibus detineant indoctum vulgus in admiratione.'

66 *Vitae*, sig. C3r: 'Ne vasa sacra vitrea, sed aut aurea, aut argentea aut stannea in inopioribus ecclesiis essent legem dixit.' Cf. sig. C2r.

67 *Vitae*, sig. C4r; cf. sig. C2r.

68 *Vitae*, sig. B8v: 'Ne Sacerdos celebraret, nisi ut minimum duo addessent ordinavit.'

69 *Vitae*, sig. H4v: 'Hic apparet, Missam esse sacrificium pro mortuis, non esse tam vetustum, neque ex institutione Christi, aut Apostolorum'. Gregory is also the last pope to whom Barnes ascribes additions to the Mass, in this case the *Quorum Solemnitas*. See sig. H4r.

70 *Vitae*, sig. H3v: 'Hic incipit bestia Romana imperare.'

in the *Vitae* to naming the papacy Antichrist – is not only closely associated with the culmination of innovations concerning eucharistic doctrine and practice; it also coincides with the first full flowering of papal pretensions to primacy, both secular and ecclesiastical. From this point Barnes begins to devote as much, if not more, attention to these two themes as he had to the sacrament. Neither, however, had been previously ignored. Almost from the beginning he had made note of the manner in which individual popes had acted to secure, or at least to assert, special privileges for the church of Rome and her clergy. In the secular sphere, for instance, he had noted the number of pontiffs who made it a point to prohibit clergy, especially bishops, from being accused by the laity or tried in secular courts.[71] Early in the church's history, however, such modest privileges were the extent of those claimed by Rome over against secular rulers.[72] But the consequences of claiming such rights are worthy of note. Though exempted from appearance in secular courts, the clergy were not thereby made immune to the coercive powers which Barnes believed to have been divinely granted to the state; instead, this power of coercion was taken up by the church itself. By way of example he records that Pope Eugenius I ordered his bishops to maintain prisons for the punishment of convicted clergy. It was with acts such as this, Barnes says, that 'they began to seize the power of the civil sword'.[73]

In Barnes's review of the papacy's growth and its frequent contests with civil authority, however, it is the long controversy concerning the papal office and its relationship with that of the emperor which receives the most attention. Thus he pauses frequently, especially throughout the early portions of his history, to emphasise the unquestioned imperial role in electing and confirming Roman bishops. When Rome was besieged by Lombards in the late sixth century, thereby preventing the city from obtaining the emperor's assent to the election of Pelagius II, Barnes makes it a point to record that a deacon was quickly sent to Constantinople to explain the extenuating circumstances. His blunt insistence that 'the election of the pontiff was dependent upon the approval of the emperor' betrays his opinion that this was more than simply a polite gesture.[74] The same was true a half century later under Pope Severinus. That confirmation of his election was sought from the imperial exarch prompts Barnes to remind his readers again that 'up to this time the confirmation of popes was overseen by the emperor'.[75] With reference to a decree of Boniface III, he notes that even the election of bishops to

[71] See, e.g., *Vitae*, sigs B4r (Evaristus), B5r (Alexander I), B7r (Pius I), C8v (Caius), D2r (Eusebius), D3r (Sylvester).

[72] Even these, however, Barnes could reasonably expect to grab the attention of the individual to whom he had dedicated his work, as the issue of clergy and courts played a prominent part in Henry VIII's early controversies with the papacy.

[73] *Vitae*, sig. G5r: 'Hic incipiunt rapere potestatem gladii civilis.'

[74] *Vitae*, sig. F6v: 'Electio pontificis pendebat ex approbatione Caesaris.'

[75] *Vitae*, sig. G3r: 'Ad huc confirmatio papae ad cesarem spectat.'

sees other than that of Rome had traditionally required the ratification of the civil authority. But the fact that Boniface had insisted in the same decree that final episcopal confirmation belongs to the pope alone was seen by Barnes as a foreshadow of things to come. 'Little by little', he comments, 'they crept into the authority of princes. But on later occasions they completely excluded them.'[76]

Despite such foreshadowing, Barnes continues to point out that popes even into the ninth century recognised the emperor's right to confirm their election. Thus he notes that Paschal I, like Pelagius II before him, was quick to send apologetic ambassadors to the emperor when circumstances prevented this protocol from being followed. And again he reads this as proof that popes to this point had not set themselves above secular rulers.[77] With the benefit of hindsight, however, Barnes regards the practice of conferring with the emperor only after the ordination of pontiffs as increasingly suspicious. In response to Hadrian II's insistence that the tumult surrounding his election made it impossible to seek imperial assent prior to the fact, Barnes sceptically commented that 'the Romans are always cunning'.[78] His suspicion was confirmed a century later with the election of Martin II, 'the first time the authority of the emperor was not awaited in creating a pontiff'.[79] This, in Barnes's judgement, had nothing to do with circumstances surrounding the election (which, he notes, were nonetheless dubious); rather, it was an intentional move by which the Romans 'loosened the power of the emperor, so that afterwards it was easier to destroy his standing'.[80] And indeed, he records that Martin's successor, Hadrian III, proposed that no further elections be subject to the emperor.[81] The culmination of these manoeuvres Barnes finally ascribes to Hildebrand, later Pope Gregory VII, who even before his own pontificate had done much to exclude the emperor from papal elections. Most notably, while Emperor Henry III's nominee to succeed Damasus II was *en route* to Rome, the monk Hildebrand intercepted him to insist that the emperor had no right to create pontiffs, but that this belonged to the Roman clergy and people alone. Not only was the nominee convinced, but so much so that upon being ordained Leo IX he immediately elevated Hildebrand to the office of cardinal.[82] Thus, Barnes remarks, 'they banished emperors from the election of pontiffs'.[83]

Clearly it is Barnes's intent to convince his readers that this banishment

76 *Vitae*, sig. G1v: 'Paulatim irrepunt in auctoritatem principum. Sed postea nacti occasionem in totum eos excludunt.'
77 *Vitae*, sig. I7v.
78 *Vitae*, sig. L7v: 'Romani semper vafri.'
79 *Vitae*, sig. M2r: 'Huius primo tempore non expectabatur imperatoris auctoritas in creando pontifice.'
80 *Vitae*, sig. M2r: 'Ita paulatim se explicant a potestate imperatorum, ut facilius eos postea predibus conterant.'
81 *Vitae*, sig. M2r.
82 *Vitae*, sigs O7v–O8r.
83 *Vitae*, sig. O7v: 'eiiciunt imperatorem ab electione pontificum'.

occurred only relatively recently in the church's history, and that by contrast 'the ancient custom is for emperors to have the right of choosing pontiffs'.[84] He makes it equally plain, however, that clarifying the historical record is not his final concern. That he believes the fundamental nature of papal doctrine, and of the papacy itself, to be bound up with the answer to certain historical questions is evident in his formulation of that which had become the central question: 'If the confirmation of pontiffs appertains to the emperor, where then is the primacy of the pope?'[85]

While Barnes traces its growth in part through the gradual rejection of an imperial role in papal elections, he also chronicles the increasingly frequent assertions that the emperor was in fact subject to the papacy. Barnes sees this beginning in the eighth century when Gregory III, despite his confirmation by Emperor Leo III, very quickly rounded on the emperor and announced him deposed. This novel power, Barnes comments, 'was not taught by Christ nor by his apostles'.[86] Thus, as he had already in his *Supplicacion*, he again criticises the papal deposition of Childeric in favour of Pepin, and asserts that the translation of empire to the Franks was done 'by the authority of the pope and not of Christ'.[87] The manner in which successive popes were able to exercise their authority over emperors reached a certain climax, in Barnes's account, under John XIII,[88] who was able to extract an oath of loyalty from Otto I before the latter received the imperial crown.[89] But once again, it is in the eleventh-century reign of Gregory VII that Barnes finds the papal subjection of emperors most thoroughly and consistently put into effect. And it is here, in his commentary on Gregory's contest with Henry IV, that Barnes's continual references to 'the beast' most clearly betray his judgement of the Roman bishopric after its adoption of the notion of papal supremacy. It is also here that he most explicitly defends the actions of those princes who have rejected the papacy. 'The beast deposed the emperor', he writes, 'and that is why other princes do not expect

[84] *Vitae*, sig. N4v: 'Vetustum est, Caesarem habere ius eligendi pontificem.'

[85] *Vitae*, sig. N3v: 'Penes cesarem erat confirmatio pontificis, ubi tunc primatus Papae?'

[86] *Vitae*, sig. H4v: 'hoc non didicit a Christo, neque ab Apostolis eius'. Despite his sources explaining that Leo was excommunicated and deposed for his opposition to images and for unorthodox opinions concerning Christ's divinity, Barnes is careful to mention only the former charge. Aside from thereby portraying Leo as a more sympathetic character than might otherwise be the case, he might also intend his readers to find some irony in the fact that one of Gregory's recent predecessors, Pope Constantine I, had himself attempted to ban certain images. In that instance they were images of heretical emperors, and Barnes had asked sarcastically, 'But what is that to the pope?' ['Sed quid hoc ad pontificem?']. *Vitae*, sig. H2r.

[87] *Vitae*, sig. H7v: 'Imperium translatum est ad francos, auctoritate papae & non christi.' Though noting that this authority was again exercised in the later translation of empire to the Germans, Barnes passes over this episode without comment. See *Vitae*, sig. M1v.

[88] In fact, this was John XII. By referring to the legendary Joan as 'John VIII' Barnes misnumbers the succeeding Popes John VIII–XIX.

[89] *Vitae*, sigs N1v–N2r.

obedience from papists'.[90] It is also why, he says, 'Princes give love to that new (as they say) doctrine by which they are freed from the beast.'[91] But that the doctrine Barnes here defends is not at all new he attempts to highlight by quoting that which he does find novel – Gregory's interpretation of the keys given to the church by Christ:

> If you have the power to bind and loose in heaven, then on earth you are also able to take away and give empires, kingdoms, and principalities, and all that which mortals possess. If you have power to judge in things which pertain to God, what do you think about these inferior and profane things?[92]

Barnes simply replies: 'The apostles exercised the authority of the keys, but not in your manner.'[93]

Barnes had emphasised in his previous works that the power of the keys was given not to Peter alone – and therefore certainly not to the papacy alone – but to the entire church. For this reason, the attention he gives to papal primacy in the *Vitae* is not limited to its growth in the temporal sphere; he is equally intent on demonstrating how Rome gradually elevated itself to a position of usurped authority in the church itself. And once again, what he finds is a long history of attempts to assert the primacy of the Roman see. At the same time, he again finds that for centuries this was both resisted and rejected. Similarly, as the confession of Roman primacy became increasingly intertwined with notions of papal infallibility, Barnes is also able to compile a catalogue of contradictions making any such claims difficult to defend in the light of history.

Barnes did not shy away from acknowledging that some insinuations, and indeed some bold assertions, of papal primacy were made quite early in the church's history. Already in the early second century, Sixtus I had announced that ministers had a right of appeal from their local bishops to the Roman see.[94] An implicit belief in Rome's superior status is also evident in Pope Anterus's decree that no bishop should be translated from one see to another without the prior consent of 'the highest pontiff'.[95] And, in fact, prior to such implicit claims, an explicit proclamation of Roman primacy had been voiced by Anacletus even before the close of the first century. According to Barnes,

[90] *Vitae*, sig. Q6r: 'Bestia Cesarem deponit, neque est cur principes aliam obedientiam sperarent a papistis'.

[91] *Vitae*, sig. Q7r: 'Principes igitur iure deberent amare istam novam (ut vocant) doctrinam, cum per eam sint liberati a bestia.'

[92] *Vitae*, sig. R4v: 'si potestis in coelo ligare, & solvere, in terra quoque imperia, regna, principatus, & quicquid mortales habere possunt,auferre, & dare vos posse. Si enim quae ad Deum pertinent, iudicare potestis, quid de his inferio ribus & prophanis censendumest?'

[93] *Vitae*, sig. R4v: 'Apostoli sunt usi auctoritate clavium, sed non ista qua tu.'

[94] *Vitae*, sig. B5v.

[95] *Vitae*, sig. C3v: 'summi ponti'.

> He claimed to be by himself the lord primate of the Roman church, over all churches by the name of Christian, because, he said, it was said of Peter, who taught and died in Rome, 'You are Peter, and upon this rock I will build my church.'[96]

But, as Barnes attempts to show in the pages which follow, such a bold assertion cannot be reconciled with the facts recorded by the historians of the church. Pointing to the canons of the council of Nicaea, for example, he notes that jurisdiction over the clergy of Egypt was given only to the patriarch of Alexandria. Expecting that none will question the Nicene canons, he simply asks, 'Where then is the primacy of the pope?'[97] Further commenting on the regard the canons show for the Jerusalem episcopate, he argues that the council expressly spoke 'against the pope's primacy'.[98]

By Barnes's account, the primacy of the Roman see was only 'established' nearly three hundred years later, under Boniface III,[99] who declared that all should recognise the Roman see as 'the head of all the churches'.[100] This pronouncement was prompted by contrary claims made by bishops of Constantinople, beginning with Boniface's contemporary John, who, in a synod convened in the reign of Pope Gregory I, had announced himself universal patriarch.[101] Barnes makes reference to this debate as 'the first contention concerning the primacy',[102] and it serves to illustrate that even in the seventh century – long after Anacletus's assertion of primacy, but long before the schism which divided the eastern and western churches – Rome's headship was far from universally acknowledged. In fact, as Barnes goes on to emphasise, even churches within such close proximity as Ravenna had long remained independent of Rome. He repeats Platina's claim that, until Pope Donus subjected that see to Rome's authority, it had long been referred to as 'alio cephalis'. 'Therefore', Barnes concludes, 'no primacy of the pope was known before.'[103] When Leo II declared soon thereafter that no bishop of Ravenna was to be elected without papal permission, Barnes demands to know, 'by what authority is the bishop of Ravenna subject, who was before equal?'[104] Being rhetorical, the question of course

96 *Vitae*, sig. B4r: 'Ab ipso domino primatum Romanae Ecclesiae super omnes Ecclesias universumque christiani nomine populum concessum esse asseruit, quia inquit Petro dicenti, & morienti Romae dixit, Tu es petrus, & super hanc petram aedificabo Ecclesiam meam.'

97 *Vitae*, sig. D4r: 'Ubi tunc erat primatus papae?'

98 *Vitae*, sig. D4r: 'Contra primatum Papae.'

99 *Vitae*, sig. G1r: 'hic stabilitur primatus Romani pont'. Even here, of course, Barnes does not find the notion truly established, as the later pages of the Vitae make clear.

100 *Vitae*, sig. G1r: 'caput omnium Ecclesiarum'.

101 See *Vitae*, sigs F8v, G1r–v.

102 *Vitae*, sig. F8v: 'Prima contentio de primatu'.

103 *Vitae*, sig. G5v: 'Ergo antea non agnovit primatum pontificis.'

104 *Vitae*, sig. G7r: 'Sed qua auctoritate subegit Ravennatem Episcopum, cum antea erat illi equalis?'

receives no answer, and he can only say that 'Against its ancient liberties the church of Ravenna was subdued by the church of Rome, and little by little the Roman beast crept into its primacy.'[105] Even with the subjection of the traditionally difficult Ravenna, however, there remained Italian churches which refused to recognise the title Rome had claimed for itself. Barnes writes, for instance, that it was only in the eleventh century that Stephen IX 'brought the church of Milan, which from the time of the apostles had been free, under obedience to the Roman pontiff'.[106] He therefore concludes that, 'at that time at least, the Roman church did not have the nature of universal head'.[107]

By drawing attention to conciliar history Barnes is further able to promote scepticism regarding papal claims to authority. He notes, for example, that Marcellus had proclaimed that no council was to be convoked without pontifical authority.[108] Yet, he emphasises, less than twenty years later the first ecumenical council was called by no Roman bishop, but by the Emperor Constantine.[109] Despite any polemical points he might have earned by playing imperial councils against papal, however, he remained unwilling to grant final authority to either. Making note of the fact that a Lateran synod convened by Pope Stephen III had anathematised the Constantinopolitan council in which images were banned,[110] Barnes remarks: 'The Holy Spirit is therefore not always in councils.'[111]

As previously noted, Barnes's attempt to undermine the doctrine of papal primacy also makes frequent appeal to those instances in which the notion of papal infallibility can be called into question. That the early church failed to give credence to any such notion he emphasises by drawing attention to the early controversies concerning the date of Easter, first under Pope Anicetus, and shortly thereafter in the pontificate of Victor. Despite 'vehement dispute', he notes that Polycarp would not be reconciled to the opinion of Anicetus; yet the pope made no move to exclude him from the church.[112] When Victor later issued a pronouncement on the subject, dispute arose once again. Rejecting what they considered a novelty, the bishops of Asia 'decreed that Easter should be celebrated according to the old custom'.[113] But, Barnes continues,

105 *Vitae*, sig. G7v: 'Ravenna Ecclesia contra antiquas libertates Romanae Ecclesiae subditur, & ita paulatim irrepit bestia Romana in suum primatum.'
106 *Vitae*, sig. P1v: 'Stephanus ecclesiam Mediolanensem, quae a temporibus Apost. libera fuit, sub obedientiam Romani pontificis redegit.' While Barnes agrees with his cited source that Stephen did subject Milan to Rome, his claim that the Milanese church had been free from the time of the apostles greatly exaggerates what Platina actually says; he had recorded that Milan had only been separated from Rome for a span of two hundred years. See Platina, *Lives of the Popes*, 1.276–7.
107 *Vitae*, sig. P1v: 'Ergo ne tunc quidem Romana ecclesia est habita pro universali capite.'
108 *Vitae*, sig. D1v.
109 *Vitae*, sig. D3v.
110 In fact the council of Hieria, convened by Emperor Constantine V in the year 754.
111 *Vitae*, sig. I1r: 'Ergo in conciliis non semper est spiritus S.'
112 *Vitae*, sig. B8r: 'vehemens concertatio'.
113 *Vitae*, sig. C1v: 'decreverunt pascha iuxta veterum consuetudinem celebrari'.

> Indeed, Victor, a firm defender of his own opinion, sent a letter to Asia. He determined to exclude the Asian bishops from the church as slanderous heretics who were unwilling to conform to the Roman church.[114]

Significantly, he concludes,

> A group of his own bishops (including Irenaeus) resisted; they advised Victor to consider more important that which is characteristic of peace, it not being worth destroying the agreement of faith on account of disagreement in ceremonies.[115]

Not only did those bishops friendly to Victor refuse to support his decree, but equally telling in Barnes's reading is that the 'agreement of faith' could not be broken by such a refusal.

Such examples, although illustrating that papal decrees had not always been received as infallible pronouncements, do not of course demonstrate that such decrees were indeed fallible. In fact, Barnes himself notes that Victor's opinion on Easter was finally approved and adopted by the council of Nicaea.[116] But he is occasionally able to highlight instances in which the pronouncements of certain popes were very clearly contradicted – and even condemned – by their successors. He records that Zachary I rejected one of the matrimonial concessions granted by his immediate predecessor, Gregory III, calling it both wicked and detestable. Making no attempt to veil his sarcasm, Barnes writes in the margin, 'And indeed, the pope is unable to err.'[117]

But Barnes gets far greater mileage out of such reversals when he finally comes to the late ninth- and early tenth-century popes, when decrees were repealed and predecessors condemned with an astonishing regularity. The controversy began with the election of Formosus, who had previously been stripped of his priestly status by Pope John VIII.[118] He was restored by Martin II, and in 891 elected to the see of Rome. Though no controversy arose in the reign of his successor (which lasted less than a month), Stephen VII, upon his succession, convened a synod which abrogated the decrees of Formosus and invalidated his official acts. Moreover, Barnes records that his body was exhumed that it might be stripped of its papal dress and have two fingers removed – those raised in

[114] *Vitae*, sig. C1v: 'Victor vero suae sententiae pertinax defensor, missis in Asiam literis, Asiaticos Episcopos ab ecclesiae excludere decrevit tanquam hereseos criminis reos, quod … Romanae ecclesiae consentire nollent.'

[115] *Vitae*, sig. C1v: 'suae factionis Episcopi (inter quos Ireneus) restiterunt, monentes victorem ut ageret potius ea quae pacis essent, indignum esse rati propter dissonantiam Ceremoniarum, fidei consonantiam rumpere'.

[116] See *Vitae*, sig. C1r.

[117] *Vitae*, sig. H5v: 'Et tamen Papa non potest errare.'

[118] Barnes does not pass up the opportunity to make a doctrinal point here; he comments: 'Thus a bishop can become a layman, notwithstanding his indelible character' ['Ergo Episcopus potest fieri laicus, non obstante caractere indelebili']. *Vitae*, sig. M3v.

priestly benediction.[119] Regarding Stephen's successor, Romanus, Barnes finds nothing worthy of record except the fact that he pronounced the acts and decrees of Stephen invalid.[120] Of Romanus's successor also Barnes records no more than that he restored those decrees which Stephen had abrogated. He does, however, give voice to the question raised by such events: 'Which of these saints erred?'[121] The answer of Pope John IX was that Stephen had erred; he convoked a synod at Ravenna in which that pope's acts were officially anathematised. Barnes himself seems to find this a suitable answer, for he remarks that 'these are the fathers who are unable to err, because they are gathered in a council'.[122] That this should be read as no more than sarcasm becomes quickly apparent, however, as he very shortly moves on to record that Sergius III once again abolished all of the acts of Formosus, even invalidating those ordinations at which he had presided.[123]

In the light of this prolonged rhythm of pronouncement and condemnation, it is hardly surprising that Barnes would praise those popes who did nothing at all during their reigns. He calls Leo V 'the best pope at that time because he did nothing bad'. But he is quick to add that this is 'certainly because he quickly died'.[124] Significantly, however, he also regularly impresses upon the reader that not all popes relinquished their office on account of death. The tenth-century Christopher was deposed.[125] So too was John XII, by a synod of Italian bishops convened at the emperor's behest, a fact which prompts Barnes to remark once again that 'the emperor now holds primacy and is the head of the church'.[126] It was also an emperor who convened the council which deposed Benedict IX, Sylvester III, and Gregory VI, all of whom sat in the seventh year of the Emperor Henry III.[127] The scandal – and, to Barnes's mind, the humour – of three popes simultaneously claiming to occupy the chair of St Peter led him to ask facetiously: 'Who would not judge these fathers to be worthy heads of the papistical church?'[128]

It is evident that Barnes's compilation of such embarrassing anecdotes is meant to undermine any and all claims to papal primacy or papal infallibility. Clearly, if popes had demonstrably and legitimately been deposed by councils, rival popes, and even emperors, any assertion of primacy rings hollow. Such also would be the case for assertions of infallibility if it can be demonstrated that the

119 *Vitae*, sig. M4v.
120 *Vitae*, sig. M4v.
121 *Vitae*, sig. M5r: 'Quis istorum sanctorum erravit.'
122 *Vitae*, sig. M5r: 'Isti sunt patres qui non possunt errare, quia sunt congregati in concilio.'
123 *Vitae*, sig. M6v.
124 *Vitae*, sig. M5v: 'Optimus pontifex, tum quia nihil egit mali tum etiam quia cito moritur.' Cf. also sigs M4r, N1v, N6v, O2r.
125 *Vitae*, sigs M5v–M6r.
126 *Vitae*, sig. N3r: 'Iam Caesar primatum tenet, & est caput Ecclesiae.'
127 *Vitae*, sig. O6r.
128 *Vitae*, sig. O5v: 'Quis non iudicaret istos patres esse digna capita papisticae ecclesiae?'

acts and decrees of historical pontiffs had not only been rejected without consequence, but also reversed and even condemned. By implication, then, papal pronouncements on a variety of issues – practical or doctrinal – need not be judged binding on the whole church. This was precisely what he had attempted to show with regard to the doctrine and practice of the Mass. Similarly, this conclusion was meant to inform his reader's judgement concerning a topic to which he had already devoted some pages of his *Sentenciae* and *Supplicacion*, the marriage of priests.

Indeed, this topic, like the eucharist, is one to which he makes frequent reference throughout the *Vitae*. In his brief introductory summary of Peter's life, the only fact he deems worthy of marginal annotation is that, according to Clement, as recorded by Eusebius, the apostle had a wife.[129] The same, he records, was true of the evangelist Luke.[130] But clerical marriage was approved not only by prominent biblical figures; the practice was certainly accepted without question through the third century, for early in the fourth century Pope Sylvester decreed that priests should not only be content with one office, but also with one wife.[131] Barnes is aware, however, that it was during Sylvester's pontificate that the issue did become a point of contention. He records the Nicene canon which stated that clerics were to avoid cohabitation with any woman other than 'a mother or a sister or an aunt'.[132] But he devotes an entire page to explaining that council's eventual refusal to condemn the marriage of priests. As he had in his *Supplicacion* of 1534, he draws upon the *Tripartite History* for the story of Paphnutius, who argued that 'marriage is honourable, and to lay with one's own wife is a pious thing; and he thereby persuaded the council not to enact a law'.[133] To further bolster his claim that the post-Nicene church respected the council's decision, he regularly flags those popes who were themselves sons of the clergy, and not only those of the lowest ranks. Deusdedit, he records, was the son of a subdeacon;[134] but many others were sons of presbyters,[135] and even of bishops.[136] At the end of the fifth century, still the only statute against clerical marriage which Barnes can find worthy of mention is that of Gelasius I, who forbade bigamists from receiving holy orders. And even here, he notes wryly, Gelasius would allow for exceptions with a papal dispensation.[137]

Only when he comes to the ninth-century reign of Nicholas I does Barnes find

129 *Vitae*, sig. B1r.
130 *Vitae*, sig. B2r.
131 *Vitae*, sig. D2v.
132 *Vitae*, sig. D3v: 'aut mater, aut soror, aut amica [*sic*!]'.
133 *Vitae*, sig. D5v: 'Coniugium honorabile esse, & concubitum cum propria Coniuge castitatem esse, persuasitque Concilio ne eiusmodi lex ferreretur'.
134 *Vitae*, sig. G2r.
135 See *Vitae*, sigs E4r (Boniface I), E7v (Felix III).
136 See *Vitae*, sigs E8r (Gelasius I), F4v (Silverus), G3v (Theodorus I).
137 *Vitae*, sig. E8r.

the papacy once again attempting to assert its authority with regard to clerical celibacy.[138] But once again he finds a 'most learned' papal opponent in the person of Bishop Huldericus of Augsburg.[139] As he had done in his *Supplicacion*, Barnes quotes in full from the letter Huldericus sent to Nicholas. The letter appeals to Scripture, the apostolic canons, Augustine's correspondence, and the history of Cassiodorus to make the case that 'clergy may be advised to celibacy, but not compelled'.[140] An earlier decree of Gregory I, which had stated the contrary, Huldericus flatly dismisses as heresy.[141] And as if to confirm the church's decision in favour of Huldericus, Barnes once again begins to highlight the number of popes born of presbyters and bishops.[142] One of these, John X, Barnes happily notes was even the son of a pope (Sergius III). Despite his joy at this discovery, the sarcasm it elicits does undermine Barnes's argument. 'A son of the highest pontiff' he exclaims, 'but nevertheless born without a mother, since his father had vowed celibacy.'[143] The insinuation that John's birth was illegitimate, and that celibacy was indeed becoming the expected ideal, seems to have forced Barnes to alter his approach in the second half of the *Vitae*.

While noting that subsequent popes increasingly pronounced against clerical marriage – in the pontificate of Leo IX, for instance, he records that a synod at Mainz perpetually damned married priests[144] – Barnes begins to focus his attention on the refusal of various national churches to recognise such pronouncements as valid or binding. Thus he returns to an episode already given some attention in his *Supplicacion*: Gregory VII's attempt to enforce celibacy in the French and German churches. Failing at first to win support in these countries, Gregory convened a synod in Rome, drew up an official decree, and forwarded this to his bishops.[145] The hostile response of the French was that the decree was not only contrary to nature, but also contrary to the words of Christ, the doctrine of Paul, the canons of the apostles, and the council of Nicaea. It was, they said, impious and heretical, 'not of the Holy Spirit, but of Satan'.[146] The clergy of Germany reacted no more favourably.[147]

[138] See *Vitae*, sig. L1r–v. Strangely, he had not earlier emphasised the anti-marital statements of Gregory I, despite later noting how strongly Bishop Huldericus condemned them. See *Vitae*, sig. L4r.
[139] *Vitae*, sig. L1v: Given that Huldericus argues from Scripture, fathers, and histories – precisely as Barnes himself does – it is perhaps unsurprising that Barnes would describe the bishop with the word 'doctissima'. For Barnes's faulty identification of Huldericus, see above at p. 104 n. 168.
[140] *Vitae*, sig. L2r: 'Clerici sunt monendi ad celibatum, non cogendi.'
[141] *Vitae*, sig. L4r.
[142] See *Vitae*, sigs L7v (Hadrian II), M7r (John X), N5v (John XIII), N7v (John XV), O5r (John XIX).
[143] *Vitae*, sig. M7r: 'Filius summi pontificis, sed natus tamen sine matre, quia pater voverat celibatum.'
[144] *Vitae*, sig. O8v.
[145] *Vitae*, sig. R8r–v.
[146] *Vitae*, sigs R8v–S1r: 'non Spiritu sancto, sed Satana'.
[147] See *Vitae*, sigs S1r–S2v.

The above is not by any means an exhaustive analysis of the content of the *Vitae romanorum pontificum*. But by highlighting some of the issues which Barnes judged to be most important, and by demonstrating the manner in which he addressed these issues, it does allow some conclusions to be made. Most importantly, it reveals that, in spite of taking up a radically different genre of literature with which to address them, Barnes's fundamental concerns remain the same as those he had first voiced in his *Sentenciae* of 1530 and reiterated again in his *Supplications* of 1531 and 1534. That is, they are largely theological concerns. The doctrine and practice of the Mass, which had first received his attention in 1530, and clerical marriage, to which he had devoted the longest chapter in his 1534 *Supplicacion*, are once again given a great deal of attention in the pages of the *Vitae*. Likewise, the very central issue of ecclesiastical authority, a subject necessarily related to each of the individual doctrines and rites of the church, is revisited at length. And once again Barnes finds reason to reject popular claims of papal or conciliar infallibility, as well as those made for papal supremacy in the temporal and spiritual realms. He certainly does not refuse to draw attention to the moral lapses of individual pontiffs, but at the same time he never allows these to become his primary concern. Whether or not the *Vitae* can reasonably be said to have one central concern – and, if so, what exactly it is – is in fact a point of some confusion in the secondary literature. In conclusion, then, it is necessary to give brief attention to the question of Barnes's motivation and to the thesis or goal which he had set for himself in this work.

The thesis and goal of the *Vitae*

Barnes explains in his dedication that he intends in the *Vitae* simply 'to pursue the study of the acts of the Roman pontiffs'. But he also qualifies this statement to specify that he has no real interest in rumour, innuendo, or private deeds; instead he will only take account of those deeds 'which they did in public'.[148] The reason for thus limiting himself can be inferred from the manner in which he describes these papal acts. Only the public acts of the Roman pontiffs are those 'by which the seat of Roman religion and its authority grows and is confirmed'.[149] And as the substance of his text goes on to make plain, it is indeed the slow but persistent rise of a distinctly Roman religion that occupies his attention. That is, he is intent on showing that 'the empirical church was an historical growth rather than a divine development'.[150] By doing so, he seems to believe, he will have undermined the authority of this empirical, historical institution. Jean-François Gilmont is therefore quite correct to describe Barnes's work not as a constructive

[148] *Vitae*, sig. A5v: 'studia sequi, qui pontificum Romanorum res gestas in publicum dederunt'.
[149] *Vitae*, sig. B2r: 'per quae Romanae sedis Religio, & auctoritas aucta, & confirmata est'.
[150] Anderson, 'The Person and Position', 219 n. 3.

piece of theology, but as an 'enterprise of destruction'.[151] Some confusion has arisen, however, in the various attempts to pinpoint precisely what it is in the institutional church that Barnes considers most deserving of destruction.

According to Rainer Pineas's study of Barnes, the 'ultimate purpose' of the *Vitae* is 'to destroy the power of the clergy within England'.[152] When all is considered, however, this hardly seems an adequate summary of his 'ultimate purpose'. Kurt Stadtwald has argued, for instance, that 'Barnes ostensibly wrote the history for his monarch, but its obvious purpose was to further Thomas Cromwell's policy of stiffening the spines of German Protestants'.[153] It does indeed seem that Barnes's intended audience included continental readers. The simple fact that he chose to write in Latin, rather than in the English with which he had first addressed his King, is telling. If he did envision a continental audience, though, it would be difficult to explain why he might choose to emphasise clerical power within the borders of England alone. But no such explanation is needed, because Barnes in fact does not emphasise the power of 'the clergy', either in England or elsewhere. The only clerical office to receive his sustained attention is that of the pope himself.[154] Thus he explains to Henry VIII the reason for first taking up his pen:

> I desired most serene King, to write this history for your royal majesty, and to aid the churches with this service ... so that it might become plain to the world how cunningly and by desperate efforts the pope and his papacy came into the church of God, and how with shameful and horrible lies they boasted the papacy to be constituted by divine right.[155]

What Barnes does not say here about his history and about the papacy is perhaps as important as what he does say. Though he claims that the papal office is not a divine institution, and that it came into existence only by studied

151 Jean-François Gilmont, 'Les Martyrologes Protestants du XVIe Siècle: Essai de Présentation Générale' (Diss., Louvain, 1966), 89; quoted by Oliver K. Olson, *Matthias Flacius and the Survival of Luther's Reform* (Wiesbaden, 2002), 233.

152 Pineas, 'Robert Barnes', 63.

153 Stadtwald, 'Pope Alexander III's Humilation', 765. It is not entirely obvious that Cromwell's influence lay behind this writing. The *Vitae* certainly cannot be considered part of the official campaign of propaganda then taking place; and, in fact, there is no extant evidence of Cromwell or the King even acknowledging the work.

154 In the light of Barnes's obviously Lutheran leanings, the comment of Bruce Gordon, 'The Changing Face of Protestant History and Identity in the Sixteenth Century', in *Protestant History and Identity in Sixteenth-Century Europe*, vol. 1, *The Medieval Inheritance*, ed. Bruce Gordon (Aldershot, 1996), 15, is especially worth noting at this point: 'the Lutheran focus upon the papacy and Rome as the source of all corruption made possible a more positive view of the other offices and structures of the church, particularly diocesan and parochial, which were retained and employed by the Protestants'.

155 *Vitae*, sig. A8r: 'Volui igitur Serenissime Rex, has historiolas ad T.R. Maiestatem scribere, & hoc iuvare beneficio Ecclesias ... [u]t mundo palam fieret, quam subdole & perditis studiis Papatum suum Papa Ecclesiae Dei intruserit, & quam turpibus & foedis mendaciis iure divino cum Papatum iactarint esse constitutum'.

deception, he does not explicitly label the papacy with the title of Antichrist. 'The doctrine that the Pope is Antichrist', Christopher Hill quite rightly notes, 'was held by Robert Barnes.'[156] And Barnes had in fact used the very term itself in his earlier *Supplicatyon* to Henry.[157] It is perhaps unsurprising, therefore, that some commentators would conclude that this work devoted entirely to papal history must have been 'organized around the thesis that the popes were the personification of the antichrist',[158] or that 'The goal is to present the papacy in the darkest possible colors, to convince all who read that it is indeed the Antichrist.'[159] But the fact that Barnes studiously avoids introducing the Antichrist title anywhere in this work must certainly be considered significant. Not only is this so because Barnes himself had previously used the term, but also because a number of his predecessors and contemporaries had done the same, but with very different and sometimes very specific implications. It has long been observed, for example, that the Lollards made frequent use of the Antichrist label, but that their identification of the pope with this biblical figure was overwhelmingly based upon moral rather than theological considerations.[160] The same was true even of those writers more closely associated with Barnes, such as the contemporary polemicist William Tyndale. Though he was unhesitating in his references to the pope as Antichrist, Tyndale's historical identification also was 'tied to, and was limited by, a theory of moral example'.[161] In the light of Barnes's unwillingness to make papal morality a major focus of his own history, it is perhaps understandable that he would avoid the introduction of terminology which might give readers the impression that moral issues were in fact central to his argument.

Another strain of Antichrist polemic, equally influential in the early sixteenth century but also, it would seem, at odds with Barnes's own project, is the eschatological and apocalyptic interpretation in which an historical Antichrist heralded the fulfilment of biblical prophecy and the advent of the last days. This historicising of biblical prophecy, first given real prominence in the medieval writings of Joachim of Fiore, became increasingly popular with many early reformers, particularly those engaged in producing their own works of history.[162] So, for example, one of Barnes's own sources, the *Chronica Carionis*, made the

156 Christopher Hill, *Antichrist in Seventeenth-Century England* (Oxford, 1971), 9.
157 See, e.g., *Supplicatyon* (1531), fos 100v, 123r.
158 Edwards, *Luther's Last Battles*, 78.
159 Anderson, 'The Person and Position', 162.
160 See, e.g., Bauckham, *Tudor Apocalypse*, 93.
161 Firth, *The Apocalyptic Tradition*, 26.
162 See, e.g., R.B. Barnes, *Prophecy and Gnosis: Apocalypticism in the Wake of the Lutheran Reformation* (Stanford, 1988), 103, who asserts that 'Apocalyptic expectancy and a growing interest in history were thus two sides of the same coin.' For Joachim and his influence, the works of Marjorie Reeves remain unparalleled; see, e.g., *The Influence of Prophecy in the Later Middle Ages: A Study in Joachimism* (Oxford, 1969), and her more recently published, *The Prophetic Sense of History in Medieval and Renaissance Europe* (Aldershot, 1999).

apocalyptic prophecies of Daniel and Elias central to its chronological and thematic organisation. Commenting upon this work, one author has in fact argued that 'there could hardly have been a work better calculated to inspire investigation into prophetic epochs and the approach of the Last Day'.[163] Nevertheless, Barnes himself did remain uninspired. At no point in his survey of Roman pontiffs does he enter into the sort of prophetic speculation concerning a papal Antichrist which was sometimes taken up even by his closest associates in Germany.[164] Indeed, Barnes offers no schematic framework at all in which to arrange the information found in his *Vitae*.[165] Cautious commentators have therefore made note of the fact that Barnes 'rejected the tendency to historicize the biblical prophecies',[166] and that 'there is no hint that this history fulfilled specific prophecies or that the world was near its end'.[167] Therefore any suggestion that his primary aim was to reveal the identity of the papacy as Antichrist must not only account for his consistent refusal to employ the term itself; it must also be qualified with the observation that Barnes's notion of Antichrist seems to have differed considerably from two of the most popular interpretations of this figure.

Because it is evident that the attention Barnes gives the papacy has nothing to do with speculative matters of prophecy and eschatology, some writers have concluded that he is predominantly concerned with very practical and even secular matters. Thus Rainer Pineas emphasises Barnes's use of 'secular' history, and notes that the *Vitae* is concerned especially with the growth of the papacy's temporal power.[168] Rosemary O'Day suggests that, in Barnes's view, 'the very decline of the Church of Rome was due in large part to the papacy's usurpation of temporal powers'.[169] Going even further, Charles Anderson has concluded that 'The whole of the *Vitae Romanorum Pontificum* is built around this thesis, and tries to demonstrate the illegal growth of papal temporal power.'[170] As has been illustrated above, Barnes certainly is concerned to trace the development of the papacy's exercise of temporal power. In fact, he had proclaimed already in his introduction that he would take pains to point out 'how disgracefully kings, princes, majesties, and crowns have been made a laughing stock'.[171] But whether this is his central thesis, or the concern of 'the whole' of his work, certainly remains questionable.

Even before Barnes wrote his introductory dedication to Henry VIII – which

163 Barnes, *Prophecy and Gnosis*, 108.
164 See, e.g., Barnes, *Prophecy and Gnosis*, 39–44, 103–7.
165 See Fairfield, *John Bale*, 57.
166 Bostick, *The Antichrist and the Lollards*, 52 n. 14.
167 Firth, *The Apocalyptic Tradition*, 29.
168 Pineas, 'Robert Barnes', 56.
169 O'Day, *The Debate on the English Reformation*, 11.
170 Anderson, 'The Person and Position', 224.
171 *Vitae*, sig. A6r–v: 'quam atrociter e Regum, Principumque maiestatibus, & coronis ludibria fecerint'.

he did several months before the work was finally published – the issue of the pope's authority over temporal rulers had been decisively concluded in England. Barnes notes, in fact, that this partially prompts his writing,

> because I understand, most serene lord King, how greatly those cowled ones and most virulent disparagers rage against the name of your royal majesty on account of that excellent deed by which you commanded the proud and damnable tyranny of the Roman popes out of your realm.[172]

The fact that Henry had already acted to exclude papal authority from his realm offered Barnes ample opportunity to flatter his prince, and indeed he does. He tells him that 'In this matter you, King, most clearly showed the highest example among kings.'[173] Continuing, he reminds Henry that

> you not only removed the auxiliaries of papal tyranny, but beat down that repulsive servitude and captivity, and left it bare to be destroyed with the imminent coming of Christ. This deed of your King's majesty, truly magnificent, excelled not only the hopes and expectations of all good and pious men, but even the boldness of papal tyranny itself (of which none is or was greater in the world).[174]

With such flattery Barnes is clearly attempting to ingratiate himself, not only by praising Henry's actions, but also more subtly by consistently addressing him as 'your majesty'. Only in the previous year had this designation begun to appear in royal statutes and proclamations, replacing traditional titles such as 'grace', 'lord', and 'highness';[175] by appealing to this title Barnes seems consciously to be playing up the King's newly discovered imperial status.

Though subtle, the vocabulary is undoubtedly significant, and it helps partially to explain that which some commentators have found puzzling. Barnes, like those before him who had drawn upon history to bolster the Royal Supremacy, gave more attention to papal-imperial conflicts than to those of a specifically English nature.[176] Contrary to the claim first made by William Clebsch and later repeated by James McGoldrick, it is not at all the case that 'The only popes on [Barnes's]

172 *Vitae*, sig. A5r: 'Cum intellexissem Sereniss. Domine Rex, quantopere in nomen tuae R. Maiestatis saevirent cucullati illi quidam & virulentissimi obtrectatores, proper illud eximium facinus, quo Romani Papae tyrannidem e tuo regno voluisti sublatum & damnatam'. Barnes's mention of 'cowled ones' is very likely meant to be a timely reference to the Observant Franciscans – the order which proved most troublesome to Henry in the first half of the 1530s – and his choice of the term 'obtrectatores' looks also to be a pun on their name.

173 *Vitae*, sig. A6v: 'In qua re tu clarissime Rex primum exemplum inter Reges ostendisti.'

174 *Vitae*, sig. A7r: 'Papali tyrannidi non solum auxilia subtraxeris, Sed foedam illam servitutem & captivitatem excusseris, nudamque reliqueris, destruendam venturo propediem Christo. Superat hoc facinus tuae Regiae maiestatis, vere regium, non solum omnium bonorum & piorum spem & expectationem, sed etiam ipsam Papae tyranni (quae nulla est aut fuit in orbe maior) confidentiam.'

175 Rex, *Henry VIII and the English Reformation*, 28.

176 See, e.g., Stadtwald, 'Pope Alexander III's Humilation', 765; Lock, 'Plantagenets against the Papacy', 154.

list to receive significant coverage are those who were noteworthy for their relations with England.'[177] In fact, in his coverage of one such pope, Alexander III, Barnes focuses only on his controversy with the German emperor and makes no mention at all of a well-known episode with which he could have capitalised on particularly English anti-papal sentiment: the conflict between Archbishop Thomas Becket and King Henry II, in which Alexander aligned himself against the King.[178] This is not to say that Barnes neglected issues of special interest to English readers. In support of the contention that there had been a Christian church in Britain long before a papal church, he repeats the legend of King Lucius being converted to Christianity with his subjects some four hundred years before 'England received the papist faith' with the arrival of the missionary Augustine.[179] And Pineas is probably correct to see a 'double appeal to English nationalism' in Barnes's record of the eighth-century papal alliance with the French, which he believes was intended to control other kings.[180]

On the whole, however, Barnes's survey of temporal rulers being subjected to the papacy does largely focus on examples drawn from imperial history. But far from being irrelevant to English circumstances, the Crown's recent assertion that 'this realm of England is an empire' made such examples both relevant and timely.[181] By giving implicit assent to Henry's imperial status, and by then highlighting the manner in which his King had put an end to centuries of papal encroachment on imperial prerogatives, Barnes was able to ingratiate himself to a far greater extent than he had in his previous works. But it is also clear that, rather than being an end in itself, the flattery made possible by highlighting Henry's expulsion of a rival authority is meant to serve as a means to another end. The rejection of the pope's most visible expression of power is, for Barnes, only the beginning of the good the King might do in his realm. This too is made apparent in his dedicatory address:

> Now surely your royal majesty will make truly glorious that title which the Roman pope gave to you (but for a very different hope and belief) and commanded you to be called – Defender of the Faith – clearly making himself in his own person a prophet. For to all people of right faith it is manifest that the pope with his papacy was and is a devastator of faith. … [Y]ou rightly ejected and devastated this devastator of your realm; you are a defender of the faith.[182]

[177] McGoldrick, *Luther's English Connection*, 146; cf. Clebsch, *England's Earliest Protestants*, 73. Clebsch names twelve such popes; but only half of these, in Barnes's account, have any significant dealings with England or her kings.
[178] See *Vitae*, sigs Y6v–Z6v. Barnes says no more than that Thomas was killed at the time, and that the papists now consider him a saint. See sig. Z6v.
[179] *Vitae*, sig. F8r: 'Anglia recepit fidem Papisticam'. Cf. sig. B8r.
[180] Pineas, 'Robert Barnes', 57. See *Vitae*, sigs H4v–H5r.
[181] *DER, 78.*
[182] *Vitae*, sig. A7v: 'Nunc certe vere gloriosum fecit T.R.M. illum titulum, quem tibi Rom. Papa

Before concluding his dedication, Barnes had subtly shifted the reader's attention from matters of politics to matters of faith. The change of verb tense is also significant. Henry had already refuted the pope's claim of supremacy in England, for which he deserved praise; but, Barnes says, now, especially in the light of Christ's 'imminent' return, the time has come to live up to the true meaning of his role as Defender of the Faith. To reject papal power is not enough; the King must also allow and promote the rejection of the papal faith. To encourage him in this endeavour, Barnes will not only outline the pope's abuse of temporal authority; he will also describe

> how horrible mendacity, idolatry, and all types of abomination devastate the church, and how so many millions of souls are led to fill up the insatiable inferno.[183]

The responsibility for this state of affairs he bluntly attributes to the false faith of Rome. Therefore he will have to demonstrate that this faith differs radically from that of the apostles, that it is in fact a novel and heretical invention.

It is this task which consumes the greatest portion of the *Vitae*, and which can reasonably be called his primary aim and thesis. This explains his consistent emphasis on essentially doctrinal topics such as the Mass and clerical celibacy. These, Barnes knew, Henry was in no great hurry to reject; yet to his mind they epitomised the novel, heretical, and in some ways central doctrines of the Roman church. He therefore set himself the goal of demonstrating the inconsistencies and contradictions evident in papal decrees, conciliar decisions, and canon law, thereby undermining not only these individual doctrines, but also the very foundation upon which all Roman doctrine was built. Barnes's 'enterprise of destruction' was first and foremost a doctrinal and theological enterprise. The *Vitae*, unlike his more explicitly theological productions, was offered to the King as a work of history; but, as Katharine Firth has rightly suggested, Barnes was a proponent of 'a Lutheran appreciation of history as the fortunes of doctrine'.[184] Just as the theological arguments set forth in his *Sentenciae* and *Supplications* might legitimately be described as 'historical' theology, so too might the sustained historical argument of the *Vitae* be characterised as a particularly 'doctrinal' history. It is this consistent interaction and mutual interdependence of history and theology in Barnes's thought which, in the next chapter, will be described as the defining, and even peculiar, characteristic of his contribution to the debates of the early sixteenth-century reformation.

dedit (Sed longe diversa spe & opinione) & defensorem fidei appellari iussit, plane sibi ipsi, & in caput suum propheta factus. Nam cum hoc omnibus rectae fidei hominibus manifestum sit, Papam cum suo Papatu, fuisse & esse vastatorem fidei. ... hunc Vastatorem e regno tuo eieceris & vastaveris, recte, fidei defensor sit'.

183 *Vitae*, sig. A6v: 'quam horribilibus mendaciis, idolatriis, omnium generum flagiciis, Ecclesiam vastaverint, & animarum tot milia, quae ipsum infernum insaturabilem, explere'.

184 Firth, *The Apocalyptic Tradition*, 110.

5

THE HISTORICAL-THEOLOGICAL PROGRAMME OF ROBERT BARNES

The emphasis of the previous two chapters has been placed on the manner in which Robert Barnes makes conscious and sustained use of historical sources and historical arguments in what is primarily a theological polemic. On the basis of the evidence there presented, it has become clear that his use of history is more than an afterthought or occasional whim; it is given a central place in his published works. As has been stressed by more than one commentator, however, evangelical appeals to history were neither inevitable nor logically necessary in the controversies of the sixteenth century.[1] This is especially true in the case of reformers such as Barnes, who, with his strong Lutheran leanings, elevated the principle of *sola scriptura* to a place of unquestioned importance in his theology. In fact, in the light of a conservative insistence on the insufficiency of Scripture alone, and a corresponding emphasis on the authority of history and tradition as necessary complements to that of Scripture, any consistent evangelical reliance on historical argument might appear quite out of place. And indeed, some authors have asserted that such dual emphases are inherently self-contradictory.[2]

Any attempt to summarise the character of Barnes's historical-theological programme must therefore give some focused attention to his conception of the nature and use of such potentially incompatible authorities. Coming to terms with Barnes's own understanding of these two authorities will then allow for some

[1] See, e.g., Alec Ryrie, 'The Problem of Legitimacy and Precedent in English Protestantism, 1539–47', in *Protestant History and Identity in Sixteenth-Century Europe*, vol. 1, *The Medieval Inheritance*, ed. Bruce Gordon (Aldershot, 1996), 78, and Thomas Betteridge, *Tudor Histories of the English Reformations, 1530–83* (Aldershot, 1999), 41, 81.

[2] See, e.g., Betteridge, *Tudor Histories*, 96–7, as well as Pontien Polman, *L'élément historique dans la controverse religieuse du XVIe siècle* (Gembloux, 1932), 539. Bruce Gordon has made a similar claim with regard to the Protestant emphasis on 'faith alone', saying this principle 'de-emphasised historical events and personalities'. Bruce Gordon, ' "This Worthy Witness of Christ": Protestant uses of Savonarola in the Sixteenth Century', in *Protestant History and Identity in Sixteenth-Century Europe*, vol. 1, *The Medieval Inheritance*, ed. Bruce Gordon (Aldershot, 1996), 107.

comparison of his programme with that of his contemporaries in England as well as on the continent. The conclusion reached by such comparison will finally allow for the formulation of a tentative answer to the question of whether Barnes's contributions to the doctrinal controversies of his day were particularly significant or in any way original.

History, theology, and authority

With regard to the question of theological authority, modern commentators have concluded that Barnes did indeed follow Luther and the majority of early evangelicals in confessing the unique status of Scripture. Neelak Tjernagel, for instance, asserts that Barnes viewed the Bible as 'the only infallible source of religious knowledge'.[3] Likewise, James McGoldrick has portrayed him as 'an unswerving exponent of the Protestant principle of *sola scriptura*'.[4] Nor are twentieth-century observers alone in having reached such conclusions. Already in the sixteenth century there were those who pronounced similar judgements. When Miles Coverdale defended his former prior against the traditionalist John Standish's attempt to blacken Barnes's posthumous reputation, he noted that Standish had been particularly vexed by the fact that Barnes 'would never willingly grant anything but what was in Scripture'.[5]

Even a brief examination of Barnes's own statements seem to confirm the above conclusions. A high regard for Scripture is already evident as early as the first controversy in which he was involved, that precipitated by his Christmas Eve sermon of 1525. Despite the extant evidence which indicates that there was very little of an explicitly evangelical nature in the sermon itself, the peculiar authority of Scripture did become a point of contention in his ensuing trial. Interviewed before the bishops of Rochester, St Asaph, and Bath and Wells, Barnes ventured to suggest that all those who died for the word of God are martyrs.[6] Though this was not an obvious or coherent articulation of the doctrine of *sola scriptura*, such a statement was of course ill-received by his conservative examiners. John Clerk, the bishop of Bath, bluntly exclaimed that he would make Barnes 'frye for thys'.[7] Although Barnes's statement at that time was not an unambiguous assertion of *sola scriptura*, when he took the opportunity to recount the events of his trial some years later he did go on in the same work to explain why those who died in the defence of Scripture might reasonably be judged martyrs. He argues in his *Supplicatyon* of 1531 that the identity of Antichrist is revealed most clearly in the

3 Tjernagel, *Reformation Essays*, 107.
4 McGoldrick, *Luther's English Connection*, 70.
5 Coverdale, *Remains*, 414.
6 *Supplicatyon* (1531), fo. 25r–v.
7 *Supplicatyon* (1531), fo. 25v.

condemnation of Scripture and those who would read it.[8] His reasoning is that 'to take away scripturs from lay men / ys as muche as to take away christ from them'.[9] The clear implication of this line of argument is that Scripture alone provides a true revelation of the person and work of Christ.[10]

What Barnes merely implied in the quotation above was also made more explicit in the same work. On the unique and necessary place of Scripture in the church he wrote,

> lett oure spreet intende as welle as he cane / studdy hys beste / a plye hym selfe to goodnes / after the uttermost of his power and yet is it but wysdom of the fleshe and hath no wytnes of god.[11]

Likewise he insists the church must 'beleve and reseve alonly his word', without which 'we cane do nothinge but erre'.[12] And this conclusion is not at all limited to Barnes's thinking in 1531. The same judgement is expressed five years later, for instance, in the Wittenberg Articles, which had been drafted with Barnes's participation. In the article devoted to original sin the authors state their belief that after the fall and apart from Scripture, 'we do not have any reliable knowledge of God'.[13] That Barnes did indeed believe this becomes all the more apparent in his comments upon alternative authorities such as autonomous human reason. Not unlike Luther, Barnes is fond of prefacing his references to 'reason' with disparaging adjectives such as 'blind presumtuous / & damnable'.[14] When he contrasts Scripture and reason such descriptive terms are especially employed. Common, for example, is his contrast of 'carnal reason' with the 'very grounde' and 'suer ancore' of the 'invincible scripturs'.[15]

Barnes's conservative opponents had not explicitly questioned the source or authority of Scripture; nevertheless, he takes some pains to explain his reasons for thinking it invincible. '[Y]ou wyll not deny', he asks, 'but scripture is geven us of god?'[16] Barnes himself refers to it as 'sent from hevyn',[17] and labels it 'the holy testament of christ Jesus'[18] and 'our father of hevyns testament'.[19] Completing his description of Scripture's trinitarian origins, he also refers to the Bible as 'the

8 *Supplicatyon* (1531), fo. 100v.
9 *Supplicatyon* (1531), fo. 108v; cf. fo. 101v.
10 See, for example, his statements concerning the relationship between Christ and Scripture at *Supplicatyon* (1531), fos 69v and 48r.
11 *Supplicatyon* (1531), fos 84v–85r.
12 *Supplicatyon* (1531), fo. 70r.
13 *DER*, 121.
14 *Supplicatyon* (1531), fo. 86r, *et passim*.
15 *Supplicatyon* (1531), fos 36v, 125v, 95r.
16 *Supplicatyon* (1531), fo. 103v.
17 *Supplicatyon* (1531), fo. 100v.
18 *Supplicatyon* (1531), fo. 101r.
19 *Supplicatyon* (1531), fo. 113v.

playne scripture of the holy gost'[20] and 'the gyft of the holy gost'.[21] This equation of the Holy Spirit with the revelation of Scripture is so regularly made that, when quoting from it, Barnes will often say no more than 'the holy gost saythe'.[22] Likewise, when he finds reason to challenge the manner in which his opponents handle particular passages, he gives free reign to his sarcasm, stating for example that 'Nowe must the holy gost change his wordes / for he hath new scole masters'.[23]

The above sufficiently illustrates Barnes's high view of Scripture, a view which certainly explains his emphasis on the authority of Scripture alone. That which Anthony Lane has stressed with reference to John Calvin's use of Scripture can therefore also be affirmed with regard to Barnes's: its place of primacy is dictated by 'a theological, not merely a humanist, principle'.[24] That is, Barnes does not simply elevate Scripture to the position of highest authority because it is the most ancient of the historical sources relevant to Christianity. Were this his justification, it would be much easier to account for the frequency with which he appeals to other historical sources. In the event, however, Barnes posits a qualitative difference between 'Scripture' and 'history'.[25] The fact that he does so, emphasising Scripture's divine origins and infallible nature while at the same time calling most frequently upon the testimony of history, undermines Pontien Polman's contention that Protestant polemicists were forced to soften their stance on infallibility in order to make use of historical argumentation.[26]

A similar conclusion must also be qualified with reference to Barnes. Polman saw in the Protestant appeal to history not only an implicit doubt concerning Scripture's infallibility, but also its sufficiency. He argued that the evangelical use of history was in some respect inevitable as reformers increasingly felt the need for an extra-biblical authority which might serve to curb the plethora of private interpretations of Scripture.[27] More recently, Leslie Fairfield has voiced a

20 *Supplicatyon* (1531), fo. 39r.
21 *Supplicatyon* (1531), fo. 104v.
22 See, e.g., *Supplicatyon* (1531), fos 52r and 57r.
23 *Supplicatyon* (1531), fo. 97r.
24 A.N.S. Lane, *John Calvin: Student of the Church Fathers* (Edinburgh, 1999), 36.
25 There is one passage in the 1531 *Supplicatyon* (fo. 52r) where this distinction might appear less than absolute. Assertions of the infallibility of Scripture inevitably give rise to questions regarding the content of Scripture and by whom it is defined. In this context Barnes claims in passing that 'if I denyed thys pystelle to be Saynt Jamys / yow coulde not prove yt by the auctoryte of the church / for she hathe allways douted of yt / as yt ys open / In ecclestica [*sic*] hystoria'. Though it is possible to read this statement as an admission that the biblical books have received their canonical, and therefore authoritative, status only by assent of the historical, institutional church, this reading is unlikely. Instead Barnes seems to be saying the opposite: the authority of the biblical books cannot be proven with reference to the lesser authority of the historical church, which, as Eusebius had pointed out, had always been indecisive.
26 Polman, *L'élément historique*, 539.
27 See Polman, *L'élément historique*, 73–6, where this argument is made with reference to Calvin. Betteridge, *Tudor Histories*, 95 and 97, makes similar observations concerning Bale.

similar judgement, describing the Protestant turn to history as part of a search for a normative period in the church's past which, though extra-biblical, could be used as a standard to measure the church's doctrines and ceremonies.[28] This is undoubtedly true with respect to a number of those who made polemical use of the historical record. Barnes's contemporary William Tyndale, whose works will be discussed more fully below, was one of many who expressed a belief in an early 'golden age' of the church's history.[29] John Bale, who serves as Fairfield's primary point of reference, took a similar view, which, Fairfield is careful to point out, differs greatly from that of Barnes. Though both, especially in their histories of the papacy, drew largely from the same sources, Fairfield notes that they 'differed radically in their attitude to the pre-Constantinian Church'.[30] Barnes, for example, was quite content to make mention of Pope Felix I instituting offices for the dead, or Calixtus I making lavish expenditures for the adornment of churches.[31] Bale, on the other hand, insists that the earlier historians who had recorded such information were nothing other than liars and blasphemers. His reason for doing so, Fairfield explains, was his desire 'to show that the pre-Constantinian Church had not been marred by the kind of superstition which he and the English Church had rejected'.[32] Fairfield's corresponding comment on Barnes's method is telling: 'Since the Bible was his only norm, he quite happily copied all the material he could find in Platina and the others which showed the early popes inventing rites and pious observances'.[33]

Rather than hindering any appeal to history, then, it would appear that Barnes's insistence on *sola scriptura* both motivated such a method and in fact enhanced his use of it. Again, comparison with Bale is instructive. Fairfield rightly emphasises that his disagreement with Barnes 'did not arise from any greater critical sense on Bale's part'.[34] What he does not go so far as to state is that the very opposite might be true. It seems, however, that this is indeed the case. That is, Bale's deductive approach to history at least partially explains the fact that Barnes 'is far more accurate than Tyndale and Bale in the polemical use of history'.[35] Unencumbered by the need to portray the early church as the doctrinally pristine institution of a golden age, Barnes was thus free to deal more honestly with his sources than prominent polemicists writing both before and after him.

28 Fairfield, *John Bale*, 100–1.

29 See O'Day, *The Debate on the English Reformation*, 8.

30 Fairfield, *John Bale*, 103.

31 *Vitae*, sigs C7r, C2v.

32 Fairfield, *John Bale*, 104.

33 Fairfield, *John Bale*, 103–4. Barnes's willingness to do so, combined with the fact that his history extends only into the twelfth century, might also necessitate the qualification of Polman's suggestion that the reformers were primarily interested in later history, where they believed the introduction of error was most obvious. See, e.g., Polman, *L'élément historique*, 185–6.

34 Fairfield, *John Bale*, 105.

35 Pineas, 'Robert Barnes', 67.

Given his frequent employment of historical argumentation, however, Barnes's judgement regarding Scripture's sufficiency must be carefully defined. This is all the more necessary as it is this point which has elicited much confusion concerning the evangelical principle of *sola scriptura*. One extreme example of such confusion is Thomas Betteridge's characterisation of this principle as the belief that all extra-biblical information is by its very nature false. Commenting, for example, upon the *Confutation of Unwritten Verities*, an anonymously edited work compiled from the notebooks of Thomas Cranmer, Betteridge summarises the evangelical conception of *sola scriptura* by saying, 'Unwritten verities, truths not found in Scripture, are untruthful except when exposing the lies of papists'.[36] Such a simplification, however, is not quite fair to the point being made in the *Confutation*; the claim there was simply that unwritten verities have no authority to establish doctrine.[37] Having missed this subtle point, Betteridge goes on to ask: 'Why should records of the past, histories, have any authority in terms of people whose beliefs are based on a direct personal interpretation of the Bible?'[38] And again:

> [I]n a world based entirely on Scripture what place is there for history? Indeed if history, and all other non-scriptural writing, lacks all authority or truthfulness as an unwritten verity what is the point of writing?[39]

Such questions, of course, are equally applicable to Barnes. But Barnes, like Cranmer and his editor, was more cautious than Betteridge allows in making claims about the nature and use of both biblical and extra-biblical sources. Barnes too claims no more than that Scripture alone is to be judged authoritative in determining doctrines which command the assent of the church.[40] Extra-biblical literature is not of itself to be impugned; only when it is judged normative or binding in doctrinal matters are its conclusions condemned as 'invencions of corrupted reson / and persuasions of the devell'.[41]

Barnes's firm distinction between the natures of Scripture and history corresponds to a similar distinction made between the proper uses of both. These clear demarcations distinguish Barnes from those contemporaries – both conservative and evangelical – who attempted to forge a mutually interdependent relationship between history and Scripture. Illustrative of the conservative attempt are those debates of the 1520s which dealt especially with the issues of ecclesiastical authority. Preceding the 1526 Disputation of Baden, for example, evangelicals

36 Betteridge, *Tudor Histories*, 94.
37 They are 'not able to prove any doctrine' and have no authority 'to make articles of our faith'. Cranmer, *Miscellaneous Writings*, 22, 36.
38 Betteridge, *Tudor Histories*, 96.
39 Betteridge, *Tudor Histories*, 97.
40 See, e.g., *Supplicatyon* (1531), fo. 66r–v.
41 *Supplicatyon* (1531), fo. 77r.

such as Zwingli had been criticised for failing to define sufficiently their understanding of the relation between Scripture and historical tradition.[42] In that disputation itself, Johann Eck attempted to prevent the same charge from being levelled against conservatives by clearly stating his own position on the matter:

> If he asks me whether a point of doctrine which is not in the Bible is also to be accepted, I answer: I proclaim that which the Church teaches or proclaims; I believe it whether it is written down or not, for example, that Mary was a virgin or that Sunday should be observed although this is not ordered by the Scripture.[43]

Eck's position is representative of the conservative argument that the historical tradition of the church remains authoritative even if it cannot be supported with a clear text of Scripture. In the same debate he also made equally plain that the church and her tradition are 'the highest court of appeal in cases where the Scripture is susceptible to different interpretations'.[44] That is, history relates to Scripture as a necessary interpretive aid. History interprets Scripture. Without recourse to the church's history – the opinions of its fathers, the pronouncements of its popes, councils, and lawyers, and the traditional rites of its congregations – Scripture will remain in part unclear.

More subtle, yet no less significant, was the manner in which many evangelicals, especially those of a historical bent, were also beginning to define the interdependent relation between Scripture and history. Simply stated, they proposed the converse of the conservative position. Scripture is not to be interpreted in the light of history, but history is to be interpreted in the light of Scripture. This inclination to make Scripture explain history is particularly evident in the growing number of chronicles and histories produced by reformers both in England and on the continent. The tendency of evangelical chroniclers, such as Johann Carion, to organise their works according to the prophetic schemes of Daniel and Elias has been previously noted. And far from being unusual, such biblically derived schemes have been described as a 'coin of common intellectual currency' in the sixteenth century.[45] The historically driven polemic of the English reformer John Bale is, once again, particularly noteworthy. Commenting on the scheme employed in Bale's history of the popes, Leslie Fairfield has rightly observed that 'this very pattern (derived from the Bible rather than the historical data) reinforced his inclination to interpret his evidence in light of the revealed Truth'.[46] In

[42] See Irena Backus, *The Disputations of Baden, 1526 and Berne, 1528: Neutralizing the Early Church* (Princeton, 1993), 10.
[43] Quoted by Backus, *The Disputations*, 44–5.
[44] Backus, *The Disputations*, 42–3.
[45] Robert Kolb, *For All The Saints: Changing Perceptions of Martyrdom and Sainthood in the Lutheran Reformation* (Macon, GA, 1987), 22.
[46] Fairfield, *John Bale*, 105.

Bale's case especially, but also in the works of English writers such as William Tyndale and George Joye, there was a concerted effort to align the history of the church not only with Scripture, but especially with the periodisation found in the book of Revelation.[47]

It was an approach to Revelation as 'a microcosm of Scripture' that encouraged the production of specifically apocalyptic histories such as those noted in the previous chapter, works in which the interdependence of Scripture and history becomes most apparent.[48] But it is precisely in such works that significant problems also become most apparent. As already noted, central to the apocalyptic conception of history was the identification of Antichrist, an identification which could only be made with reference to Scripture. As Howard Hotson has astutely observed, however, any historical identification of Antichrist on the basis of Revelation had also to deal with the preceding millennium described in that book's twentieth chapter. As a consequence, wherever the idea of a papal Antichrist was accepted, the idea of a past millennium was also accepted.[49] The particular difficulty caused by this fact is described by Hotson:

> [Z]ealous investigation into the origins of papal supremacy and the theological, liturgical and ecclesiastical usages associated with it soon revealed that they were rather older than the doctrine of a medieval millennium could comfortably accommodate.[50]

This would have especially been the case for an historical investigation such as that carried out in Barnes's *Vitae romanorum pontificum*, where, unlike Bale, he does concede the very early introduction of questionable theological and liturgical innovations.

As intimated in his preface to that work, Barnes did not remain unaffected by certain apocalyptic notions, such as a belief in the imminent return of Christ. But by refusing to impose such beliefs upon his historical method he is able to avoid some of the problems inevitably raised by attempting to establish an interdependent relationship between Scripture and history. For example, he avoids the potential tensions highlighted by Thomas Betteridge, who has suggested that

> the appearance of apocalyptic imagery in a work of history radically undermines the truthfulness of the historical text by introducing an inherently ahistorical, if not anti-historical, truth into its midst. In other words, once an event becomes apocalyptic it implicitly becomes not of history and, in a sense, drops out of a historical discourse; it becomes scriptural.[51]

47 See Parish, 'Beastly is their living', 139.
48 Parish, 'Beastly is their living', 152.
49 Howard Hotson, 'The Historiographical Origins of Calvinist Millenarianism', in *Protestant History and Identity in Sixteenth-Century Europe*, vol. 2, *The Later Reformation*, ed. Bruce Gordon (Aldershot, 1996), 164.
50 Hotson, 'Historiographical Origins', 170.
51 Betteridge, *Tudor Histories*, 15–16.

Upon examining Barnes's works one is forced to wonder if, as Katharine Firth suggests, 'The materials for the apocalyptic tradition were being assembled without any commitment to the thematic structure of prophecy',[52] or if, having perceived the problems inherent in such a structure, Barnes moved beyond a simple lack of commitment to a very conscious rejection of any such commitment.

As Barnes himself offers no explanation for proceeding as he does, no absolutely decisive answer can be offered. It is worth noting, however, that his largely historical argumentation not only fails to make any significant use of Revelation; it makes comparatively little use of biblical exegesis at all. As William Clebsch has bluntly stated upon examination of Barnes's works, 'he made no original study of the Bible'.[53] Clebsch is not mistaken; in none of Barnes's writings does an original, or even an extensive, interpretation of Scripture appear. Quotations abound, but detailed analysis is rare indeed. In fact, Barnes's biblical quotations come far more frequently from the vernacular New Testament of William Tyndale than they do from the authoritatively accepted Vulgate. Likewise, despite the often repeated suggestion that he was an admirer, and perhaps even a one-time pupil, of Erasmus, nowhere does he give evidence of having made use of that humanist's critical edition of the New Testament in its original Greek. Indeed, the only indications that Barnes had any knowledge of that biblical language at all are a few scattered uses of Greek terms, none of which provide readers with any more information than their Latin or English equivalents.[54]

Whether prompted by choice or necessity, Barnes's evident unwillingness to engage in any sustained examination of, or commentary upon, the biblical texts sets him apart from the great majority of his evangelical counterparts. It also sheds further light on the intentions which motivate his writing. Because he believes Scripture to be the sole authority for the establishment of Christian doctrine, yet nevertheless offers little in the way of biblical analysis which might support specifically evangelical dogma, it would appear that Barnes's intentions lie elsewhere. By so often making historical argumentation his choice of polemical method, but by refusing to relate history too closely to the nature and purpose of Scripture, he steers a middle way between his evangelical and conservative contemporaries. Against conservative claims such as those made by Eck, he is able to demonstrate that a simple belief in what the 'historical church' teaches and proclaims is insufficient and unsustainable in the light of the church's many self-contradictions and reversals of opinion. Objectionable doctrine is thereby undermined while the necessity of *sola scriptura* is at the same time re-affirmed;

52 Firth, *The Apocalyptic Tradition*, 29.

53 Clebsch, *England's Earliest Protestants*, 74.

54 See, e.g., *Vitae*, sigs C6r, D4v, D7v, H2v.

this, for Barnes, seems to be enough.[55] Therefore he stops short of those evangelicals who, sharing his belief in *sola scriptura*, would attempt to make it so wide-ranging a principle as to find Scripture the sole norm and authority even outside the realm of dogma. In Barnes's thought, Scripture and history each have their limits. History cannot be judged normative as a basis for establishing doctrine or for interpreting Scripture. But conversely, neither can Scripture be judged normative as an interpreter of history.

Contemporary polemics: comparisons and contrasts

In order to shed further light on Barnes's distinctive understanding of the relationship between Scripture, history, and the theological and polemical use of each, some comparison of his thought with that of influential contemporaries is warranted. Although the views of any number of evangelical reformers might here be examined, two personalities in particular recommend themselves. On the continent and in England respectively, Martin Luther and William Tyndale undoubtedly stand as the two most influential figures of early Protestantism. And this is not only the case in general, but especially with regard to Robert Barnes, who was closely associated with the person and work of each. Furthermore, both Tyndale and Luther have some claim to a significant influence on the development of sixteenth-century Protestant historical thought. The question to be addressed here is to what extent, if any, they might have influenced the historical-theological programme of Barnes himself.

Because Martin Luther made no extended foray into church history, some comparison of his theological programme with that of Robert Barnes might not immediately suggest itself. Luther was, both by training and vocation, an exegete, and it is true that the great majority of his publications are lectures and commentaries on the Old and New Testaments. Though this fact can sometimes be obscured by historians who tend to place a greater emphasis on those tracts and treatises which Luther produced in controversy with his opponents, it remains the case that 'His larger and smaller topical writings too are saturated with quotations

55 Thus Pineas's observation that on those occasions where Barnes does attempt positively to state his position on particular doctrines, he simply resorts to the 'rather pedestrian allegation' of biblical authority. Pineas, *Tudor Polemics*, 140. Even these occasions are, comparatively speaking, rare; Clebsch, *England's Earliest Protestants*, 77, has fairly described Barnes's thought as 'more polemical than constructive', and Barnes himself as '[a]lways quicker to pick out what he took to be theological error than to articulate what he took to be theological truth'. Whether Barnes conceived of his published works as in some sense no more than prolegomena, and would himself have turned eventually to the production of positively stated expressions of dogma built upon a more thorough exegesis of Scripture, is of course an unanswerable question. But given his commitment to a specifically Lutheran theology, and taking into account the large number of Lutheran works which had already made such expressions public, it is perhaps reasonable to suggest that Barnes would have found such a task superfluous.

from Scripture and are largely exegetical in character.'[56] Despite the demonstrably exegetical bent of Luther's vast output, however, it cannot be denied that he had more than a passing interest in matters historical, especially those pertaining to the history of the church.[57] It has even been asserted by one scholar that 'Luther was the creative genius in the new church history as well as in other phases of the Reformation'.[58]

Robert Barnes's commitment to Lutheran doctrine, as well as his long personal association with Luther himself, has been previously demonstrated. Given the evidence of Luther's influence on Barnes's theology, as well as Luther's notable interest in ecclesiastical history, it is worth asking whether these two reformers held shared views concerning the nature and use of history in theological polemic. Indeed, since it was Luther who contributed the preface to Barnes's *Vitae romanorum pontificum*, it is perhaps logical to assume a fundamental agreement between the two. Also supporting such an assumption is Kurt Stadtwald's suggestion that Luther might even have had some influence on the content of Barnes's *Vitae*.[59] As will be discussed in more detail below, Luther certainly maintained a consistently high view of this work.[60] Yet this is not the same as saying that the two shared an identical position on the theological use of history.

Where agreement between Luther and Barnes certainly is evident is in their shared refusal to grant history or tradition a normative role in the formulation of Christian dogma. John Headley has adequately summarised Luther's principle of *sola scriptura* in terms similar to those used of Barnes above:

> As Luther's principle of authority in matters of faith, *sola scriptura* asserted first the clarity and sufficiency of Scripture in revealing its own meaning, and secondly it signified that the content or meaning of Scripture stood as judge to all other authorities and could accept none which opposed Scripture.[61]

Headley here makes several points clear. First, *sola scriptura* for Luther, as for Barnes, is the principle of authority primarily 'in matters of faith'.[62] Headley also rightly emphasises that for Luther *sola scriptura* is fundamentally an assertion of Scripture's 'clarity and sufficiency'. Like Barnes, Luther dismisses the suggestion that unwritten traditions or post-apostolic interpretations are necessary for a

56 Paul Althaus, *The Theology of Martin Luther*, tr. R.C. Schultz (Philadelphia, 1966), 3.
57 Thus entire monographs have been devoted to the subject. See, e.g., Ernst Schäfer, *Luther als Kirchenhistoriker* (Gütersloh, 1897), and John M. Headley, *Luther's View of Church History* (New Haven and London, 1963).
58 Lewis Spitz, 'History as a Weapon in Controversy', *Concordia Theological Monthly* 18 (1947), 753.
59 Stadtwald, 'Pope Alexander III's Humilation', 765.
60 See below at pp. 174–5, 198–201, and 208–10.
61 Headley, *Luther's View of Church History*, 83–4.
62 See, e.g., *AE*, 28.76–7 (*WA*, 36.500).

proper understanding of Scripture. Instead, he will maintain that Scripture serves as its own interpreter.[63] Not only does the Bible's clarity mean that extra-biblical sources are unnecessary for its right understanding, but also the sufficiency of Scripture means that they can provide nothing necessary to the Christian faith. As early as 1510, long before he was forced to defend his theology publicly, he had been willing to state about the doctrine revealed in Scripture: 'whatever is added beyond the faith is most certainly human invention'.[64] But as his position was refined and confirmed in subsequent controversies he came to express himself more forcefully, bluntly stating that 'Whatever is taught in the church of God without the Word of God is a godless lie'.[65]

The logical conclusion of such a view, as Headley notes, is Luther's sharp distinction between Scripture and all other sources of ecclesiastical authority, with the former being the highest court of appeal in controversy. In fact, in the early 1520s Luther would argue that making this distinction clear is the ultimate goal of his teaching and writing. Writing in 1521 against the Leipzig theologian Jerome Emser, he would ask, 'What else am I fighting about but precisely this? I do it so that everyone may understand the true difference between divine Scripture and human teaching'.[66] Likewise, in the previous year he had argued that 'those things which have been delivered to us by God in the sacred Scriptures must be sharply distinguished from those that have been invented by men in the church'.[67]

The reference here to those things 'delivered to us by God' explains Luther's insistence on a necessary distinction between authorities. For Luther the word of God is precisely that: God's own words recorded by human authors. Thus he can say that 'God and the Scripture of God are two things, no less than the Creator and the creature'.[68] Because Scripture is God's creation, containing God's own words, Luther can assert that 'all apostles who are sent to us by a sure decree of God are infallible teachers'.[69] Thus Scripture itself, he insists, stands in contrast to all other authorities as that 'which has never erred'.[70]

No attempt has been made here to distinguish between Luther's 'early' or

[63] See, e.g., *WA*, 10/3.238: 'die schrifft selbs auszlegt', and *WA*, 7.97: 'sui ipsius interpres'.
[64] *WA*, 9.62: 'quicquid supra fidem additur, certissimum est figmentum esse humanum'.
[65] *AE*, 34.354 (*WA*, 54.425).
[66] *AE*, 39.198 (*WA*, 7.667).
[67] *AE*, 36.96 (*WA*, 6.553).
[68] *AE*, 33.25 (*WA*, 18.606).
[69] *WA*, 39/1.48: 'omnes Apostoli, qui certo Dei decreto nobis sunt infallibiles Doctores missi'.
[70] *AE*, 32.11 (*WA*, 7.315). Many twentieth-century authors have questioned Luther's commitment to the inspiration and inerrancy of Scripture, preferring to see him as a proponent of a more modern, 'Barthian' position. But even Paul Althaus, who himself disagreed with Luther on this point, concluded that Luther accepted the Bible 'as an essentially infallible book, inspired in its entire content by the Holy Spirit'. Althaus, *Theology of Martin Luther*, 50. For a summary of some of the last century's literature on Luther and Scripture, see E.F. Klug, 'Word and Scripture in Luther Studies since World War II', *Trinity Journal* n.s. 5 (1984), 3–46.

'late' writings because he himself indicates that he held such opinions quite early in his career. He claimed, for instance, that it was his Nominalist professors at Erfurt from whom he learned that Scripture alone commanded faith while all other authorities must be judged mere opinions.[71] Therefore it is not entirely correct to state, as Bernhard Lohse has, that before the Leipzig Debate of 1519 Luther considered councils and fathers to have authority equal to that of Scripture.[72] But it certainly is true that the events associated with Leipzig confirmed Luther's belief that a radical distinction must be made between Scripture and all other authorities. Equally significant is the fact that it was the events associated with Leipzig which contributed to his growing appreciation for the study of ecclesiastical history. It might even be argued that Leipzig was the determining factor in the development of Luther's view of the relationship between Scripture and history.

Prompting his detailed consideration of the matter was the Dominican Sylvester Prierias, who served on the commission which introduced canonical proceedings against Luther in 1518. In this role Prierias produced his *Dialogus de Potestate Papae*, in which he argued that neither church, councils, nor popes could err, and which asserted that 'Whoever does not rest on the doctrine of the Roman church, and of the Roman pontiff, as on an infallible rule of faith, from which even holy Scripture draws its strength and authority, is a heretic'.[73] Claims such as this drove Luther not only to an intensive study of Scripture as he prepared for the Leipzig debate, but also to an historical study of the church's alternative authorities – popes and councils. One consequence of this research was his realisation that even the highest authority in the church, the papacy, had no clear foundation in Scripture or the earliest church. 'It was this shock', many have concluded, 'that drove him to Holy Scripture as the only reliable and irrefutable source of all Christian doctrine'.[74] While undoubtedly true, it is also commonly

71 See, e.g., *WABr*, 1.171.

72 Bernhard Lohse, *Martin Luther's Theology: Its Historical and Systematic Development* (Edinburgh, 1999), 187.

73 *Dokumente zur Causi Lutheri (1517–1521)*, ed. P. Fabisch and E. Iserloh, *Corpus Catholicorum* 41 (Münster, 1988), 55: 'Quicunque non innititur doctrine Romane ecclesie, ac Romani pontificis, tanquam regule fidei infallibili, a qua etiam sacra scriptura robur trahit et auctoritatem, hereticus est.' While some commentators have suggested that Prierias's position was extreme and unrepresentative, it does not differ significantly from other prominent theologians writing against Luther at the time. Johann Eck, Luther's primary opponent at Leipzig, would argue in his *Enchiridion* that 'the power of the church is over Scripture' ['potestas ecclesiae super scriptura'], and that 'Scripture is not authentic without the authority of the church' ['Scriptura non est autentica sine authoritate ecclesiae']. Commenting on the councils and their decrees he likewise insisted that 'Without the authority of councils, everything in the church will be ambiguous, doubtful, undecided, and uncertain' ['Tollatur conciliorum authoritas, et omnia in ecclesia erunt ambigua, dubia, pendentia, incerta']. Johann Eck, *Enchiridion Locorum Communium adversus Lutherum*, ed. Pierre Fraenkel, *Corpus Catholicorum* 34 (Münster, 1979), 30, 27, 38.

74 Hermann Sasse, 'Luther and the Word of God', in *Accents in Luther's Theology*, ed. H.O. Kadai (St Louis, 1967), 58.

accepted that even after his own historical studies, Luther would not have willingly announced this novel position had he not been forced to do so by the proceedings of the disputation itself. By compelling Luther to admit publicly that some of the propositions of Jan Hus were falsely condemned by the council of Constance, Eck had forced Luther to deny the infallibility of church councils.[75]

Though Luther's preparation for and participation in the Leipzig debate proved to be a watershed in his understanding of *sola scriptura*, it was also, as previously suggested, a significant moment in the development of his historical understanding. Despite his conclusion that Scripture alone is the church's ultimate authority, this conclusion was partly based upon his study of the church's past. And, indeed, during the debate itself, 'Luther urged with remarkable skill the authority of history'.[76] He goes so far, in fact, as to ascribe something like objective truth to historical knowledge. Responding to Eck's criticism of his use of Platina's history of the popes, he stated, 'I attribute nothing to Platina, but to history which is the mother of truth, and which Platina writes'.[77] But such a statement must not be misunderstood as suggesting that history by itself reveals independent and authoritative truths on a par with those of Scripture. To the contrary, the truth of history is, in Luther's view, dependent upon that of revelation. Or, as Headley summarises, 'The authority and veracity of history as a knowledge derive from its agreement with Scripture'.[78]

This is especially evident in Luther's important identification of the Roman papacy with the Antichrist. It was the study of papal history undertaken by Luther in preparation for Leipzig which made the most significant contribution to his growing understanding of the papal Antichrist. This identification in turn 'led to giving greater attention to apocalyptic ideas', ideas which begin to become especially apparent in his second series of Psalms lectures, begun in the same year as the Leipzig debate and in which the papacy's antichristian nature is a recurring theme.[79] This theme cannot be underestimated in any attempt to understand Luther's estimate of history. It is no exaggeration to say, for instance, that 'The apostasy of the bishop of Rome, the rise of the Antichrist, formed the focal point of Luther's concern with the history of the world since Christ's time'.[80] This is a view shared by Robin Barnes, who argues that

[75] Luther's rejection of received authorities did not stop with pope and councils. The opinions of the fathers were also rejected in favour of *sola scriptura*. Thus he complained that his opponents at Leipzig relied too heavily on the fathers for their interpretation of Scripture, while noting at the same time that the fathers can err and have erred. See Julius Köstlin, *The Theology of Luther in its Historical Development and Inner Harmony*, 2 vols (Philadelphia, 1897), 1.314–15.
[76] Headley, *Luther's View of Church History*, 45.
[77] *WA*, 2.289: 'Platyne nihil tribuo, sed historie que est mater veritatis, quam scribit Platyna'.
[78] Headley, *Luther's View of Church History*, 44; and cf. 46: 'the authority and truth of history lie ultimately with the fact that history is God's work and must therefore agree with the Bible'.
[79] Lohse, *Martin Luther's Theology*, 126.
[80] Kolb, *For All The Saints*, 23.

> The image of the Antichrist, then, was central to Luther's eschatological understanding. Perhaps more than any other single idea, it gave shape to his vision of church history.[81]

Though Luther's belief in the antichristian nature of the papacy was perhaps initially suggested by his reading of ecclesiastical history, he quickly sought confirmation of this suspicion in Scripture. Unsurprisingly, he found the apocalyptic books of Daniel and Revelation especially significant in this regard. Though famously criticising Revelation as obscure and perhaps non-canonical in his 1522 preface to its translation, Luther by no means ignored the book. Indeed, the development of Luther's biblical-historical views, which had begun with the events of Leipzig, reached its culmination at the end of the next decade when he revised and republished the preface to his own translation of the book of Revelation. This has been noted by Avihu Zakai, who suggests that the 'relationship between history and prophecy is nowhere more clearly seen than in Luther's change of opinion in his exegesis of Revelation, from an allegorical interpretation of prophecies to a literal interpretation and a tendency to perceive them in historical terms'.[82] In this revised preface Luther does not hesitate to read Revelation as a commentary on the history of both church and world.[83] Also suggesting 1530 as the culmination of Luther's understanding of history interpreted by Scripture is the fact that it was in this year that he concluded his vernacular translation of Daniel, and it too was provided with an illuminating preface. In this preface Luther argues that Daniel's prophecy so clearly outlines church and world history until the second coming of Christ that 'one cannot miss the Last Day or have it come upon him unawares'.[84] Luther himself had no doubt, for example, that the kingdoms of his own day were mentioned in Daniel 7, or that the eleventh chapter unambiguously described the papal Antichrist.[85] In fact, so important was Daniel's description of the papal Antichrist for Luther that John Headley has gone so far as to assert that it was 'his central endeavor to identify the papacy with Antichrist according to the prophecy of Daniel'.[86]

Particularly relevant in the above summary of Luther's thought are the points at which his views on history can be compared and contrasted with those of

[81] Barnes, *Prophecy and Gnosis*, 44.

[82] Avihu Zakai, 'Reformation, History, and Eschatology in English Protestantism', *History and Theory* 26 (1987), 304. Zakai's judgement is shared by Barnes, *Prophecy and Gnosis*, 41, who also claims that 'Luther regarded the apocalyptic passages of the Bible as predictive prophecies with real ... historical meaning'. It should be noted, however, that Zakai is mistaken in dating Luther's 1530 revision of this preface to 1545.

[83] See, e.g., the summary in M.E. Schild, 'Luther's Interpretations of Daniel and Revelation', in *Theologia Crucis: Studies in Honour of Hermann Sasse*, ed. H.P. Hamann (Adelaide, 1975), 107–18.

[84] *AE*, 35.314 (*WA*, *Deutsche Bibel*, 11/2.126).

[85] See Barnes, *Prophecy and Gnosis*, 39–40.

[86] Headley, *Luther's View of Church History*, 32.

Robert Barnes. As is evident, Luther, like Barnes, was firmly committed to a principle of *sola scriptura* which denied history and tradition any independent authority in doctrinal matters. Just as significantly, Luther's commitment to Scripture alone is developed in concert with his realisation that traditional historical authorities – popes, councils, and fathers – are demonstrably subject to error. At the same time, it was this very realisation, especially with regard to the papacy, which encouraged Luther's further interest in history and its theological use. To this point it is possible to recognise a fundamental agreement between Luther and Barnes on the relationship between history and theology. But it is also here that their views noticeably diverge. Unlike Barnes, who gives evidence of a conscious effort to treat history and Scripture independently, Luther proves more willing to suppose their necessary interdependence. That is, Luther makes the interpretation and subsequent use of history dependent on the authority of Scripture. Thus one of the most influential treatments of Luther's historical thought finally concludes not only that 'Luther's view of history was biblical', but that 'in every feature it imparted its scriptural origins'.[87] Moreover, these origins can be found especially in those biblical books described as apocalyptic, allowing one to say that Luther 'developed his understanding of history hand in hand with his acceptance of apocalyptic ideas'.[88] Or, as another author has concluded, 'Apocalyptic expectancy and a growing interest in history were thus two sides of the same coin'.[89]

As important as the notable difference between Luther and Barnes is on this central point, even more significant is the fact that the position of Luther outlined above had received coherent formulation by 1530. That is, the culmination of this particular view had been achieved by the very year in which Barnes produced his first work for publication. Living and writing in Wittenberg, both in 1530 and frequently throughout the next decade, Barnes would have had ample opportunity to imbibe not only Luther's theological opinions, but also his historical views. That only the former find a place in his published works is telling, and again suggests that Barnes's own conclusions about history and its theological use were developed independently, and even in contrast to popular alternatives.

This conclusion can be further strengthened by some comparison with another influential contemporary, William Tyndale. Some comparison with Tyndale is warranted because, as Luther did among Barnes's German associates, 'Tyndale indeed occupied the leading position among the early English Protestants'.[90] It has also been argued that this is especially the case with regard to the establishment of a historical-theological polemic. Glanmor Williams, for instance, does

87 Headley, *Luther's View of Church History*, 267.
88 Lohse, *Martin Luther's Theology*, 126.
89 Barnes, *Prophecy and Gnosis*, 103.
90 Clebsch, *England's Earliest Protestants*, 137.

not hesitate to assert that 'Not one of the others among the first generation of English reformers showed himself to be as historically minded as Tyndale'.[91] That Barnes's own historical efforts owe a great debt to Tyndale has been frequently assumed. With reference to Tyndale, John King bluntly states that Barnes and other Englishmen merely 'followed their master'.[92] This judgement is shared by Katherine Firth, who suggests that 'Tyndale's *Practice of Prelates* established a pattern of English argument from history that remained virtually unchanged throughout the decade', and concludes that 'Robert Barnes made use of the same approach'.[93] Whether these assumptions are more than superficially true, however, can only be determined after a more detailed comparison of their respective positions.

Once again beginning with the question of ecclesiastical authority, it can be said of Tyndale no less than of Luther and Barnes that the principle of Scripture alone was foundational. Popular works such as *The Parable of the Wicked Mammon* demonstrate what has been described as Tyndale's 'inflexible adherence to *sola scriptura*'.[94] Indeed, in this work, which is in large part simply a translation and expansion of one of Luther's own sermons, parallels with the German's expressions of this principle are only to be expected. Thus Tyndale writes,

> Seek the word of God in all things; and without the word of God do nothing, though it appear never so glorious. Whatsoever is done without the word of God, that count idolatry.[95]

But this emphasis on Scripture's sufficiency especially comes to the fore in his vigorous debate with Thomas More, which 'centered on the question whether the final authority in matters of church practice and doctrine should be the scriptures or the traditions of the Church'.[96] In the tract which opened the debate, the *Dialogue against Heresies*, More had scoffed at the idea of Scripture being a sufficient source for defining the Christian faith.[97] Instead, in all of his polemical works, More appeals to the inerrant and infallible authority of the church and her traditions. So frequent and so fundamental is this appeal that one author has described it as his '*deus ex machina*'.[98]

91 Williams, *Reformation Views of Church History*, 30. And again on the next page he states that 'of this first generation it is clearly Tyndale who matters most'.
92 John N. King, *English Reformation Literature: The Tudor Origins of the Protestant Tradition* (Princeton, 1982), 4.
93 Firth, *The Apocalyptic Tradition*, 29.
94 McGoldrick, *Luther's English Connection*, 72.
95 William Tyndale, *Doctrinal Treatises and Introductions to Different Portions of the Holy Scriptures*, ed. H. Walter (Cambridge: Parker Society, 1848), 103.
96 R. Pineas, 'William Tyndale's Use of History as a Weapon of Religious Controversy', *Harvard Theological Review* 55 (1962), 123.
97 See his prolonged treatment of the issue in *CWM*, 6/1.113–62.
98 Mozley, *William Tyndale*, 231.

In this, of course, More is united with his conservative counterparts on the continent; and in fact, he shows more than a passing familiarity with the arguments of those who had already written against Luther on this subject. Not only had he read the work of Luther's early opponent Johannes Cochlaeus, but it appears that Cochlaeus continued to provide More with information concerning the state of the controversy on the continent. Nor was More unfamiliar with the works of Johann Eck, whom he had met during that Dominican's travels in England.[99] But Tyndale's familiarity with the history of the church and her doctrine would not allow him to agree with either More or those who shared his position. Therefore, in his *Answere unto Sir Thomas More's Dialoge*, he immediately asks his readers to judge 'whether their authority be above the scripture; whether all they teach without scripture be equal with the scripture; whether they have erred, and not only whether they can'.[100] Because he will consistently reject the traditional answer to such questions, it can be asserted that Tyndale's belief in the authority of Scripture alone is 'the presupposition of everything'.[101]

Because this is indeed Tyndale's presupposition, it is not surprising that the great majority of his writings are biblical and exegetical in character. Thus when James McGoldrick compares the works of Barnes and Tyndale he can state that 'Barnes wrote polemic with the fervor of a tractarian. Tyndale wrote from that perspective too, but more often from the standpoint of an exegetical theologian.'[102] David Daniell has more specifically observed that, for instance, in his *Obedience of a Christian Man*, Tyndale 'builds his sentences, paragraphs and pages out of the bricks of Scripture', and that 'from start to finish it is about the Bible'.[103] Even in his polemical exchange with More, Tyndale spends a great deal of time justifying his controversial translation and interpretation of certain biblical terms. Because this constant return to exegetical arguments is evident in nearly all of his works, it has reasonably been concluded that Tyndale consciously slights historical arguments in favour of those from Scripture alone. Stating this conclusion most forcefully, Rainer Pineas has argued that 'Tyndale regarded all nonscriptural study – including the study of history – with suspicion, indulging it only as a necessary evil'.[104]

This is not to say that Tyndale does not make frequent references to history. In fact he does. Again and again he exhorts his readers to 'Read the chronicles of

99 See David Daniell, *William Tyndale: A Biography* (New Haven and London, 1994), 260–1.
100 Tyndale, *An Answer*, 9.
101 E. Flesseman-van Leer, 'The Controversy about Scripture and Tradition between More and Tyndale', *Nederlandsch Archief voor Kerkgeschiedenis* 43 (1959), 144.
102 McGoldrick, *Luther's English Connection*, 82.
103 Daniell, *William Tyndale*, 226, 243.
104 R. Pineas, 'William Tyndale's Influence on John Bale's Polemical Use of History', *Archiv für Reformationsgeschichte* 53 (1962), 85.

England',[105] and to 'Look in the chronicles'.[106] He tells Thomas More to 'Read the stories of your popes and cardinals',[107] and urges his King to 'look in the chronicles, what the popes have done to kings in time past'.[108] What he does not so consistently do, however, is himself turn to these sources in order to build an extended argument from them. To the contrary, it has been rightly noted that, although 'he refers to them extensively, he seems to do so almost reluctantly'.[109] Indeed, despite his frequent exhortations to take up the chronicles, he at the same time actively discourages his readers from doing so. He tells them 'not to believe a tale of Robin Hood, or Gesta Romanorum, or of the Chronicles, but to believe God's word'.[110] And he openly gives voice to his suspicion of non-biblical sources, saying 'I doubt not but they [the papists] have put the best and fairest for themselves ... for I suppose they make the chronicles themselves'.[111] Further indicating Tyndale's actual discouragement of reading history is the fact that his references to ecclesiastical history are 'made with a vagueness which we shall find to be characteristic of his references to history generally'.[112] That is, only very rarely does he reveal which particular histories his audience might read with benefit. It has been pointed out that in the entire corpus of Tyndale's writings only one work of ecclesiastical history is referred to by name; likewise, only once does he name a source of secular history.[113]

Forcing one to qualify this portrait of Tyndale as an historical sceptic is the single work on which his reputation as an historian rests, his 1530 *Practice of Prelates*. Only this work among Tyndale's publications 'has any pretensions to being a historical piece'.[114] Despite its subtitle, which indicates that Henry's divorce will be a major focus, only the final pages touch on this subject. 'For the most part', William Clebsch observes, 'the book was a pejorative rehearsal of the

105 Tyndale, *Doctrinal Treatises*, 338.
106 Tyndale, *An Answer*, 138.
107 Tyndale, *An Answer*, 129.
108 Tyndale, *Doctrinal Treatises*, 335.
109 Pineas, 'Tyndale's Use of History', 122.
110 Tyndale, *Doctrinal Treatises*, 328.
111 Tyndale, *Doctrinal Treatises*, 338. This complaint about the presumed bias of 'official' histories is significant. More so than Luther or his continental counterparts, Tyndale was well aware of the unwritten, 'secret' history of the church as lived out in movements such as native Lollardy. Almost certainly this knowledge influenced his low regard for those histories which ignored or disparaged what Tyndale believed to be true Christianity. In this light it is all the more significant that Barnes – no less aware of this secret history than Tyndale – would actually emphasise his reliance on 'official' histories.
112 Pineas, 'Tyndale's Influence', 79.
113 Pineas, 'Tyndale's Influence', 79, and 'Tyndale's Use of History', 122. Both references appear in the *Practice of Prelates*; the one is to Platina's lives of the popes, the other to Higden's *Polychronicon*. See William Tyndale, *Expositions and Notes on Sundry Portions of the Holy Scriptures, Together with The Practice of Prelates*, ed. H. Walter (Cambridge: Parker Society, 1849), 267 and 294.
114 Williams, *Reformation Views of Church History*, 23.

history of the Church.'[115] Though Clebsch's assessment is accurate, it must also be noted that, for Tyndale, the history of the church was not necessarily to be equated with the history of the church's teaching. On the contrary, when he turned his attention to the church's past he 'confined his polemical use of history largely to the political sphere'.[116] For this reason Thomas Betteridge can state that the 'motivation of this text is recounting the full deeds of the Pope and his henchmen in their subversion of royal power'.[117] Nor is Betteridge alone in this analysis. Rainer Pineas has likewise concluded that clerical subversion of temporal authority is Tyndale's 'central historical thesis'.[118] According to this thesis, 'the pope and his clergy wrested the government of the European states from the lawful rulers' and pursued a subversive programme 'so that no single state will be in a position to counter the territorial ambitions of Rome'.[119] Glanmor Williams agrees:

> The object of the *Practice of Prelates* was to show that the actions of men like Anselm, Becket, Stephen Langton, Thomas Arundel or Thomas Wolsey in England were but one ramification of a vast international conspiracy headed by the pope. Its object was to elevate clerical authority and subordinate secular monarchy to it completely.[120]

This emphasis on temporal affairs contributes to yet another distinctive feature of Tyndale's historical thought. Rather than pressing history into the service of a specifically theological polemic, he chooses instead to highlight the moral failings of the church. Thus when his focus was on the papacy, his 'examples were marshalled to sustain a theme of Roman treachery and immorality rather than to trace a growth of papal power'.[121] And when he turned his attention to lower ecclesiastical offices he argued that 'out of the deacons sprang all the mischief';[122] being appointed to oversee the church's goods, they quickly forfeited 'pure religious zeal' for temporal wealth and temporal power. Because Tyndale does assume that there existed an era of 'pure religious zeal', Clebsch has not unfairly described his historical effort as one 'written under the spell of the renaissance humanists' view of the past', one in which 'A pure, golden age of following the *philosophia christi* prevailed until distorted'.[123] This is also the conclusion of Katherine Firth, who agrees that 'Tyndale's conception of history

[115] Clebsch, *England's Earliest Protestants*, 160.
[116] Pineas, 'Tyndale's Influence', 95; cf. also 85, where Pineas states that, as a general rule, 'Tyndale emphasized secular over ecclesiastical history in his controversial works'.
[117] Betteridge, *Tudor Histories*, 52.
[118] Pineas, 'Tyndale's Influence', 82.
[119] Pineas, 'Tyndale's Use of History', 124, 129.
[120] Williams, *Reformation Views of Church History*, 27.
[121] Firth, *The Apocalyptic Tradition*, 26.
[122] Tyndale, *Expositions and Notes*, 256.
[123] Clebsch, *England's Earliest Protestants*, 160.

was as strongly tied to, and limited by, a theory of moral example as Erasmus's was'.[124] Indeed, by the time Tyndale came to write his *Practice of Prelates*, history no less than theology had become for him a 'handmaid to morality'.[125]

Despite occasional assertions to the contrary, the above serves to illustrate that Tyndale not only brought very different presuppositions to his historical study, but that, compared with Barnes, he also pursued very different ends. Barnes, for example, will certainly not neglect opportunities to highlight the papacy's attempts to undermine the authority of temporal rulers, but neither will he allow this to become his primary focus. Nor does he adopt the pronounced emphasis on morality which was popular in humanist historiography and eagerly continued by Tyndale. Perhaps most telling, however, is Tyndale's noted reluctance to encourage his readers to examine available histories, and his consistent unwillingness to cite his historical sources. This reluctant attitude is particularly noteworthy in the light of further observations regarding Tyndale's historical methodology.

Though the *Practice of Prelates* does rehearse a great deal of English ecclesiastical history, it is also apparent that 'the dominant matter of the last half' concerns contemporary events, especially those revolving around the person and power of Cardinal Wolsey.[126] This is especially significant because, as Rainer Pineas has convincingly suggested, 'it is quite likely that Tyndale's view of history was colored by the events of his own day', and that he 'generalized on the contemporary situation'.[127] More specifically:

> He interpreted this body of history guided by one organizing principle – the conviction that all actions he regarded as evil emanated ultimately from the pope and his clergy. It is not unlikely that Tyndale was led to this conclusion from observing the activities of Wolsey.[128]

What leads Pineas to this conclusion is the fact that,

> while he refers in conveniently vague terms to 'hystories' in support of his charges, giving his readers the impression that he is merely citing what has already been recorded, very often the event, and almost invariably the interpretation, has no basis in the chronicles.[129]

Indeed, compared with Barnes, there is in Tyndale a 'habit of manufacturing events not recorded at all', and a tendency 'to read into the chronicles what simply was not there'.[130] Although it cannot be claimed that Barnes wrote with unbiased

124 Firth, *The Apocalyptic Tradition*, 26.
125 Clebsch, *England's Earliest Protestants*, 203, and cf. 163.
126 Daniell, *William Tyndale*, 203.
127 Pineas, 'Tyndale's Use of History', 127, 140.
128 Pineas, 'Tyndale's Use of History', 131.
129 Pineas, 'Tyndale's Use of History', 140; cf. also 134.
130 Pineas, 'Tyndale's Use of History', 131, 135. For specific examples, see especially 132–4.

objectivity, his methodology, especially when compared to that of Tyndale, is far less influenced by obvious theological presuppositions. And with his constant references to the sources upon which he relies, Barnes effectively invites readers to confirm his argument. As has been noted with regard to Luther, the fact that Tyndale had developed a distinctive approach to history before Barnes himself began to write is significant. Being familiar with Tyndale and his work, Barnes could simply have 'followed his master', as Firth and King assume he did. All evidence, however, seems to suggest that he did not.

It has become clear that Barnes shares with both Luther and Tyndale a high view of Scripture, a view which leads each to conclude that it alone is to be granted authoritative status in the establishment of doctrine. But it is also clear that this common view does not lead the three authors to a common conception of the relationship between Scripture and history, either in theory or in use. Tyndale's appreciation for *sola scriptura* produces in him a suspicion of historical sources and arguments which not only encourages his predisposition to exegetical polemic, but which also seriously undermines the credibility of those historical arguments into which he does enter. Unlike Tyndale's, Luther's realisation that the church's history demonstrates the fallibility of its institutions and traditions serves to prompt his further interest in history. His distinction between the reliability of Scripture and history, however, leads him to insist that the authority of the latter is dependent upon its agreement with the former. Working with the assumption that these two authorities are thus interdependent, Luther seeks to establish an agreement between the recorded events of the church's history and the apocalyptic prophecies of the Old and New Testaments.

Tyndale's presupposition that history is inherently unreliable results not only in a general neglect of historical sources, but also in what seems to be a willing distortion of the information found in those sources. Because the chronicles must be untrue, Tyndale takes it upon himself to rewrite the history of the church 'under the influence of his *idée fixe*, which was that there had been in operation for eight hundred years a huge clerical conspiracy to dominate the territory of Europe and the minds of its rulers'.[131] Though Luther cannot be similarly charged with a neglect of history, he too brings an *idée fixe* to its study and use. The apocalyptic notion of the papal Antichrist is central to his historical thought, and therefore plays a large part in determining his interpretation of the past. Because both Tyndale and Luther – the two individuals most often cited as being responsible for the development of Barnes's historical thought – had arrived at their positions in the decade before Barnes began to publish, and because Barnes certainly despised the opinions of neither, it would not have been unreasonable for him simply to have adopted one of the positions put forward by his influential

131 Pineas, 'Tyndale's Use of History', 131.

contemporaries. Because he chose not to do so, it is necessary to attempt a summary of Barnes's own historical-theological programme.

A summary Barnes's programme

As was noted at the beginning of this chapter, an appeal to history by those for whom the principle of *sola scriptura* was an unquestioned presupposition was not, strictly speaking, a logical necessity. But precisely for this reason it is all the more significant that an evangelical reformer like Robert Barnes did choose to give historical argumentation a central place in his theological polemic. Of course, the use of arguments which were logically unnecessary does not by itself make such arguments original. It cannot be denied that even the many reforming movements of the medieval church 'hinged on a historical argument whose logic held that through the course of human history the church had repeatedly fallen away from the intentions of its founder and was in need of correction'.[132] The reform movement of the early modern era did, however, differ from its predecessors in significant respects. The most important of these was a novel conception of that which was in need of correction. Unlike the predominantly moral and organisational reforms implemented in monastic orders and encouraged by a number of medieval councils, the issues which came to the fore in the early sixteenth century were overwhelmingly doctrinal. The reformers were charged with introducing novel and heretical doctrines, which doctrines in turn became the foundation of a new and false church. The often raised question, 'Where was your church before Luther?', was one that could not be ignored by reformers either in England or on the continent.

The fact that both English and continental reformers alike took it upon themselves to answer this historical question does not, however, mean that they arrived at the same conclusion. Despite any broad distinction which might be made between the concerns for reform evident in the medieval and early modern churches, one cannot simply conclude that there was a single type of 'reformation history' or 'Protestant history'. On the contrary, it is 'manifestly evident that there was no one Protestant view of history, but several, and each acquired its voice and character from the local circumstances out of which it arose'.[133] This conclusion has become evident even in the brief survey of the differing views held by Martin Luther and William Tyndale. Overarching statements such as those made by Avihu Zakai – 'Protestant historiography based itself upon an historical interpretation of prophecies and regarded the Apocalypse as the guide to history'[134] – or

132 Gordon, 'The Changing Face', 3.
133 Gordon, 'The Changing Face', 6–7. See also O'Day, *The Debate on the English Reformation*, 5–6.
134 Zakai, 'Reformation, History, and Eschatology', 300.

May McKisack – 'Heavy moralizing is a characteristic common to nearly all sixteenth-century historians'[135] – can therefore be accepted only with caution. What might be accepted less cautiously is the assertion that 'moralism' and 'apocalypticism' are defining characteristics of two particular, and very popular, strains of sixteenth-century evangelical historiography. The argument of this chapter, as well as the previous two, however, is that the historical-theological programme of Robert Barnes can be defined by neither of these terms. And because Barnes's programme is noticeably different, questions must be asked about 'the local circumstances out of which it arose'.

In spite of Barnes's frequent travels in Germany and his consistent adherence to the doctrine of the Wittenberg reformers, there is little doubt that his programme took shape in the context of those events related to the reform of the church in England. It was to the English King that three of his four published works were dedicated. It was promotion to a respectable position in the English church that he so frequently requested. Even much of the time he spent in the company of the German reformers was at the behest of, and in the employ of, the English Crown. And despite the King's hope that his ambassador would persuade the Wittenbergers to accept a theological settlement based upon mutually agreeable compromises, it seems clear that Barnes, like his mentor Thomas Cromwell, was in fact secretly promoting England's full acceptance of those reforms already implemented in Saxony. Although his significance can by no means be restricted to the English church, it is to England especially that one must look for the context in which Barnes's programme was developed. And the distinctly historical bent of this programme might partially be explained by this context, as it has been noted that it was especially among English reformers that 'reforming rhetoric pressed historical precedent with a singular intensity'.[136]

This fact can perhaps be traced to the tone set by the English King himself, both in his early defence of the papacy and in his later search for a means by which to break with Rome. Responding to Luther's treatise on the 'Babylonian captivity' of the church, Henry himself laid down an historical challenge. If grievous error had been introduced since the time of the apostles, he argued in his *Assertio Septem Sacramentorum*, then surely someone should 'recall this to our memory from the histories'.[137] In presenting this challenge Henry had especially in mind that dogma concerning papal authority. And this authority, as he understood it, necessarily included the liberty to promulgate Christian doctrine and

[135] McKisack, *Medieval History in the Tudor Age*, 123.
[136] W.P. Haaugaard, 'Renaissance Patristic Scholarship and Theology in Sixteenth-Century England', *Sixteenth Century Journal* 10 (1979), 51. See also Dickens and Tonkin, *The Reformation in Historical Thought*, 59.
[137] Henry VIII, *Assertio Septem Sacramentorum* (Rome, 1521 [facs. Ridgewood, NJ, 1966]), sig. b4r: 'in memoriam nobis rem redigat ex historiis'.

regulate ecclesiastical practice. If such authority were no divine right, if it had been usurped in the course of the church's history, then there could be no lack of evidence for such an assertion. Thus it has been reasonably argued that 'The problem which, above all others, forced the participants in the Reformation ecclesiastical controversies to appeal to the record of human experience was that of authority'.[138] And it was precisely to this problem that Barnes would turn his attention in his published works. In his earliest, the *Sentenciae ex doctoribus collectae*, he turned not only to Scripture, but, as the title suggests, to fathers, councils, and canon law in order to demonstrate that many doctrines and rites of the contemporary church had been clearly rejected or condemned by the very authorities this church championed as normative. The two editions of his *Supplication* would argue the same point in more detail, once again referring not only to Scripture, but to traditional authorities and available chronicles.

Although arguably effective from a polemical point of view, this concentrated emphasis on historical authorities was not without its own theological problems. The foremost of these was simply the question of how much the historical record itself could be considered authoritative, and on what basis. The answer of Tyndale, as illustrated above, was that the extant sources, especially the chronicles, were so flawed by the dubious motives of their authors that they warranted only suspicion. While Luther's answer would grant history some authoritative status, this was only the case insofar as history agreed with Scripture. Barnes adopted neither of these conclusions, preferring instead to assume the veracity of the historical record without forcing it into a specifically biblical paradigm. Like both Luther and Tyndale, however, he would not permit even incontrovertible historical evidence to displace or complement Scripture in establishing doctrine. But more than either of his contemporaries, he recognised that it could be a formidable weapon in the refutation of doctrinal claims based upon non-scriptural authority. He saw that historical arguments certainly had their limitations; but, if persuasively presented, 'they were potentially highly effective at stiffening the morale of the converted and the half-converted'.[139] To Barnes, who in the early 1530s was presenting his case to a King already embroiled in controversy with Rome, Henry himself could only appear to be one of the 'half-converted' to whom a historical argument might appeal. And indeed, in the light of the historical research sponsored by the King in preparation for his break with Rome and assertion of imperial authority, here is little doubt that such arguments were in fact appealing.[140] Thus Barnes's associate Thomas Swinnerton could make a

[138] A.B. Ferguson, *Clio Unbound: Perception of the Social and Cultural Past in Renaissance England* (Durham, NC, 1979), 132.

[139] Ryrie, 'The Problem of Legitimacy', 81.

[140] In particular, Henry was very appreciative of the historical arguments presented to him in the *Collectanea satis copiosa* of 1530. Barnes certainly would have been familiar with this text and the

special point of praising Henry and his advisors for having sought out the historical truth about the pope and his power.[141]

As Henry's anti-papal position became increasingly unqualified, culminating in the 1534 rejection of all papal authority, Barnes grasped the opportunity to focus his historical-theological polemic even more sharply. He was, in fact, virtually invited to do so. Shortly after the Oath to Succession had been administered, all English clergy were exhorted to preach 'against the usurped power of the bishop of Rome'.[142] In June 1535, in the months immediately preceding the completion of Barnes's *Vitae romanorum pontificum*, the clergy were commanded to 'publishe and shewe to the people how the Pope hath usurped and taken upon him contrarie to Christes faythe'.[143] And there is some indication that there was a real need for persuasive arguments concerning the rise of the papacy as an institution and the false doctrine which emanated from it. Even Stephen Gardiner, frequently though not entirely accurately portrayed as a willing participant in the rejection of Roman primacy, would later claim that this was an unpopular move. In a statement that probably reflects his own early perceptions of the break as much as it does the simple historical fact, he noted that 'Parlament was with most great crueltie constrained to abolish and put away the primacie from the bishops of Rome'.[144] If this was indeed the case, Barnes would have had good reason to believe that the carefully documented historical argument outlined in his *Vitae* might make a significant contribution to the theological debate. This is especially the case because, as Irena Backus has pointed out, this appeal to historical method and historical sources was radically out of step with the arguments employed by previous critics of the papacy. Even those of the preceding century, she notes, typically limited their attacks on Rome's primacy to a few select quotations from Augustine.[145]

King's opinion of it. Edward Foxe, with whom Barnes would become closely involved during the Anglo-Lutheran dialogues of the mid-1530s, seems to have been the leading figure in its preparation. Also involved at this time with the collection of evidence in support of Henry's annulment and his claim to supremacy were two of the individuals with whom Barnes would spend time during his 1531 visit to England: Stephen Gardiner and Nicholas de Burgo. For the best brief discussion of the *Collectanea* see G. Nicholson, 'The Act of Appeals and the English Reformation', in *Law and Government under the Tudors*, ed. C. Cross, D. Loades, and J.J. Scarisbrick (Cambridge, 1988), 19–30. For the involvement of Barnes's associates, see E. Surtz and V. Murphy, *The Divorce Tracts of Henry VIII* (Angers, 1988), xix–xx.

141 Swinnerton does so in his 1534 *A litel treatise ageynste the mutterynge of some papistes in corners* (STC 23551.5), which can be found reprinted in *Records of the Reformation: the Divorce, 1527–1533*, ed. Nicholas Pocock, 2 vols (Oxford, 1870), 2.539–52. See especially at 2.544.

142 Rex, *Henry VIII and the English Reformation*, 30.

143 Wriothesley, *A Chronicle of England*, 1.30.

144 *A&M*, 2.1485.

145 Irena Backus, *Historical Method and Confessional Identity in the Era of the Reformation, 1378–1615* (Leiden, 2003), 374. It should be noted that Backus attributes this original, historical approach to those involved in the compilation of the later *Magdeburg Centuries*. In fact, as will be

The conclusions of those who have found Barnes's thought wholly unoriginal, then, simply cannot stand without serious qualification. This conclusion, for example, is stated especially forcefully by Charles Anderson, who says of Barnes: 'the hope for a novel "hook" upon which to hang his theological system is proven fruitless; the desire for, if not new concepts, at least new approaches, is also doomed to disappointment'.[146] The present examination of Barnes's thought has attempted to show that such a conclusion, if not entirely wrong, is at least greatly overstated. Barnes's sources, of course, are by no means original. But the presuppositions with which he approaches them, the manner in which he uses them, and the ends to which they are employed, do indicate that Barnes was consciously developing a rather novel historical-theological programme. In fact, the suspicion that there was indeed something distinctive about Barnes's programme is implicit in a number of studies. A.G. Dickens and John Tonkin, for example, recognise Barnes as one of those Henrician theologians who 'had been writing an English scenario more radical than the official one, yet likewise largely based on historical considerations'. And, they note, these historical considerations had one principal aim: 'to prove the Roman Church guilty ... of doctrinal innovations'.[147] F.J. Levy, who claims that the use of history in the English reformation was primarily secular, acknowledges Barnes as one of only two exceptions to this rule.[148] Even in Rainer Pineas's study of six Tudor polemicists, the chapter dealing with Robert Barnes is the only one to give primary consideration to the use of historical argumentation.[149] Barnes's historical, though at the same time distinctly theological, emphasis certainly comes to the fore in his history of the papacy. But it is just as significantly present in his earlier works, the sources, methods, and goals of which set the agenda for this final publication.

On the basis of his doctrinal conclusions, it is true that Barnes cannot be judged an original theologian. Likewise, when taking into account his foremost concerns, it would be difficult simply to label him an historian. It certainly is possible to recognise him as 'a searching, critical student of history, however credulous and biased he can be at times'.[150] But it must be emphasised that his approach to history was neither 'moralistic' nor 'apocalyptic', despite the popularity of such views among his contemporaries. Consciously and consistently employing history in a discussion of matters which were pre-eminently doctrinal,

discussed below, the Centuriators merely follow – more critically and in much greater detail – the lead taken by Barnes several decades earlier.

146 Anderson, 'The Person and Position', 262.

147 Dickens and Tonkin, *The Reformation in Historical Thought*, 63.

148 Levy, *Tudor Historical Thought*, 87. The other noted exception is John Bale, for whom Barnes was both a source and an inspiration. See below at pp. 216–19.

149 Pineas, *Tudor Polemics*, also examines Thomas More, William Tyndale, Simon Fish, John Frith, and Christopher Saint-German.

150 Anderson, 'The Person and Position', 163.

Barnes can perhaps best be described as an early proponent of 'dogmatic' history, or what would later come to be known as historical theology.[151] Barnes's history was, as well, a very distinctly 'apologetic' history. That is, his use of historical argumentation served to prove no particular doctrine, but only to undermine any based upon an authority other than Scripture. His programme 'consists primarily in the dissolution of the stability of Rome'.[152] Because Barnes's polemical use of history was strictly limited by his conception of *sola scriptura*, he, and any who adopted his particular approach to Scripture and history, 'could hope for nothing else for their cause than to shake the position of the opposition; they could not hope to substantiate their own cause'.[153] Developed in the early years of the English reformation, when the 'dissolution of the stability of Rome' was the primary goal of both evangelical and secular reformers alike, this novel programme was particularly appropriate. As pursued by Barnes, however, it was never so narrowly focused as to be irrelevant outside of England or beyond the 1530s. Thus, as following chapters will demonstrate, his programme was soon adopted and adapted by later polemicists in England and on the continent. Because this was the case, the question which must now be asked is how this programme was received and revised by his contemporaries and successors.

[151] Contra Spitz, 'History as a Weapon in Controversy', 755, who very curiously says of Barnes's historical programme: 'The history of dogma, which certainly must be regarded as the great moment in a religious controversy, was not included'.
[152] Werner Elert, *The Structure of Lutheranism*, tr. W.A. Hansen (St Louis, 1962), 491. Elert here speaks of Lutheran historiography in general, and draws heavily on that of the late sixteenth and early seventeenth centuries. On the basis of the above, however, it seems that in the early years of the reformation this description is suited to Barnes's particular programme better than any other.
[153] Elert, *The Structure of Lutheranism*, 482.

Part III

THE RECEPTION AND REVISION OF BARNES'S PROGRAMME

6

THE EVANGELICAL EVALUATION OF BARNES'S PROGRAMME

If the conclusions of the previous section are correct, and if the programme pursued by Robert Barnes can best be described as one of historical-theological polemic, it must be asked why this particular interpretation has not been previously put forward. Though there is by no means an overabundance of literature on the life and work of Barnes, those authors who have ventured to offer an analysis of his significance for the sixteenth-century reformation almost invariably reach one of two conclusions. Especially among those writers whose unmistakable agenda is to illustrate the Lutheran origins of England's reformation, Barnes's significance is summarised with the description of him as 'Luther's English connection'.[1] That is, Barnes was the most prominent of the English reformers to maintain a consistently Lutheran confession of faith, as well as the individual who most clearly promoted this confession among his countrymen. As a large number of Lutheran works composed in Latin were circulating in England even before Barnes began to publish, it should be noted that this conclusion typically gives special weight to Barnes's promotion of Lutheran doctrine in the vernacular, especially by means of his *Supplications* to the King. Even if such authors were not narrowly focused on the reception of Lutheran doctrine in England, it is not difficult to see how such an emphasis on Barnes's *Supplications*, and a corresponding neglect of his Latin writings, might result in their failure to stress the historical bent which is most discernible in his Latin works. This is especially true in those cases where the *Supplicatyon* is read in its 1531 edition,[2] which did not include what is by far the most historically driven article to be published under that title, that concerning clerical marriage.

While the portrait of Barnes primarily as a populariser of Luther has certainly

[1] Hence, for example, the title of McGoldrick's *Luther's English Connection*.

[2] And it is this edition which, until the recent publication of Douglas H. Parker's *A Critical Edition of Robert Barnes's* A Supplication Unto the Most Gracyous Prince Kynge Henry The .VIIJ. *1534*. (Toronto, 2008), was the most readily available, being published in a facsimile reprint (New York, 1973).

detracted from an investigation of his own more original programme, this is also the case with the even more common emphasis on Barnes as martyr. This has been highlighted by Alec Ryrie, for instance, who describes Barnes as a 'more or less worthy footsoldier of the Reformation, then; but not a man whose life and works were especially worthy of memorialization', and who goes on to argue that 'it was principally the manner of Barnes' death which secured what posthumous fame he had'.[3] Given the nature of Barnes's death, and the circumstances in which it occurred – following a protracted public debate with Stephen Gardiner, taking place on the same day that three conservative priests were also martyred, and following only two days after the death of Thomas Cromwell – it is not at all surprising that several publications quickly sought to capitalise on the event, either praising the King for the just manner in which he dealt with such a heretic, or lamenting the death of yet another pious confessor.[4] And with the first of a number of English editions of John Foxe's *Actes and Monuments* coming off the press only two decades later, Barnes's status as a martyr would not soon be forgotten by the English public. When the nature, purpose, and popularity of Foxe's martyrology is considered, it is quite understandable that it was especially Barnes's death which many sixteenth- and seventeenth-century evangelicals most vividly remembered about him. But the influence of Foxe's work not only in the century after Barnes's death, but especially as a resource for modern scholars, has also served to obscure the fact that many of his contemporaries and successors viewed Barnes not only – and not even primarily – as a source of martyrological propaganda, but as a significant influence on their own historical and theological polemics. This will become increasingly clear as the evangelical evaluation of Barnes's programme is further examined.

Early modern commentary on Barnes's programme

Even with his expected emphasis on martyrdom, it remains easy to see why Foxe's earliest readers would recognise that there was more to Barnes than his death. Barnes was neither, as so many of Foxe's martyrs were, a simple layman, nor even a country priest with reformist leanings. He was not only well-educated,

[3] Alec Ryrie, ' "A saynt in the devyls name": Heroes and Villains in the Martyrdom of Robert Barnes', in *Martyrs and Martyrdom in England, c. 1400–1700*, ed. Thomas S. Freeman and Thomas F. Mayer (Woodbridge, 2007), 151.

[4] See, e.g., Barnes's *Protestation*, its refutation by John Standish, *A lytle treatyse composyd by John Standysshe* (London, 1540 [STC 23209]), and the response of Miles Coverdale, *A confutacion of that treatise, which one John Standish made* (Zürich, 1541 [STC 5888]); George Joye, *George Joye confuteth Vvinchesters false articles* (Antwerp, 1543 [STC 14826]), and the reply of Stephen Gardiner, *A declaration of suche true articles* (London, 1546 [STC 11588]); John Huntington's *The Genealogye of heresye*, printed together with the response of John Bale, *A mysterye of inyquyte* (Antwerp, 1545 [STC 1303]); and the anonymous *The metynge of Doctor Barons and Doctor Powell at Paradise gate* (London, 1548 [STC 1473]).

but, as Foxe acknowledges, a doctor of the church. And while Martin Luther would claim that the reason Barnes was known on the continent by the pseudonym Antonius Anglus was that he was too humble to lay claim to his doctoral title,[5] it is clear that Barnes's humility – real or pretended – was simply ignored in his homeland, where few evangelicals referred to him without mention of his doctorate. Typical in this regard is Miles Coverdale's refutation of John Standish, who had been quick to publish a rebuttal of Barnes's last words at the stake.[6] Throughout the whole of Coverdale's treatise, the author will not refer to Barnes without also ascribing to him the designation of doctor. Even forty years later this trend remains discernible, very notably so in *A Booke of Notes and Common Places*.[7] Compiled by John Merbecke, who was otherwise best known for his musical contributions to English evangelicalism, this locus-by-locus refutation of Roman doctrine will cite Barnes by name more than sixty times, with only a few of these references lacking the doctoral title. The significance of such ascriptions certainly must not be overestimated; they do, after all, merely make note of what was a fact. At the same time, however, they must not be underestimated, especially since there were those, such as Thomas More, who had studiously refused to acknowledge the title.[8]

Even when the title itself was not the issue, Barnes's learning came to be a constant point of reference. Foxe's brief account of his life and death, for example, emphasises the effect Barnes had on the academic environment of Cambridge. Noting that Barnes returned from Leuven to his friary 'having some feeling of better learning and authors', he goes on to claim that 'he caused the house shortly to florish with good letters, and made a great part of the house learned', adding that even those outside of the friary 'sojourned there for learnings sake'.[9] While the historian John Speed merely follows Foxe in describing Barnes as 'the first reducer (as M. Foxe reporteth) of the University of Cambridge from rudeness and barbarity, unto good literature and learning',[10] there are those who could testify to the same independently of Foxe. The most notable is John Bale, who, though not otherwise known for modesty or humility, would claim that while they were together at university Barnes easily and greatly surpassed him 'in literary matters'.[11] Bale was also quick to defend Barnes

5 *WA*, 51.449.
6 Coverdale's *Confutacion* is reprinted together with Standish's *Lytle treatyse* and Barnes's original *Protestation* in Coverdale, *Remains*, 320–449.
7 John Merbecke, *A booke of notes and common places* (London, 1581 [STC 17299]).
8 More had instead attempted to score polemical points by consistently referring to 'frere Barns', highlighting the scandal of Barnes's earlier flight from his order. See especially the eighth book of his *Confutation of Tyndale's Answer* in *CWM*, 8.831–992.
9 *A&M*, 2.1192.
10 John Speed, *The history of Great Britaine* (London, 1611 [STC 23045]).
11 Bale, *Catalogus*, 667: 'in re literaria'.

against any who might impugn his learning. Responding to the sometime conservative polemicist John Huntington, who disparagingly referred to 'Barnes the blynde',[12] Bale insists that he was rather 'a man lerned'.[13] He also goes on to quote the book of Proverbs, applying its words especially to Barnes:

> Preciosi spiritus / vir eruditus. A preciouse sprete hath he that is lerned / speciallye of God. Though youre whole generacion denyeth him this / yet is it known to the Christen worlde by his godlye workes to youre utter confusyon and shame.[14]

Nor was Bale the only evangelical to defend Barnes in this way. When, referring to their meetings only shortly before Barnes's death, Stephen Gardiner called himself the reformer's schoolmaster, George Joye contemptuously replied that Barnes was 'better learned than his maister'.[15]

As important as the memory of Barnes's death might have been to early modern evangelicals, especially as a polemical device, it was never by itself allowed to define or to limit his importance. Thus, even into the middle of the seventeenth century, while Puritans like William Prynne could not resist references to Barnes's status as a martyr, he could not be referred to as only a martyr. Instead, he was 'Dr. Barnes a learned Martyr',[16] or 'Our learned Martyr Doctor Barnes'.[17] In fact, still in the sixteenth century, less than a generation after his death, it is evident that there were some evangelicals who knew less – or cared less – about Barnes's martyrdom than they did about his publications. So, for instance, when writing against the Portuguese bishop Jerome Osorius, the classicist Walter Haddon makes great use of the *Vitae romanorum pontificum* in his 'description of the Antiquities of Rome out of the Chronographers', itself largely a history of the popes. When he finds cause to comment on the author of the *Vitae*, however, he can only venture a guess that he was one of the 'Famous men martyred under Queene Mary'.[18] It was a safe guess, to be sure, but the fact that it

[12] Bale, *A mysterye of inyquyte*, fo. 57r. John Huntington's poem, *The Genealogye of heresye*, remains extant only in Bale's response to it. But see also its reconstruction in *Notes and Queries* 237 (1992), 282–4.

[13] Bale, *A mysterye of inyquyte*, sig. A4v.

[14] Bale, *A mysterye of inyquyte*, fo. 59v.

[15] George Joye, *The refutation of the byshop of Winchesters derke declaration* (London, 1546 [STC 14828.5]), fo. 2r.

[16] William Prynne, *The Church of Englands old antithesis to new Arminianisme* (London, 1629 [STC 20457]), 63, and cf. 69.

[17] William Prynne, *The antipathie of the English lordly prelacie* (London, 1641 [Wing P3891A]), 306; cf. also William Prynne, *A looking-glasse for all lordly prelates* (London, 1636 [STC 20466]), sig. a3r.

[18] Walter Haddon, *Against Jerome Osorius* (London, 1581 [STC 12594]), fo. 338v. Barnes is listed among Haddon's sources at fo. 284v. This work was begun by Haddon in 1567. Upon his death, it was continued by John Foxe, who brought it to completion in 1577. The English edition of 1581 was translated by James Bell.

was wrong by at least thirteen years suggests that, in Haddon's mind at least, Barnes was more 'famous' for what he wrote than for how he died.

Something of this view is expressed even by John Foxe himself, who did so much to promote the remembrance of Barnes as a martyr. In *The Whole workes of W. Tyndall, John Frith and Doct. Barnes*, which can with some warrant be judged a 'companion volume' to the *Actes and Monuments*,[19] Foxe encourages his readers not only to remember Barnes's death, but especially to read his works. He does so because Barnes is, he says, one of the 'learned fathers', 'chiefe ryngleaders',[20] and 'principall teachers of this Churche of England',[21] a man endowed with 'special giftes of fruitfull erudition, and plentifull knowledge'.[22] What is more, even on the continent, where Barnes's martyrdom would never hold the same significance it did in England, prominent evangelicals were voicing the same opinion. It was in the midst of praising Barnes that Philip Melanchthon was prompted to say England had never before produced 'so many distinguished lights of genius'.[23] This was a sentiment repeated even more pointedly by Melanchthon's co-religionist Friedrich Myconius, who called Barnes the 'most learned, most able man that all of England had'.[24]

The question which must be asked, of course, is on what basis did so many evangelicals find such consistent praise of Barnes's learning justified? Unsurprisingly, perhaps, the answer is not always the same. When Foxe draws attention to Barnes as the one who reformed the Augustinian friary at Cambridge, it is obviously the biblical and classical leanings of that reform which he applauds. When Hugh Latimer said 'he is alone in handling a piece of scripture, and in setting forth of Christ he hath no fellow', it is Barnes's learned preaching that receives the emphasis.[25] And contemporaries such as Thomas Swinnerton especially praise the convincing manner in which his writings expound the doctrine of justification.[26] John Bale's recollection that Barnes had been his better 'in literary matters' is perhaps too vague to pursue with any confidence; but, recognising that Bale had always been 'more interested in history than in theology', it is tempting to read an historiographical allusion into this statement.[27] And there may be some small justification for succumbing to this temptation. In his *Catalogus*, the work in which he describes Barnes as above, Bale, while providing a complete list of all

[19] Ryrie, 'A saynt in the devyls name', 144.
[20] Foxe, *Whole workes*, sig. A2r.
[21] Foxe, *Whole workes*, sig. A1r.
[22] Foxe, *Whole workes*, sig. A3r.
[23] *CR*, 2.1264: 'tam multa egregia lumina ingeniorum' (*LP*, 8.384).
[24] Friedrich Myconius, *Historia reformationis vom Jahr Christi 1517 bis 1542* (Leipzig, 1718), 59: 'hochgelerten allergeschicksten Mann, den ganz Engeland hatte'.
[25] Latimer, *Sermons and Remains*, 389.
[26] See, e.g., Rex, *A Reformation Rhetoric*, 129, 143.
[27] Firth, *The Apocalyptic Tradition*, 38.

of Barnes's publications, only finds his most obviously historical work worthy of mention in the narrative itself. In glowing terms, he writes:

> In Latin, and from many authors, this most faithful minister of the divine word wrote to Henry VIII, the King of England, a history of the matters between Popes and Emperors, so that it would be difficult for another to do so with better judgement.[28]

This high regard for Barnes's historical efforts especially is in fact frequently evident in Bale's writings. Addressing the Roman church in *A mysterye of inyquyte*, he would claim that the 'labours ye have taken and how busylye ye have applyed yt to set up the kyngedome of the devyll by all madde mastryes of ydolatre / the Chronycles declareth at large', adding that 'Barnes here in England was not all behynde with his part'.[29] He picks up this theme again in the same work:

> What Barnes was in the juste quarell of God agaynst youre blynde beastlye kyngedome of Antichrist / we are not so blynde but we knowe. And yf oure testimonye shulde fayle / the workes which he compyled are sufficient wytnesses to declare his godlye wytt and lernynge / of the whiche we have seane more than .x. undre diverse tyttles. So blynde is youre popishe generaction that they never yet were able to answre one of them. Which of you all with youre dyrtye divynite hath yet soluted but the least of his arguments in his boke of prestes matrymoney or yet of the Masses abusyon?[30]

Significantly, Bale here highlights the two *loci* under which, in his distinctly dogmatic works, Barnes most effectively brought his historical research to bear: clerical marriage and the Mass.

In addition to such explicit statements of approval, further evidence of Bale's respect for Barnes's specifically historical arguments, and his *Vitae romanorum pontificum* in particular, is found in the fact that Bale himself took up the task of compiling an index to the *Vitae*, a clear indication of his belief that this volume was not only worthy to be read, but also to find continued use as a work of reference.[31] And Bale was not alone in singling out Barnes's historical efforts as his most significant contribution to the controversies of the reformation. In 1564 James Pilkington, the first evangelical bishop of Durham, wrote to his brother-in-law Andrew Kingsmill, who was at that time a fellow of All Souls College in Oxford. In recommending a course of reading in the historians, he

28 Bale, *Catalogus*, 667: 'Scripsit fidelissimus divini verbi minister Latine ad Henricium octavum Anglorum regem, ex multi authoribus, historiam eorum quae inter Papas & cesares sunt gesta, ut vix alius meliori iudicio possit.'

29 Bale, *A mysterye of inyquyte*, fo. 29r.

30 Bale, *A mysterye of inyquyte*, fos 57v–58r.

31 See W.T. Davies, 'A Bibliography of John Bale', *Oxford Bibliographical Society, Proceedings and Papers* 5 (1940), 217.

urges Kingsmill to read Josephus concerning the era before Christ and Eusebius for the centuries from Christ to Pope Gregory the Great. He then continues by saying 'master Barnes succinctly and with sufficient clarity describes the tyranny of the popes after Gregory the Great'.[32] What is more, in addition to placing Barnes in the company of such venerated authors as Josephus and Eusebius, Pilkington concludes by making it clear that he could have recommended any number of alternate historians. 'There is an infinite number of historians', he writes, 'but for ease you can use these'.[33] Likewise, even a century later, by which time a plethora of papal histories had been produced by anti-Roman polemicists, Eton provost Sir Henry Wotton would specifically mention Barnes as one of three 'notable Writers of Popes lives'.[34] And, once again, it must be noted that such sentiments were not limited to Barnes's fellow Englishmen. So, for example, the Königsberg court preacher Johann Funck expressed himself in terms very similar to those of John Bale when he said, 'Robert Barnes wrote a history of the Roman pontiffs with such care and order that another could scarcely have done it with better judgement'.[35]

For the earliest reaction to Barnes's historical-theological programme, however, the continental reformers most logically to be consulted are those who offered their unqualified approval and recommendation by writing prefaces to his various publications. The first to do so was the Wittenberg reformer Johann Bugenhagen, whose regard for the programme Barnes pursued in his *Sentenciae* was such that he not only provided separate prefaces for the first and later editions of this work, but also immediately set about translating and republishing it for a wider audience. It is clear that Bugenhagen has no illusions about the possibility of the work converting opponents of reform; playing on the words of Christ in Luke 16:31, he writes, 'they will not believe even if Augustine rises from the dead'.[36] But resurrecting the teaching of 'the holy bishops Augustine, Ambrose, and others' is precisely what Barnes has done in the *Sentenciae*, setting them against 'impious monks ... and other ministers of Satan'.[37] Therefore Bugenhagen encourages his evangelical readers: 'that you might see either their

32 James Pilkington, *The Works of James Pilkington*, ed. J. Scholefield (Cambridge: Parker Society, 1842), 682: 'post Gregorium Magnum paparum tyrannidem succincte et satis luculenter descripsit dominus Barnes'.

33 Pilkington, *Works of James Pilkington*, 682: 'Chronographorum infinitus est numerus; sed illis per otium poteris uti'.

34 Henry Wotton, *The state of Christendom* (London, 1657 [Wing W3655]), 172. The two authors mentioned together with Barnes are Platina and Illescas.

35 Funck's opinion is quoted in the 'Testimonia Quorundam doctorum vivorum' in the 1555 Basle edition of the *Vitae*, sig. β2v: 'Robertus Barns ea diligentia, eoque ordine historiam de Romanis pontificibus scripsit, ut vix alius meliori iudicio possit'.

36 *Sentenciae*, sig. A2v: 'credituri non sine si resurrexerit ex mortuis Augustinus'.

37 *Sentenciae*, sig. A2r: 'sanctorum episcoporum Augustini, Ambrosii & aliorum'; 'impios Monachos ... & alios Satanae ministros'.

[the papists] ignorance or their impudence, look for yourselves in this little book of the sentences of the doctors, whom they are wont to condemn'.[38]

Unfortunately, no separate preface is attached to Barnes's second publication, his *Supplicatyon* to Henry VIII. This is not altogether surprising given the fact that, although he was writing in English for an English audience, Barnes prepared the first edition of his *Supplicatyon* while he was yet in Germany. Despite the lack of a proper preface, however, some early evangelical endorsements do survive in the form of letters sent to England with the first copies of the work. Stephen Vaughan, Cromwell's agent in the attempt to recruit polemicists in support of the King's cause, had forwarded a copy of the *Supplicatyon* to Cromwell on 24 October 1531, requesting that it be specially presented to the King. When, by 14 November, Cromwell had not confirmed its receipt, Vaughan wrote again, forwarding a second copy.[39] He once again requested that it be presented to the King, saying, 'it is suche a piece of worke as I yet have not syn one like unto it', adding that 'the comen people have never byn so muche moved to geve credence to any worke that before this, hathe byn put forthe in thenglish tongue, as they wil be unto this'. Vaughan's reason for regarding the *Supplicatyon* as a unique contribution to the debates of the day is explained when he concludes that Barnes 'presumithe to prove his lernyng as well by the scripture, as by the Doctours and the popes law'.[40] As Vaughan had up to this point been primarily interested in the works of William Tyndale, and since he had in fact sent Tyndale's exposition of 1 John along with the first copy of the *Supplicatyon*, it can hardly be assumed that Barnes's use of Scripture was what he thought particularly novel and noteworthy. Almost certainly, then, it was Barnes's emphasis on the extra-biblical evidence he found in historical sources such as the fathers and canon law which influenced Vaughan's enthusiasm for this work.

It was unquestionably this historical evidence which Luther found most valuable in Barnes's *Vitae romanorum pontificum*, for which he would write the preface. There Luther extolled the value of history in general, suggesting that Antichrist would not have entered – or, at least, not so easily entered – the temple of God if the church had been armed with 'some faithful histories'.[41] But, reflecting on the neglect of ecclesiastical history even in the earliest church, as well as the histories produced in the age which followed, he expresses no surprise when stating that 'rather than histories, we scarcely have some torn fragments of histories'.[42] Given such circumstances, Luther takes some pleasure in the fact that

38 *Sentenciae*, sig. A2r: 'ut videas ipsorum vel egnorantiam vel impudentiam, ecce tibi in hoc libello doctorum sententias, quas ipsi damnare solent'.
39 BL Cottonian MS Titus B.I, fo. 373 (*LP*, 5.532).
40 PRO SP 1/68, fos 51–2 (*LP*, 5.533).
41 *Vitae*, sig. A3v: 'aliquot fidelibus historicis'.
42 *Vitae*, sig. A2v: 'nos vix lacera quaedam historiarum fragmenta verius quam historias habeamus'.

he has been able 'to arouse the minds of the saints and friends of Christ to the investigating of the pope's tyranny and his inviolable church'.[43] He also takes delight in being able to announce that, now, as a result of such historical investigations, 'we have a worthy and just history' compiled by Barnes.[44] Therefore, what he would two years later say in his preface to the Italian Galaetius Capella's history of the reign of Francesco II Sforza – that 'histories are ... a very precious thing',[45] and that 'historians, therefore, are the most useful people and the best teachers, so that one can never honor, praise, and thank them enough'[46] – he can already express in even more pointed terms when speaking of Barnes's own programme:

> they know that they offer the highest and most pleasing sacrifice of praise by being able to recite, teach, and write against this bloody, blasphemous, and sacrilegious harlotry of the Devil. Indeed, in the beginning, not having much expertise in history, I attacked the papacy *a priori* (as is said), that is, from the holy Scriptures. Now I wonderfully rejoice that others are doing this *a posteriori*, that is, from history. And I seem to myself clearly to triumph since, with the light becoming clear, I perceive that the histories agree with the Scriptures. For what I have learned and taught from the teachers St Paul and Daniel, that the pope is the Adversary of God and of all, this history proclaims to me, pointing out this very thing with its finger, not revealing it in general (as they say), and not merely the genus or the species, but the very individual.[47]

What Barnes had done, Luther explains, is not only to offer confirmation of what he himself had long suspected on the basis of his biblical investigations, but to do so with a thoroughness and an exactness which would seem to prevent any further debate of the question.

But, of course, further debate was not prevented. If anything, it was intensified; and, quite frequently in the following decades, the grounds on which the theological battle was fought were those of the church's history. Therefore it is not surprising that, in the light of such consistently positive evangelical responses to the historical and theological programme pursued in Barnes's writings, these

43 *Vitae*, sig. A4r: 'pias & Christi amantes animas accendere, ad investigandum ... de Papali tyrannide & sacrosancta Ecclesia eiusdem'.
44 *Vitae*, sig. A3r: 'dignam et iustam historiam habeamus'.
45 *AE*, 34.275 (*WA*, 50.383).
46 *AE*, 34.276 (*WA*, 50.384).
47 *Vitae*, sig. A4r–v: 'sciant, sese offerre summum & gratissimum laudis sacrificium, quicquid contra hanc cruentam, blasphemam & sacrilegam meretricem Diaboli, legere, dicere, scribere possunt. Ego sane, in principio non valde gnarus nec peritus historiarum a priori (ut dicitur) invasi papatum, hoc est, ex scripturis sanctis. Nunc mirifice gaudeo, alios idem facere a posteriori, hoc est, ex historiis. Et plane mihi triumphare videor cum luce apparente, historias cum scripturis consentire intelligo. Nam quod ego S. Paulo & Daniele Magistris didici et docui, Papam esse illum Adversarium Dei & omnium, hoc mihi historiae clamantes, re ipsa velut digito monstrant, & non genus neque speciem, sed ipsum individuum, non vagum (ut vocant) ostendunt.'

works were judged worthy to be reprinted for continued use in the debate with Rome.

The republication of Barnes's works

It is the conclusion of Richard Rex that 'The writings of early evangelical humanists like Robert Barnes ... were crucial in broadening the appeal of the new doctrines' of the reformation;[48] and the preceding pages confirm that Barnes's writings were indeed well received. But these conclusions need not – and should not – be applied only to the original editions of Barnes's works. Something more of the favour with which they were regarded can also be discerned by taking note of the number of times these works were deemed worthy of republication, where, by whom, and under what circumstances.

An examination of later printings is perhaps best served by beginning with the *Supplication*, since only with this work was Barnes himself involved in a later edition. It may seem questionable, however, to return to the 1534 *Supplicacion* as if it were simply a reprinted version of the 1531 edition. The revisions made by Barnes himself are certainly significant enough to justify viewing it as a wholly new work; and in an earlier chapter it was indeed treated as such. Despite the many changes, however, much of the work does remain the same. The retention of the title indicates an intended continuity; it also suggests that those who brought the revised edition into print did so because they found much in the original edition which was judged worthy of wider reception.[49] The important question, though, is why? As no editorial comments accompany this new edition, the answer to the question of why the printer thought it worth the financial risk to republish is not obvious. But circumstantial evidence may offer some clues.

It was previously suggested that the original edition of the *Supplicatyon* was especially welcomed – at least by the individual who forwarded copies to the King and his minister – for its reliance on historical sources such as church fathers and canon law. Barnes's addition of even more historical material, especially in the new section pertaining to clerical marriage, further indicates that those promoting the evangelical cause in England were consciously seeking historical arguments to bolster their particular programme of reform. It is especially

[48] Richard Rex, 'The Role of English Humanists in the Reformation up to 1559', in *The Education of a Christian Society: Humanism and the Reformation in Britain and the Netherlands*, ed. N.S. Amos et al. (Brookfield, VT, 1999), 24.

[49] Though the suggestion can be only tentative, it is probable that the 1534 edition enjoyed a full print run of around 1300 copies, whereas the 1531 edition was likely a half run. During his brief stay in Antwerp during the first printing, Barnes had little in the way of reputation or financial support, whereas the 1534 edition was almost certainly backed by Cromwell as part of the propaganda push of that year (see below). Furthermore, the production quality of the second edition, much higher than the first, suggests the increased time and attention associated with the greater financial commitment of a full print run.

significant that this republication of the *Supplicacion* took place in the very year of the Royal Supremacy, the claims for which were largely based on historical arguments built on research sponsored by the Crown. That the 1531 edition made a favourable impression on Henry VIII is evident in his almost immediate willingness to grant Barnes a safe conduct to return to England. And once again, it is not unreasonable to suppose that the King appreciated this work for the same reasons Stephen Vaughan had: it outlined a programme of reform based on a rejection of papal inventions, it defended royal authority in ecclesiastical affairs, and it supported both by appealing to ancient authorities.

Despite the favourable reception of the *Supplicatyon* in 1531, however, it is not possible simply to assert that its republication three years later was part of the official campaign of propaganda directed by the Crown. Barnes was not at this time employed by the government; nor was his work published by the royal printer, Thomas Berthelet.[50] But his printer, John Byddell, was, along with Berthelet, one of the most important working in early sixteenth-century England.[51] His pedigree partially reveals why. An assistant to Wynkyn de Worde, and later executor of his will, Byddell would inherit de Worde's Fleet Street shop in 1535, making him heir to the business once owned by England's pioneer printer, William Caxton.[52] Even before de Worde's death, however, from March 1534, Byddell began printing under his own name.[53] It was almost immediately upon his beginning to print independently, then, that the *Supplicacion* was chosen for republication. And it would seem that, also from an early stage, Byddell's choice of publications was guided at least in part by the desires of the Crown. So, for example, in 1535 it was Byddell who printed the injunctions circulated in the diocese of Lincoln, which commanded the clergy to publicly preach the Royal Supremacy.[54] A few years later, but linking him even more closely with the government, it is Byddell who prints Richard Taverner's translation of Scripture, not on his own behalf but on behalf of Berthelet.[55]

Also drawing Byddell into government circles was William Marshall, the publisher who backed several of his publications and who, with Taverner, was at the time translating evangelical tracts for Cromwell.[56] In this context Marshall frequently corresponded with Cromwell on the topic of which books might best

[50] On the importance of these criteria see G.R. Elton, *Policy and Police: The Enforcement of the Reformation in the Age of Thomas Cromwell* (Cambridge, 1972), 172–3.
[51] Colin Clair, *A History of European Printing* (London, 1976), 254.
[52] See E.G. Duff, *The Printers, Stationers, and Bookbinders of Westminster and London* (Cambridge, 1906), 138–9; Colin Clair, *A History of Printing in Britain* (London, 1965), 59.
[53] E.G. Duff, *A Century of the English Book Trade* (London, 1948), 20.
[54] See Pamela Neville-Sington, 'Press, Politics and Religion', in *The Cambridge History of the Book*, vol. 3, *1400–1557*, ed. L. Hellinga and J.B. Trapp (Cambridge, 1999), 591.
[55] Neville-Sington, 'Press, Politics and Religion', 593.
[56] William Underwood, 'Thomas Cromwell and William Marshall's Protestant Books', *The Historical Journal* 47 (2004), 517–39.

serve the evangelical cause. Though no evidence remains to suggest that the two discussed Barnes's *Supplicacion*, they did discuss the equally polemical treatise attributed to the Swiss humanist Joachim Vadianus, *Of ye Olde God [and] the Newe*.[57] This work, originally published on the continent ten years previously, in many ways anticipated the historical-theological programme which Barnes himself would pursue. In it the author writes:

> who soever list to know his [the pope's] newe faith, his lyfe and his governaunce, let hym rede the canon lawe whiche he hath made / and let hym compare it to the holy scrypture, and to the olde faythe of Christ: and it shall appere to him more clerly then the sonne, that he is a newe god and a newe faythe / let ony man searche thoroughe out the cronycles, and hystoryes, and he shall fynde.[58]

The English translation of this work, funded by Marshall, came off Byddell's press at the same time as Barnes's *Supplicacion*. Also printed by Byddell in the same year was Thomas Swinnerton's *A mustre of scismatyke bysshopes of Rome*, another anti-papal polemic relying heavily on historical argument.

In the company of such similar publications, it would appear that the *Supplicacion* was intended to be part of a deliberate historical-theological programme of printing which Byddell was at that time pursuing. This programme was certainly appreciated by the Crown, and Cromwell's involvement with at least some of Byddell's output strongly suggests his hand at work in the republication of Barnes's *Supplicacion*. At the very least, its printing had his tacit approval since, from 1530, the Crown had effectively assumed oversight of all printing and distribution of books in England, even issuing its own index of prohibited works.[59] And especially in London, where Byddell's shop was located, it would prove nearly impossible to print unapproved books without notice.[60]

Despite the passing of fourteen years, there are striking similarities between the circumstances in which Byddell put the *Supplicacion* into print and those in which it was again reprinted in 1548.[61] As they had in 1534 with the proclamation of the Royal Supremacy, the political and ecclesiastical environments changed rapidly and radically with the death of Henry VIII in 1547. With the succession of Edward VI, evangelicals had reason to hope that the reformation introduced, but increasingly reined-in, by his father would once again receive active royal support. One tangible reason for such hope was the parliamentary statute – one of the first of Edward's reign – abolishing the previously instituted restrictions on

57 Duff, *The Printers*, 203.
58 Vadianus [attr.], *A worke entytled of ye olde god [and] the newewww*, sigs K2v–K3r.
59 D.M. Loades, *Politics, Censorship and the English Reformation* (London, 1991), 130.
60 Andrew Pettegree, 'Printing and the Reformation: The English Exception', in *The Beginnings of English Protestantism*, ed. Peter Marshall and Alec Ryrie (Cambridge, 2002), 167. Byddell himself would find this out in 1543, when he was briefly imprisoned. See Duff, *A Century*, 20.
61 As *The supplication of doctour Barnes* (London, 1548 [STC 1472]).

religious printing.[62] It was this new environment of toleration which prompted Hugh Singleton to return from the continent in 1548, and at once to open his own printing house in Paul's Yard.[63]

A 'stout Protestant', Singleton, like Byddell, became an especially important printer in sixteenth-century England.[64] Despite more than one conflict with the Crown,[65] he consistently remained in the good graces of those who controlled the printing trade, including the government. He was an original member of the Stationers' Company.[66] For several years in the 1560s he acted as a company agent for the search and seizure of illegally printed and imported literature.[67] And in 1584 he would succeed John Daye as printer to the city of London.[68]

A significant similarity is also to be noted in the fact that Singleton's edition of the *Supplication* was, as it had been with Byddell, printed almost immediately upon his taking control of his own press. Despite having been out of print for more than a decade, then, Barnes's work not only remained sufficiently well known to attract the attention of an individual who had been in the country for less than a year, but also sufficiently well-regarded to justify its being put into print as soon as possible.[69] The theoretical possibility, with the overturning of Henrician restrictions, of once again publishing vigorous evangelical polemic did not, however, mean that printers were in fact given absolute freedom with regard to

62 See Pettegree, 'Printing and the Reformation', 172.

63 H.J. Byrom, 'Edmund Spenser's First Printer, Hugh Singleton', *The Library*, 4th series, 14 (1933–34), 123. The effects of Edward's succession on publishing are especially evident in the drastic increase in the number of printing presses and the number of books coming off those presses in the years immediately following Henry's death. From about 25 London presses and 100 titles in 1547, the numbers rose to 39 presses and 225 titles in 1549. Loades, *Politics, Censorship and the English Reformation*, 114. Pettegree, 'Printing and the Reformation', 172, puts the number of titles in 1548 at 269.

64 J.F. Mozley, *John Foxe and His Book* (London, 1940), 31.

65 It is widely assumed, though by no means certain, that Singleton is the printer alluded to in *The Diary of Henry Machyn* (London, 1848), 72, in which Machyn notes that 'John Day … and an odur prynter' were imprisoned in October 1554 'for pryntyng of noythy bokes'; and Singleton himself confessed in 1557 to having been imprisoned 'on religious grounds', in relation to some unflattering remarks he had made about Northumberland. See Christina Garret, 'The Resurreccion of the Masse by Hugh Hilarie – or John Bale(?)', *The Library*, 4th series, 21 (1941–42), 154, and cf. Byrom, 'Edmund Spenser's First Printer', 127. His most serious offence, however, was the 1579 printing of *The discoverie of a gaping gulf* (STC 23400), denounced by Elizabeth I for having disparaged her proposed marriage to Henry III of France. Singleton was arrested and, though himself exonerated, the author, John Stubbes, and the publisher, William Page, both lost hands for the offence. See Leona Rostenberg, *The Minority Press and the English Crown* (Nieuwkoop, 1971), 82; and F.S. Siebert, *Freedom of the Press in England, 1476–1776* (Urbana, 1952), 91–2.

66 Duff, *A Century*, 148.

67 Siebert, *Freedom of the Press*, 82–3.

68 Byrom, 'Edmund Spenser's First Printer', 131.

69 In fact, since the *Supplicacion*, like all of Barnes's writings, had been banned in the later years of Henry VIII, it could not legally have been printed much earlier than 1548, the year after his death. See John King, 'The Book-Trade under Edward VI and Mary I', in *The Cambridge History of the Book*, vol. 3, *1400–1557*, ed. L. Hellinga and J.B. Trapp (Cambridge, 1999), 166.

what went through their presses. Had Edward's evangelical councillors shared the suspicions of conservatives like Stephen Gardiner, believing that certain arguments in Barnes's *Supplication* served to undermine royal authority, they surely would have continued to prevent its publication. And it comes as no surprise that Henrician proclamations of 1538 and 1543, which forbade the printing of English books without the licence of the privy council, were again reiterated in Edward's reign.[70] Nevertheless, Singleton republished the *Supplication* without any evident controversy.

There is some small indication, however, that the motivation for its republication might have changed slightly. Andrew Pettegree has observed that the first few years of Edward's reign were dominated by three types of printed material: translations from the works of continental reformers; new works written by rising evangelical leaders or those returning from exile; and reprints of what he calls 'classics of the early English Reformation'.[71] The *Supplication*, like most of Singleton's early output, clearly falls into the third category. Unlike the early works of Byddell, however, with their historical and polemical bent, the titles reprinted by Singleton reveal a predilection especially for devotional and catechetical material. In 1548, for example, the *Supplication* was printed alongside translations of select sermons by Luther and Oecolampadius, as well as a Swiss doctrinal confession and the *Instruccyon* of Urbanus Rhegius.[72]

This devotional and catechetical emphasis is discernible throughout Singleton's career, and it therefore seems quite likely that the *Supplication* was reprinted for its catechetical nature as a locus-by-locus commentary on disputed doctrines and practices. This is not to suggest that Singleton was uninterested in the historical emphases found in Barnes's treatment of these matters. The opposite is more likely the case, that the *Supplication* was put into print because its historical treatment of disputed matters lent credence to Edwardian claims to be restoring to the English church older and purer doctrines and practices.[73] Some support for this suggestion can be found in Singleton's association at this time with those who would soon become the most prominent proponents of an historical approach to ecclesiastical controversies: John Foxe and John Bale. At this early stage in his career, Foxe was printing exclusively with Singleton, and provided him with more than half of the titles put through his press in 1548.[74]

70 See Loades, *Politics, Censorship and the English Reformation*, 101, 102, 113.

71 Pettegree, 'Printing and the Reformation', 172.

72 Martin Luther, *A frutfull sermon* (STC 16983); Johannes Oecolampadius, *A sarmon, of Jhon Oecolampadius* (STC 18787); Anon., *The confescion of the fayth of the Sweserla[n]des* (STC 23553); Urbanus Rhegius, *An instruccyon of Christen fayth* (STC 20847).

73 Pettegree, 'Printing and the Reformation', 173, notes for instance that the vast majority of new writings during this period are concerned either with the Mass or with 'the construction of the new Church'.

74 Mozley, *John Foxe*, 243; Byrom, 'Edmund Spenser's First Printer', 123. Singleton began printing for Bale in the early 1550s.

Foxe's early association with Singleton is all the more noteworthy because it was Foxe who eventually oversaw the final incarnation of the *Supplication* in the so-called *Whole workes* of Tyndale, Frith, and Barnes. Also involved in this 1573 printing was the man who had by this time become Foxe's primary printer, Singleton's long-time associate John Daye.[75] Daye, who had founded his own press the year before Singleton, seems in fact to have been not only the printer, but also the publisher of the final edition of the *Supplication*.[76] It was Daye who had met the costs of printing Foxe's *Actes and Monuments*, and, as previously noted, Foxe himself viewed the *Whole workes* as a companion volume to that more famous work. Some hint of Daye's financial support is evident even in the preface to the *Whole workes*, where Foxe praises printers like Daye, who by their own 'industrie and charges' preserve the 'fruitfull workes and monumentes of auncient writers, and blessed Martyrs'.[77] Elizabeth Evenden has even gone so far as to suggest that Daye himself was the 'driving force' behind this particular project.[78]

The question once again, however, is what incentive Foxe and Daye had to reprint a work now forty years old. The common and pragmatic incentive of certain financial gain seems unlikely. Indeed, the very size of the edition in which it would appear not only dramatically increased the production costs, but also severely limited the number of buyers who could afford it.[79] Furthermore, despite being reprinted under every Tudor monarch of evangelical leanings, the *Supplication* had never been a runaway best-seller. No printer, for instance, seems to have sought a monopoly on the work as they did with more popular titles, such as those of Thomas Becon. Moreover, had the *Supplication* been thought unworthy of republication on other grounds, it is unlikely to have been licensed in any case. Thus the Elizabethan injunctions of 1559 made explicit provisions for royal licensing 'because there is a great abuse in the printers of books, which for covetousness chiefly regard not what they print, so they may have gain'.[80] But Foxe

[75] The association of Daye with 1553–54 titles printed by the pseudonymous 'Michael Wood, Rouen' is well established. See especially Elizabeth Evenden, 'The Michael Wood Mystery: William Cecil and the Lincolnshire Printing of John Day', *Sixteenth Century Journal* 35 (2004), 383–94. The involvement of Singleton in this venture is less certain, but cf. C.L. Oastler, *John Day, The Elizabethan Printer* (Oxford, 1975), 11, and Loades, *Politics, Censorship and the English Reformation*, 132. Singleton later succeeded Daye as the City Printer in London; and shortly after Daye became Warden of the Stationers' Company, Singleton was chosen by him to investigate the pirating of books. See Elizabeth Evenden, *Patents, Pictures and Patronage: John Day and the Tudor Book Trade* (Aldershot, 2008), 79.

[76] Evenden, *Patents, Pictures and Patronage*, 146.

[77] Foxe, *Whole workes*, sig. A2r.

[78] Evenden, *Patents, Pictures and Patronage*, 146.

[79] See Elizabeth Evenden and Thomas S. Freeman, 'John Foxe, John Day, and the Printing of the "Book of Martyrs" ', in *Lives in Print: Biography and the Book Trade from the Middle Ages to the 21st Century*, ed. Robin Myers, Michael Harris, and Giles Mandelbrote (London, 2002), 23–54.

[80] *Visitation Articles and Injunctions of the Period of the Reformation*, 3 vols, ed. W.H. Frere (London 1910), 3.24.

was especially determined to avoid such charges, arguing in his preface that printing provides a great service to religion and should not be abused by 'thrusting into the worlde every unworthy trifle that commeth to hand'.[81] That influential court figures did not consider it an unworthy trifle is evident in the light of its patronage by Daye's most prominent supporters, William Cecil and Archbishop Matthew Parker.[82]

Fortunately, it is easier to discern the motives of Foxe and Daye than some of their predecessors. Unlike Byddell and Singleton, Foxe contributed a preface to the *Whole workes* which partially explains his decision to include Barnes in the volume. As early as 1570 he had mentioned his intention to publish the works of Tyndale, Frith, and Barnes in a single volume.[83] When he did so, he explained on the title page that he considered Barnes and his companions to be 'principall teachers of this Churche of England', and went on to refer to them as 'learned fathers of blessed memory' and 'chiefe ryngleaders in these latter tymes'.[84] Some modern commentators have found Barnes's work out of place in such company, however. Alec Ryrie has suggested that 'the inclusion of Barnes is a little unexpected. ... Barnes was the Cinderella of the volume.'[85] He further ventures the opinion that 'If Barnes had not been martyred, he would perhaps not have been republished.'[86] There is much to this. Especially given the theological leanings of Foxe and Daye, Barnes makes awkward company with Tyndale and Frith. Equally true is that Barnes's martyrdom certainly did raise Foxe's opinion of him, and the tale of his death is included in the volume by way of introduction to the *Supplication*. But it is also notable that, of the three martyrs whose works are here reprinted, it is only Barnes who most obviously shares Foxe's methodological predilection for historical argument.

This fact may help to explain the somewhat cryptic statement in Foxe's preface:

> whatsoever thou art, if thou be yong, of John Frith: if thou be in middle age, of W. Tyndall: if in elder yeares of D. Barnes, matter is here to be founde, not onely of doctrine to enforme thee, of comfort to delyte thee, of godly ensample to direct thee: but also of speciall admiration, to make thee to wonder at the workes of the Lord.[87]

[81] Foxe, *Whole workes*, sig. A2r.
[82] Parker was especially supportive of the work, even having presentation copies bound in Lambeth Palace. Evenden, *Patents, Pictures and Patronage*, 109–11. For Cecil's consistent patronage of Daye's larger works, see also Elizabeth Evenden and Thomas S. Freeman, 'Print, Profit and Propaganda: The Elizabethan Privy Council and the 1570 Edition of Foxe's "Book of Martyrs" ', *English Historical Review* 119 (2004), 1288–1307.
[83] Mozley, *John Foxe*, 81.
[84] Foxe, *Whole workes*, sig. A2r.
[85] Ryrie, 'A saynt in the devyls name', 145.
[86] Ryrie, 'A saynt in the devyls name', 145.
[87] Foxe, *Whole workes*, sig. A2v.

J.F. Mozley reads this statement as suggesting that 'Men of every age can learn here, the young from Frith, the middle-aged from Tyndale, the elder from Barnes'; but he does not offer an explanation of why Frith should be best suited to younger readers, while Barnes is to be recommended to the older.[88] An explanation might be offered, however, on the basis of the methodology evident in each author's works. As an exegete, Frith simply offers a presentation of evangelical doctrine as found in Scripture – precisely what is needed by the young. Tyndale provides the same, but also allows himself occasional historical asides. But those thoroughly grounded in biblical doctrine, who are also interested in the faith of the fathers and the question of how the biblical and patristic faith was eventually corrupted under the papacy, can be directed to Barnes for answers. This would also explain why Foxe and Daye chose to include translations from Barnes's Latin *Sentenciae* in the *Whole workes*, despite only reprinting the English works of the martyrs throughout the rest of the volume. The decision to do so will be touched on below, in a consideration of Barnes's works in translation, but it deserves mention here as it further reveals Foxe's special interest in the patristic and historical aspects of Barnes's writings. It also reveals further motive for Cecil and Parker to patronise such a volume, as each was eager to encourage the publication of propaganda undermining the historical claims of Rome and asserting the antiquity of the English church and its 'Protestant' doctrine.[89]

By way of brief summary, certain conclusions can be reached concerning each republication of the *Supplication* from 1534 to 1573. Each time the work was reprinted, it received either the implicit or explicit approval of the government. The first two reprintings took place in similar contexts of recent political and ecclesiastical changes, and seem consciously intended to support or further the reform of the church. Likewise, in all three instances, the aspects of the *Supplication* which seem to have convinced printers and publishers of its worthiness were not only its evangelical doctrinal conclusions, but especially the historical evidence marshalled in support of those conclusions.

Similar judgements can also be made with respect to the printing history of Barnes's first published work, the *Sentenciae ex doctoribus collectae*. The first Latin reprinting of the *Sentenciae* was carried out in 1536 by the Wittenberg printer Joseph Clug. Clug's press was an obvious choice. Not only did he print for all of Barnes's Wittenberg companions – Luther, Melanchthon, and Bugenhagen – but it was Clug himself who had printed the *editio princeps* of 1530. It was also Clug who first printed Barnes's *Vitae romanorum pontificum*, in the same year that the *Sentenciae* was republished. In fact, in a year in which Clug's output was otherwise dominated by textbooks,[90] Barnes's theological and polemical works

88 Mozley, *John Foxe*, 81.
89 Evenden, *Patents, Pictures and Patronage*, 137–8.
90 E.g., the *Syntaxis* and *De dialectica libri quatuor recogniti* of Melancthon, as well as Georg Joachim Rheticus's *In arithmeticen praefatio*.

stand out; and they were probably intended to complement one another.[91] A survey of titles printed throughout Clug's career also reveals a particular interest in major themes addressed by the *Sentenciae*, notably those of clerical marriage, the sacrament of the altar, and the issues of biblical and patristic authority. A further interest in the method of the *Sentenciae* is also evident in Clug's output, and can be noted in titles such as Melanchthon's *Sentenciae Veterum aliquot Scriptorum de Coena Domini* (1530), his collected *Sententiae* on worship, and Urbanus Rhegius's confutation of sacramental reception in only one kind, in which he argues 'ex scripturis et patribus'.[92]

Most revealing, however, is the new preface appended to the *Sentenciae* (now the *Sententiae*) in 1536. In the new edition Bugenhagen, who had also supplied the original preface of 1530, added quite considerably to his previous remarks.[93] He begins by lamenting the oppression of the church which had taken place under the papacy, where 'publicly to hear and see the preaching of Christ was not allowed'.[94] Without such preaching, he asks, what can remain of the true church?

> If the writings of the prophets are not worthless, if that church is holy which is apostolic – that is, believing in Christ with the doctrine of the apostles (just as Christ said in his prayer: 'I ask this not only for myself, but also for those who will believe in me on account of the word') – if, in short, it stands on that article of faith which is recited – the remission of sins on account of Christ, the Son of God, who was conceived by the Holy Spirit, born of the virgin Mary, suffered under Pontius Pilate, was dead, resurrected, and reigns at the right hand of the Father – what is all the justifying doctrine in the papacy and monasticism other than blasphemy, error, hypocrisy, idolatry, a negation of the remission of sins by Christ, a negation of the mercy of God the Father and of the blood of our Lord Jesus Christ? [95]

[91] This suggestion is further supported by the fact that later reprints of the *Vitae* by Johannes Oporinus and Nicolaus Bassaeus would also include the *Sentenciae* as an appendix.

[92] Philip Melanchthon, *Sentenciae Veterum aliquot scriptorum de Coena Domini* (Wittenberg, 1530); Philip Melancthon, *Sententiae ex sacris scripturis collectae, quae docent praecipuum cultum Dei esse, promovere Evangelium* (Wittenberg, 1539); Urbanus Rhegius, *Confutatio libelli cuiusdam Luneburgi occulto adfixi, quo scriptor ille, quisquis fuerit, usum unius speciei in sacramento, conatur ex scripturis et patribus probare* (Wittenberg, 1538).

[93] He also added to the text of Barnes's work itself, including additional biblical and patristic quotations. See, e.g., the entries under the first article, where a dozen new quotations are provided from Ambrose alone.

[94] *Sententiae ex doctoribus collectae* (Wittenberg, 1536), sig. A2r: 'Christi audire publice & videre non licet'.

[95] *Sententiae* (1536), sig. A2v: 'Si Prophetarum scripta non sunt inania, Si Ecclesia sancta, illa est, quae Apostolica est, id est Apostolorum doctrina credens in Christum, quem admodum Christus in oratione ait, Non rogo tantum pro eis, sed etiam pro illis, qui per verbum eorum crediturі sunt in me. Si denique stat ille fidei articulus, qui dicitur, Remissio peccatorum per Christum filium Dei, conceptum de Spiritu sancto, natum ex Maria virgine, passum sub Pontio Pilato, mortuum, resuscitatum, & regnantem in dextara patris. Quid est omnis iusticiaria doctrina in Papatu & monachatu aliud, quam blasphemia, error, hypocrisis, idolatria, negatio remissionis peccatorum per Christum, negatio misericordiae Dei Patris & sanguinis Domini nostri Iesu Christi?'

He explains this sad state of affairs by simply asserting that in Rome 'falsehood reigns; truth is hated: the traditions of men are everything; the word of God is nothing'.[96] And again:

> If you offer to them Scripture, they condemn it, as though to say, 'What is the word of God? What are the prophets? What are the apostles? It is heresy, it is seduction, it is the devil.'[97]

In spite of such complaints, however, the reader is counselled not to despair,

> because the church will not perish, as even thus far under the Turk and under papal tyranny Christ preserved it for himself. It certainly does not follow that since the scribes and pharisees are deceivers, therefore the people are damned.[98]

Responding to Roman claims that the church is the 'pillar of truth', Bugenhagen does not disagree. Rather he asserts the same even more firmly, saying the church therefore cannot be a pillar of falsehood, 'falsehood being the doctrines of demons, another faith, the condemnation of the gospel, the prohibition of the sacraments, the prohibition of marriage'.[99] But such errors are defended, he notes, because

> they flee as if to their sacred anchor, so that they cry 'Fathers, Fathers'. Here God, the Christ, the Holy Spirit, the whole Trinity, the prophets, and the apostles are not fathers, so that they do not recognise the one holy catholic and apostolic church.[100]

Such a critique of the Roman dependence on patristic authority might seem rather out of place in the preface to a work which is itself largely a collection of patristic citations. But Bugenhagen is by no means so naive as to condemn the use of the fathers or their authority. Instead he simply rejects their misuse. And it is for misusing the patristic writings that he attacks his Roman opponents, because,

> from the fathers upon whom they call, they seize some dictum either erroneous, or poorly understood, or wrongly interpreted, or which even allows itself to be perverted, so that with this darkness they are able to obscure the great radiance of the sun of the gospel. But nevertheless, not

96 *Sententiae* (1536), sig. A2v: 'falsitas regnat, veritas odium parit, traditiones humanae sunt omnia, verbum Dei nihil est'.
97 *Sententiae* (1536), sig. A4v: 'si eis scripturam obiicias, contemnunt quasi dicant, quid est verbum Dei? quid prophetae? quid apostoli? haeresis est, seductio est, diabolus est.'
98 *Sententiae* (1536), sig. A3v: 'quod non peritura sit Ecclesia, quam etiam hactenus sub Turca & sub Papistica tyrannide Christus sibi servavit. Non enim sequitur. Scribae & Pharisaei sunt seductores Ergo totus populus est damnatus.'
99 *Sententiae* (1536), sig. A5r: 'falsitatem autem esse doctrinas daemoniorum fiduciam alienam, damnationem Evangelii, prohibitionem Sacramenti, prohibitionem coniugii'.
100 *Sententiae* (1536), sig. A5r: 'confugiunt ceu ad sacram anchoram, ut clament, Patres Patres, hic Deus, Christus, spiritus sanctus, tota, Trinitas, Prophetae, & Apostoli non sunt patres, ne agnoscant Unam Sanctam Catholicam & Apostolicam Ecclesiam'.

> even an angel from heaven, if proclaiming a gospel other than the gospel of the apostles, is to be believed. And to their fathers is not given the authority to teach novelties or other matters.[101]

Bugenhagen's complaint is not simply that Rome calls upon the fathers, but that it quotes these authorities in contradiction to Scripture – even when the fathers themselves intended no such thing. This he bluntly calls 'madness, to condemn God in his word and to be willing to believe men without the word of God, even, indeed, against the word of God and the understanding of the Christian faith'.[102] Nor is this an unintentional error, according to Bugenhagen, but deliberate deception:

> They want to believe those speaking without the word of God if that which is said suits them. But they are not willing to believe those speaking for the word of God and for our salvation, because this does not suit them.[103]

It especially does not suit them, in Bugenhagen's view, because the great majority of the fathers spoke in agreement with the evangelical faith. So he asserts that 'those whom they call doctors of the church confess with us the same faith in Christ according to the word of God',[104] and concludes: 'This is certain: if they continue to damn us on account of teaching the word of God, they will also damn their own fathers'.[105]

This, finally, is Bugenhagen's motivation for reprinting the *Sententiae*. Doing so will provide evangelicals with the means by which to refute papal opponents 'with the fathers themselves, who also teach us', and to reveal 'that which they often confess in their writings concerning grace, the profit of Christ, the remission of sin, the worthlessness of human righteousness, the sacraments, etc.'[106] Unbiased readers, he hopes, will then be able to 'see in return their [Rome's]

[101] *Sententiae* (1536), sig. A5r: 'ex patribus, quos vocant, arripiant aliquod dictum vel erroneum vel male intellectum vel non recte interpretatum vel etiam quod ipsis liceat depravare, ut hisce tenebris immensum solis Evangelii iubar possint obscurare, cum tamen ne angelo quidem e coelis [aliud] praeter Evangelium Apostolorum Evangelizanti, credendum sit; & Patribus eorum non sit data autoritas nova, aut alia docendi'.

[102] *Sententiae* (1536), sig. A5v: 'dementia est, contemnere Deum in suo verbo & velle credere hominibus sine Dei verbo atque adeo contra Dei verbum & fidei Christianae rationem'.

[103] *Sententiae* (1536), sig. A5v: 'Sine verbo Dei loquentibus credere volunt si ipsis commodum est quot dicitur, pro verbo autem Dei & saluta nostra loquentibus credere nolunt, quia hoc incommodum ipsis videtur.'

[104] *Sententiae* (1536), sig. A6r: 'quos vocant Doctores Ecclesiae eandem in Christum fidem nobiscum secundum verbum Dei confessos'.

[105] *Sententiae* (1536), sig. A6r: 'Hic, certe si pertexerint nos eadam ex verbo Dei docentes damnare, damnabunt etiam suos patres'.

[106] *Sententiae* (1536), sig. A5v: 'quod ipsorum patres, idem quod nos docuerunt, id quod confessi sunt saepe in suis scriptis, de gratia, de usu Christi, de remissione peccatorum, de reprobata iusticia humana, de Sacramentis, &c.'

manifest impiety'.[107] Significantly, but unsurprisingly, Bugenhagen also claims to be doing no more by reprinting the *Sententiae* than Barnes himself intended by compiling the work.

> For this reason, therefore, namely so that this last refuge of the papists might also be destroyed, the bold man and master, the Englishman Robert Barnes, doctor of theology and faithful minister of the word, lays out this excellent and most clear work. By himself he most diligently presents these sayings from the fathers of the church of God.[108]

Likewise, he claims to be fulfilling Barnes's intention not only in his wish to refute Roman errors, but also in his desire to confirm and strengthen the faith of evangelicals accused of novelty. He argues that Barnes compiled the *Sententiae*

> not only to refute adversaries, but also for ourselves, in order to have such sentences of the fathers by which they often confessed their faith and taught their churches, so that our faith is confirmed, because we are also in the very same church, having the same God, one Lord Christ, the same gospel, the same sacraments, the same faith, the same calling to eternal life in Christ alone.[109]

Such conclusions, he believes, will be obvious to the reader. Therefore he quickly concludes his preface, 'so as not to delay you from the reading of these sentences, which without me will sufficiently be commended to you as good'.[110]

Bugenhagen's concerns were shared some years later by his fellow Lutheran Eberhard Haberkorn, pastor in the Hessian town of Oberursel. Writing in 1558 to Count Ludwig of Stolberg and Königstein, who had introduced the reformation in Oberursel, Haberkorn expressed his great delight in the fact that there

> lately came into my hand so many sentences of certain illustrious fathers, especially concerning the articles of controversy in our age, collected here from the doctors of the church and of the schools about twenty years ago by the reverend doctor of holy memory, Robert Barnes, the English doctor of theology, and four years later strengthened by his martyrdom in London.[111]

107 *Sententiae* (1536), sig. A5v: 'videas rursum manifestam eorum impietatem'.

108 *Sententiae* (1536), sig. A6r–v: 'Ad hanc itaque rem, nempe ut etiam hoc ceu ultimum asylum Papistis auferatur, egregiam impendit operam Clarissimus vir & dominus .R. Barns Anglus Theologiae Doctor & fidelis verbi minister. Is a se diligentissime haec Patrum dicta Ecclesiae Dei offert.'

109 *Sententiae* (1536), sig. A6v: 'non solum contra adversarios sed etiam pro nobis habere tales Patrum sententias, quibus saepe fidem suam confessi sunt, & suas Ecclesias docuerunt, ut confirmetur fides nostra, quod cum ipsis in eadem Ecclesia sumus, habentes eundem Deum, unum Dominum Christum, unum Evangelium, eadem Sacramenta, eandem fidem, eandem vocationem vitae aeternae in solo Christo'.

110 *Sententiae* (1536), sig. A7r: 'ne te morer ab istarum sententiarum lectione, quae sine me tibi satis probabuntur'.

111 *Sententiae ex doctoribus collectae* (Oberursel, 1558), sig. *3r: 'nuper adeo mihi in manus

Haberkorn had good reason to suspect that Ludwig would share his delight in Barnes's work and desire to see it republished. Not only had the count introduced the reformation to Oberursel, but it was also Ludwig himself who had invited the printer Nikolaus Henricus to set up his press there in 1557.[112] Immediately upon doing so, Henricus began a sponsored campaign of printing which can only be described as 'Gnesio-Lutheran' in character. Over the next forty years he saw through his press a steady stream of works attacking the papacy, the Reformed followers of Calvin and Zwingli, and even those 'Philippist' Lutherans accused of compromising the theology of Luther and the Lutheran confessions.[113]

Haberkorn therefore immediately declares his intentions to be in accord with those of his ruler, saying 'we hear and examine the word of God; we teach the whole truth with the utmost care; we compare and seek one sure and uninterrupted meaning of Holy Scripture'.[114] It is his desire, he explains, to transmit to posterity 'that manner of doctrine which is fully proved with the evidence of Scripture and the experience of the testimony of conscience'.[115] This 'uninterrupted' interpretation of Scripture, which is also proved by the 'testimony of conscience', Haberkorn believes can be demonstrated with reference to patristic and historical sources. But he does of course confess that there is 'nevertheless a huge difference among the writings and decrees of the fathers, councils, and also the martyrs, so that we religiously regard and uphold Holy Scripture'.[116] Unlike the fathers, affected by sin and therefore liable to err, Haberkorn asserts that Scripture 'is truly immune and set apart from the stain of all errors', and therefore must remain the final judge in doctrine.[117] For this reason he, like Bugenhagen, feels obligated to repeat the common evangelical quotation of St Paul's anathema pronounced on all 'new' doctrines (Galatians 1:8), as well as to add his own: 'I therefore detest and abhor all doctrine in the church, worship, and religion, which opposes that Scripture'.[118]

venerint, illustres quaedam Patrum, de praecipuis nostra aetate articulis controversis sententiae, ante viginti plus minus annus, per R.D. sanctae memoriae Robertum Barnum, Theologiae Doctorum Anglum, hinc inde ex Ecclesiasticis & Scholasticis Doctoribus collectae, & quadriennio post Londini martyrio corroboratae.' Working with the 1536 edition, Haberkorn was evidently unaware that the first edition had been printed even earlier.

112 John L. Flood, 'The Book in Reformation Germany', in *The Reformation and the Book*, ed. Jean-François Gilmont, tr. Karin Maag (Aldershot, 1998), 31.

113 Josef Benzing, *Buchdruckerlexicon des 16. Jahrhunderts* (Frankfurt, 1952), 141.

114 *Sententiae* (1558), sig. *2r: 'verbum DEI audiamus & inspiciamus: verum summa cura sicamus, conferamus, unamque certam ac perpetuam sacrae Scripturae sententiam quaeramus'.

115 *Sententiae* (1558), sig. *3r: 'illud doctrinae genus, quod evidentibus scripturae & peritae conscientiae testimoniis convictus'.

116 *Sententiae* (1558), sig. *3v: 'ingens tamen discrimen inter Patrum, Conciliorum, & martyrum quoque scripta ac decreta, ut sanctam Scripturam religiose ponimus & observamus'.

117 *Sententiae* (1558), sig. *3v: 'vero ab omnis erroris labe immunem & alienam'.

118 *Sententiae* (1558), sig. *3v: 'Ideo detestor & abominor omnem in Ecclesia doctrinam, cultum et religionem, cum hac Scripura pugnantem.'

Yet the sentences compiled by Barnes, he feels, proclaim nothing new; they only reiterate and demonstrate the 'one sure and uninterrupted meaning of Holy Scripture'. Therefore Haberkorn promotes it as a 'little book of many distinguished judgements' and expresses his desire that it be used as 'a guide for the future'.[119] In offering Barnes's work for republication, he says he only wishes to follow 'the good example of this holy martyr of Christ'.[120] But he does so not only by reproducing Barnes's articles; he notes also that 'I enriched them in large part'.[121] And indeed, Haberkorn's additions are evident under each locus, where he not only includes further biblical citations, but also numerous patristic quotations, conciliar decrees, and passages copied from ecclesiastical histories. Rather significantly, the greatest number of additions are to be found 'indeed, especially in those [articles] which are written concerning the sacrament of the altar, the invocation of saints, and the origin and parts of the Mass'.[122] As noted elsewhere, these articles – and especially the last – are some of those to which Barnes himself had given the most historical attention. By singling them out for special attention, and by then greatly increasing the historical testimonies pertaining to each, Haberkorn highlights his approval of Barnes's own favoured methodology.

Because the *Sentenciae* by its very nature is more specifically an historical-theological work than the *Supplications*, it is not at all surprising that those who reprinted it were especially interested in the contribution it made to the debates concerning the history of doctrine. But it is worth noting that this conclusion is further strengthened by the fact that the *Sentenciae* was not only republished independently. It also went into three more printings – two in 1555, and another in 1567 – as an appendix to Barnes's most obviously historical work, the *Vitae romanorum pontificum*. It is to the publishing history of this final work, then, that some attention must now be given.

The favour with which the *Vitae* was received among evangelicals both in England and on the continent has already been noted. And this favour, especially among Lutherans, no doubt rests upon the fact that it was one of the 'pioneer works in confessional historiography from the Lutheran side'.[123] Its endorsement by Luther himself certainly did nothing to diminish the esteem in which it was held. In fact, Luther's preface made its own contributions to the more philosophical questions of ecclesiastical history. There, for instance, he wondered whether the general lack of historical writings in the church had been a blessing or a curse. He especially noted the likelihood that if fewer hagiographical histories of saints had been produced the church would have been less inclined to venerate them.

119 *Sententiae* (1558), sig. **5v: 'libellum pluribus insignibus sententiis'; 'profutura comitatum'.
120 *Sententiae* (1558), sig. *3r: 'sancti martyris Christi bono exemplo'.
121 *Sententiae* (1558), sig. *3r: 'magna parte locupletavi'.
122 *Sententiae* (1558), sig. *3r: 'maxime vero in his, qui inscribuntur de SACRAMENTO ALTARIS, de SANCTORUM INVOCATIONE, & de ORIGINE ac partibus MISSAE'.
123 Pullapilly, *Caesar Baronius*, 50.

But at the same time he argued that it was a lack of reliable historical knowledge which had led to the invention of so many saints.[124] More significantly perhaps, Luther here applied his distinction between the visible and invisible churches to the course of history. He suggested, for example, that where the Turks rule the visible church is profaned and destroyed; but one is at least allowed to believe the gospel. By contrast, the pope is determined only to protect the visible, institutional church, while at the same time oppressing the true faith upon which the invisible church is built.[125] It is his raising of such issues that has led to the conclusion that 'Luther had also outlined the general course of a new historical approach to Church history' in his 1536 preface to the *Vitae*.[126]

In this light, at least one author has asserted that the *Vitae* enjoyed so many reprints and translations – more than any of Barnes's other works – only because it bore Luther's preface.[127] But this conclusion must be seriously questioned on several grounds. The first is simply economic, and it bears repeating that 'Printing was first and foremost a business.'[128] When the production of a single edition typically cost more than the initial equipping of a print shop,[129] and when the cost of paper alone could easily surpass that of the total wages for all involved in a printing,[130] it would make little economic sense to reprint a text of three hundred pages whose chief value lay in its brief preface.[131] The printer who did so would hardly fit the description of 'a hard-driving, self-made man of affairs'.[132] This is all the more true when the work in question is one of history, which 'was certainly not a "major" subject for either most readers or their booksellers' in the sixteenth century.[133] It is for this reason that D.R. Woolf, after emphasising that it was the reader who 'ultimately shaped the commercial boundaries of what could be published', was able to conclude: 'Unless a historical work proved a surprise best-seller ... it was unlikely to go into reissues or new editions'.[134] And yet not only did the *Vitae* go into reissues and new editions; it has been regarded as 'among the sixteenth century's unrare books'.[135]

[124] *Vitae*, sigs A2v–3r.
[125] *Vitae*, sigs A3v–4r.
[126] Pullapilly, *Caesar Baronius*, 50.
[127] Clebsch, *England's Earliest Protestants*, 73.
[128] Loades, *Politics, Censorship and the English Reformation*, 99.
[129] Lucien Febvre and Henri-Jean Martin, *The Coming of the Book: The Impact of Printing, 1450–1800*, tr. David Gerard, ed. Geoffrey Nowell-Smith and David Wootton (London, 1976), 111.
[130] Robert M. Kingdon, 'Patronage, Piety and Printing in Sixteenth-Century Europe', in *Church and Society in Reformation Europe*, ed. R.M. Kingdon (London, 1985), 27.
[131] For an overview of the economic factors involved in printing, see especially Febvre and Martin, *The Coming of the Book*, 109–27.
[132] Elizabeth Eisenstein, *The Printing Press as an Agent of Change*, 2 vols (Cambridge, 1979), 1.393.
[133] D.R. Woolf, *Reading History in Early Modern England* (Cambridge, 2000), 322.
[134] Woolf, *Reading History*, 6, 42.
[135] Andrew Pettegree, 'The Latin Polemic of the Marian Exiles', in *Humanism and Reform: The Church in Europe, England, and Scotland, 1400–1643*, ed. James Kirk (Oxford, 1991), 313–14.

The endorsement of the *Vitae* by a figure of Luther's prominence certainly would have contributed to the work's popularity; and there can be no doubt that his preface was originally requested for this very reason. But the claim that Luther's preface was solely or even primarily responsible for the popularity of the *Vitae* must finally be rejected on account of the simple fact that more than one printer released editions which omitted this preface.[136] And finally, it must be noted that the work was not only reprinted, but in some instances continued by later authors.[137] Together these observations strongly suggest that, despite the undoubted importance of Luther's preface, what was found to be most significant was quite simply the content of the *Vitae* itself.

Among those holding this opinion can be counted the Basle printer Johannes Oporinus, whose 'printing program was guided primarily by his scholarly tastes'.[138] Both of his 1555 printings of the *Vitae* are introduced with an attempt to emphasise the scholarly nature of the work by offering the testimonies of contemporary historians who extol Barnes as 'a great man and professor of the gospel of Jesus Christ'.[139] A brief and newly added preface, in verse, explains:

> The Englishman Robert Barnes presents this history; no history which he has narrated, has he narrated better than of the evil popes. But if you desire to know more, friendly reader, you want to know the author, not just his name.[140]

Its author also reveals what he believes to have been Barnes's goal in writing the *Vitae*: 'He taught men utterly to condemn as foolish all hope and faith which was of this world.'[141]

Who wrote this unsigned preface is not entirely clear, but at least one likely suggestion can be put forward. As previously mentioned, John Bale is known to have compiled an index to the *Vitae*, which has not survived independently. But here in the first reprinting of Barnes's work an extensive index is provided at the

136 E.g., the 1615 edition of Lydius, the 1565 Czech translation of Glatovinus, and all of the reprinted portions published in German translation.
137 This is again the case with the editions of Lydius and Glatovinus.
138 *The Oxford Encyclopedia of the Reformation*, 4 vols, ed. H.J. Hillerbrand (Oxford, 1996), 3.175.
139 *Vitae romanorum pontificum* (Basle, 1555), sig. ß2v; cf. also sig. ß3r. Although one of these printings is obviously a newly set edition, the other probably does not deserve to be called such. Despite the resetting of the typeface for the title page, the catalogue of authors, and the testimonies of contemporary doctors, as well as the changing of the initial capitals found both at the beginning of the text and in the prefaces by Luther and Barnes, the body of the text itself remains unaltered. Nevertheless, the changes noted here have gone unmentioned in the secondary literature, and no other author seems to have recognised that the *Vitae* went through at least two separate printings on Oporinus's presses.
140 *Vitae* (1555), sig. α1v: 'Exhibit historiam Robertus Barnsius Anglus, Nulla malos melius qua dedit ante Papas. Sed si plura cupis cognoscere Lector amice, Nec solo autorem nomine nosse velis.'
141 *Vitae* (1555), sig. α1v: 'docuit nugas hominum contemnere prorsus, Tota in queis mundi spesque fidesque fuit'.

end.[142] As one would expect, it is not credited, and there is no definitive proof that it was compiled by Bale, or that its composer was the same individual who wrote the opening verses. But these verses do reappear two years later in Bale's *Catalogus* under his entry on Barnes, 'concerning whom these verses were published', and may very well be his own handiwork.[143] It is also worth noting that Bale's name is further associated with the 1555 edition of the *Vitae*, as a long quotation from his 1548 *Illustrium Maioris Brittaniae Scriptorum* is listed among the 'testimonies' previously mentioned. Both Bale and his fellow exile John Foxe are known to have been working for Oporinus when the Basle edition of the *Vitae* was published.[144] And as will become evident in the next chapter, each would make great use of the *Vitae* in his own commentary on papal history. It seems most probable, then, that one or both historians, already recognising its value, had some influence on the printer's decision to republish it. That those who would become the pre-eminent polemical historians of the English reformation had a hand in keeping the *Vitae* in print speaks highly of its presumed importance for historical and theological controversy. Likewise, the involvement of these English exiles further reinforces the conviction that, although it was never printed in England, Barnes's work continued to hold the interest of the English evangelical community.[145]

None of this is to suggest, however, that Oporinus himself was otherwise uninterested in historical works which might contribute to the evangelical cause. It was of course Oporinus who would become a printer not only for Foxe and Bale, but also for the most ambitious historical-theological project of the century, the multi-volume *Magdeburg Centuries*. And similar historically oriented works were being issued by Oporinus at the same time as the *Vitae*. In the following year, for example, he printed Francois Baudouin's *Constantinus Magnus*, a history of Roman law in which Baudouin emphasised – for the benefit of the bishops then sitting at the council of Trent – that even the most exemplary council of Nicaea was controlled by neither pope nor bishops. Baudouin further revealed his historical and polemical leanings by expressing a willingness to contribute the fruits of his own research to the compilation of the *Magdeburg Centuries*.[146]

The legal and historical emphases evident in the works of polemicists like Baudouin and Barnes were precisely those favoured by the next printer of the

142 The inclusion of such an index further confirms the impression that the *Vitae* was viewed as a 'scholarly' volume, intended by those who printed it to find use as a work of reference.
143 Bale, *Catalogus*, 667: 'De quo sunt editi versus'.
144 For Foxe, see Mozley, *John Foxe*, 50–1; for Bale, see Martin Steinmann, *Johannes Oporinus* (Basel, 1967), 95.
145 In any case, the fact that the *Vitae* was never printed in England offers no proof that it received little interest there. It has been acknowledged that English readers looking for Latin books 'inevitably looked abroad'. Pettegree, 'Printing and the Reformation', 161; see also 162.
146 Peter Bietenholz, *Basle and France in the Sixteenth Century* (Geneva, 1971), 149.

Vitae, Nikolaus Bassaeus. And yet the 1567 edition of the *Vitae* stands out as something of an anomaly among the works produced in the thirty-seven-year career of this Frankfurt printer, publisher, and bookseller. Bassaeus printed largely in German, and only rarely dealt in theological offerings, so his decision to publish Barnes's work sheds further light on how the *Vitae* was both perceived and received in the sixteenth century. While Bassaeus printed a number of popular classics, the bulk of his output consisted of texts devoted to the disciplines of medicine and law. Noteworthy, however, is that even under these headings, a significant number of titles are specifically historical in nature. Thus it was Bassaeus who published Joachim Strupp's medical history, the Swiss botanist and physician Kaspar Bauhin's history of plants, and – one of his most frequently reprinted publications – the *Historischer Processus Iuris* of the lawyer and imperial notary Jakob Ayrer.[147] Even when Bassaeus ventured beyond his fields of speciality, history continued to hold his attention. He would print an edition of Matthias Delius's *Meditationum de Historia Mundi* in 1584; and in the next decade he published the epitome of sacred and profane histories compiled by another Wittenberg student, the lawyer Nicolaus Reusner, as well as the *Annales Suevici sive Chronica* of classicist Martin Crusius.[148] With the exception of Lukas Osiander's *Epitomes Historiae Ecclesiasticae*, abridged from the *Magdeburg Centuries*, however, Bassaeus seems not to have taken a particular interest in specifically ecclesiastical or theological history. Given his primary interest in works of a legal nature, his publication of the *Vitae* seems best explained in the light of Barnes's historical approach to the laws of the church as they were developed and expressed both in conciliar canons and in Gratian's *Decretum*.[149]

Barnes's attention to the history of ecclesiastical law – especially where it conflicted with the established legal rights of temporal rulers – was clearly a motivating factor in Frankfurt minister Johannes Lydius's decision to make the *Vitae* available yet again in 1615. This edition, published by the Amsterdam bookseller Hendrick Laurensz and printed in Leiden by Joris Abrahamsz van der Marsce, included not only the *Vitae romanorum pontificum*, but also John Bale's *Acta romanorum pontificum*, which both built upon Barnes's work and brought it forward to 1559. In addition, Lydius himself continued the work up to the pontificate of Paul VI in his own day. His determination to reveal as much as possible

[147] Joachim Strupp, *Consensu celebriorum, medicorum historicorum, et philosophorum* (Frankfurt, 1574); Kaspar Bauhin, *Animadversiones in Historiam generalem plantarum* (Frankfurt, 1601); Jakob Ayrer, *Historischer Processus Iuris* (Frankfurt, 1598, etc.).
[148] Matthias Delius, *Matthaei Delii Meditationum De Historia Mundi* (Frankfurt, 1584); Nicolaus Reusner, *Ephemeris, sive Diarium Historicum* (Frankfurt, 1590); Martin Crusius, *Annales Suevici sive Chronica* (Frankfurt, 1595, etc.).
[149] Unfortunately, as this 1567 edition includes no new foreword or comments provided by printer or publisher, a clearer picture of Bassaeus's motives cannot be offered.

about the history of papal misdeeds is revealed partially in his preface, and can be further discerned by taking note of similar works prepared by Lydius.

Already in 1608 he had republished the polemical *De Primatu Papae Romani* of Nilus Cabasilas, fourteenth-century Archbishop of Thessalonica. Vigorously opposed to attempts to reunite the eastern and western churches, Cabasilas, to the delight of later reformers, had penned this letter as a refutation of the Roman notion of papal infallibility.[150] Along the same lines, Lydius five years later compiled the complete works of Nicolaus of Clémanges, the fifteenth-century reformist student of Jean Gerson and Pierre d'Ailly; he was motivated in part by the inclusion of *De Corrupto Ecclesiae Statu*, which was at the time attributed to Nicolaus. In his preface to the works of Barnes and Bale, Lydius refers to further works which he had prepared in the attempt to undermine the historical claims of the papacy. He makes note of his *Glossarium Latinobarbarum* of 1613, in which 'we traversed certain writings of the middle ages and, defying the accounts of the adulterers, brought together etymologies and authorities' in support of the evangelical cause.[151] And referring to Gabriel DuPréau's *Narratio Historica Conciliorum Omnium Ecclesiae Christianae*, which he had published with corrections and additions in 1610, Lydius explains that 'we previously gave their councils, now their lives'.[152] He also makes use of this preface to announce his intention to publish 'the constitutions of the apostolic chancellery (however many we are able to collect)'.[153]

In this light, Lydius's decision to reprint Barnes's *Vitae* is clearly revealed to be part of a conscious programme of historical-theological polemic. He explains his choice of authors – despite subtly criticising their 'vulgar style of writing'[154] – by noting that he sought only the most reliable sources, 'and therefore we chose Barnes and Bale and passed over the Italians, because they were less fawning, flattering, and charming with regard to the pope'.[155] Likewise, he desires to impress upon his readers that 'the English also assert that he is worshipped as the whore of Babylon'.[156] Because Lydius dedicates this volume to the members of the Estates-General, the highest representative governing institution of the Netherlands, he also feels obligated to note its political value.

[150] Lutheran polemicist Matthias Flacius Illyricus, for example, had the work printed in 1555 under the title *Nili Thessaloncensis libellus de primatu romani pontificis*.
[151] *Scriptores Duo Anglici, Coaetanei ac Conterranei; De Vitis Pontificum Romanorum* ... (Leiden, 1615), sig.)(3v: 'scriptores quosdam mediae aetatis percurrimus, & vocum adulterinarum rationes, etymologias & auctoritates congessimus'.
[152] *Scriptores*, sig.)(4r: 'Dedimus olim ipsorum concilia, nunc vitas.'
[153] *Scriptores*, sig.)(4v: 'Constitutiones Cancellariae Apostolicae (quotquot colligere potuimus)'.
[154] *Scriptores*, sig.)(3r: 'scripta stylo vulgari'.
[155] *Scriptores*, sig.)(2v: 'ideoque Barnum ac Baleum selegimus & Italis praetulimus, quod minus assentando, blandiendo Papis adulati fuissent'.
[156] *Scriptores*, sig.)(2v: '& facie anglica adoretur scortum Babylonis'.

> I offer to you the labours of two years, the history of those pontiffs at whose names all good men shudder, of whose frequent fraud and deceit you are well aware, who by violence or deceit desire to destroy your greatness as well as all Christian monarchs.[157]

And, significantly, he again highlights the particular benefits of history for proving this thesis. 'Indeed', he writes, 'Scripture proclaims and at the same time reveals the son of perdition, but in history it is made manifest how true the divine oracles are'.[158] Therefore, again referring to the works of Barnes and Bale, he concludes: 'From the two histories conjoined it will become known how much injury they inflict on the Republic'.[159] Finally, further confirming the general impression that the *Vitae* was especially intended to be used as a work of reference or a debating handbook, he explains that this work is being reprinted so 'it is possible to impugn the papacy with arguments'.[160]

The frequency with which, and the purposes for which, Barnes's works were reprinted both in England and on the continent indicates quite strongly that the evangelicals who praised these works were not merely flattering the memory of a friend or martyr. A significant number of them felt strongly enough about the value of these works that they willingly took the financial risk of making them available for new generations of reformers. Even more tellingly, those works in which Barnes dedicated himself most obviously to historical theology – his *Sentenciae* and *Vitae* – were not only reprinted and even continued by others; they were also soon translated for an even wider readership.

The translation of Barnes's works

While any work put through a sixteenth-century press involved the printer in some financial risk-taking, these risks would not have been quite so pronounced with many Latin publications. Especially with works such as those produced by Barnes, intended primarily as reference texts or debating handbooks, a printer might reasonably expect to find a market among the growing number of evangelical clergy and theologians. But whether such works would appeal to the laity, or

157 *Scriptores*, sig.)(2v: 'offero vobis labores bienii, Historiam Pontificum illorum, ad quorum nomen omnes exhorrent boni, quorum fraudes & dolos soepius estis experti, qui vestras Amplitudines, omnesque Christianos Monarchas, vi aut dolo extinctos vellent'. As contemporary proof of this, he notes that the Jesuits 'are now everywhere, not only confusing pure doctrine, but overturning states and publicly teaching people not to pay you any tribute'; sig.)(4r: 'qui nunc passim, non solum doctrinae puritatem conturbant, sed politiam evertunt, & publice docent, non esse vobis ulla tributa solvenda'.

158 *Scriptores*, sig.)(2v: 'Clamat quidem Scriptura & simul monstrat filium perditionis, sed in historia patefit, quam vera sint divina oracula.'

159 *Scriptores*, sig.)(4r: 'Ex utraque historia coniuncta innotescet, quantum Reipublica damnum intulerint'.

160 *Scriptores*, sig.)(4v: 'papatum ... possumus rationibus impugnare'.

to those who could not read Latin, was a question any publisher would have to consider seriously before committing them to a printer. This was, of course, a question which would also demand consideration by anyone taking up the laborious task of translation itself. That the Latin works of Barnes were indeed judged worthy of being published in vernacular editions is thus further testimony to their immediate and continued popularity.

The perceived value of the *Sentenciae*, for example, is again revealed in its very early translation into the vernacular. Even in the first Latin edition of 1530, Bugenhagen had noted in his foreword:

> if we see that they have been satisfied we shall later, if God wills it, repeat the book somewhere for the people with our annotations, or another whole book collected out of Augustine alone.[161]

The *Sentenciae* apparently did satisfy, for already in the next year Bugenhagen was fulfilling his promise of an edition 'for the people'. He himself took up the task of translating it into German, though he did not, as suggested, add to Barnes's work in any substantial fashion.[162] In addition to translating, Bugenhagen also seems to have taken upon himself the responsibility of seeing this new edition through the press; the printer, Johannes Petreius of Nuremberg, had issued a number of Bugenhagen's works in the previous decade.[163] Despite the apparent popularity of the first Latin edition, however, Petreius seems not to have foreseen a great market for a vernacular edition. It appears that he quickly dismantled the formes with which the first German edition was printed, because a second edition was printed later in the same year with the typeface completely reset.[164]

The immediate desire for a vernacular edition of the *Sentenciae* in Germany was not replicated in Barnes's native country. It would be a mistake, however, to interpret this as indicative of an English disregard for the work. By the time the Latin *Sentenciae* would have become known to an English audience Barnes's first *Supplicatyon* was already available. Being essentially an enlargement of his earlier publication, this work would have made an English version of the *Sentenciae* somewhat superfluous. Some forty years later, however, when John

161 *Sentenciae*, sig. A2v: 'haec boni consulere, quae si probari viderimus, dabimus postea, si deus voluerit, in publicum, cum Annotationibus nostris, integrum aliquem librum vel ex solo Augustino collectum'.

162 It is in the later 1536 Latin edition that Bugenhagen does add a great deal to Barnes's text, as mentioned above.

163 Most of Bugenhagen's publications with Petreius were commentaries and lectures on Scripture; but one, *De coniugo episcoporum et diaconorum* (Nuremburg, 1525), shows clear affinities with the subject matter of the *Sentenciae*.

164 *Furnemlich Artickel der Christlichen kirchen* (Nuremberg, 1531). Examples of both 1531 editions can be found in the British Library, London. They would seem to be the only editions in German, contrary to the claim of William Clebsch, *England's Earliest Protestants*, 49, that another was also printed in 1536. The 1536 publication was a new Latin edition, discussed above.

Foxe sought to reprint the 'whole workes' of Barnes, it became evident that even the 1531 and 1534 *Supplications* together did not repeat all of the articles found in the *Sentenciae*.

This fact is addressed by an otherwise anonymous 'T.G.' in his preface to 'A generall collection out of Doctour Barnes Workes of all the testimonyes, auncient fathers, Councels, and of the Popes owne lawes, alleaged by hym to proove these articles folowyng'.[165] He explains that, in spite of Barnes's historical testimonies being available with commentary in the *Supplication* newly reprinted, 'it was thought more expedient by the advise of the learned, and for the better edifying of the Reader, to have those testimonyes for every article collected severally by themselves'.[166] This is a significant admission of the particular value of the historical emphases found in Barnes's works. Their importance is further highlighted by the fact that the compiler not only draws these testimonies from the *Supplication*, but

> added also thereunto foure other articles translated into Englishe out of hys Booke De Doctorum Sententiis, whiche bee confirmed in the lyke sorte onely by bare testimonyes of scriptures, fathers, councels, & lawes. Which foure articles, and the treatise beefore of the originall of the masse, were omitted in hys English workes.[167]

The precise reason for judging these sources especially worthy of emphasis is also noted by the editor. They serve to reveal how much the church has changed in the course of history, and how starkly the contemporary papal church contrasts with the church of the fathers. Very closely following the exhortation provided by Barnes himself in the 1531 *Supplicatyon*, he writes:

> Now hast thou gentle reader to consider of these auncient testimonyes: desiring thee for the confirming and establishyng of thy doubtfull conscience, to compare these sayinges of Doctors, holy fathers, and of the Popes own law, unto the saying of the Pope and his Papisticall byshops, that bee in these latter dayes, and to their late practises, where their power

[165] Foxe, *Whole workes*, 358. This is perhaps the same 'T.G.' responsible for translating Pierre Boquin's *Assertio veteris ac veri Christianismi* (London, 1581 [STC 3371]) and for compiling *The friers chronicle* (London, 1623 [STC 11510]), a scurrilous account of cloistered life. But the suggestion of Clebsch, *England's Earliest Protestants*, 60 n. 3, that Thomas Good (Goad) was the man involved with the *Whole workes*, based on Good's seventeenth-century publication of Frith's works, must be dismissed for the simple reason that the *Whole workes* was compiled four years prior to Good's date of birth.

[166] Foxe, *Whole workes*, 358.

[167] Foxe, *Whole workes*, 358. The four mentioned articles are those on auricular confession, monasticism, fasting, and excommunication. As alluded to here by the author, Barnes's treatise on the origin of the Mass, the single most historically driven article in the 1530 *Sentenciae*, is not simply included among the appended articles, but translated in its entirety and placed among the articles reproduced from the two editions of the *Supplication*. This also strongly suggests a desire on the part of Foxe and his assistants to give particular attention to Barnes's historical research.

> is, or hath beene receaved: and then geeve sentence howe they doe agree. If they doe accorde, then is it lyke they bee of the true Church, whereof these holy fathers were. But if they agree not, then mayest thou suspect, that they have gone astray, and that the devill hath transfigured hym selfe into an Aungell of light, and that they are his ministers.[168]

Given this clearly stated objective, as well as the titular indication that Barnes's 'whole workes' are reprinted in this volume, it is surprising that his most overtly historical work is not included. Foxe himself had access to the *Vitae romanorum pontificum*, and he certainly considered it a valuable resource. Yet, in contrast to their treatment of the *Sentenciae*, the editors do not even attempt to explain its exclusion. Though this can be no more than a tentative suggestion, it is quite possible that Foxe himself simply found its inclusion unnecessary. It has been previously noted that the *Whole workes* was conceived as a companion volume to his *Actes and Monuments*, a work which contained its own account of the history of the popes. It is likely that this English history – itself dependent on Barnes's work – was deemed sufficient, especially since the work of translating and reprinting the *Vitae* would have greatly increased the labour and expense involved in an already large volume.

Though less probable, the issue of expense might also partially explain why the first vernacular edition of the *Vitae* was not a translation of the complete work, but only of the concluding sections concerned with the reigns of Popes Hadrian IV and Alexander III.[169] Three separate editions of this work, under the title *Bapsttrew Hadriani iiii. und Alexanders iii. gegen Keyser Friderichen Barbarossa geübt*, were printed in 1545, one in Strassburg and two more in Wittenberg.[170] As with the original Latin edition of the *Vitae*, Luther provided a foreword for these German editions. On this basis it has often been assumed that Luther himself was also the translator.[171] Ernst Schäfer, who offers the earliest and most extensive analysis of this translation, also attributes it to Luther on the basis of further internal evidence. He argues that the humour, sarcasm, and certain German expressions found in it are consistent with Luther's own writings.[172] The 'ponderous and archaic' style, he also notes, is reminiscent of that found in Luther's earlier translation of the Donation of Constantine.[173]

168 Foxe, *Whole workes*, 358. Cf. *Supplicatyon* (1531), unnumbered folio = sig. U1r.

169 Stadtwald, 'Pope Alexander III's Humilation', 755–68, convincingly argues that only these sections were translated and published because they most concisely illustrated the papal threat to temporal authority, and that the *Papsttreu* was published as part of a wider campaign of pro-imperial propaganda then taking place.

170 The work was reprinted twice more in Luther's *Gesamtausgaben* of Wittenberg, 1551, and Jena, 1558.

171 See, e.g., Schäfer, *Luther als Kirchenhistoriker*, 107; Stadtwald, 'Pope Alexander III's Humilation', 766 n. 40.

172 Schäfer, *Luther als Kirchenhistoriker*, 107–8.

173 Schäfer, *Luther als Kirchenhistoriker*, 107: 'schwerfällig und archaistisch'.

This conclusion, however, has been challenged by the editor of the critical edition found in *Luthers Werke*; he argues that the sober style of the translation was 'natural for people used to writing Latin, and it is not at all unusual with historical writers'.[174] Brenner, the editor, also points out that much of the German vocabulary found in this tract is not only uncommon in Luther's works, but rare in Wittenberg as a whole.[175] Citing its more frequent use in the Alsace region of south-west Germany, Brenner argues for the origin of the translation, and its first edition, in Strassburg. This would also account for the fact that the two Wittenberg editions are sloppily set and corrected, something unlikely to have been allowed if Luther had a direct hand in its printing. By Brenner's account, then, Luther's foreword was most likely written on the basis of his knowledge of the original edition of the *Vitae*. Without having seen the translation, he would have sent his foreword to Strassburg, where it was first printed; this printed edition would have subsequently been acquired by Joseph Clug in Wittenberg, who republished it without Luther's involvement.[176]

Brenner's is a convincing analysis of the *Papsttreu*'s origins. If correct, it also provides additional testimony concerning the popularity enjoyed by the *Vitae*. Given Luther's high regard for the original edition, it would have been unsurprising if he had initiated its later translation and publication. That this project was pursued independently, however, further reveals its influence outside of Wittenberg. Something more of this influence might also be evident in the fact that Wendel Rihel, the Strassburg printer of the *Papsttreu*, seems to have shown little interest in historical works before Barnes's text was brought to his press. Beginning in that year, however, Rihel would go on to print a number of works similar to the *Vitae* in both content and method. Printed in the same year, for example, was the ironically titled work of the Anabaptist Gerhard Westerburg: *That the Most Holy Pope Cannot Err*.[177] Perhaps most significantly, however, only one year later Bartolomeo Platina's *Historia von der Bäpst und Keiser Leben* was put through the same press. Like the *Papsttreu* and the *Historia*, many of the historical titles Rihel would publish over the next decade were German translations of earlier Latin works.[178]

174 *WA*, 54.305: 'natürliche für Leute, die lateinisch zu schreiben gewohnt waren, und bei historischen Schriftstelern gar nicht ungewöhnlich'. Brenner's conclusion is followed by Martin Brecht, *Martin Luther*, 3 vols, tr. J.L. Schaaf (Philadelphia, 1985–93), 3.361, who simply says, 'The translation and work's marginal notes can scarcely have come from Luther.'
175 *WA*, 54.305–6.
176 *WA*, 54.306.
177 Gerhard Westerburg, *Das der allerheiligster Papst ... nicht ihrren können* (Strassburg, 1545).
178 Many of which were translated by the Strassburg humanist Caspar Hedio, including the *Histori des burgundischen Kriegs* (1551) by Philippe de Commines, as well as his *Histori von König Carle* (1552). Two Latin histories worth mention are Foxe's *Commentarii rerum in ecclesia gestarum* (1554) and Johann Sleidan's *De statu religionis commentarii* (1555).

Rihel's sudden interest in such ecclesiastical histories was precisely the reaction desired by the author of the *Papsttreu*'s preface. In terms similar to those with which he had praised the first edition of the *Vitae*, Luther opened his foreword by proclaiming that 'next to holy Scripture, it is very good to have as proof for oneself the histories of the emperors'. But their primary benefit, he continues, is not to be found in what they reveal about the emperors. Instead they are especially valuable because in them 'one sees how the pope is certainly filled with the devil'.[179] Describing him in increasingly common terms, Luther labels the pope 'the arch-enemy of our Lord and Saviour, and the disturber of his holy Christian church'.[180]

Such name-calling is not, however, merely *ad hominem* abuse. Rather, it is a consequence of conclusions Luther had reached in his own study of history, partially influenced by the writings of Barnes himself. Luther can conceive of the pope as the principal opponent of Christ and disturber of the church because he believes him to hold an office not instituted by Christ for the sake of the church. Thus he can ask here why the pope, 'who is no bishop, still has an office in the church'.[181] The question is particularly pertinent because, as the *Papsttreu* attempts to demonstrate, those who have held this office have habitually persecuted those appointed to a true office established by God. Luther describes the emperor's station as 'ordained of God and at his command',[182] and thus the emperor himself as 'a person so elevated in God's law'.[183]

Pressing this point even further, Luther equates such a divinely ordained office-holder with the person of Christ himself. Dismissing the pope's self-identification with the figure described in Psalm 91, Luther retorts: 'one justly says that the hellish cobra and lion, asp and basilisk, Alexander III, walks on and tramples on the neck of a Christian prince – and in the prince, Christ himself'.[184] This is an assertion repeated twice more in his short preface. What is done to emperors, he insists, is done 'to the Christ in the highest majesty';[185] popes act unjustly against 'Christ and God himself, just as his father the devil also does, from whom he has learned to do this'.[186]

This stark identification of emperors with Christ and popes with the devil is

[179] *WA*, 54.307: 'neben der heiligen schrifft, seer wol die historien von den Keysern, darin man sihet, wie die Bepste voller Teuffel sind gewest'.
[180] *WA*, 54.307: 'den Ertzfeind unsers HERRN und Heilands und verstörer seiner heiligen Christlichen kirchen'.
[181] *WA*, 54.309: 'der kein Bischoff noch einiges ampt in der Kirchen hat'.
[182] *WA*, 54.308: 'von Gott geordent und zu ehren geboten'.
[183] *WA*, 54.308: 'solcher hohen person von Gott gesetzt'.
[184] *WA*, 54.308: 'man billicher sagen, das der hellische Trache und Lewe, Otter und Basilisce Alexander iii. gehet und tritt einem Christlichen fürsten und in dem Fürsten Christo selbst auff den hals'.
[185] *WA*, 54.309: 'den Christen in den höhesten Maiesteten'.
[186] *WA*, 54.308: 'Christo und Gott selbs, thun, wie sein Vater der Teufel auch thut, Und in solchs zu thun geleret hat'.

common in Luther's thought. While the comments cited above are made with specific reference to the events described in the *Papsttreu*, they are simply one manifestation of his wider conviction that, in history, both God and the devil operate behind 'masks'. For the benefit of church and world, God acts in and through ordained offices such as that of the emperor. The false office of the papacy, however, Luther here and elsewhere condemns as nothing other than 'the devil's mask and attire'.[187] It is because he believes these conclusions to be manifestly evident in the record of papal-imperial relations that he can say 'it is very good to have as proof for oneself the histories of the emperors'.

The unqualified praise of political authority found in Luther did not figure prominently in the next, fuller translation of the *Vitae*, a Czech edition published in 1565 under the simple title of *Kroniky*. In fact, this edition is one of those in which no foreword by Luther is included at all, despite the lengthy influence of Lutheranism in Bohemia. Not only had Luther established ties with both the Bohemian Brethren and the Utraquists, but already in the 1520s Lutheran preachers were crossing the borders of Saxony into the German-speaking communities of northern and western Bohemia. And travelling in the opposite direction, large numbers of students left Bohemia to study in Wittenberg in the next decade.[188] With the blessing of nobles and urban magistrates, many of Bohemia's clergy in the 1530s and 1540s moved toward Lutheranism and a 'quasi-Lutheran' neo-Utraquism.[189]

Despite the popularity of Luther's thought in his lands, however, the Bohemian King Ferdinand I, brother of Emperor Charles V, attempted in the 1540s to draw Bohemian troops into the Schmalkaldic War against the estates of Lutheran Germany. Rather than comply, his subjects revolted, leading to Ferdinand's seizure of Prague in 1547 and the expulsion of all Lutheran preachers in the same year. The memory of Ferdinand's pro-imperial and anti-Lutheran campaign might partially explain why those who published Barnes's *Vitae* twenty years later chose not to include the high praise for imperial authority found in Luther's earlier writing.[190] What it does not by itself explain is the fact that even Luther's

187 *WA*, 54.309: 'die Teuffels larven und putzen'. This idea will be examined again in the next chapter, when attention is turned to further works written by Luther while under the influence of Barnes's historical analysis of the papacy.

188 Winfried Eberhard, 'Bohemia, Moravia and Austria', in *The Early Reformation in Europe*, ed. Andrew Pettegree (Cambridge, 1992), 30.

189 Winfried Eberhard, 'Reformation and Counterreformation in East Central Europe', in *Handbook of European History, 1400–1600*, vol. 2, ed. T.A. Brady, H.A. Oberman, and J.D. Tracy (Leiden, 1995), 555. Eberhard's 'quasi-Lutheran' tag refers to the party's defence of the principle of *sola scriptura*, a reduction in the number of sacraments from seven to two, and a rejection of the Mass as a sacrifice.

190 The translator of the *Vitae* was the mayor of Prague's Old Town in 1547, the year of the revolt. As discussed in more detail below, however, his sympathies seem to have been more in line with the Old Utraquists than the Lutherans.

original preface to the *Vitae* was excised in this new translation. This is especially peculiar in the context of the renewed prominence of Lutheran preaching in Bohemia after the 1555 Peace of Augsburg.[191] Even in the Old Utraquist stronghold of Prague, Lutheranism remained strong through the second half of the sixteenth century, with Luther's works being more widely read there than those of the native reformer Jan Hus.[192] This is particularly noteworthy because it was in Prague and in response to ecclesiastical developments in that city that the Czech *Vitae* originated.

The Prague translator of Barnes's work was a man of some distinction. Simon Ennius Glatovinus had been the mayor of the Old Town when Ferdinand seized the city in 1547. Only a few years earlier he had served as rector of Prague's university, a traditionally Utraquist institution, but one which maintained correspondence with Melanchthon.[193] His academic credentials at the time of his rectorship seem to have been established primarily through an influential work on mathematics published in the 1530s; but a decade later he authored an even more popular textbook of the Czech and German languages. The work was in no way polemical, so it cannot be assumed that Glatovinus's encouragement of German literacy was meant to further the cause of a distinctly German theology.[194] In fact, the evidence suggests that Glatovinus was not a convinced supporter of Luther or Lutheranism. One of his patrons even in the late 1540s was the Roman bishop of Vienna; and Glatovinus himself seems to have held some hope that the council of Trent would result in a reunification of western Christendom.[195]

If not overtly Lutheran, Glatovinus was nevertheless decidedly anti-papal. In addition to his translation of Barnes's papal history, he is also named as the translator of the *Obandwach Antykrystuow*, an extended comparison of the rule of Christ with those of Mohammed and the popes.[196] Furthermore, Glatovinus not only translated the *Vitae* for a Czech audience, but also continued it through the

[191] See Graeme Murdock, 'Eastern Europe', in *The Reformation World*, ed. Andrew Pettegree (New York and London, 2000), 195, and Eberhard, 'Bohemia', 36.

[192] Jirí Pešek, 'Protestant Literature in Bohemian Private Libraries *circa* 1600', in *The Reformation in Eastern and Central Europe*, ed. Karin Maag (Aldershot, 1997), 43. Pešek concludes that 'the writings of the Lutheran authors represented the core of religious literature in the Protestant libraries of Prague'.

[193] See Andrew Pettegree and Karin Maag, 'The Reformation in Eastern and Central Europe', in *The Reformation in Eastern and Central Europe*, ed. Karin Maag (Aldershot, 1997), 9, and Eberhard, 'Reformation', 555.

[194] Pešek, 'Protestant Literature in Bohemian Private Libraries', 40–1, notes that the greatest number of all books in sixteenth-century Bohemia were printed in Germany, not merely those of a religious nature.

[195] Zdenek David, *Finding the Middle Way: The Utraquists' Liberal Challenge to Rome and Luther* (Washington, DC, 2003), 154. Though dismissing them, David does note that some MS notes in Glatovinus's copy of the *Epistulae Familiares* of Aeneas Silvius speak more favourably of Lutheranism than of Czech Utraquism.

[196] The copy in the University Library, Cambridge, is bound together with the *Kroniky*.

sixteenth-century reign of Pope Pius IV, especially emphasising 'particular Utraquist grievances against the popes, as well as against the General Councils of the period'.[197] In this, Zdenek David suggests, Glatovinus simply expresses his agreement with the Old Utraquists, who had

> justified the office of the pope on biblical grounds, and were ready to welcome a catalog of the popes' historical misdeeds to document their assertion that the popes had misused their office to accumulate unwarranted powers and wealth.[198]

Thus, he argues, the translator's work 'probably should not be seen as stemming from a historical or theological connection with Luther or his heritage'.[199]

Concrete motivation for the publication of the *Kroniky* can, however, be discerned in events then taking place in Prague. From the mid-1550s Jesuits began entering the city to train Roman priests,[200] and in the following years Jesuit colleges were established not only in Prague, but also in Brno and Olomouc.[201] The concerted effort to re-establish Bohemia as a centre of Roman orthodoxy is especially evident in the consecration of an archbishop to the see of Prague, which had remained vacant since 1471.[202] Though Glatovinus himself had died in the 1550s, and the *Kroniky* would not actually be printed until 1565, its anonymous preface bears the date 1561, the very year in which the archbishopric of Prague was finally filled. There can be little doubt that the publication of Barnes's work 'was timed to coincide with the restoration of the Roman archbishopric in Prague', and to help 'mobilize theological resources by the Utraquists for the coming encounters with, and challenges of, the agencies of the Roman curia'.[203]

The parallels here with the 1615 Latin reprint of the *Vitae* are significant. According to Johannes Lydius, who would edit and continue that edition, it too was published as part of an attempt to counter recent Jesuit activity.[204] Of equal import is that the author of the Czech preface, like that of the 1615 Latin preface, especially emphasises the value of the *Kroniky* as a work of history. He suggests that all historians should be praised, because, he believes, even the chroniclers of temporal affairs 'were certainly and undoubtedly inspired by the Holy Spirit'.[205]

197 David, *Finding the Middle Way*, 153.
198 David, *Finding the Middle Way*, 153. Two pages later David also argues that Glatovinus likewise 'accepted the papal role in succession to that of the Apostle Peter', but disliked 'the attempts of some popes to force certain human inventions, which actually opposed the law of Christ, on the faithful'.
199 David, *Finding the Middle Way*, 153. It is in support of this that he also notes the previously mentioned omission of Luther's foreword.
200 C.A. Pescheck, *Reformation and Anti-Reformation in Bohemia* (London, 1845), 47.
201 Murdock, 'Eastern Europe', 202.
202 Murdock, 'Eastern Europe', 194.
203 David, *Finding the Middle Way*, 153.
204 See especially *Scriptores*, sig.)(4r.
205 *Kronyky. A žiwotuow sepsánij naywrchnegssych biskupuow Ržijmskych ginac Papežuow*

But any such praise of papal histories warrants some qualification, for 'there are not so many good chroniclers of popes'. The author does assert, though, that 'some historians are more reliable and trustworthy'.[206]

> Such was the great and famous scholar Doctor Robert Barnes, a teacher of holy Scripture, an Englishman by origin, who in this short work collected, recorded, and connected their lives, deeds, administration, learning, provisions, ordinances, holy wars, conspiracy, revolts (against some Christian emperors, kings, princes, and towns), and also many councils.[207]

Noting that Barnes's work ended with the pontificate of Alexander III, the author explains that the lives of later popes were collected from other histories, and he expresses his desire that the work be further continued in the future.[208] He is especially anxious that the volume be read by the Bohemian clergy, as it will 'suit their education so that they not support and protect their many fabricated provisions against Jesus Christ'.[209] The author's confidence in the effectiveness of the *Kroniky* seems at least partially influenced by his erroneous belief that it was responsible for the earlier English rejection of the papacy. He suggests it was written 'on the request of Henry VIII, the King of England, who longed to know about the lives, deeds, and administration of the Roman bishops',[210] and concludes:

> Henry read this brief writing on the lives, learning, and administration of some popes, and particularly of the last ones, and found and discovered that all the things Luther wrote against the pope were true. When he had discovered this, as they said, he left the Roman church, rejected its learning and provisions, and ordered the following of Christ's pure gospel.[211]

As the preface draws to a close, the author affirms that the *Vitae* was translated with similar hopes for Bohemia.

> Having seen and considered it good and needed, a man of learning, the late Simon Ennius Glatovinus, in order to save the Czech nation and convert it to true religion and evangelical piety, and to the following of Christ's learning, industriously translated the histories of popes by the above mentioned Robert Barnes from Latin into Czech.[212]

(Nuremburg, 1565), sig. 2r. All translations from the *Kronyky* are those of Blanka Frydrychova Klimova, to whom I am extremely grateful for her time and labour.

206 *Kronyky*, sig. 2r.
207 *Kronyky*, sig. 2r–v.
208 *Kronyky*, sig. 3v.
209 *Kronyky*, sig. 4r.
210 *Kronyky*, sig. 2v.
211 *Kronyky*, sig. 3r.
212 *Kronyky*, sig. 5r.

That the *Vitae* would have an influence even in Bohemia offers further evidence of Barnes's importance as an historical theologian.[213] It is especially noteworthy that, while history had enjoyed some previous popularity in Bohemia, it was only with the coming of the reformation that there was 'an immense increase in the writing of history'.[214] That Barnes's history was one of the first to be made accessible in the Czech language is even more significant in the light of the fact that the Bohemian Brethren would not even produce a Czech translation of the Bible until more than a decade later.[215]

The above reveals Charles Anderson to have been mistaken in his off-hand assertion that the *Vitae* is a work unworthy of translation.[216] This was clearly not the opinion of sixteenth-century reformers. Nor do they seem to have believed, as Alec Ryrie suggests, that 'it was principally the manner of Barnes's death that secured such posthumous fame as he had'.[217] While this is to some extent true in England, with which Ryrie is primarily concerned, even there Barnes's status as an historian rivalled his memory as a martyr or an evangelical theologian. That his doctrinal influence would soon wane, especially outside of Germany, is perfectly understandable in the light of his confessionally Lutheran leanings.

But it is also for this reason that his value as an historian continued to be recognised, not only in England, but throughout Europe. Barnes's historical works could be pressed into service even by those who ultimately disagreed with his theological conclusions. The arguments presented in the *Vitae*, and to a lesser extent in the *Sentenciae*, could be manipulated to suit ends not pursued by their original author. Thus, for instance, Wendel Rihel could selectively reprint that portion of the *Vitae* which most effectively supported a largely political agenda. And likewise, the Prague Utraquists could find the work a useful corrective to certain papal abuses, while not adopting its author's complete rejection of the papal office. The manner in which Barnes's historical works could be manipulated for use by a variety of theological parties will become even more evident in a survey of their use as sources and models for later polemicists.

[213] On the influence of the *Vitae* in Bohemia see also Miroslava Hejnová, 'Barnesovy "Kroniky" a jejich ceské pokracování', *Folia Historica Bohemica* 13 (1990), 590, where the contemporary censors's awareness of the work is noted.

[214] Norbert Kersken, 'Reformation and the Writing of National History in East-Central and Northern Europe', in *The Reformation in Eastern and Central Europe*, ed. Karin Maag (Aldershot, 1997), 70–1.

[215] Murdock, 'Eastern Europe', 200.

[216] Anderson, 'The Person and Position', 163 n. 2.

[217] Ryrie, 'A saynt in the devyls name', 151.

7

ROBERT BARNES: HIS SUCCESSORS AND HIS LEGACY

Despite the high regard in which the Latin works of Robert Barnes were held, the conclusion should not be reached that his English works were without influence. They clearly were. But, as suggested above, the extent to which they could be put to fruitful use was limited not only by the language in which they were written, but also by their doctrinally Lutheran leanings. To be sure, in the early days of the reformation, before confessional lines became rigidly fixed, and when much debate centred upon the doctrine of justification, such leanings were less controversial. So, for example, writing in the 1530s, Thomas Swinnerton showed no hesitation in recommending Barnes's *Supplicatyon* to his own readers, especially for its treatment of justification by faith.[1] And even after the splintering of the reform movement there were those who, overlooking or reinterpreting Barnes's personal convictions, could make great use of the *Supplication* in internecine Protestant controversies. Thus the Puritan controversialist William Prynne relies heavily on this work in his refutation of Arminianism, chiefly citing Barnes's articles on justification and free will.[2] Nevertheless, a survey of Prynne's works and the works of others reveals that many later theologians and polemicists found even the *Supplication* most useful for its historical data rather than for its doctrinal conclusions.

Barnes's works as early modern sources

Writing in the mid-seventeenth century, it is to Barnes's English work that Prynne will appeal when asserting that 'their was no great Clarke in the Church of God

1 See Rex, *A Reformation Rhetoric*, 129, 143. Throughout the whole of Swinnerton's *Tropes* Barnes is one of only three contemporary authorities cited.
2 See, e.g., Prynne, *The Church of Englands old antithesis*, 53, 54, 63, 69, 73, 74, 109, 110. Prynne's reliance on these two articles in refuting Arminianism is especially noteworthy since these very articles were the two republished in the next century by no less an Arminian than John Wesley. See his *Two Treatises* (London, 1739).

this 400. yeares',[3] and that it was 'the ancient policy of Lordly Prelates ... to speake most against popery, when they are busiest to bring it in'.[4] But it is also in the pages of the *Supplication* that Prynne finds the historical details in support of such assertions, especially as they relate to the church in England. He relies on Barnes, for instance, for his account of the contentious election of Canterbury Archbishop Stephen Langton in the thirteenth century, as well as for his account of the fifteenth-century Archbishop of York, Richard Scrope, inciting rebellion against King Henry IV.[5] In the same work Prynne lifts a quotation of no fewer than twenty-one pages from the *Supplication*, in which Barnes had outlined the historical consequences of the papal oath of loyalty sworn by English clergy, often to the detriment of royal prerogatives.[6] Likewise, in arguing that the popish books of the previous five hundred years had failed to encourage obedience to princes, Prynne notes that Barnes had sufficiently proved this with examples from history.[7]

That Prynne perceived Barnes primarily as an historian is made even more evident in his 1637 work, *A quench-coale*, where he cites Barnes among those whom he calls 'our Historians and writers'.[8] This designation is all the more noteworthy as Prynne relies most heavily on that work by Barnes which is the least historical; only rarely does he reference his *Vitae romanorum pontificum*. Significantly, when Prynne does cite the *Vitae*, he illustrates how readily the information supplied by Barnes in a relatively objective manner could be put to polemical use by those who followed him. While Barnes had simply recorded that it was Pope Vigilius who decreed that priests should face eastward during the celebration of the Mass, Prynne employs this as an argument in favour of the Puritan rejection of altars standing against the eastern walls of churches: 'their superstitious easterly adoration', he says, was 'derived from Necromancers, and those heathen Idolaters, Ezech. 8.16. whoe worshipp the risinge sunne'.[9]

Similar use of the *Vitae* is made by George Downame, a conformist contemporary of Prynne. Attempting to prove that, in the earliest church, Christians of the same city did not all assemble in the same place for worship, he quotes Barnes concerning Evaristus's distribution of city parishes among presbyters.[10] Sir Henry Wotton, who, as previously noted, would declare Barnes one of 'three notable Writers of Popes lives', calls upon his testimony in proof of the

3 Prynne, *A looking-glasse*, sig. a3r.
4 William Prynne, *The Popish royall favourite* (London, 1643 [Wing P4039]), 70.
5 Prynne, *The antipathie*, 33, 528.
6 Prynne, *The antipathie*, 101–22.
7 Prynne, *The antipathie*, 526–7.
8 William Prynne, *A quench-coale* (Amsterdam, 1637 [STC 20474]), 14; cf. 44.
9 Prynne, *A quench-coale*, 23.
10 George Downame, *A defence of the sermon preached at the consecration of the L. Bishop of Bath and VVelles* (London, 1611 [STC 7115]), 93.

contention that early popes were not superior to emperors. On the contrary, Barnes had shown, when they were not being martyred by Roman emperors they were having their elections approved and confirmed by them.[11] The *Vitae* was likewise quoted by the arch-conformist Archbishop John Whitgift to show that this imperial prerogative, even after having been relinquished to the people of Rome, was actually restored by a reigning pope, Leo VIII.[12] And even one of Whitgift's most vocal detractors, the Presbyterian agitator John Field, found the *Vitae* a useful source from which he could draw illustrations of the contemptuous manner in which English kings had been treated by their bishops.[13]

This casual use of Barnes's works in later theological controversies partially reveals the extent to which even those with widely divergent views on doctrine and church polity could find his historical data to be of continuing relevance. And this was the case not only in England, but also on the continent. It appears quite likely, for example, that the Genevan reformer John Calvin made use of Barnes's *Sentenciae*.[14] Heinrich Bullinger was certainly conversant with his *Vitae*, making special reference to it in his refutation of the papal bull promulgated against Queen Elizabeth I.[15] But because Barnes is so frequently portrayed as a disciple of Luther – and often as no more than a disciple of Luther – it is especially worth noting Luther's apparent debt to Barnes. The German's high praise of the *Vitae* has already been noted. In the light of such praise, Ernst Schäfer was undoubtedly correct in stating that 'We may regard it as certain that, from this point on [i.e., its publication], Barnes's writing was a particularly eagerly read component of Luther's library.'[16] Circumstantial evidence in support of this supposition can be found in the fact that, while Luther confessed that he had not previously been well versed in history, the years immediately following saw him publish an impressive number of treatises addressing the very issues of papal and conciliar history covered by Barnes.[17] The common estimate of these writings, in comparison with Luther's earlier polemics, is that they are 'richer and more sophisticated, for they have gained a historical dimension'.[18]

[11] Wotton, *The state of Christendom*, 172.

[12] John Whitgift, *The Works of John Whitgift*, 3 vols, ed. J. Ayre (Cambridge: Parker Society, 1851), 1.403–04.

[13] John Fielde, *A caveate for Parsons Hovvlet* (London, 1581 [STC 10844]), sig. F2r.

[14] See Lane, *John Calvin*, 132 n. 127, 139 n. 164, and 140 n. 174.

[15] Heinrich Bullinger, *Bullae Papisticae ante biennium contra ... Reginam Elizabetham ... promulgatae, refutatio* (London, 1571 [STC 4043]), fo. 75r. See below for his more extensive use of the *Vitae* in compiling his own papal history.

[16] Schäfer, *Luther als Kirchenhistoriker*, 87: 'Wir dürfen es als gewiss ansehen, dass dieses Schriften des Barns fortan einen besonders eifrig gelesenen Bestandteil von Luthers Bibliothek gebildet hat.'

[17] See, e.g., the titles listed in *WA*, 50.494–6, and the commentary in Edwards, *Luther's Last Battles*, 77–96.

[18] Edwards, *Luther's Last Battles*, 96.

Though Luther will not cite Barnes by name in these works,[19] one example of the Englishman's intimate involvement with his developing thought can be seen in Luther's request that Barnes participate in a 1536 Wittenberg disputation on the power of church councils. Written shortly after his foreword to the *Vitae*, Luther's disputation theses reveal his conviction that the historical record encourages a sceptical view of both papal and conciliar authority.[20] His prefatory remarks set the tone:

> Among other monstrosities in the church, and that which is not the least, is that the power of holy councils lays waste the church. Before the council of Nicaea a pope was below a council; but afterward the pope himself rejected not only the church, but also councils, so that he might be the head of the council.[21]

For his part, Barnes weighed in by treating Augustine's often quoted assertion that he would not have believed the gospel if he had not been moved to do so by the church. Putting this remark in context, Barnes notes that 'Augustine has two arguments, one *a priori*, another *a posteriori*'.[22] He points out that Augustine had equated the church with the apostles, those who believe and proclaim the gospel. 'Those same were called the church who themselves have the true gospel', Barnes explains, and, with an eye toward Rome, concludes that 'the church, which believes the gospel, condemns you, you who set the church above the gospel'.[23]

That Luther arranged for this disputation so quickly after having read the *Vitae*, and that he would request Barnes's involvement, is especially worthy of note because the arguments put forward at this time 'anticipate many of the arguments Luther advanced in his 1539 masterwork, *On the Councils and the Church*'.[24] Noting this connection, at least one author has suggested that the understanding of history first expressed in Luther's foreword to the *Vitae* is that which defines this later treatise.[25] And, indeed, the dual emphases of Luther's 1539 work – that 'the present position of the church in the papacy is woefully at variance (as is evident) with the ways of the councils and fathers',[26] and that 'the

19 Citing authorities, especially contemporaries, was something Luther rarely did.

20 It is impossible to date the disputation precisely. While some have tentatively suggested October 1536, Brecht favours a date early in the year. As evidence places Barnes in England in both September and November 1536, the later date is most unlikely. For a discussion of the details see *WA*, 39/1.181–3, and cf. Brecht, *Martin Luther*, 3.132 and 3.177.

21 *WA*, 39/1.188: 'Inter caetera monstra in Ecclesia et illud non est minimum, quod Ecclesiam devastat potestas sancti concilii. Ante concilium Nicaenum papa erat sub concilio, sed postea sibi reiecit papa non solum Ecclesiam, verum et concilia, ita ut esset caput concilii.'

22 *WA*, 39/1.191: 'Augustinus duo habet argumenta, unum a priori, alterum a posteriori'.

23 *WA*, 39/1.191: 'Ipsi se vocabant Ecclesiam, utqui verum haberent Evangelium'; 'Ecclesia, quae credit Evangelio, damnat vos, vos supra Evangelium ponitis Ecclesiam.'

24 Edwards, *Luther's Last Battles*, 79.

25 See *WA*, 50.498.

26 *AE*, 41.14 (*WA*, 50.515).

councils are not only unequal, but also contradictory'[27] – are precisely those so frequently put forth by Barnes himself. And Luther makes no secret of his reason for such conclusions: they are 'based on history'[28] he says; 'history clearly shows' them to be true,[29] and the facts are 'strongly borne out by the histories'.[30] The sustained and highly informed argument present in *On the Councils* has led many to agree that this treatise represents 'the most sophisticated historical analysis to come from Luther's pen',[31] and that it is 'eminently persuasive ... by virtue of its logic and historical examples'.[32]

Nearly a decade later Luther would engage in an equally historical attack on the papacy. Believing Charles V to have encroached on papal authority at the 1544 Diet of Speyer, Pope Paul III censured the emperor in a letter of August that year. When Luther learned of this, he set to work on a treatise in which he argued that papal authority was hardly what Paul III imagined it to be. The pope, he said, was not the supreme head of Christendom; emperors had a better claim to convening councils than did popes; and imperial authority did not derive from the papacy. Though much less refined than his earlier work, *Against the Papacy at Rome, An Institution of the Devil* reveals that Luther could still 'produce a persuasive argument using historical examples'.[33] Partly explaining this, almost certainly, is the fact that Luther began this work at the very moment his attention had once again been turned to Barnes's *Vitae*.

In February 1545, the Wittenberg theologian Justus Jonas wrote to a colleague: 'Against the pope and his counterfeit council the Reverend Doctor Luther is writing two, or, if I am not mistaken, three thunderous little books'.[34] Jonas here refers to *Against the Papacy*, as well as to the Wittenberg artist Lucas Cranach's separately published illustrations, for which Luther composed descriptive verses. The mention of a third 'little book' can only be a reference to the *Papsttreu*, that German translation from the *Vitae* for which Luther was then writing a preface. Undoubtedly this was one of the works Luther had in mind when he declared it evident 'from all the histories' that the bishops of Rome exercised none of their present power before the reign of Boniface III.[35] Just as it had been in 1539, Luther's constant refrain once again became 'you must read the histories'.[36]

[27] *AE*, 41.20 (*WA*, 50.520).
[28] *AE*, 41.23 (*WA*, 50.522).
[29] *AE*, 41.43 (*WA*, 50.539).
[30] *AE*, 41.120 (*WA*, 50.604).
[31] J. Pelikan, *Obedient Rebels: Catholic Substance and Protestant Principle in Luther's Reformation* (London, 1964), 53; cf. 27, 56.
[32] Edwards, *Luther's Last Battles*, 93.
[33] Edwards, *Luther's Last Battles*, 185.
[34] Quoted in *WA*, 54.300: 'Contra papam et eius simulatum concilium scribit rev. d. Lutherus duos aut, ni fallor, tres fulmineos libellos'.
[35] *AE*, 41.290 (*WA*, 54.228).
[36] *AE*, 41.372 (*WA*, 54.296); cf. *AE*, 41.295 (*WA*, 54.232).

While Luther always remained primarily an exegetical theologian, the impact of the *Vitae* certainly 'pulled Luther deeper into history', as one modern editor of his works has suggested.[37] But other continental reformers especially, in whose thought history played a more central role, found in Barnes a kindred spirit and a source of ready information to supplement their own research. Thus, for example, his name is to be found among the sources for French cleric Jean de Hainault's ecclesiastical history, *L'estat de l'Eglise*.[38] As previously mentioned, the Königsberg preacher and historian Johann Funck also found the *Vitae* a useful source for his *Commentarius in Chronologiam*, not only citing Barnes within the text, but commenting that 'another could scarcely have written with better judgement'.[39] A similar estimate was given by the Lutheran theologian Christophorus Hoffman in his *De Christiana religione et de regno Antichristi*, a work in three books devoted to locating the origins of Antichrist, tracing his growth in the church, and outlining his usurpation of temporal authority. 'Surely Doctor Robertus judges correctly', he declares.[40] In his final book especially, Hoffman is careful to note by name those histories in which his assertions find support. Taking up the life of Hildebrand he cites the works of Platina, Nauclerus, and a third historian: 'Hoc est, Doctoris Roberti Barus'.[41] Significantly, both Platina and Nauclerus are cited in Barnes's own survey of Hildebrand's life, raising the suspicion that Hoffman is making exclusive use of Barnes, and simply multiplying his witnesses by noting those also mentioned in the *Vitae*. This suspicion, in fact, is elsewhere confirmed. With the first mention of Barnes, Hoffman will admit: 'his little book of the lives of the Roman pontiffs is extant, which work I use, especially for the sake of brevity, in reference to several following examples'.[42] And citing the *Vitae* again towards the end of his work, he refers to 'Doctor Robert Barnes, the words of whom I have thus far used entirely in this recitation of the lives of the Roman pontiffs'.[43]

In Barnes's England a similar reliance upon the *Vitae* can be observed in the works of those who gave special weight to historical argumentation. Among these is one of the most popular and prolific authors of sixteenth-century England, Thomas Becon. *The relikes of Rome*, in which he catalogues the history of church

[37] *WA*, 50.498: 'Tiefer ziehen ... Luther in die Historie hinein'.

[38] Jean de Hainault, *L'estat de l'Eglise avec le discours des temps depuis les apostres jusques à présent sous Charles V* (Geneva, 1556), sig. *5v, and cited throughout.

[39] See above at p. 173, and below at p. 220.

[40] Christophorus Hoffman, *De Christiana religione et de regno Antichristi* (Frankfurt, 1545), fo. 156v: 'Recte vero censet D. Robertus'.

[41] Hoffman, *De Christiana religione*, fo. 163v.

[42] Hoffman, *De Christiana religione*, fo. 155r: 'Nam eius extat libellus de vitis Pontificum Romanorum, cuius scripto vel compendii gratia, & in sequentium aliquot exemplorum relatione utar'.

[43] Hoffman, *De Christiana religione*, fo. 169r: 'D. Rob. Barus. Cuius verbis hactenus fere usus sum, in hac recitatione exemplorum vitae Ro. Pontificum'.

architecture, furnishings, rites, sacraments, and doctrines, offers a particularly striking example of Barnes's continuing usefulness. Becon announces his intent to show 'how, by whome, and at what tyme, everye one of theyr beggerlye Ceremonyes dyd creape or rather was violently intruded into the Churche of Christe',[44] and he provides a lengthy list of authors upon whom he will rely to do so. Not only is Barnes himself included in this list, but, unsurprisingly, so too are more than a dozen of those authors previously named in the *Vitae*.[45] Barnes alone is cited no fewer than seventy times, with more than half of these references pertaining to the development of the Roman Mass. Rather significantly, even the heading under which Becon treats many of these developments – 'Of the Masse & all the partes therof' – is reminiscent of the nineteenth article of Barnes's *Sentenciae*: 'De Origine Missae et Omnibus eius Partibus'.[46] Similar linguistic parallels are evident in another of Becon's treatises, *The displaying of the Popish Masse*. While he here makes even more plain the radical differences between his own eucharistic theology and that of the more conservative Barnes, Becon can still echo Barnes's earlier conclusion that the Latin Mass is 'an hotch-potch devised and made by a number of Popes', and that it resembles a 'beggers cloke, cobbled, clouted, and patched with a multitude of popish ragges'.[47]

The fact that Becon, while sharply disagreeing with Barnes's theology, was nevertheless willing to rely so heavily on his historical conclusions once again illustrates the manner in which Barnes remained valued more as an historian than a theologian. The same is further revealed in a work such as Henrician exile William Turner's *The huntyng & fynding out of the Romishe fox*. Though Turner, unlike Becon, will not mention Barnes by name, it has been observed that this work seems to indicate 'a close reading' of the *Vitae*.[48] Indeed, Turner's historical survey of Roman rites and ceremonies does quite consistently parallel that of Barnes.[49] Any who might disbelieve his accounts, though, he urges to examine the evidence found in Platina, Sabellicus, Volaterranus, and other pre-reformation historians.[50] While Barnes's status as a theologically biased evangelical might be good reason to exclude him from such a list, it is surely more than coincidence that most of those authors named by Turner are also to be found cited in the *Vitae*. In fact, it is undoubtedly Barnes's papal history to which Turner refers when he mentions that

44 Thomas Becon, *The relikes of Rome* (London, 1560 [STC 1754]), sig. A5r.
45 See Becon, *The relikes*, sigs A7v–8r.
46 Becon, *The relikes*, sig. A6v; *Sentenciae*, sig. K5r.
47 Thomas Becon, *The displaying of the Popish Masse* (London, 1637 [STC 1719]), 140; cf. *Sentenciae*, sig. K7v.
48 Anderson, 'The Person and Position', 307 n. 2.
49 William Turner, *The huntyng & fynding out of the Romishe fox* (Basle [i.e., Bonn], 1543 [STC 24353]). See especially sigs A7r–B2r.
50 Turner, *The huntyng & fynding out*, sig. B4rv.

> about seven yere ago when men preched ernestly agaynst the pope / and he with all hys ordinances was lyke to be dryven out of Englond / a certain man to set hym forward gathered together out of platina and such other writers / what popes had made all the ceremonies that are now in the church / and to every ceremoni he assygned on pope or other / whiche thyng made the ceremonies to be less regarded then they wer before.[51]

In 1543, when Turner was writing, it was exactly 'seven yere ago' that the *Vitae* had been first published.

It is not wholly surprising that Barnes would come to be esteemed as a valuable source for historical-theological polemic. But the argument that his particularly historical offerings were most appreciated is also suggested by the use made of him even by those not otherwise given to theological controversy. The poet and dramatist George Whetstone, for instance, would make use of Barnes's papal history in *The English myrror*, a work more concerned with the promotion of civil morality than with the condemnation of papal rites or doctrines.[52] Likewise, another playwright and poet, Thomas Heywood, would find in the *Vitae* a source for his *Gynaikeion*, a novel seventeenth-century survey of history's notable women.[53]

Though this brief sampling of authors is by no means exhaustive, it does serve sufficiently to illustrate that Barnes was not only remembered, but also used with some regularity by those who succeeded him. And while he could on rare occasions be cited as a theological authority, he was more often perceived as a source of historical information. It is this that helps to account for his continued popularity not only among Lutherans, but even among those with Calvinist or Zwinglian leanings. Even those controversialists who frequently wrote against one another – men such as Whitgift and Field, or Prynne and Heywood – were able to find Barnes's works a fruitful resource. But Barnes did more than provide useful information; his programme would also become an early model for the rapidly developing genre of Protestant historical theology.

Barnes's works as early modern models

While the novelty of Barnes's historical approach to theological issues surely contributed to the early – and sometimes continued – use of his works, the programme pursued especially in his *Vitae* would not remain unique for long. It is noteworthy, for example, that Protestant histories of the papacy came off English and continental presses by the dozens in the one hundred years following the

51 Turner, *The huntyng & fynding out*, sig. B8v.
52 George Whetstone, *The English myrror* (London, 1586 [STC 25336]), 50.
53 Thomas Heywood, *Gynaikeion: or, Nine bookes of various history* (London, 1624 [STC 13326]), 197.

publication of Barnes's work.[54] Despite the acknowledgment that Barnes wrote 'the first Protestant history of the papacy',[55] it of course cannot be assumed that his work therefore provided the model for all that followed. However, it is clear that Barnes's text was not ignored. Furthermore, as will become evident, even where Barnes himself receives no mention, there often remain very good reasons to posit his influence on certain directions taken in later reformation historiography.

In any account of sixteenth-century Protestant historiography the figure of John Foxe deservedly finds a prominent place. While a superficial reading of his most famous work, the *Actes and Monuments*, may suggest no obvious debt to Barnes, Foxe's involvement in the republication of his *Vitae romanorum pontificum* has already been noted. Given his clear respect for this work, it would be strange indeed if it had no influence on Foxe's own historical and theological programme. In fact, the too simple description of the *Actes and Monuments* as a 'martyrology' partially obscures the fuller programme Foxe pursued in this work. That his intent went beyond producing a 'book of martyrs' is revealed even by the nature of the sources from which he gained both information and inspiration. He drew not only on the common historical tradition found in the lives of the saints, but also on 'the history of dogma and doctrine, which originated with the Lutheran Reformation'.[56] These two influences and emphases are further evident in Foxe's decision to divide the first edition of his work into two parts. While the more familiar second section surveys the lives and acts of the martyrs, the first is given the title 'Actes and Monumentes touching things done and practiced by the prelates of the Romishe Church'.[57] It is, as the title might suggest, largely a history of the papacy. And beyond Foxe's noted interest in Barnes's *Vitae*, there is further reason to believe this work served in some part as a model for Foxe's own. Not only does he overwhelmingly rely on the very sources previously cited in the *Vitae*, drawing from them the same information his predecessor found important; he also tips his hand by citing Barnes himself.[58]

It is true that Barnes is not referenced often. That the *Vitae* appears to have been one of Foxe's implicit models, while not figuring more explicitly as a source, is in large part a result of the parameters Foxe sets for his work. Whereas the *Vitae* covers only the first twelve centuries of papal history, Foxe quickly passes over the church's first millennium. He explains this decision in part by saying that, compared to the five hundred years preceding the reformation, the first thousand 'might seme a golden age full of muche light, vertue, and true

54 See, e.g., those listed in seventeenth- and eighteenth-century bibliographies such as Louis Jacob, *Bibliotheca Pontificalia* (Lyon, 1643), 453–78; Augustini Oldoini, *Athenaeum Romanum* (Perugia, 1676), 671–9; Johann Georg Walch, *Bibliotheca Theologia Selecta*, 4 vols (Jena, 1762), 3.523–57.

55 McGoldrick, *Luther's English Connection*, 14.

56 Firth, *The Apocalyptic Tradition*, 74.

57 *A&M* (1563), 1–84, with p. 84 misnumbered as 74.

58 See, e.g., *A&M* (1563), 11.

felicitie'. But he also offers another reason. Previous historians had already outlined the abuses which occurred during this time. Therefore Foxe is 'referring the Reader rather to other writers, which have sufficiently committed those things to memory'.[59] That Barnes should be considered one of these 'other writers' is suggested not only by his inclusion among Foxe's cited sources, but also by an introductory summary which bears a remarkable resemblance to that found in the *Vitae*. Referring to the earliest form of the Mass, Foxe argues that it had

> neither Confiteor nor Misereatur, nor office with Gloria patri, nor Graile, nor Sequence, nor communion with post communion, nor Qui pridie the Cannon, nor the Agnus, nor Gloria in excelsis, nor Ita missa est, nor the Collect of the day, nor Cope, nor Albe with Tunickle. &c. Whiche all wer brought in after, as by the grace of the lord here after shall appere.[60]

This list does not precisely parallel that found in Barnes's introduction, but the similarities in placement, content, and purpose are unmistakable.[61]

That Foxe perceived the *Vitae* to be a valuable model for his own historical theology is perhaps more clearly revealed in an even earlier work. *A solemne contestation of diverse popes*, printed in London in 1560, is a shorter and more narrowly focused survey of the papal usurpation of both temporal and spiritual authority. While it was not published under Foxe's name, Thomas Freeman has convincingly argued that this work – included unchanged in every edition of the *Actes and Monuments* from 1570 forward – undoubtedly originated with the martyrologist. It attracts particular attention because, as Freeman points out, while its theme was not uncommon in sixteenth-century English Protestant histories, 'very few of the ones written in the first half of the sixteenth century dealt with the growth of papal power on the continent before Wiclif's time'.[62] Barnes's *Vitae*, though not mentioned by Freeman, stands out as a notable exception to this observation; and Foxe's citation of this work makes it an obvious influence.[63] The novelty of the *Contestation* must be further qualified by correcting one of Freeman's assertions. While he suggests that no previous work had relied on both Platina and Cardinal Benno for information concerning the life of Gregory VII, the *Vitae* had in fact done just that.[64] This minor correction in no way discredits Freeman's central thesis, however; indeed, it strengthens it. His discussion concludes with the statement that Foxe was 'deeply influenced by Lutheran historical writings, [which] suggests that the Lutheran influence on the

59 *A&M* (1563), 2.
60 *A&M* (1563), 2.
61 See *Vitae*, sig. B1r–v, quoted above at p. 116.
62 Freeman, '*A Solemne Contestation*', 37.
63 Anon. [John Foxe], *A solemne contestation of diverse popes* (London, 1560 [STC 20114]), sig. B9v.
64 Freeman, '*A Solemne Contestation*', 39; cf. *Vitae*, sig. R6v.

English Reformation extended beyond the confines of theology'.[65] Though Freeman especially has in mind Lutheran historians such as Johann Carion and Matthias Flacius Illyricus, Robert Barnes wears that title no less comfortably.

The influence of Barnes's 'Lutheran historical writings' also extended in England beyond the person and work of John Foxe. The use of the *Vitae* as a model is even more obviously evident in the publications of John Bale, despite the fact that this debt is often downplayed or unacknowledged by modern commentators. Matthew Fitzsimons's survey of historiographical development, for example, discusses Bale's *Acta romanorum pontificum* without any mention of Barnes's earlier, and similarly titled *Vitae romanorum pontificum*.[66] Andrew Pettegree at least notes that the *Acta* is 'a work similar in style and purpose to Robert Barnes' *Lives of the Roman Pontiffs*'.[67] And while F.J. Levy goes so far as to say Bale wrote 'under the influence of Tyndal and Barnes',[68] Glanmor Williams expressly denied any close similarities. 'Although at first sight it [the *Acta*] seems to be following the precedent set by Barnes's *Vitae Pontificum*', he writes, 'it is in fact a much more learned, ingenious and subtle onslaught on the papacy than Barnes's pedestrian offering.'[69] A close examination of the text and context of Bale's work, however, reveals Katharine Firth to be closer to the truth in her conclusion that it both 'owed and acknowledged a tremendous debt to Robert Barnes's *Vitae Romanorum Pontificum*'.[70]

It has already been noted that Bale was, like Foxe, working for the Basle printer Johannes Oporinus when he reprinted Barnes's *Vitae*. Likewise, mention has been made of the probable involvement of both exiles in this project. What has not thus far been discussed in any detail is that Oporinus was also during this period printing Bale's original works. He not only published the first edition of Bale's *Acta* in 1558, but he was also responsible for its previous incarnation in Bale's *Catalogus* of 1557. As is the case with Foxe's *Actes and Monuments*, the *Catalogus*, a biographical and bibliographical survey of Britain's notable authors, does not immediately strike one as a likely heir of the *Vitae*. But first impressions are again deceptive, because Bale, like Foxe, introduced papal history as an integral component of this otherwise dissimilar work. In fact, while intending the *Catalogus* to be something more akin to a history of England itself,[71] Bale himself asserts that English history cannot be understood without a knowledge of papal

65 Freeman, '*A Solemne Contestation*', 41.

66 Matthew Fitzsimons et al., *The Development of Historiography* (Harrisburg, PA, 1954), 124.

67 Pettegree, 'The Latin Polemic', 310.

68 Levy, *Tudor Historical Thought*, 95.

69 Williams, *Reformation Views of Church History*, 41. Cf. also King, *English Reformation Literature*, 5, who considers the *Acta* a 'notable exception' to the 'sub-literary' works of Barnes and his contemporaries.

70 Firth, *The Apocalyptic Tradition*, 78. Peter Happé, *John Bale* (London, 1996), 22, even suggests that 'This work may have been a kind of homage to Bale's long-dead colleague, Robert Barnes.'

71 See Fairfield, *John Bale*, 99; O'Day, *The Debate on the English Reformation*, 20.

history.[72] This conviction, considered together with Bale's involvement in the printing of the *Vitae*, as well as the speed with which his *Catalogus* followed with its own papal history, leads almost inevitably to the conclusion that Barnes's work was the primary model for Bale's history of the popes. This is especially the case since it has been recognised that the Marian exiles produced a large amount of literature which 'fell easily into patterns already set by the Henrician exiles', including Barnes.[73]

Bale's debt to Barnes is further evident in an examination of the text of the *Acta romanorum pontificum*. Here the brief papal biographies which appeared as appendices in the *Catalogus* are presented in a continuous narrative, supplemented with a new introduction and several minor revisions and additions.[74] Not only does the new title and arrangement suggest the influence of the *Vitae*, but so too does the content. Barnes's name is found among the more than one hundred cited in the bibliography; and among the modern authors mentioned in Bale's introduction, Barnes is placed first.[75] With only a few important methodological and ideological exceptions, Bale adopts almost wholesale the material first compiled by Barnes. Because these exceptions are important, and have in some cases obscured Bale's reliance on Barnes, they deserve some brief comment.

The first notable difference between the two works results from the different theological presuppositions of their authors. Bale, for example, refuses to accept information in the *Vitae* which portrays the centuries before Constantine as anything other than a 'golden age' of the church.[76] Of equal import is the fact that Bale, unlike Barnes, lays much more stress on the moral corruption of the papacy. As Firth has noted, while primarily relying on the text of the *Vitae*, Bale 'augmented particularly good examples of corrupt popes'.[77] This, again, is best explained with reference to Bale's personal presuppositions, since, he assumed, 'allegations of sexual misconduct were as fruitful as detailed theological argument'.[78]

But by far the greatest difference between these two works is the interpretive scheme Bale imposes on Barnes's historical data. Unlike his predecessor, Bale was driven by the theological desire to illustrate the papacy's fulfilment of apocalyptic prophecy. Beginning with Barnes's text, 'Bale superimposed on this material the argument from prophecy and the structure of the Apocalypse'.[79] In fact, this apocalyptic framework has been described as 'the special mark and method of his book'.[80] It is, of course, this mark and method which led Williams

72 Fairfield, *John Bale*, 99, 106; cf. Bale, *Catalogus*, sigs a3v–a4r.
73 Firth, *The Apocalyptic Tradition*, 71–2.
74 For some of these additions, see Fairfield, *John Bale*, 99–100.
75 John Bale, *Acta romanorum pontificum* (Basle, 1558), sig. a2r.
76 See Fairfield, *John Bale*, 103–4, and p. 141 above.
77 Firth, *The Apocalyptic Tradition*, 78.
78 Parish, 'Beastly is their living', 151. Cf. Betteridge, *Tudor Histories*, 74.
79 Firth, *The Apocalyptic Tradition*, 79; cf. 110.
80 Firth, *The Apocalyptic Tradition*, 109.

to conclude that the *Acta* is a much more 'ingenious' work than Barnes's 'pedestrian' *Vitae*. This, though, is a value judgement with which not all would agree. Oliver Olson, for example, refers to the organisation of the later *Magdeburg Centuries* into divisions of one-hundred-year periods as ultimately arbitrary, 'but an advance over the typical medieval organization of history according to the four monarchies of Daniel'.[81] Likewise, Bale's apocalyptic scheme, rather than being an advance on that of Barnes, might be viewed as a regression to an essentially medieval approach.

Though each of Bale's modifications results in a text significantly different from the *Vitae*, the differences largely concern interpretation rather than information. Bale's regular references to and citations of Barnes and his sources reveal that the *Acta* is unashamedly built upon the foundation first laid by the *Vitae*.[82] Moreover, this is precisely what one might expect from an author who rarely makes claims to originality, but most frequently refers to himself more humbly as a 'compiler' or 'collector'.[83] One result of this approach is that the *Acta*, like the *Vitae* before it, quickly became a much used and often reprinted reference volume. After the first printing of 1558, Latin issues and editions appeared again in 1559, 1560, 1567, and 1615. Two editions of a French translation were printed as early as 1561; German translations appeared in 1566 and 1571; and an expanded English translation came off the press in 1574.[84] Not only does Bale's work exhort readers also to examine the *Vitae* – 'Vide Barnum in Pontificum vitis'[85] – but even those who read only the *Acta* were digesting much of what Barnes had originally composed.[86]

Although much less certain, it is not unlikely that Bale was also involved with another papal history which hints at some affinity with Barnes's own. The anonymous *A breve Cronycle of the Bysshope of Romes blessynge*, printed by John Daye in 1549, is regularly attributed to Bale. Though composed in rhyming verse, and focusing only on events in England, the preface to this short work proclaims:

> Who lyst to loke aboute
> May in Cronicles soon finde out
> What sedes the Popysshe route

81 Oliver K. Olson, 'Matthias Flacius Illyricus, 1520–1575', in *Shapers of Religious Tradition in Germany, Switzerland, and Poland, 1560–1600*, ed. Jill Raitt (London, 1981), 14.

82 For sample citations of Barnes himself, see, e.g., Bale, *Acta*, 126, 147, 166, 193, 238, 255.

83 King, *English Reformation Literature*, 69. As Betteridge, *Tudor Histories*, 186, points out, the same was true of Foxe, at least during the production of the 1563 *Actes and Monuments*.

84 In addition, the original *Catalogus* went into another edition of 1557, followed by three more printings in 1559. For the bibliographical information, see Davies, 'A Bibliography of John Bale', 203–79, and the updated bibliography in Fairfield, *John Bale*, 165–71.

85 Bale, *Acta*, 193.

86 Indeed, as Happé, *John Bale*, 29, has pointed out, 'there are places where Bale seems to be relying upon Barnes verbatim'.

> In England hath sowen
> Because the tyme is shorte
> I shall bryvely reporte
> And Wryte in dewe sorte
> Therin what I have knowen.[87]

It is not a rhyme which can be traced to any of Barnes's printed works, but, as previously noted, it had already been put in Barnes's mouth by the similarly anonymous author of a 1548 pamphlet concerning his death.[88] Such a tenuous connection cannot be pressed too far, of course; but it does reinforce the impression that Barnes's work and memory were not far removed from the wide variety of early English papal histories.

In fact, this is true not only of early English histories, but also of those produced on the continent. And once again, Bale's influence is not wholly absent. One of those to whom Bale had dedicated his *Acta*, for instance, was soon at work on his own history of the popes. Heinrich Bullinger's deep interest in history began to find expression in the 1560s, when both his *History of the Reformation* and his unfinished *Swiss Chronicle* were printed. In 1568 he produced yet another historical work, which, because it went unpublished, remains relatively unknown. This *Pontifices Romani*, a survey of papal lives from Peter to Pius V, was an ambitious undertaking which drew on more than eighty acknowledged authors in the process of building a case against the papacy as Antichrist.[89] Not unexpectedly, Barnes – and the many authors named in his own work – is found among the authorities cited.[90] Whether it was Bale's *Acta*, received by Bullinger a decade earlier, which first brought Barnes to his attention is uncertain; but the influence of Barnes and his English successor is unmistakably evident in the *Pontifices Romani*. While adopting much of the historical information found in the *Vitae*, Bullinger follows Bale in arranging this material within an apocalyptic framework. Dividing his work into seven books, each covering what he judges to be a distinct historical epoch, Bullinger arrives at a decidedly apocalyptic understanding of papal history, which culminates with the revelation of Antichrist in the sixth epoch, commencing with the reign of Gregory VII.

While following Barnes's lead in compiling an evangelically biased history of

87 Anon., *A breve Cronycle of the Bysshope of Romes blessynge* (London, 1549 [STC 11842a]), sig. A1v.

88 Anon., *The metynge of Doctor Barons*, sig. A5v; see above at p. 75.

89 Heinrich Bullinger, *Pontifices Romani*, Zentralbibliothek Zürich, MS Car I 161. For much of the information in this paragraph I am indebted to Christian Moser, who not only spoke on 'Heinrich Bullinger and the History of the Papacy' at the 2004 Sixteenth Century Studies Conference in Toronto, but who also very graciously provided me with important copies from the *Pontifices Romani*. For further details, see his '"Papam esse Antichristum": Grundzüge von Heinrich Bullingers Antichristkonzeption', *Zwingliana* 30 (2003), 65–101, especially 94–7.

90 Zentralbibliothek Zürich, MS Car I 161: Barnes is named on the third unnumbered folio of authors cited; for use of his work in the text itself, see, e.g., fos 49v–50r.

the popes, Bullinger's theological interpretation of history ultimately led him to rely on Bale's work as his most immediate model. This was not, however, always the case with continental historians. Johann Funck, for instance, was far more interested in producing a history detached from an explicitly apocalyptic framework. This he did in his extremely popular two-volume *Chronologia*, in which he dedicates volume one to chronological tables of temporal and ecclesiastical rulers, and then moves on in the second volume to a narrative survey. Barnes's importance for Funck becomes obvious in the latter half of this second volume. Beginning at the end of its eighth book, which concludes the eighth century, Funck unashamedly cites the *Vitae* on almost every other page. He quotes at length from documents he finds reprinted in the *Vitae*.[91] He makes no attempt to conceal the fact that 'I am repeating from Robert Barnes's little book concerning the popes'.[92] And even when he might assume a posture of objectivity by mentioning only pre-reformation authorities, he will instead admit that it is Barnes from whom he gains his knowledge of such sources. So, for example, concerning the information he includes on Alexander III, he writes:

> This Robert Barnes most studiously collects from Nauclerus, Albert Crantz, Cardinal Benno, Lambert of Schaffhausen, Vincent, Antoninus, and the Abbot of Ursberg.[93]

For the great culmination of Barnes's historical and theological programme, however, attention must be turned to the most ambitious of sixteenth-century Protestant historical projects, the *Magdeburg Centuries*. The *Ecclesiastica Historia*, as the *Centuries* was officially titled, assumes a special importance not only because the Centuriators might be considered the 'fathers of modern intellectual history',[94] but because the great scope, detail, and documentation of their research allowed it to succeed in a way that Barnes's more modest offering could not. Indeed, as even one modern Catholic commentator has conceded, confronted with the *Centuries*,

> Catholics felt defeated, humiliated and despondent on the very territory of tradition and history on which defending their right of possession had seemed so simple and certain.[95]

Despite the obvious differences between Barnes's 'little book' and the multi-volume *Centuries*, the success of the latter is at least partially attributable to

91 See, e.g., Johann Funck, *Chronologia*, 2 vols (Basle, 1554), 2.174.
92 Funck, *Chronologia*, 2.183: 'integram ex R. Barns libello de Pontificibus'.
93 Funck, *Chronologia*, 2.203: 'Haec R. Barns ex Naucler. Alb. Crantzio, Bennone cardinale, Lam. Schaffnerio, Vincentio, Antonino, & Abbate Urspurgensi, summo studio collegit'. Cf. also 2.188.
94 N.L. Jones, 'Matthew Parker, John Bale, and the Magdeburg Centuriators', *Sixteenth Century Journal* 12 (1981), 35.
95 Angelo Roncalli, *Baronius* (Einsiedeln, 1963), 49–50; quoted by Olson, 'Matthias Flacius Illyricus', 14.

its return to the emphases found originally in Barnes's work, but overshadowed by some of his successors. Most notably, unlike Bale and others, Matthias Flacius Illyricus and his fellow Centuriators largely limited their attention to the public doctrines and official acts of the church of Rome. Chapter titles highlight these emphases by singling out such topics as doctrine, ceremonies, ecclesiastical polity, and church councils. In fact, the authors did not hesitate to criticise earlier Protestants for being sidetracked by attacks on the moral faults of individual churchmen.[96] This is not to suggest that the Centuriators did not benefit greatly from works such as Bale's *Acta romanorum pontificum*; they certainly did. In fact, Bale seems to have played an important role in the production of the *Centuries*, not only by means of his written works, but also in a personal capacity. As early as 1553 Bale had been informed of the historical project proposed by Flacius.[97] In the next year, Flacius himself wrote to Bale with a request for assistance.[98] Bale's direct involvement becomes most evident in the summer of 1560, however. Hoping to gain the patronage of Queen Elizabeth, Flacius dedicated the fourth volume of the *Centuries* to her. Along with the dedication copy he also sent a note requesting her aid in the acquisition of books needed to complete further volumes. Elizabeth handed the request over to her Archbishop, Matthew Parker, who then turned to Bale for guidance. Significantly, among the works requested by Flacius, church histories and papal histories headed the list.[99]

Given the popularity of the *Vitae* on the continent, it is likely that the Centuriators had previously come into possession of this work. And, in fact, their request for papal histories from England mentions only those 'nondum impressae'.[100] But Bale, responding to Parker's request, cannot refrain from also mentioning the *Vitae*, 'printed but now of late'.[101] And it is notable that the Centuriators first begin to make use of the *Vitae* only in their fifth volume, the first to be printed after their appeal to England.[102] From this point forward, regular use is made of Barnes's work, most frequently in the tenth chapter of each century, which treats Barnes's own theme: 'Episcoporum et doctorum vitis'.

The groundbreaking nature of the *Magdeburg Centuries* – both in scope and method – inaugurated a new era in the writing of church history and historical theology, not least because the *Centuries* prompted an almost immediate reaction from the church of Rome. The detailed responses produced by traditionalists such

96 See Gordon, 'This Worthy Witness', 103.

97 See the letter to Bale from Alexander Alesius in Honor C. McCusker, *John Bale: Dramatist and Antiquary* (Freeport, NY, 1971), 68–9.

98 See McCusker, *John Bale*, 69–70.

99 Jones, 'Matthew Parker, John Bale, and the Magdeburg Centuriators', 36–9. For similar requests, see 39–40.

100 Jones, 'Matthew Parker, John Bale, and the Magdeburg Centuriators', 38.

101 Graham and Watson, *The Recovery of the Past*, 19. Bale's letter is printed in full at 17–30.

102 Matthias Flacius et al., *Ecclesiastica Historia*, vol. 5 (Basle, 1565), cent. 8, cap. 7, col. 491.

as Robert Bellarmine and Caesar Baronius, who were virtually forced by the Centuriators to seek out the best original sources available, effectively prevented any further Protestant reliance upon simple summaries, or even collections, of historical documents. For obvious reasons, this would especially be the case if such works had been compiled by men known to be sympathetic to the new faith. As will be suggested in conclusion, then, the very method employed by Robert Barnes – though his work would remain valuable to later Protestants – inevitably led to the exclusion of his name from later generations of historical-theological polemic.

The reformation significance of Robert Barnes

The argument that Barnes's works, though uncited, continued to serve as historical-theological sources and models must almost inevitably remain an argument from silence. So, for example, those suggesting that the Scottish reformer John Knox employed the *Vitae* in his preaching,[103] or that Barnes's frequent commentary on the development of the Mass 'may even have stimulated the interest of Cranmer himself',[104] have wisely refrained from stating their cases too emphatically. And yet circumstantial evidence – including the fact that the *Vitae* would be reprinted even in the seventeenth century – does lend weight to the suspicion that Barnes was not simply abandoned by later generations of reformers.

Works such as those by the turn-of-the-century Huguenot Philippe de Mornay, for instance, cover much of the ground previously surveyed both in Barnes's *Sentenciae* and in his *Vitae*, though doing so much more thoroughly. His *De l'institution, usage, et doctrine du sainct sacrement de l'euchariste, en l'eglise ancienne*, in which he treats not only the historical development of the Mass, but also the gradual imposition of clerical celibacy, is a notable example. As one might expect, de Mornay relies on many of the sources previously cited by Barnes, repeats many of the same stories, and often quotes at length from the same documents.[105] He nowhere makes reference to Barnes himself, but further similarities between the works of the two authors are noticeable in verbal parallelisms similar to those previously observed in the works of Becon. Where the nineteenth article of Barnes's *Sentenciae* had taken up 'De Origine Missae et Omnibus eius Partibus', for example, de Mornay also states that the first book of his work will be given over to 'l'origine & progrez de la Messe; selon toutes ses parties'.[106]

What is true of de Mornay's work on the Mass is equally true of his *Mystere*

[103] Firth, *The Apocalyptic Tradition*, 117.
[104] Fisher, 'The Contribution of Robert Barnes', 104.
[105] See, e.g., Philippe de Mornay, *De l'institution, usage, et doctrine du sainct sacrement de l'euchariste, en l'eglise ancienne* (Geneva, 1599), 458 and 440–1.
[106] De Mornay, *De l'institution*, sig. ¶¶¶¶8r; cf. *Sentenciae*, sig. K5r.

d'iniquité, a history of the papacy first published in 1611. He makes much use of the sources cited in the *Vitae* and, again, while never referring to Barnes himself, does echo certain sentiments expressed in the Englishman's history. Where Barnes had described the papacy as so many Domitians, Diocletians, and Neros, de Mornay similarly concludes that in the papal office one observes 'remarquer nombre de Nerons, de Caligules, d'Heliogabales'.[107] And despite his failure to mention Barnes as either a source or a model, it must be noted that de Mornay also studiously avoids mention of any other evangelical authors; and the reason for such exclusions is not left unstated. Writing specifically in response to the histories of Bellarmine and Baronius, de Mornay recognises that he must draw his information from the 'books and titles which we have in common, or from the monks themselves'.[108] Indeed, even more explicitly he will say,

> we are reduced to making use of their writings, to take straight from their documents, to draw our evidence from their breast and their own mouth, to make ... their histories, councils, and decrees speak.[109]

As previously noted, such a refusal to name any but pre-reformation authorities must prevent one from insisting that de Mornay made any use of Barnes's works. But a comparison of de Mornay's method with that of more transparent authors might suggest that this is not at all unlikely. The evangelical Spanish exile Cipriano de Valera, for instance, reflected precisely the same concerns as de Mornay when he wrote his *Dos Tratados*, two treatises published together in 1588. The first of these, like de Mornay's *Mystere d'iniquité*, outlines the growth of the papacy, while the second treats the subject of de Mornay's *De l'institution* – the development of the Mass.

The reason for addressing these two topics specifically is clearly stated by de Valera; echoing a common evangelical sentiment, he refers to them as 'the two pillars of the church' of Rome.[110] Not unexpectedly, then, he will appeal to the same sources Barnes had used in his own attempt to topple these pillars. As Barnes had done in his *Sentenciae*, de Valera reaches the conclusion that the Mass did not originate with Christ or the apostles; and by way of proof he also provides

107 Philippe de Mornay, *Mystere d'iniquité, c'est a dire, L'histoire de la papauté* (Saumur, 1611), 603; cf. *Vitae*, sig. A6r.

108 De Mornay, *Mystere d'iniquité*, 598: 'livres & titres qui nous sont communs, ou par les particuliers des Moines mesmes'.

109 De Mornay, *Mystere d'iniquité*, 598: 'nous sommes reduicts à nous servir de leurs productions, à prendre droict de leurs documens, à tirer nos preuves de leur sein, & de leur propre bouche; à faire parler ... leurs Histoires, Conciles & Decrets'.

110 Cipriano de Valera, *Dos Tratados: el primo es del papa, ... el segundo es de la missa* (London, 1588), sig. A7v: 'las dos colunas de la yglesia'. Despite Barnes's clear interest in the papacy and the Mass, he had nowhere been so explicit as de Valera in identifying them as Rome's 'two pillars'. Nicholas Ridley, however, had done so in 1554. See *The Works of Nicholas Ridley*, ed. H. Christmas (Cambridge: Parker Society, 1843), 366. Graham Windsor has also pointed out that in the writings of English Protestants and Catholics from the middle of the sixteenth century the predominant issues of

an unembellished recitation of additions introduced, noting the relevant dates and popes involved.[111] His conclusion, reflecting Barnes's statement that the Latin Mass had been 'patched together',[112] is that 'The Mass is patched together like a beggar's cloak.'[113] Most significantly, though, de Valera reveals that such similarities are not mere coincidence. In previously treating the reign of Pope Alexander III, he had noted that his information could also be found in the work of Barnes.[114] Though this is the only time the English reformer is mentioned, it is enough to confirm that de Valera at least had access to the *Vitae*. The fact that the *Vitae*, when reprinted in Latin, was most often published together with the *Sentenciae* might also go some way toward explaining the parallels between the *Sentenciae* and de Valera's treatise on the Mass.

A similar piece of evidence is to be found in the seventeenth-century *Historia Pontificum Romanorum* of the Dutch poet and theologian Jacob Revius. Despite the late date of its publication, its content and method still suggest the influence of Barnes. Not only are the same sources employed, but, more than most contemporary papal historians, Revius imitates Barnes's literary style (or, indeed, lack thereof). Rather than providing an extended narrative, he favours brief, tersely written entries which note only the significant events of each papal reign and, like the *Vitae*, the length of each reign and the vacancy which followed. The fact of Barnes's influence would remain unprovable, however, if not for a single parenthetical comment made early in the treatise. Revius explains that the early fourth-century Pope Miltiades ordained that neither Sundays nor Thursdays be observed as days of fasting; then, in a passing display of critical-mindedness, he notes: 'for Thursday, Barnes reckons Tuesday'.[115]

As the examples of Revius and de Valera indicate, even when Barnes's works could no longer be deemed scholarly or objective enough to warrant frequent and explicit citation, those following in his footsteps would not neglect them. Despite the recognition that Barnes's brief and not unbiased accounts would do little to

dispute were primacy and the Mass. See Graham Windsor, 'The Controversy between Roman Catholics and Anglicans from Elizabeth to the Revolution' (unpublished Ph.D. Thesis, Cambridge, 1967), 27. Twenty years before Ridley wrote, while Barnes was composing his *Vitae*, Luther had made a slightly different conclusion in identifying the two pillars; he referred to the Mass and clerical celibacy as the 'zweien stücken' of the Roman Antichrist. See *WA*, 38.271. The German ambassadors to England in 1538, of whom Barnes was one, concluded similarly, calling private Masses, communion in one kind, and clerical celibacy the 'three heads, and the foundation, of papal tyranny and idolatry' ['tria … capita, et fundamentum Tyrannidis et idolatriae pontificiae']. BL Cottonian MS Cleopatra E.V, fo. 188 (*LP*, 13/2.37).

111 De Valera, *Dos Tratados*, 306–7. De Valera only once disagrees with the information provided by Barnes; but it should also be noted that he does not include all of the additions recorded in the *Vitae* or in the *Sentenciae*.

112 *Sentenciae*, sig. K7v: 'consutam'.

113 De Valera, *Dos Tratados*, 308: 'La Missa remendada como Esclavina.'

114 De Valera, *Dos Tratados*, 99.

115 Jacob Revius, *Historia Pontificum Romanorum* (Amsterdam, 1632), 17: 'pro quinta feria Barus diem martis ponit'.

sway those under the influence of more thorough papal historians, it is evident that his work remained a useful reference. If the new climate of intensified historical-theological polemic arising in the late sixteenth and early seventeenth centuries effectively dictated that Barnes could not be named as an authority, it is also true that his ostensibly objective method of citing and quoting from ancient and medieval sources meant that he need not be named. His evidence could simply be taken up and cited independently by later writers. Ironically, then, it was the very methodology employed by Barnes – so valuable to his successors – which allowed him eventually to be written out of later Protestant historiography.

* * *

Despite Barnes's eventual disappearance from the literature of sixteenth- and seventeenth-century history and theology, the evidence presented in the preceding chapters makes clear that, for at least a century, Barnes figures much more prominently in the controversies of the reformation than is often acknowledged. Made especially evident is the important but previously unexamined role which Barnes played in these controversies. In spite of previous emphases, he was not only a marginally important – if ultimately unsuccessful – English proponent of Lutheranism. Nor was he, as is still often argued, chiefly significant for his death and subsequent 'canonisation' as an evangelical martyr. There can be no doubt that these elements of his biography contributed to the popular relevance of Barnes, especially in sixteenth-century England. One result of the foregoing, however, should be the recognition that Barnes's significance was not limited to the reformation in sixteenth-century England. It was, especially as the result of his Latin writings, international in scope, and extended even into the seventeenth century.

Furthermore, a more thorough examination of the text and context of these writings, their reception, and their subsequent use reveals that Barnes's greatest influence – both in England and throughout Europe – is to be located in his endeavours as a polemical historian of the church, its ceremonies, and its theology. In this light, the common perception of Robert Barnes as 'Luther's English connection' must also be modified to account for the fact that he did not simply promulgate Luther's theological programme in England; Luther, as well as a substantial number of reformers not necessarily in agreement with him, were also promulgating Barnes's historical programme on the continent.

That this was the case should not be entirely surprising. Though usually only as asides, and frequently without any further substantiation, the significance of Barnes's novel approach to theological polemic has often been noted. His has been called 'the first Protestant history of the papacy',[116] one of 'the earliest

[116] McGoldrick, *Luther's English Connection*, 14.

excursions of the Reformers into Church history',[117] and 'the earliest full-length history of the English Reformation'.[118] Likewise it has been judged one of 'the pioneer works in confessional historiography',[119] and the 'first important contribution of the Protestant camp'.[120] As the present examination demonstrates, even such passing comments must be taken seriously, for they seem clearly to reflect the sentiments of Barnes's contemporaries and immediate successors. Conclusions to the contrary – those which suggest, for example, that the *Vitae* 'had no great significance for the development of the English Reformation',[121] or that Barnes would have been quickly forgotten 'If his claim to be remembered rested solely upon his one and only historical work'[122] – are no longer tenable. If they are not wholly rejected, they must at least be heavily qualified.

Finally, the realisation that Barnes's programme, while relatively novel, did not long remain unique necessitates an acknowledgement of his minor but unquestionably important position in the development of that historiographical tradition which had its roots in the controversies of the reformation.[123] As Graham Windsor has rightly noted, Barnes was one of those who 'introduced the use of history into the debate'.[124] While this was already becoming evident in his *Sentenciae*, and to some extent in his *Supplications*, it is especially true of the approach taken in his *Vitae romanorum pontificum*. It is therefore worth noting Robin Barnes's observation that, unlike the medieval attempt to predict the biography of Antichrist, Protestant authors would instead stress the study of the history of the papacy.[125] As the first evangelical author to make this his special concern, Barnes exercised a small but decisive influence on the shape of later Protestant historiography. In the light of the evidence in support of this contention, the received interpretations of Robert Barnes as a Lutheran populariser and an evangelical martyr must now be complemented by the view which those of his own age seem most often to have had of him: as an early and influential proponent of historical theology.

117 Rupp, *The Righteousness of God*, 39.
118 Parish, *Clerical Marriage*, 78.
119 Pullapilly, *Caesar Baronius*, 50.
120 Barnes, *A History of Historical Writing*, 123.
121 N.S. Tjernagel, 'Robert Barnes and Wittenberg', *Concordia Theological Monthly* 28 (1957), 650. Indeed, contrary to Tjernagel, and especially with regard to the matter of clerical celibacy, Helen Parish has recently noted that the *Vitae* 'was to exert considerable influence' in England. And referring to Barnes's summary of the reign of Gregory VII, she further states that it 'was to be the staple of subsequent Protestant histories of his pontificate'. Parish, *Clerical Marriage*, 14, 111.
122 Fisher, 'The Contribution of Robert Barnes', 99.
123 See, e.g., the conclusion in Pineas, *Tudor Polemics*, 220.
124 Windsor, 'The Controversy between Roman Catholics and Anglicans', 8.
125 Barnes, *Prophecy and Gnosis*, 43. Strangely, while noting this fact, Barnes himself does not go on to give any significant attention to the papal histories produced by sixteenth- or seventeenth-century Protestants.

BIBLIOGRAPHY

Early modern sources in manuscript

British Library, London
  Cottonian MSS: Galba, Titus, Cleopatra, Vitellius, Nero.
  Harleian MS 288.
  Lansdowne MS 515.
National Archives (formerly Public Record Office (PRO)), London
  C.65: Parliament Rolls.
  E.36: Exchequer, Treasury of the Receipt, Miscellaneous Books.
  SP 1: State Papers, Henry VIII, General Series.
Warwickshire Record Office, MS DR 801/12.
Zentralbibliothek Zürich, MS Car I 161: Heinrich Bullinger, *Pontifices Romani*.

Early modern sources in print

Aarsberetninger fra det Kongelige Geheimearchiv, 7 vols, ed. C.F. Wegener (Copenhagen, 1852–83).

Anglus, Antonius [i.e., Robert Barnes]. *Furnemlich Artickel der Christlichen kirchen* (Nuremberg, 1531).

——. *Sentenciae ex doctoribus collectae* (Wittenberg, 1530).

——. *Sententiae ex doctoribus collectae* (Wittenberg, 1536).

——. *Sententiae ex doctoribus collectae* (Oberursel, 1558).

Anon. *A breve Cronycle of the Bysshope of Romes blessynge* (London, 1549 [STC 11842a]).

Anon. *Chronicle of King Henry VIII of England*, ed./tr. M.A.S. Hume (London, 1889).

Anon. *The friers chronicle* (London, 1623 [STC 11510]).

Anon. *The metynge of Doctor Barons and Doctor Powell at Paradise gate* (London, 1548 [STC 1473]).

Anon. *This lytle treatyse declareth the study and frutes of Barnes borned in west smyth felde* (London, 1540 [STC 1473.5]).

Anon. [John Foxe], *A solemne contestation of diverse popes* (London, 1560 [STC 20114]).

Bale, John. *Acta romanorum pontificum* (Basle, 1558).

——. *A mysterye of inyquyte* (Antwerp, 1545 [STC 1303]).

——. *Scriptorum Illustrium maioris Brytanniae ... Catalogus* (Basle, 1557).
Barnes, Robert. *Bekanntnus dess Glaubens die Doctor Robertus Barus* (Wittenberg, 1540).
——. *A Critical Edition of Robert Barnes's* A Supplication Unto the Most Gracyous Prince Kynge Henry The .VIIJ. *1534.*, ed. Douglas H. Parker (Toronto, 2008).
——. *Kronyky. A živwotuow sepsánij naywrchnegssych biskupuow Ržijmskych ginac Papežuow* (Nuremburg, 1565).
——. *Scriptores Duo Anglici, Coaetanei ac Conterranei; De Vitis Pontificum Romanorum ...* (Leiden, 1615).
——. *A supplicacion unto the most gracious prynce kynge Henry the .viii.* (London, 1534 [STC 1471]).
——. *The supplication of doctour Barnes* (London, 1548 [STC 1472]).
——. *A supplicatyon made by Robert Barnes* (Antwerp, 1531 [STC 1470]).
——. *Two Treatises* (London, 1739).
——. *Vitae romanorum pontificum* (Wittenberg, 1536)
——. *Vitae romanorum pontificum* (Basle, 1555).
——. *Vitae romanorum pontificum* (Frankfurt, 1567).
Becon, Thomas. *The displaying of the Popish Masse* (London, 1637 [STC 1719]).
——. *The relikes of Rome* (London, 1560 [STC 1754]).
Boquin, Pierre. *Assertio veteris ac veri Christianismi* (London, 1581 [STC 3371]).
Bugenhagen, Johann. *De coniugo episcoporum et diaconorum* (Nuremburg, 1525).
——. *Dr Johannes Bugenhagens Briefwechsel*, ed. O. Vogt (Stettin, 1888).
Bullinger, Heinrich. *Bullae Papisticae ante biennium contra ... Reginam Elizabetham ... promulgatae, refutatio* (London, 1571 [STC 4043]).
Burnet, Gilbert. *History of the Reformation of the Church of England*, 7 vols, ed. N. Pocock (Oxford, 1865).
Calendar of State Papers, Spanish, 15 vols, ed. P. de Gayangos et al. (London, 1862–1954).
Concilia Magnae Britanniae et Hiberniae, 4 vols, ed. David Wilkins (London, 1737).
Correspondance Politique de MM. De Castillon et de Marillac, Ambassadeurs de France en Engleterre, ed. Jean Kaulek (Paris, 1885).
Coverdale, Miles. *Remains of Myles Coverdale*, ed. G. Pearson (Cambridge: Parker Society, 1846).
Cranmer, Thomas. *Miscellaneous Writings and Letters of Thomas Cranmer*, ed. J.E. Cox (Cambridge: Parker Society, 1846).
Documents of the English Reformation, ed. G. Bray (Cambridge, 1994).
Dokumente zur Causi Lutheri (1517–1521), ed. P. Fabisch and E. Iserloh, *Corpus Catholicorum*, vol. 41 (Münster, 1988).

Downame, George. *A defence of the sermon preaached at the consecration of the L. Bishop of Bath and VVelles* (London, 1611 [STC 7115]).

Eck, Johann. *Enchiridion Locorum Communium adversus Lutherum et alios Hostes Ecclesiae*, ed. Pierre Fraenkel, *Corpus Catholicorum*, vol. 34 (Münster, 1979).

Fielde, John. *A caveate for Parsons Hovvlet* (London, 1581 [STC 10844]).

Flacius, Matthias, et al. *Ecclesiastica Historia*, 13 vols (Basle, 1554–74).

Foxe, John. *Actes and monuments of matters most speciall and memorable*, 2 vols (London, 1583 [STC 11225]).

——. *Actes and monuments of these latter and perilous dayes* (London, 1563 [STC 11222]).

——. *The Acts and Monuments of John Foxe*, 7 vols, ed. J. Pratt (London, 1877).

——. *The Whole workes of W. Tyndale, John Frith, and Doct. Barnes* (London, 1573 [STC 24436]).

Funck, Johann. *Chronologia*, 2 vols (Basle, 1554).

Gardiner, Stephen. *A declaration of suche true articles* (London, 1546 [STC 11588]).

——. *The Letters of Stephen Gardiner*, ed. J.A. Muller (Cambridge, 1933).

Haddon, Walter. *Against Jerome Osorius* (London, 1581 [STC 12594]).

Hainault, Jean de. *L'estat de l'Eglise avec le discours des temps depuis les apostres jusques à présent sous Charles V* (Geneva, 1556).

Hall, Edward. *Hall's Chronicle Containing the History of England* (London, 1809).

Henry VIII, King of England. *Assertio Septem Sacramentorum* (Rome, 1521 [facs. Ridgewood, NJ, 1966]).

Heywood, Thomas. *Gynaikeion: or, Nine bookes of various history* (London, 1624 [STC 13326]).

Hoffman, Christophorus. *De Christiana religione et de regno Antichristi* (Frankfurt, 1545).

Holinshed, Raphael. *Holinshed's Chronicles of England, Scotland, and Ireland*, 6 vols (London, 1807–08; repr. New York, 1976).

Jacob, Louis. *Bibliotheca Pontificalia* (Lyon, 1643).

Jewel, John. *The Works of John Jewel, Bishop of Salisbury: The First Portion*, ed. John Ayre (Cambridge: Parker Society, 1845).

——. *The Works of John Jewel, Bishop of Salisbury: The Fourth Portion*, ed. John Ayre (Cambridge: Parker Society, 1850).

Joye, George. *George Joye confuteth Vvinchesters false articles* (Antwerp, 1543 [STC 14826]).

——. *The refutation of the byshop of Winchesters derke declaration* (London, 1546 [STC 14828.5]).

Latimer, Hugh. *Sermons and Remains of Hugh Latimer*, ed. G.E. Corrie (Cambridge: Parker Society, 1845).

Letters and Papers, Foreign and Domestic, of the Reign of Henry VIII, 23 vols, ed. J.S. Brewer et al. (London, 1862–1932).
The Lisle Letters, 6 vols, ed. Marie St Clare Byrne (London, 1981).
Luther, Martin. *D. Martin Luthers Werke, Kritische Gesamtausgabe, Briefwechsel*, 10 vols (Weimar, 1930–47).
——. *D. Martin Luthers Werke, Kritische Gesamtausgabe, Deutsche Bibel*, 12 vols (Weimar, 1906–61).
——. *D. Martin Luthers Werke, Kritische Gesamtausgabe, Schriften*, 62 vols (Weimar, 1883–1986).
——. *Luther's Works, American Edition*, 56 vols, ed. J. Pelikan and H. Lehmann (Philadelphia and St Louis, 1955–86).
Machyn, Henry. *The Diary of Henry Machyn* (London, 1848).
Matricule de L'Université de Louvain, 10 vols, ed. A. Schillings et al. (Brussels, 1903–80).
Melanchthon, Philip. *Corpus Reformatorum, Philippi Melanthonis Opera*, 28 vols, ed. C.G. Bretschneider (Halle, 1836).
Merbecke, John. *A booke of notes and common places* (London, 1581 [STC 17299]).
Merriman, R.B. *Life and Letters of Thomas Cromwell*, 2 vols (Oxford, 1902).
More, Thomas. *The Complete Works of St. Thomas More*, 15 vols, ed. C.H. Miller et al. (New Haven, 1963–97).
Mornay, Philippe de. *De l'institution, usage, et doctrine du sainct sacrement de l'eucharistie, en l'eglise ancienne* (Geneva, 1599).
——. *Mystere d'iniquité, c'est a dire, L'histoire de la papauté* (Saumur, 1611).
Myconius, Friedrich. *Historia reformationis vom Jahr Christi 1517 bis 1542* (Leipzig, 1718).
Oldoini, Augustini. *Athenaeum Romanum* (Perugia, 1676).
Original Letters Illustrative of English History, ed. H. Ellis, 1st series, 3 vols (London, 1824–46).
Original Letters Relative to the English Reformation, 2 vols, ed. H. Robinson (Cambridge: Parker Society, 1846–47).
Pilkington, James. *The Works of James Pilkington*, ed. J. Scholefield (Cambridge: Parker Society, 1842).
Platina, Bartolomeo. *Lives of the Popes*, 2 vols, tr. W. Benham (London, 1888).
Prynne, William. *The antipathie of the English lordly prelacie* (London, 1641 [Wing P3891A]).
——. *The Church of Englands old antithesis to new Arminianisme* (London, 1629 [STC 20457]).
——. *A looking-glasse for all lordly prelates* (London, 1636 [STC 20466]).
——. *The Popish royall favourite* (London, 1643 [Wing P4039]).
——. *A quench-coale* (Amsterdam, 1637 [STC 20474]).
Records of the English Bible, ed. A.W. Pollard (London, 1911).

Records of the Reformation: the Divorce, 1527–1533, 2 vols, ed. Nicholas Pocock (Oxford, 1870).
Revius, Jacob. *Historia Pontificum Romanorum* (Amsterdam, 1632).
Rex, Richard (ed.). *A Reformation Rhetoric: Thomas Swynnerton's The Tropes and Figures of Scripture* (Cambridge, 1999).
Ridley, Nicholas. *The Works of Nicholas Ridley*, ed. H. Christmas (Cambridge: Parker Society, 1843).
Speed, John. *The history of Great Britaine* (London, 1611 [STC 23045]).
The Statutes of the Realm, 12 vols, ed. A. Luders et al. (London: Record Commission, 1963).
Strype, John. *Ecclesiastical Memorials*, 3 vols in 6 (Oxford, 1822).
Swinnerton, Thomas. *A mustre of scismatyke bysshopes of Rome* (London, 1534 [STC 23552]).
Turner, William. *The huntyng & fynding out of the Romishe fox* (Basle [i.e., Bonn], 1543 [STC 24353]).
Tyndale, William. *An Answer to Sir Thomas More's Dialogue, The Supper of the Lord ... and Wm. Tracy's Testament Expounded*, ed. H. Walter (Cambridge: Parker Society, 1850).
——. *Doctrinal Treatises and Introductions to Different Portions of the Holy Scriptures*, ed. H. Walter (Cambridge: Parker Society, 1848).
——. *Expositions and Notes on Sundry Portions of the Holy Scriptures, Together with The Practice of Prelates*, ed. H. Walter (Cambridge: Parker Society, 1849).
Vadianus, Joachim [attr.]. *A worke entytled of ye olde god [and] the newe* (London, 1534 [STC 25127]).
Valera, Cipriano de. *Dos Tratados: el primo es del papa, ... el segundo es de la missa* (London, 1588 [STC 24579]).
Visitation Articles and Injunctions of the Period of the Reformation, 3 vols, ed. W.H. Frere (London 1910).
Walch, Johann Georg. *Bibliotheca Theologia Selecta*, 4 vols. (Jena, 1762).
Westerburg, Gerhard. *Das der allerheiligster Papst ... nicht ihrren können* (Strassburg, 1545).
Whetstone, George. *The English myrror* (London, 1586 [STC 25336]).
Whitgift, John. *The Works of John Whitgift*, 3 vols, ed. J. Ayre (Cambridge: Parker Society, 1851).
Wotton, Henry. *The state of Christendom* (London, 1657 [Wing W3655]).
Wriothesley, Charles. *A Chronicle of England during the Reigns of the Tudors*, 2 vols, ed. W.D. Hamilton (London, 1875–77).

Secondary literature

Althaus, Paul. *The Theology of Martin Luther*, tr. R.C. Schultz (Philadelphia, 1966).

Anderson, Charles. 'Robert Barnes on Luther', in *Interpreters of Luther*, ed. J. Pelikan (Philadelphia, 1968), 35–66.

Aston, Margaret. 'Lollards and the Reformation: Survival or Revival?', in *Lollards and Reformers*, ed. Margaret Aston (London, 1984), 219–42.

Backus, Irena. *The Disputations of Baden, 1526 and Berne, 1528: Neutralizing the Early Church* (Princeton, 1993).

——. *Historical Method and Confessional Identity in the Era of the Reformation, 1378–1615* (Leiden, 2003).

Barnes, H.E. *A History of Historical Writing* (New York, 1963).

Barnes, R.B. *Prophecy and Gnosis: Apocalypticism in the Wake of the Lutheran Reformation* (Stanford, 1988).

Bauckham, Richard. *Tudor Apocalypse* (Oxford, 1978).

Bauer, Stefan. *The Censorship and Fortuna of Platina's* Lives of the Popes *in the Sixteenth Century* (Turnhout, 2006).

Bautz, F.W., and T. Bautz (eds). *Biographisch-Bibliographisches Kirchenlexicon*, 24 vols (Hamm, Herzberg, and Nordhausen, 1975–2005).

Benzing, Josef. *Buchdruckerlexicon des 16. Jahrhunderts* (Frankfurt, 1952).

Bernard, G.W. *The King's Reformation: Henry VIII and the Remaking of the English Church* (New Haven, 2007).

Betteridge, Thomas. *Tudor Histories of the English Reformations, 1530–83* (Aldershot, 1999).

Bietenholz, Peter. *Basle and France in the Sixteenth Century* (Geneva, 1971).

Bostick, C.V. *The Antichrist and the Lollards: Apocalypticism in Late Medieval and Reformation England* (Leiden, 1998).

Brecht, Martin. *Martin Luther*, 3 vols, tr. J.L. Schaaf (Philadelphia, 1985–93).

Breisach, Ernst. *Historiography: Ancient, Medieval, and Modern* (Chicago, 1983).

Brigden, Susan. *London and the Reformation* (Oxford, 1989).

——. 'Popular Disturbance and the Fall of Thomas Cromwell and the Reformers, 1539–1540', *The Historical Journal* 24 (1981), 257–78.

——. 'Thomas Cromwell and the "Brethren" ', in *Law and Government under the Tudors*, ed. C. Cross, D. Loades, and J.J. Scarisbrick (Cambridge, 1988), 31–49.

Brooke, Christopher, et al. (eds), *A History of the University of Cambridge*, 4 vols (Cambridge, 1988–2004).

Brooks, P.N. *Thomas Cranmer's Doctrine of the Eucharist*, 2nd edn (Basingstoke, 1992).

Byrom, H.J. 'Edmund Spenser's First Printer, Hugh Singleton', *The Library*, 4th series, 14 (1933–34), 121–56.

Cargill Thompson, W.D.J. 'The Sixteenth-Century Editions of *A Supplication Unto King Henry the Eighth* by Robert Barnes, D.D.: A Footnote to the History of the Royal Supremacy', *Transactions of the Cambridge Bibliographical Society* 3 (1960), 133–42.

—— . 'The "Two Kingdoms" and the "Two Regiments": Some Problems of Luther's *Zwei-Reiche-Lehre*', in *Studies in the Reformation*, ed. C.W. Dugmore (London, 1980), 42–59.

Carlyle, A.J. *A History of Medieval Political Theory in the West*, 6 vols (Edinburgh, 1927).

Chester, A.G. *Hugh Latimer: Apostle to the English* (Philadelphia, 1954).

—— . 'Robert Barnes and the Burning of the Books', *The Huntington Library Quarterly* 3 (1951), 211–21.

Clair, Colin. *A History of European Printing* (London, 1976).

—— . *A History of Printing in Britain* (London, 1965).

Clark, F. *Eucharistic Sacrifice and the Reformation* (London, 1960).

Clebsch, W.A. *England's Earliest Protestants: 1520–1535* (New Haven, 1964).

Cooper, C.H., and T. Cooper. *Athenae Cantabrigienses*, 2 vols (Cambridge, 1858–61).

Craig, J., and K. Maas. 'A Sermon by Robert Barnes, c. 1535', *Journal of Ecclesiastical History* 55 (2004), 542–51.

Dallmann, William. 'Dr. Robert Barnes: The English Lutheran Martyr', *Theological Quarterly* 9 (1905), 22–32.

—— . *Robert Barnes: English Lutheran Martyr* (St Louis, n.d.; repr. Decatur, IL, 1997).

D'Alton, Craig. 'Cuthbert Tunstal and Heresy in Essex and London, 1528' *Albion* 35 (2003), 210–28.

—— . 'The Suppression of Lutheran Heretics in England, 1526–1529', *Journal of Ecclesiastical History* 54 (2003), 228–53.

Daniell, David. *William Tyndale: A Biography* (New Haven and London, 1994).

David, Zdenek. *Finding the Middle Way: The Utraquists' Liberal Challenge to Rome and Luther* (Washington, DC, 2003).

Davies, W.T. 'A Bibliography of John Bale', *Oxford Bibliographical Society, Proceedings and Papers* 5 (1940), 203–79.

Dickens, A.G. *The English Reformation* (London, 1964).

Dickens, A.G., and J.M. Tonkin. *The Reformation in Historical Thought* (Oxford, 1985).

Doernberg, Erwin. *Henry VIII and Luther: An Account of their Personal Relations* (London, 1961).

Dowling, M., and J. Shakespeare. 'Religion and Politics in mid-Tudor England through the Eyes of an English Protestant Woman: The Recollections of Rose Hickman', *Bulletin of Historical Research* 55 (1982), 94–102.

Duff, E.G. *A Century of the English Book Trade* (London, 1948).

——. *The Printers, Stationers, and Bookbinders of Westminster and London* (Cambridge, 1906).

Dugmore, C.W. *The Mass and the English Reformers* (London, 1958).

Eaves, R.G. 'The Reformation Thought of Dr. Robert Barnes, Lutheran Chaplain and Ambassador for Henry VIII', *The Lutheran Quarterly* 28 (1976), 156–65.

Eberhard, Winfried .'Bohemia, Moravia and Austria', in *The Early Reformation in Europe*, ed. Andrew Pettegree (Cambridge, 1992), 23–48.

——. 'Reformation and Counterreformation in East Central Europe', in *Handbook of European History, 1400–1600*, vol. 2, ed. T.A. Brady, H.A. Oberman, and J.D. Tracy (Leiden, 1995), 551–84.

Edwards, Mark U. *Luther's Last Battles: Politics and Polemics, 1531–46* (Leiden, 1983).

Eisenstein, Elizabeth. *The Printing Press as an Agent of Change*, 2 vols (Cambridge, 1979).

Elert, Werner. *The Structure of Lutheranism*, tr. W.A. Hansen (St Louis, 1962).

Elton, G.R. *Policy and Police: The Enforcement of the Reformation in the Age of Thomas Cromwell* (Cambridge, 1972).

——. 'Thomas Cromwell's Decline and Fall', *Cambridge Historical Journal* 10 (1951), 150–85.

Estes, J.M. 'Luther on the Role of Secular Authority in the Reformation', *Lutheran Quarterly* n.s. 17 (2003), 199–225.

Evenden, Elizabeth. 'The Michael Wood Mystery: William Cecil and the Lincolnshire Printing of John Day', *Sixteenth Century Journal* 35 (2004), 383–94.

——. *Patents, Pictures and Patronage: John Day and the Tudor Book Trade* (Aldershot, 2008).

Evenden, Elizabeth, and Thomas S. Freeman. 'John Foxe, John Day, and the Printing of the "Book of Martyrs" ', in *Lives in Print: Biography and the Book Trade from the Middle Ages to the 21st Century*, ed. Robin Myers, Michael Harris, and Giles Mandelbrote (London, 2002), 23–54.

——. 'Print, Profit and Propaganda: The Elizabethan Privy Council and the 1570 Edition of Foxe's "Book of Martyrs" ', *English Historical Review* 119 (2004), 1288–1307.

Fairfield, Leslie P. *John Bale: Mythmaker for the English Reformation* (West Lafayette, 1976).

Febvre, Lucien, and Henri-Jean Martin. *The Coming of the Book: The Impact of Printing, 1450–1800*, tr. David Gerard, ed. Geoffrey Nowell-Smith and David Wootton (London, 1976).

Ferguson, A.B. *Clio Unbound: Perception of the Social and Cultural Past in Renaissance England* (Durham, NC, 1979).
Firth, Katharine. *The Apocalyptic Tradition in Reformation Britain, 1530–1645* (Oxford, 1979).
Fitzsimons, Matthew, et al. *The Development of Historiography* (Harrisburg, PA, 1954).
Flesseman-van Leer, E. 'The Controversy about Scripture and Tradition between More and Tyndale', *Nederlandsch Archief voor Kerkgeschiedenis* 43 (1959), 143–65.
Flood, John L. 'The Book in Reformation Germany', in *The Reformation and the Book*, ed. Jean-François Gilmont, tr. Karin Maag (Aldershot, 1998), 21–103.
——. ' "Safer on the battlefield than in the city": England, the "Sweating Sickness", and the Continent', *Renaissance Studies* 17 (2003), 147–76.
Freeman, Thomas. '*A Solemne Contestation of Diverse Popes*: A Work by John Foxe?', *English Language Notes* 31 (1994), 35–41.
Gairdner, J. *Lollardy and the Reformation in England*, 4 vols (London, 1908–13).
Garret, Christina. 'The Resurreccion of the Masse by Hugh Hilarie – or John Bale(?)', *The Library*, 4th series, 21 (1941–42), 144–59.
Gogan, B. 'Fisher's View of the Church', in *Humanism, Reform and the Reformation*, ed. B. Bradshaw and E. Duffy (Cambridge, 1989), 131–54.
Gordon, Bruce. 'The Changing Face of Protestant History and Identity in the Sixteenth Century', in *Protestant History and Identity in Sixteenth-Century Europe*, vol. 1, *The Medieval Inheritance*, ed. Bruce Gordon (Aldershot, 1996), 1–22.
——. ' "This Worthy Witness of Christ": Protestant uses of Savonarola in the Sixteenth Century', in *Protestant History and Identity in Sixteenth-Century Europe*, vol. 1, *The Medieval Inheritance*, ed. Bruce Gordon (Aldershot, 1996), 93–107.
Graham, T., and A. Watson (eds). *The Recovery of the Past in Early Elizabethan England: Documents by John Bale and John Joscelyn from the Circle of Matthew Parker* (Cambridge, 1998).
Greenslade, S.L. *The English Reformers and the Fathers of the Church* (Oxford, 1960).
Grisar, Hartmann, and Franz Heege. *Luthers Kampfbilder*, Heft 5, *Der Bilderkampf in den Schriften von 1523 bis 1545* (Freiburg im Breisgau, 1923).
Haaugaard, W.P. 'Renaissance Patristic Scholarship and Theology in Sixteenth-Century England', *Sixteenth Century Journal* 10 (1979), 37–66.
Hall, B. 'The Early Rise and Gradual Decline of Lutheranism in England', in *Reform and Reformation: England and the Continent, c.1500–c.1750*, ed. D. Baker (Oxford, 1979), 103–31.
Happé, Peter. *John Bale* (London, 1996).

Headley, John M. *Luther's View of Church History* (New Haven and London, 1963).

Hejnová, Miroslava. 'Barnesovy "Kroniky" a jejich ceské pokracováni', *Folia Historica Bohemica* 13 (1990), 588–92.

Hill, Christopher. *Antichrist in Seventeenth-Century England* (Oxford, 1971).

Hillerbrand, H.J. (ed.). *The Oxford Encyclopedia of the Reformation*, 4 vols (Oxford, 1996).

Hotson, Howard. 'The Historiographical Origins of Calvinist Millenarianism', in *Protestant History and Identity in Sixteenth-Century Europe*, vol. 2, *The Later Reformation*, ed. Bruce Gordon (Aldershot, 1996), 159–81.

House, S.B. 'An Unknown Tudor Propaganda Poem, c. 1540', *Notes and Queries* 237 (1992), 282–5.

Hume, Anthea. 'English Protestant Books Printed Abroad, 1525–1535: An Annotated Bibliography', in *The Complete Works of St. Thomas More*, ed. C.H. Miller et al. (New Haven, 1963–97), vol. 8, 1063–91.

Jacobs, H.E. *The Lutheran Movement in England* (Philadelphia, 1916).

James, M.R. 'The Catalogue of the Library of the Augustinian Friars at York', in *Fasciculus Joanni Willis Clark dictatus*, ed. J.W. Clark (Cambridge, 1909), 2–96.

Jones, N.L. 'Matthew Parker, John Bale, and the Magdeburg Centuriators', *Sixteenth Century Journal* 12 (1981), 35–49.

Kelly, J.N.D. *The Oxford Dictionary of Popes* (Oxford, 1986).

Kersken, Norbert. 'Reformation and the Writing of National History in East-Central and Northern Europe', in *The Reformation in Eastern and Central Europe*, ed. Karin Maag (Aldershot, 1997), 50–71.

King, John. 'The Book-Trade under Edward VI and Mary I', in *The Cambridge History of the Book*, vol. 3, *1400–1557*, ed. L. Hellinga and J.B. Trapp (Cambridge, 1999), 164–78.

——— . *English Reformation Literature: The Tudor Origins of the Protestant Tradition* (Princeton, 1982).

Kingdon, Robert M. 'Patronage, Piety and Printing in Sixteenth-Century Europe', in *Church and Society in Reformation Europe*, ed. R.M. Kingdon (London, 1985), 19–36.

Klug, E.F. 'Word and Scripture in Luther Studies since World War II', *Trinity Journal* n.s. 5 (1984), 3–46.

Knappen, M.M. *Tudor Puritanism* (Chicago, 1929).

Kolb, Robert. *For All The Saints: Changing Perceptions of Martyrdom and Sainthood in the Lutheran Reformation* (Macon, GA, 1987).

Köstlin, Julius. *The Theology of Luther in its Historical Development and Inner Harmony*, 2 vols (Philadelphia, 1897).

Kronenberg, M.E. 'Forged Addresses in Low Country Books in the Period of the Reformation', *The Library*, 5th series, 2 (1947), 81–94.

Lamberts, Emiel, et al. (eds). *Leuven University, 1425–1985* (Leuven, 1990).
Lane, A.N.S. *John Calvin: Student of the Church Fathers* (Edinburgh, 1999).
Levy, F.J. *Tudor Historical Thought* (San Marino, 1967).
Liliencron, R. von, et al. (eds). *Allgemeine Deutsche Biographie*, 56 vols (Leipzig, 1875–1912).
Loades, D.M. *Politics, Censorship and the English Reformation* (London, 1991).
Loane, M.L. *Pioneers of the Reformation in England* (London, 1964).
Lock, Julian. 'Plantagenets against the Papacy: Protestant England's Search for Royal Heroes', in *Protestant History and Identity in Sixteenth-Century Europe*, vol. 1, *The Medieval Inheritance*, ed. Bruce Gordon (Aldershot, 1996), 153–73.
Lohse, Bernhard. *Martin Luther's Theology: Its Historical and Systematic Development* (Edinburgh, 1999).
Lusardi, J.P. 'The Career of Robert Barnes', in *The Complete Works of St. Thomas More*, ed. C.H. Miller et al. (New Haven, 1963–97), vol. 8, 1365–1415.
Maas, Korey. 'Thomas Bilney: "simple good soul?" ', *The Tyndale Society Journal* 27 (July 2004), 8–20.
MacCulloch, Diarmaid. 'Putting the English Reformation on the Map', *Transactions of the Royal Historical Society* 15 (2005), 75–95.
——. *Thomas Cranmer: A Life* (New Haven, 1996).
McCusker, Honor C. *John Bale: Dramatist and Antiquary* (Freeport, NY, 1971).
McEntegart, R. *Henry VIII, the League of Schmalkalden and the English Reformation* (Woodbridge, 2002).
McGoldrick, James. *Luther's English Connection* (Milwaukee, 1979).
McKisack, M. *Medieval History in the Tudor Age* (Oxford, 1971).
Maclure, M. *The Paul's Cross Sermons, 1534–1642* (Toronto, 1958).
Marius, R. 'Thomas More and the Early Church Fathers', *Traditio* 24 (1968), 379–407.
Marshall, Peter. 'The Shooting of Robert Packington', in *Religious Identities in Henry VIII's England*, ed. Peter Marshall (Aldershot, 2006), 61–79.
Moser, Christian. ' "Papam esse Antichristum": Grundzüge von Heinrich Bullingers Antichristkonzeption', *Zwingliana* 30 (2003), 65–101.
Mozley, J.F. *John Foxe and His Book* (London, 1940).
——. *William Tyndale* (London, 1937).
Muller, J.A. *Stephen Gardiner and the Tudor Reaction* (London, 1926).
Murdock, Graeme. 'Eastern Europe', in *The Reformation World*, ed. Andrew Pettegree (New York and London, 2000), 190–210.
Neville-Sington, Pamela. 'Press, Politics and Religion', in *The Cambridge History of the Book*, vol. 3, *1400–1557*, ed. L. Hellinga and J.B. Trapp (Cambridge, 1999), 576–610.
Nicholson, G. 'The Act of Appeals and the English Reformation', in *Law and*

Government under the Tudors, ed. C. Cross, D. Loades, and J.J. Scarisbrick (Cambridge, 1988), 19–30.

Oakley, F. 'Christian Obedience and Authority, 1520–1550', in *The Cambridge History of Political Thought, 1450–1700*, ed. J.H. Burns (Cambridge, 1994), 159–92.

Oastler, C.L. *John Day, The Elizabethan Printer* (Oxford, 1975).

O'Day, R. *The Debate on the English Reformation* (London, 1986).

O'Donnell, Anne M. 'Augustine in *Unio Dissidentium* and Tyndale's Answer to More', *Reformation* 2 (1997), 241–60.

Olson, Oliver K. *Matthias Flacius and the Survival of Luther's Reform* (Wiesbaden, 2002).

——. 'Matthias Flacius Illyricus, 1520–1575', in *Shapers of Religious Tradition in Germany, Switzerland, and Poland, 1560–1600*, ed. Jill Raitt (London, 1981), 1–18.

Parish, Helen. ' "Beastly is their living and their doctrine": Celibacy and Theological Corruption in English Reformation Polemic', in *Protestant History and Identity in Sixteenth-Century Europe*, vol. 1, *The Medieval Inheritance*, ed. Bruce Gordon (Aldershot, 1996), 138–52.

——. *Clerical Marriage and the English Reformation* (Aldershot, 2000).

Parker, Douglas H. (ed.). *A Critical Edition of Robert Barnes's* A Supplication Unto the Most Gracyous Prince Kynge Henry The .VIIJ. *1534*. (Toronto, 2008).

Pelikan, J. *Obedient Rebels: Catholic Substance and Protestant Principle in Luther's Reformation* (London, 1964).

Pescheck, C.A. *Reformation and Anti-Reformation in Bohemia* (London, 1845).

Pešek, Jirí. 'Protestant Literature in Bohemian Private Libraries *circa* 1600', in *The Reformation in Eastern and Central Europe*, ed. Karin Maag (Aldershot, 1997), 36–49.

Peters, Robert. 'The Enigmatic *Unio Dissidentium*: Tyndale's "Heretical" Companion', *Reformation* 2 (1997), 233–40.

——. 'Who Compiled the Sixteenth-Century Patristic Handbook *Unio Dissidentium*?', in *Studies in Church History*, vol. 2, ed. G.J. Cuming (London, 1965), 237–50.

Pettegree, Andrew. 'The Latin Polemic of the Marian Exiles', in *Humanism and Reform: The Church in Europe, England, and Scotland, 1400–1643*, ed. James Kirk (Oxford, 1991), 305–29.

——. 'Printing and the Reformation: The English Exception', in *The Beginnings of English Protestantism*, ed. Peter Marshall and Alec Ryrie (Cambridge, 2002), 157–79.

Pettegree, Andrew, and Karin Maag. 'The Reformation in Eastern and Central Europe', in *The Reformation in Eastern and Central Europe*, ed. Karin Maag (Aldershot, 1997), 1–18.

Pineas, R. 'Robert Barnes' Polemical Use of History', *Bibliotheque d'Humanisme et Renaissance* 26 (1964), 55–69.
——. *Thomas More and Tudor Polemics* (Bloomington, IN, 1968).
——. 'William Tyndale's Influence on John Bale's Polemical use of History', *Archiv für Reformationsgeschichte* 53 (1962), 79–96.
——. 'William Tyndale's Use of History as a Weapon of Religious Controversy', *Harvard Theological Review* 55 (1962), 121–41.
Pollard, A.W., and G.R. Redgrave. *A Short-title Catalogue of Books Printed in England, Scotland and Ireland, and of English Books Printed Abroad, 1475–1640*, 2nd edition, 3 vols (London, 1976–91).
Polman, Pontien. *L'élément historique dans la controverse religieuse du XVIe siècle* (Gembloux, 1932).
Porter, H.C. *Reformation and Reaction in Tudor Cambridge* (Cambridge, 1958).
Powicke, Maurice. *The Reformation in England* (London, 1941).
Prüser, F. *England und die Schmalkaldner* (Leipzig, 1929).
Pullapilly, C.K. *Caesar Baronius: Counter Reformation Historian* (Notre Dame, 1975).
Reeves, Marjorie. *The Influence of Prophecy in the Later Middle Ages: A Study in Joachimism* (Oxford, 1969).
——. *The Prophetic Sense of History in Medieval and Renaissance Europe* (Aldershot, 1999).
Rex, Richard. 'The Early Impact of Reformation Theology at Cambridge University, 1521–1547', *Reformation & Renaissance Review* 2 (1999), 38–71.
——. *Henry VIII and the English Reformation* (London, 1993).
——. *A Reformation Rhetoric: Thomas Swynnerton's The Tropes and Figures of Scripture* (Cambridge, 1999).
——. 'The Role of English Humanists in the Reformation up to 1559', in *The Education of a Christian Society: Humanism and the Reformation in Britain and the Netherlands*, ed. N.S. Amos et al. (Brookfield, VT, 1999), 19–40.
——. *The Theology of John Fisher* (Cambridge, 1991).
Riordan, Michael, and Alec Ryrie. 'Stephen Gardiner and the Making of a Protestant Villain', *Sixteenth Century Journal* 34 (2003), 1039–63.
Rostenberg, Leona. *The Minority Press and the English Crown* (Nieuwkoop, 1971).
Roth, Francis. *The English Austin Friars, 1249–1538*, serialised in *Augustiniana*, vol. 8 (1958), 22–47, 465–96, vol. 11 (1961), 533–63, vol. 12 (1962), 93–122, 391–442, vol. 13 (1963), 515–51, vol. 14 (1964), 163–215, 670–710, vol. 15 (1965), 175–236, 567–628; vol. 16 (1966), 204–63, 446–519, vol. 17 (1967), 84–166, with primary source documents serialised in *Augustiniana*, vol. 8 (1958), 1*–108*, vol. 9 (1959), 109*–294*, vol. 10 (1960), 295*–464*, vol. 11 (1961), 465*–572*.
Rupp, E.G. *The Righteousness of God* (London, 1953).

——. *Studies in the Making of the English Protestant Tradition* (Cambridge, 1966).

Ryrie, Alec. 'The Problem of Legitimacy and Precedent in English Protestantism, 1539–47', in *Protestant History and Identity in Sixteenth-Century Europe*, vol. 1, *The Medieval Inheritance*, ed. Bruce Gordon (Aldershot, 1996), 78–92.

——. ' "A saynt in the devyls name": Heroes and Villains in the Martyrdom of Robert Barnes', in *Martyrs and Martyrdom in England, c. 1400–1700*, ed. Thomas S. Freeman and Thomas F. Mayer (Woodbridge, 2007), 144–65.

Sasse, Hermann. 'Luther and the Word of God', in *Accents in Luther's Theology*, ed. H.O. Kadai (St Louis, 1967), 47–97.

Scarisbrick, J.J. *Henry VIII* (Harmondsworth, 1968).

Schäfer, Ernst. *Luther als Kirchenhistoriker* (Gütersloh, 1897).

Schild, M.E. 'Luther's Interpretations of Daniel and Revelation', in *Theologia Crucis: Studies in Honour of Hermann Sasse*, ed. H.P. Hamann (Adelaide, 1975), 107–18.

Schoeck, R.J. 'The *Cronica Cronicarum* of Sir Thomas More and Tudor Historians', *Bulletin of the Institute of Historical Research* 35 (1962), 84–6.

Scribner, R.W. 'Demons, Defecation and Monsters: Popular Propaganda for the German Reformation', in *Popular Culture and Popular Movements in Reformation Germany*, ed. R.W. Scribner (London, 1987), 277–99.

Siebert, F.S. *Freedom of the Press in England, 1476–1776* (Urbana, 1952).

Smith, P. 'Englishmen at Wittenberg in the Sixteenth Century', *English Historical Review* 36 (1921), 422–33.

Southgate, W.M. *John Jewel and the Problem of Doctrinal Authority* (Cambridge, MA, 1962).

Spitz, Lewis. 'History as a Weapon in Controversy', *Concordia Theological Monthly* 18 (1947), 747–62.

Stadtwald, Kurt. 'Pope Alexander III's Humilation of Emperor Frederick Barbarossa as an Episode in Sixteenth-century German History', *Sixteenth Century Journal* 23 (1992), 755–68.

Steinmann, Martin. *Johannes Oporinus* (Basel, 1967).

Stephen, L., and S. Lee (eds). *Dictionary of National Biography*, 63 vols (London, 1885–1900).

Strauss, Gerald. 'The Course of German History: The Lutheran Interpretation', in *Enacting the Reformation in Germany*, ed. G. Strauss (Aldershot, 1993), 665–86.

Strayer, J.R. (ed.). *Dictionary of the Middle Ages*, 12 vols (New York, 1982–89).

Surtz, E., and V. Murphy (eds). *The Divorce Tracts of Henry VIII* (Angers, 1988).

Talbert, Ernest W. 'A Lollard Chronicle of the Papacy', *Journal of English and Germanic Philology* 41 (1942), 163–93.

Tentler, T.N. *Sin and Confession on the Eve of the Reformation* (Princeton, 1977).

Tierney, Brian. *The Crisis of Church and State, 1050–1300* (Toronto, 1988).

Tjernagel, N.S. *Henry VIII and the Lutherans: A Study in Anglo-Lutheran Relations from 1521 to 1547* (St Louis, 1965).
——. *Lutheran Martyr* (Milwaukee, 1982).
——. *The Reformation Essays of Dr. Robert Barnes* (London, 1963).
——. 'Robert Barnes and Wittenberg', *Concordia Theological Monthly* 28 (1957), 641–53.
Trueman, C. *Luther's Legacy: Salvation and the English Reformers, 1525–1556* (Oxford, 1994).
——. ' "The Saxons be sore on the affirmative": Robert Barnes on the Lord's Supper', in *The Bible, the Reformation and the Church*, ed. W.P. Stephens (Sheffield, 1995), 290–307.
Underwood, William. 'Thomas Cromwell and William Marshall's Protestant Books', *The Historical Journal* 47 (2004), 517–39.
Venn, J., and J.A. Venn (eds). *Alumni Cantabrigienses: A Biographical List of All Known Students, Graduates and Holders of Office at the University of Cambridge, from the Earliest Times to 1751*, 10 vols (Cambridge, 1922–54).
Wabuda, Susan. ' "Fruitful Preaching" in the Diocese of Worcester: Bishop Hugh Latimer and his Influence, 1535–1539', in *Religion and the English People, 1500–1640: New Voices, New Perspectives*, ed. Eric Joseph Carlson (Kirksville, MO, 1998), 49–74.
Williams, Glanmor. *Reformation Views of Church History* (London, 1970).
Wing, D.G. *A Short-title Catalogue of Books Printed in England, Scotland, Ireland, Wales and British America, and of English Books Printed in Other Countries, 1641–1700*, 2nd edition, 4 vols (New York, 1982–98).
Wingren, Gustaf. *Luther on Vocation*, tr. C. Rasmussen (Edinburgh, 1958).
Woolf, D.R. *Reading History in Early Modern England* (Cambridge, 2000).
Zakai, Avihu. 'Reformation, History, and Eschatology in English Protestantism', *History and Theory* 26 (1987), 300–18.

Unpublished theses

Anderson, Charles. 'The Person and Position of Dr. Robert Barnes, 1495–1540: A Study in the Relationship between the English and German Reformations' (unpublished Th.D. Thesis, Union Theological Seminary, New York, 1962).
Fisher, N.H. 'The Contribution of Robert Barnes to the English Reformation', (unpublished M.A. Thesis, University of Birmingham, 1950).
McEntegart, R. 'England and the League of Schmalkalden 1531–1547: Faction, Foreign Policy and the English Reformation' (unpublished Ph.D. Thesis, London School of Economics, 1992).
Nicholson, G. 'The Nature and Function of Historical Argument in the Henrician Reformation' (unpublished Ph.D. Thesis, Cambridge, 1977).

Tjernagel N.S. 'Dr. Robert Barnes and Anglo-Lutheran Relations, 1521–1540 (unpublished Ph.D. Thesis, University of Iowa, 1955).

Windsor, Graham. 'The Controversy between Roman Catholics and Anglicans from Elizabeth to the Revolution' (unpublished Ph.D. Thesis, Cambridge, 1967).

INDEX

STUDIES IN MODERN BRITISH RELIGIOUS HISTORY

Previously published volumes in this series

I
Friends of Religious Equality
Non-Conformist Politics in mid-Victorian England
Timothy Larsen

II
Conformity and Orthodoxy in the English Church, c.1560–1660
edited by Peter Lake and Michael Questier

III
Bishops and Reform in the English Church, 1520–1559
Kenneth Carleton

IV
Christabel Pankhurst
Fundamentalism and Feminism in Coalition
Timothy Larsen

V
The National Church in Local Perspective
The Church of England and the Regions, 1660–1800
edited by Jeremy Gregory and Jeffrey S. Chamberlain

VI
Puritan Iconoclasm during the English Civil War
Julie Spraggon

VII
The Cult of King Charles the Martyr
Andrew Lacey

VIII
Control of Religious Printing in Early Stuart England
S. Mutchow Towers

IX
The Church of England in Industrialising Society
The Lancashire Parish of Whalley in the Eighteenth Century
M. F. Snape

X
Godly Reformers and their Opponents in Early Modern England
Religion in Norwich, c.1560–1643
Matthew Reynolds

XI
Rural Society and the Anglican Clergy, 1815–1914
Encountering and Managing the Poor
Robert Lee

XII
The Church of England and the Holocaust
Christianity, Memory and Nazism
Tom Lawson

XIII
Religious Politics in Post-Reformation England
edited by Kenneth Fincham and Peter Lake

XIV
The Church of England and the Bangorian Controversy, 1716–1721
Andrew Starkie

XV
Martyrs and Martyrdom in England, c.1400–1700
edited by Thomas S. Freeman and Thomas F. Mayer

XVI
John Henry Williams (1747–1829): 'Political Clergyman'
War, the French Revolution, and the Church of England
Colin Haydon

XVII
Religion, Reform and Modernity in the Eighteenth Century
Thomas Secker and the Church of England
Robert G. Ingram

XVIII
The Royal Army Chaplains' Department, 1796–1953
Clergy under Fire
Michael Snape